RAILWAYWOMEN

"Woman labour
is the kind of thing
that raises trouble."

LORD RUNCIMAN, 1915,
SPEAKING OF RAILWAYS

Published September 2005

The Hastings Press
PO Box 96 Hastings TN34 1GQ
hastings.press@virgin.net
www.hastingspress.co.uk

ISBN 1-904-109-047
British Library Cataloguing in Publication Data
A catalogue record for this book is available from the British Library

Dedicated website: www.railwaywomen.co.uk

Cover, book design and typesetting by the author
Set mainly in Gentium 10/12
Printed by T J International, Padstow, England

RAILWAYWOMEN

EXPLOITATION
BETRAYAL
AND
TRIUMPH
IN THE
WORKPLACE

HELENA WOJTCZAK

Acknowledgements

Writing a book is a solitary process, and it has been particularly so for me. Sixteen years ago I approached the work as a working railwaywoman with no contact with anyone knowledgeable or even interested in railway history. Over the years I have made the (mostly electronic) acquaintance of many people who have given me snippets of information and photographs, and to whom I owe thanks. Among them are Chris Dadson, Paul Martin, Jon Elphick and other members of the SEmG Group, Adrian Vaughan, Gerald Sandison, Brian McDermott, Edward Talbot, Derek Sharpe, Patrick Howat, Fred Richardson, Glyn Waite, Oliver Green, David Allan, John Hinson, Frank Archer, Marc Nussbaumer, the D Binns Collection, Malcolm Wallace (TSSA), Paul Whiting (*Railnews*), PCs Steve Daly, Kevin Gordon, Peter Robinson, Helen Thorpe, Kevin Robertson, Paul Rouet, the TSSA, David Bownes (TFL), Yvonne Oliver (IWM), Helen Ashby, Richard Taylor and Keira Meheux (NRM). I am grateful to the late Gertrude Tuckwell for her wonderful cuttings collection at the TUC Library, and to the staff of the NUR both at Frant Place (who entrusted me with their archived minute books) and at Unity House (who allowed me to peruse hundreds of back copies of *The Railway Review*). I also wish to thank the many former and current railwaywomen who shared their first-hand experiences.

Warmest thanks to Gail Braybon and Alan Scott for much needed encouragement and helpful guidance in the book's early days and to my friends Cameron Moffett, Adrian Hancock and Eric Bond Hutton for their helpful comments and support.

This book has been a long time in the making and if I have omitted to mention anyone who contributed information or photographs I hope they will forgive me.

Helena Wojtczak
Sussex, 2005

Contents

ABBREVIATIONS

ASLEF	Associated Society of Locomotive Engineers & Firemen
ASRS	Associated Society of Railway Servants
BR/BRB	British Rail/British Railways Board
BTC	British Transport Commission
EC	Executive Committee of the NUR/RMT (now, Council of Executives)
GCR	Great Central Railway
GER	Great Eastern Railway
GNR	Great Northern Railway
GSWR	Glasgow & South Western Railway
GWR	Great Western Railway
LBSCR	London, Brighton & South Coast Railway
LCDR	London, Chatham & Dover Railway
LNER	London & North Eastern Railway
LNWR	London & North Western Railway
LSWR	London & South Western Railway
LUL	London Underground Limited
LYR	Lancashire & Yorkshire Railway
MR	Midland Railway
NBR	North British Railway
NER	North Eastern Railway
NUR	National Union of Railwaymen (now RMT)
RCA	Railway Clerks' Association
RCH	Railway Clearing House
REC	Railway Executive Committee
RMT	Rail, Maritime and Transport Workers' Union (formerly NUR)
RSJ	*Railway Service Journal* (RCA magazine)
SDA	Sex Discrimination Act
SECR	South Eastern & Chatham Railway
SER	South Eastern Railway
SR	Southern Railway (to 1923, thence) Southern Region
TSSA	Transport Salaried Staffs' Association

PHOTOGRAPH CREDITS

Though every effort has been made to trace the owners of photographs and acknowledge copyright there remain some whose origins are unknown. The publisher offers apologies and welcomes amendments.	
Darwin	Darwin, B. (1946) *War on the Line*
IWM	Imperial War Museum
Kenning/Vaughan	Adrian Vaughan/W L Kenning Collection
NRM	National Railway Museum
TFL	Transport for London

FOREWORD

By Colin Divall
BSc, MSc, PhD, FRHistS
Professor of Railway Studies
Head of the Institute of
Railway Studies & Transport History, York

Britain's railways have always been largely a man's world. Yet almost from the railways' earliest stirrings as adjuncts of the coal mining industry in the 1600s through to the modern system of high-speed passenger and heavy-haul freight trains, women have been there. Almost every type of job on the railway has at some time or another been filled by a female. In 1717 Lady Jane Clavering took over a wooden waggonway in north-east England on which chaldrons of coal were pulled by horses; nowadays women drive Eurostar trains under the Channel from London to Paris and Brussels. During the Second World War, women could be found doing pretty well any manual task except locomotive driving and firing, in addition to the numerous clerical and administrative jobs in which they were also employed in their thousands.

The story of women's role on Britain's railways is, however, largely an obscure one, and it is so because very few historians have bothered to look for the evidence. One reason then warmly to welcome the fruits of Helena Wojtczak's extensive research over a period of many years. She shows not only just how numerous female railway workers were, particularly during the two world wars, but also how varied were the tasks undertaken by them, often under particularly trying and dangerous conditions. But this is not just a book about recovering evidence of women's participation, essential though that task is, for the author also explains why women have found it so difficult to participate in anything like equal numbers with men or with equal responsibility. In part long-standing attitudes concerning women's suitability for anything other than the most traditionally feminine of tasks were to blame, but this is not the complete story. As with many other occupations dominated by men, women were often regarded by male colleagues as a threat— for taking jobs which should rightfully have gone to other male family bread-winners, and for being prepared to work for less pay than men and thus providing a source of cheaper labour. Thus for different (and occasionally the same) reasons, (male) trades unionists and (male) railways managers long shared attitudes and policies which resulted in women's marginalisation on the railways.

It would be pleasant to record that the renewal of feminist thinking from the 1960s plus the last quarter-century's equal-rights legislation meant that women were now as welcome on the railway as their male counterparts. There has been progress, certainly, but in bringing the story of women on Britain's railways firmly up to the present day Helena Wojtczak shows just how deeply entrenched old ways of thinking can be. Unlocking the secrets of the past, as this book does so engagingly, may yet help build a better and fairer railway in the future.

Author's Note

This book makes no claim to be complete. To compile a detailed history of all grades of railwaywomen over 170 years is an impossibility because there are no comprehensive records available from employers, unions or national archives. Previous railway histories have either excluded women or made only brief references to them. All that exist are thousands of scraps of information such as press cuttings, photos (often without descriptions), rare and brief references in trades union minutes' books and conference reports and the odd relevant paragraph amongst thousands of others within railway magazines and railway companies' staff records. These are held in various locations across Britain and I have travelled hundreds of miles and searched through many thousands of words to unearth often disappointingly small amounts of information; on some rare occasions, I found treasure trove. In short, this has been needle-in-a-haystack work.

Thousands of interesting facts and key people are absent simply because they did not come to light. Many anecdotes are buried in the memories of thousands of women who did not see the many appeals I published, who were uninterested or who were too busy to contribute to this book. The employers' 'gagging clause', which forbids staff to speak to the press, made many female colleagues feel unable to speak to me 'on the record' or to allow their names to appear. BR refused to give information on individual staff and most train operating companies even ignored my request for statistical data.

The history of women in higher railway management since the 1980s and the story of women's involvement with the railway unions since the 1950s would each fill a book, and are covered only briefly. The past half-century's complex and convoluted negotiations and agreements between the unions and management about grading, promotion, transfer, redundancy and pay would have made very dull reading and are almost completely omitted for this reason. I have chosen instead to give the space to personal histories that relate in direct, human terms the experience of being a woman on the railway.

The main focus of this work is on women in operational roles (such as track, station and train staff) and those involved in building and maintaining trains. Less attention is given to the operational periphery (shipping, engineering, catering, administration, senior management, etc,) except where the subject matter was one of great significance or was exceptionally interesting. The emphasis changes according to the era under discussion. In the early days railwaywomen were so few that every obtainable piece of information has been included about any woman in any grade, but by the late 20th century far more women worked on the railways and, for reasons of space, I have had to be more discriminating and to focus on women working on the operational side. Geographically, this work covers the British mainland. I did not conduct research specific to the London Underground, but when snippets of information or photographs presented themselves I included them.

Pre-1971 wages mentioned in this book are in '£sd' (librae, solidi, denarii) more commonly known as pounds, shillings and pence. There were 12 pence in a shilling and 20 shillings in a pound.

1: Before the First World War

As near as a hundred percent as made no matter, the railway service was a man's world.

J.A.B. Hamilton

Railways developed from horse-drawn waggonways. As early as 1645 tracks made of stone and iron carried waggons* from mines and quarries to the docks of the River Tyne. The first woman to own one was probably Dame Jane Clavering, who in 1717 inherited the Byermoor Colliery Waggonway near Newcastle from her husband, Sir John Clavering of Whitehouse. Not long after, Elizabeth Blakiston of Gibside teamed up with another woman to build a waggonway 'in the teeth of cartel opposition, and by skilful wayleave sabotage destroyed a way of their opponents'. [1] The tracks of waggonways were crossed at intervals by roads protected by gates, and women were often employed as crossing keepers to open and close the gates and as numbertakers to count the number of waggons that crossed, to enable the company to charge the correct tolls.

The passenger railways we know today were built between the 1820s and 1890s by itinerant navvies drafted in by contractors to construct what is known as the permanent way (i.e. the strip of land on which the rails are laid). They created the cuttings, tunnels and embankments by hand and the work was both exceptionally heavy and exceedingly dangerous: many men were killed by explosions, land-falls and collapsing tunnels.[2]

Italian women were spotted working as navvies near Pisa in 1862[3] but none has been recorded by eyewitnesses in Britain. Intriguingly, the 1851 Census listed three women 'railway labourers' working on the construction of the South Eastern Railway between Tunbridge Wells and Robertsbridge: Mary Smith, aged 40; Elizabeth Taylor, 20; and Elizabeth Waters, 21. They were all unmarried and living in lodgings, one in a public house, which suggests that, like the men, they were itinerant. The same Census records that Hannah Hamilton, a Scot aged 32, was a 'railway labourer' living in 'the railway hut' at Bexhill, London, Brighton & South Coast Railway (LBSCR) with her Irish husband and their three children. The National Railway Museum owns a photograph taken by J. B. Pyne about 1865, which is captioned: 'Workmen and women during the construction of the mile-long Belsize Tunnel'.[4] This implies that the women were workers; however, they were almost certainly the navvies' wives, bringing lunch to their husbands on the site. The only woman who definitely laboured alongside men as a navvy was Elizabeth Ann Holman, who worked on the Great Western Railway (GWR) in Cornwall for 14s a week in the 1850s. She managed to obtain the job by masquerading as a man, something she had done since the age of 13.[5]

* The spelling has since changed and a single 'g' is now used.

Early Railway Workers

Once the lines were built and operative, railways became profitable businesses employing over 250,000 workers by the 1870s. Staff were employed not only in running trains and stations but also in docks and shipping, goods, engineering, telegraphy, locomotive and carriage building, track laying and maintenance, and hotels and catering. As well as the obvious uniformed and administrative employees, railway companies employed a huge range of peripheral workers including printers, rat-catchers, bootblacks, horse-keepers, bakers, police, ship's captains, blacksmiths, painters, chemists, French polishers, gas fitters and seamstresses.* By 1900 five per cent of the population of Britain was employed by a railway company.

A railwayman's job dominated not only his life but also that of his family: domestic routine was organised around his shifts. Men benefited from travel concessions, free uniforms and cheap coal. About one-tenth of the workforce lived in railway-owned houses† and their families joined institutes, schools, churches and societies provided by their employer. Many rented allotments from the company. It was common for sons to follow fathers into the service, for daughters to marry railwaymen and for widows to seek jobs with their late husbands' employer.

Railwaymen were drawn from the poorly educated classes‡ and given responsibility for people's lives and expensive equipment, so it was crucial that they were sober and, above all, well disciplined. Railway companies based staff-management relations on military practice, which meant a strict hierarchy of rank and workers being controlled by 'a combination of reprimands, cautions, fines, suspensions and dismissals'.[6] The companies sought control over their employees' behaviour both on and off duty. For example, the Taff Vale Railway rule book of 1856 forbade staff to exhibit 'levity' at work and required them to attend church every Sunday. Fines were levied and staff disciplined for even minor misdemeanours. Instant dismissal was common in cases of absence without leave or for insubordination and there was no appeals procedure till 1912. Each company notified the others of dismissals, so that a person sacked from one railway could not obtain work with another.

Paradoxically, it was essential for staff to be constantly alert and observant despite having sometimes to work shockingly long hours. The theoretical 12-hour maximum working day was habitually exceeded. In 1871 the Chief Inspector of Railways revealed instances of 18, 25 and even 37 hours' continuous duty. Companies paid scant attention to the safety of staff and accidents were frequent. In 1875, 767 railwaymen were killed on duty; between 1875 and 1899 an average of ten railwaymen were killed every week and a further 50 were injured, some of whom lost limbs or were otherwise maimed. Whether an accident affected passengers, staff or equipment, managers blamed workers' lack of vigilance rather than the gruelling pattern of excessive hours and rotating shifts. At one

* Railways also employed people with the baffling titles of gobber, gongsman, teemer, hanger-on, improver, pondsman, rulley shifter, bye worker, strapper and sleeper pickler but, as none of them was female, we need not concern ourselves with deciphering what their duties were.

† Collectively, the companies were among the largest landlords in Britain. Figures are available only for 1944, when the railway companies owned 51,000 houses — almost five times the number of signalboxes they possessed.

‡ A random sample of 87 LBSCR station staff in 1856 revealed that all were illiterate.

point parliament attempted to introduce a law to restrict railwaymen's daily hours to 12, but railway directors and shareholders in the House of Lords blocked it, fearing a reduction in profits.

All railway companies were fiercely opposed to trade unions and refused to recognise them for several decades. Any worker who took a grievance to management was labelled as a 'troublemaker' to distinguish him from those considered to be 'loyal' to the company. Such an act would also have destroyed any prospect he might have had of advancement. The NUR's historian Philip Bagwell commented that most railwaymen 'were careful not to jeopardize their positions by such reckless indiscretions as joining a trade union and taking part in strikes,'[7] but a few small groups of railwaymen did campaign for better conditions, and this took enormous courage because pay rises, bonuses, promotion and even a person's continued employment were conditional upon 'good conduct', a term which – although undefined – would certainly not encompass complaint and agitation. There were no unemployment or other welfare benefits, and so men were placed under immense pressure not to risk their families' livelihoods. Under the circumstances it is remarkable that so many railwaymen had the courage to petition for improvements and some even went on strike, knowing what the consequences might be. Provision of railway housing for staff gave the companies even more control over their workforce, for a man risked his home as well as his job: in 1871 engine drivers at Camden Town were evicted from their railway cottages after striking.

Despite everything, railway employment was much sought after – the relatively high pay was one reason for this* – and the typical railwayman felt immense pride in his profession. Staunch loyalty to one's railway company was expected and, in most cases, given. Everyone knew his place in the pecking order and those in the higher grades – line superintendents, station masters, passenger guards, engine drivers and signalmen – felt a great sense of superiority and jealously protected their status, especially with regard to the demarcation between themselves and the lower ranks.

THE STATUS OF RAILWAYWOMEN

Women's history is different from that of men, because women were subject to special laws and social customs which governed every part of their lives. This is particularly true of employment. While it is not the task of this book to describe the genesis of women's subordinate position in the workforce, it is necessary to explain that, when railways began, women had little or no control over anything that affected their lives. They were completely subjugated to men socially, politically, legally, educationally, financially and professionally. It was men and not women who decided which areas of work would be open to the female sex and how much women should be paid. As a result, women were excluded from well-paid employment and few occupations were open to them other than domestic service, laundering, unqualified nursing, elementary teaching, cleaning and dressmaking. In the few workplaces in which women performed identical work to men they were paid less, just for being female.

Railway staff were (and still are) divided into two broad categories: wages grades and salaried grades. The former were the manual workers on stations and trains, etc, and the latter were those in administration, booking offices and technical departments and all

* A porter in the 1840s earned about 18s. An agricultural labourer earned between 8s and 11s.

supervisory and managerial staff overseeing both wages and salaried grade staff. Each category was subdivided into male and female grades. In addition, a handful of grades could be filled by either sex and these will be termed 'unisex'. From the 1830s till 1915, most railwaywomen worked in female wages grades, some were in unisex grades and a tiny number filled male grades.

In common with other employers, Victorian railway companies routinely allocated to women those jobs with the lowest status and the least prospects. Menial work, especially that which resembled domestic tasks, was women's domain. The abstract of the national Census of 1851 lists 54 railwaywomen but their jobs were not revealed; they were placed under the heading 'Railway driver, etc, porter, etc, labourer, platelayer'; but, as women were barred from all the named grades, they must have formed part of the 'etc'. Fifty years later the number had increased thirty-fold: the 1901 Census reported that 1,633 women worked in railway wages grades. A decade later this had more than doubled to 3,787.[8] In addition, 1,120 women had obtained jobs in railway offices and 2,263 were employed in their workshops, hotels and in various types of railway catering — a grand total of 7,170.[9] This figure almost doubled again in the next three years: by 1914, 13,046 of the railways' 630,000 staff were female. The number of women in wages grades had risen by only 300; the greatest increase was in the other categories. Roughly 6,200 worked in hotels and catering and 800 were in the workshops, while the number in office work had doubled to 2,300.*

The lack of more detailed statistics is not surprising, for even at the peak of their pre-war numerical strength — in 1914 — women comprised only 2% of the workforce, distributed between 178 railway companies. When they compiled returns of staff the companies did not enumerate women by grade. For example, a GWR census listed male staff by job title but gave merely the numbers, wages and hours of 'female employées' lumped together at the end.

As in every other industry, there was an enormous gulf between the pay of male and female employees. Women were paid one-third to one-half the wages of men, even if engaged in the same work. In 1869 a porter earned about 36s; a guard, 44s; a signalman, 42s; and a booking clerk, 35s. Taking the lower grades, juniors and lads into account the average weekly pay of a wages-grade railwayman was 26s 8d while a railwaywoman generally earned between 8s and 15s a week. For women to have expected equal pay would have constituted a stance so radical that it could not have been taken seriously. It was universally assumed that all men had dependent wives and children and that all working women were either young spinsters merely filling in time till marriage, or wives who worked for 'pin money'. The fact that neither assumption was true was irrelevant.

Only three examples have come to light of railwaywomen's receiving equal pay. The first was spotted in the 1891 GWR staff census: of 114 female office staff, all but three earned under 15s while the three supervisors earned between 15s and 22s; of the 294 male staff, half earned over 15s while 14 earned 20s-25s. However, the men worked 60 hours while the women averaged 47.5 and were paid more for overtime. These discrepancies brought women's 'take-home' pay up to the level of men's. The two other cases were

* In *75 Years of Industrial Trade Unionism* Philip Bagwell erroneously states: 'Before the war, only 4,565 women were employed on the railways, mainly in clerical jobs.' Leaving aside the discrepancy in numbers, the majority were in wages grades, not clerical work.

instances of individual women employed in a male grade. When the signalman responsible for Britain's worst train crash, at Quintinshill,[10] was sentenced to three years' imprisonment, his employer (the Caledonian Railway) showed compassion by offering his wife a job as cloakroom attendant at Carlisle. Mrs Tinsley began work on 4th October 1915 at a wage of 21s a week, the male rate for that grade.[11] The other example was a woman attendant at Ouseburn Viaduct. Part of it served as a footbridge, for the use of which she collected tolls from pedestrians.* Her pay was 19s a week – again, the male rate.

The free travel granted to spouses and children of railwaymen was systematically withheld from their female colleagues. In 1908 the London Electric Railway made women's low status clear in a circular that emphatically decreed: 'No passes of any description will be supplied to any female employees whether clerks, telephone operators, ticket sorters, car cleaners or lavatory attendants.'

Women were on the margins of railway life. They were afterthoughts whose terms and conditions were added as footnotes to those of the male workforce. On pre-printed employment application forms the words 'he' and 'him' were crossed through when a woman applied, and substituted with 'she' and 'her' in ink. Even the status of women workers was different from that of men, but nobody seemed to know quite what their classification was, or even what to call them. The North Eastern Railway (NER) tried to clear up the matter by issuing a notice to clarify women's employment status. Waiting room attendants, cooks, housekeepers, housemaids, barmaids, seamstresses and hostel attendants, together with attendants, waitresses and manageresses of tea-rooms, it said, were permanent staff; but office cleaners were not permanent, nor were women crossing keepers who gave only 'a portion of their day to the company'.[12] By 'a portion', the company meant anything less than 24 hours.

There were also some interesting differences in the terminology used when referring to women, and it is clear that social class played a part; for example, the London, Brighton & South Coast (LBSCR) referred to 'lady' clerks, 'women' carriage cleaners and 'female' French polishers!

Wages Grades

In the early years the only female names on any list of station staff were those of the office cleaners (or charwomen). Before long, mess-rooms and canteens began to be provided at depots, workshops and stations, and women were engaged to serve and clean up after the staff who used them. From the 1890s companies built lodging hostels, where long-distance engine crews, guards and dining car stewards slept overnight before their return journeys. They were staffed by matrons who, in addition to their domestic duties, had to wake the railwaymen in time to work their trains. The pay in some cases was quite high for 'women's work'; for example, Mrs Adams, the matron at Chester 'lodge' (as the men called the hostels) was appointed in 1874 (aged 40) at a wage of 19s 3d.

Victorian railwaywomen were, with very few exceptions, barred from 'men's work'. Research revealed only one being engaged as a porter: 22-year-old Sarah Battersby, who appears in the 1871 Census as an 'Innkeeper/Railway Porter' at Barrow-in-Furness. At

* Toll-collecting on turnpike roads had for many decades been a typical female occupation outside of the railways.

least two daring women impersonated men to gain railway employment. One was the aforementioned navvy Elizabeth Holman, the other Mary Walker, who obtained a job on the GWR as a porter in the 1860s by dressing in male attire and calling herself Thomas.[13] She had tricked her way into men's jobs for many years and had previously been a sailor, and — most remarkably of all, in view of the arduousness of the labour — a stoker on a Cunard steamer. Her true sex was eventually discovered and she stood trial in 1867, after which a ballad was written about her. Of course, we only know about these two because they were caught; there may have been more.

Ladies' Attendants

Ladies' waiting rooms were at one time ubiquitous when segregation by sex was as important as segregation by class. Indeed the larger stations had both first and second class ladies' rooms.* Women were often nervous of travelling alone and 'ladies-only' accommodation was a welcome facility. The rooms contained bench seating (sometimes upholstered), tables, coal fires, lace tablecloths, vases of flowers and reading material — generally, a bible. A connecting door led to toilets and washbasins.

Overseeing these facilities gave employment to thousands of women nationally. The first was probably Mary Counsell, engaged by the GWR at Paddington on 25th May 1838 as a 'Female Attendant'.[14] By the 1870s, ladies' waiting room attendants were employed at most stations. They were generally over 35 and usually related to railwaymen. One LBSCR staff register shows that at Bexhill the attendants between 1900 and 1920 were a crossing keeper's wife, the station master's unmarried daughter and the widow of a guard. At Victoria and London Bridge 80% of the ladies' waiting room attendants were widows of railwaymen. There was no uniform, but white lace caps and aprons were provided, to be worn with a simple, dark dress.

Those working for the LBSCR between 1889 and 1917 earned 12s to 14s a week in coastal or rural areas and 18s in London. At Worcester, GWR, in 1873 Ladies' Attendant Mrs Dale earned 10s (the same as Mrs Spencer, the office cleaner), while in 1874 ladies' attendants at Huddersfield earned 12s 6d. Here is a comparison of their pay compared with that of the male station staff:

Huddersfield station, 1874	*Worcester station, 1873*
Slip boy, 9s	Female office cleaner, 10s
Parcel boy, 10s	Ladies' attendant, 10s
Ladies' attendant, 12s 6d	Ticket examiners, 18s and 20s
Porter, 17s 6d	Porters, 16s and 17s
Cloakroom clerk, 20s	Cloakroom porter, 19s
Parcel deliverer, 21s	Inspector, 34s

* 'Ladies-only' carriages were also sometimes offered. The first were inaugurated in 1845 by the Grand Junction Railway (which was subsumed into the LNWR in 1846), closely followed by the London & Brighton Railway (later the LBSCR).

Although working as a waiting room attendant must have had its pleasant moments and perhaps the occasional tip or small gift from a lady passenger, the job was menial. Sustaining exemplary conduct while enduring this humble work for a decade or more might lead to promotion — for a few — to inspectress. This was the highest rank a woman could achieve on the railways and the only female uniformed grade. The duties included travelling the company's network to check that the ladies' accommodation and its staff were spick and span, and to act as the first line of supervision for all female staff on a station, including office cleaners. Welsh staff records reveal that Mary Ellen Lenton was appointed district inspectress at Llandudno Junction in 1886; Mrs Emma Livesey was waiting room inspectress at Chester in 1897 and Annie Ingham took her place in 1902; and Mary Ann Pauter became the inspectress at Rhyll in 1911.

In 1898 Ellen Rees, waiting room attendant at London Bridge, gained her '15 minutes of fame' for picking out Louisa Masset in an identification parade. Masset had murdered her child at Dalston Junction station and, partly owing to Mrs Rees's evidence, she was hanged in 1900.

Ladies' room attendant was a good job compared with other women's work during Victoria's reign[15] and they rarely left unless forced to by ill health. As a result, a number of them achieved very long service. Mrs Palmer was the first class ladies' waiting room attendant at Liverpool Lime Street, LMS, for 34 years, from 1890 till 1924. Mrs Allen was the waiting room attendant at Henley-on-Thames, GWR, from 1908 till 1938. Mrs Stemp joined the SECR as a ladies' room attendant in 1904 and worked at several locations before settling at London Victoria. During the Second World War, despite being in her mid 70s, she was still working 7 a.m. to 3 p.m. and 2 p.m. to 10 p.m. alternate weeks, 13 days a fortnight. She retired in 1946 with 42 years' service.

Laundresses

Railways generated a huge amount of dirty linen from station catering establishments, restaurant cars, sleeping cars and steamships. Everything presented to the public had to be spotless and perfectly ironed. Laundering was typical women's work, and so it is not surprising that when companies opened steam laundries women were engaged to staff them. In 1881 a laundry owned by the London & North Western Railway (LNWR) at Liverpool employed 13 female staff and one male van driver. All the women were widows or spinsters and they lived on the premises.[16]

A laundry was one of the few areas in which a woman might be appointed manager. The GER opened a steam laundry at Colchester in 1888 and by 1890 it was handling 949,000 items every year, among them napkins and tablecloths, towels, aprons, antimacassars,* tray cloths, doilies, cleaning cloths, tea towels, sheets, blankets, pillowcases and tick covers. From 1893 Mrs Bellchambers and her husband were joint managers, and they lived in a company house on site. By 1912 they had 59 girls and 12 men in their charge, processing 3.4 million articles per annum.[17]

Some of the longest-serving laundresses were sisters Mary and Rose Steele, who began work in 1914 and 1915 at the Highland Railway's Station Hotel at Inverness and retired together in 1957.

* Antimacassars are napkins for the backs of seats, used to prevent soiling of the fabric by the head.

THE POETRY OF THE RAIL

We have already pointed out the alteration likely to be made in poetry and song-writing by the introduction of Railroads, and we this week give another specimen of the probable effect of the change. We shall hear no more now of the Lily of the Vale or the Village Rose, but the Pearl of the Refreshment-room and the Daisy of the Rail will supersede the once popular maidens alluded to. The following touching ballad is supposed to be addressed by one of the luggage superintendents to one of the female waiters at the same station, and may be called –

THE PORTER TO HIS MISTRESS

Oh maiden, but an instant stay,
And let me breathe my vow;
I know the train is on its way,
I hear its thund'ring row.

Another moment crowds will stand
Where now to thee I kneel;
And hungry groups will soon demand
The beef, the ham, the veal.

Turn not away thy brow so fair,
'Tis that, alas! I dread;
For thou hast given me, I swear,
One fatal turn a-head.

I've linger'd on the platform, love,
My brow with luggage hot;
A voice has whisper'd from above,
'Porter, take heed, love knot!'

O'er thee mine eye doth often range:
I've mark'd thee take the pay
From those who, ere you bring their change,
Rush to the train away.
Turn not, &c. &c.

A cartoon about romance between railway workers, probably the first representation of a female railway employee to appear in any publication. *Punch*, c1845

Catering Workers

Before the birth of railways, passengers travelled by stagecoach, whose 'stations' were inns and taverns, so they were accustomed to being able to purchase food and drink at each end of their journey and at stops en route. In replacing road transport, the railways also provided catering and accommodation for their passengers.

The first railway hotel opened at London's Euston station in 1839 and over the next 74 years a further 91 appeared. About one-third of all female railway employees worked in these establishments as cooks, chambermaids, kitchen assistants, cleaners, laundresses and waitresses. The highest female grades were housekeeper and tea-room manageress.

Today's station buffets bear no resemblance to the great catering enterprises of the Victorian era. The fullest description available of an early railway refreshment room is of one owned not by a railway company but by Dethier & Vantini, a catering firm. However, it serves well as an example of station refreshment rooms in general. Written by Sir Francis Bond Head, it describes the establishment at Wolverton, LNWR, in 1849, at which time it was staffed by a matron — 'or generallissima' — called Leonora Hibbert, seven young waitresses, two scullery-maids, two housemaids, a still-room maid (engaged solely to make tea and coffee) and a kitchen maid, as well as several male staff. The 13 female staff lived on the premises and 85 pigs and 'piglings' were kept in the yard. That they were overworked is evident: they performed 16-hour shifts, either 7 a.m. till 11 p.m. or 12 noon till 4 a.m. Their laborious day was punctuated at irregular intervals by frantic episodes in which crowds of passengers would race in from trains during the customary 10-minute refreshment stops.[18]

The Victorians developed a derogatory stereotype of railway refreshment rooms, which supposedly had stale buns, suspicious meat pies, coffee like ditchwater and insolent servants. While one cannot comment on the quality of the provisions, it is known that the companies exercised great care in choosing staff; for example, the LNWR at one time employed only daughters of railway workers, and Sir Francis Head assured readers that 'the breath of slander has never ventured to sully the reputation of any' at Wolverton.

Some concern was shown for the welfare of young women in railway catering. The barmaids at Liverpool Street were invited to reside in the GER hostel at Hackney, where they received full board. The company boasted that every convenience — from a housekeeper to a piano — was provided for them. By the 1890s a Barmaids' Guild existed at Wolverton and a House of Rest was provided for them by Lady Wolverton.

Catering workers were not entirely isolated from the grim incidents that occasionally occurred out on the track. When two trains were involved in a fatal collision in 1910 at Willesden Junction, LNWR, refreshment room assistant Mrs Ginger ran out to the scene and dispensed brandy to the shocked and injured passengers.[19]

Many women enjoyed lengthy careers in railway catering. Some of the longer-serving were Miss Swift, who worked at Snow Hill, Birmingham, GWR, for 42 years (1913-1955);[20] Miss M. Stephenson, who was at Middlesbrough, NER, for 48 years (1908-1956);[21] and Miss Reece, who was employed in the refreshment room at Swindon, GWR, for 29 years. Each started at the lowest grade and was manageress by the time she retired.

Description of gatekeepers' work

The old axiom, that the strength of any chain is the strength of its weakest link, has many illustrations, and one may be found in the great chain of workers employed upon our various railway systems, the effective working of which systems depends upon the fitness and reliability of every link. One of these links, the importance and value of which are apt to be underrated by the general public, is the gatekeeper at a public-level crossing, whose duty it is to open a gate whenever a vehicle has to cross the railway; a simple and prosaic act, requiring very little skill in its performance, and apparently entailing very little responsibility upon the incumbent of the office. But with all its apparent monotony and simplicity the duty of a gatekeeper, in common with all other duties connected with the actual railway, has its measures of responsibility, and is a matter of equal importance both to railway company and to the travelling public.

Gatekeepers are perhaps the most nondescript class of railway employees; for while guards, signalmen, ticket collectors, shunters, &c., are recruited from among porters, gatekeepers are drawn from no particular class, but are furnished by all classes indiscriminately, and sometimes the gatekeeper is a woman.

The men who are employed as gatekeepers have always served the company in some other capacity, and no man is ever engaged as a gatekeeper who has not had some experience of railway work. In the majority of cases they are men who have received, in some other branch of the service, injuries which unfit them for any active duty requiring the use of all limbs; while in some instances the gatekeeper has grown old in the company's service and to such the gatehouse offers a well-earned and much coveted retirement from active duty. Thus, while one crossing has as its guardian a man who as a guard lost a leg, the next may have been a shunter who has lost an arm; another may have a porter who has been crushed between trucks; and an adjoining gatekeeper may have a goods-porter worn out with hard work, or even an old station-master no longer able to cope with the increasing demands of developing traffic.

Each gatekeeper is supplied with a tricolour hand-lamp, some detonating signals and two flags, one red, one green, in order to signal when necessary to approaching trains, for it does sometimes happen that a vehicle breaks down on the railway while crossing over it; and the prompt use of signals by the gatekeeper is necessary to prevent a train running into the obstruction and so causing a general smash-up. Not long since, at a crossing kept by a woman — the wife of a platelayer — a load of straw broke down, blocking both lines, at a time when a passenger train was within ten minutes of being due. Away went the woman with her red flag to meet the approaching train, which she succeeded in stopping before it reached the obstruction; her presence of mind and prompt obedience to orders being suitably acknowledged by the company she served.

Other instances might be quoted in which the prompt action of the gatekeeper prevented a temporary block from becoming a serious accident.

The relations of the gatekeeper to the public may be described as various, depending to a large extent upon the temperament and temper of both parties. Sometimes when the gentleman who wants the gates opened and the gentleman who has to open them are both of an irascible disposition, these relations are a little strained and not infrequently call forth some vigorous language from the occupant of the trap, which the man at the gate has to bear as best he may, well knowing that retaliation on his part would lead to him being reported and probably fined.

Chambers' Journal of Popular Literature, Science & Arts, 1889

Track and Trains

Railway operating was men's work. Carriages, wagons and the steam locomotives that hauled them were built by craftsmen in railway workshops and cleaned by men in the sheds. Platelayers and lengthsmen laid and maintained the track. In sidings and marshalling yards, shunters made up or divided a train by attaching or detaching wagons and carriages to engines, which involved handling heavy couplings, frequently going between vehicles and clambering on and off moving carriages, wagons and locomotives. Alongside the engine driver, a fireman shovelled coal into the firebox. Train movements on running lines were controlled by signalmen, who had to operate levers to move points and change signals, and some of the lever-pulling demanded considerable muscular effort. The work of platelayers, shunters and goods guards was carried out in the vicinity of moving vehicles at all hours in all weathers and was physically challenging, even for men. Passenger guards were promoted from goods guards, and their role – taking charge of a train in transit – called for personal qualities thought to be found only in men.

The mere suggestion that women might attempt any of the above railway work would have reduced railwaymen to helpless mirth.* Few would have heard of Mrs Town, maybe the first and perhaps the only signalwoman in Victorian Britain. She took over a small signalbox at Morebath Junction, between Taunton and Barnstaple, GWR, in 1890. The traffic was light: just fourteen trains a day and a few more on market days. In 1913, after 23 years' service, Mrs Town told the press that she was 'very proud' of her occupation and intended to continue indefinitely.[22]

A small number of women worked as carriage cleaners but it was a man's job and women's duties were restricted. Early industrial vacuum cleaners were heavy and cumbersome, and the long dresses and tight corsets worn by Victorian women severely hindered their movement, rendering climbing in and out of carriages from the track difficult and dangerous. It was, of course, impossible for women so dressed to climb up the sides of carriages onto their roofs either to clean and light carriage lamps or to refill the water tanks of train lavatories. Much carriage cleaning took place in sidings, amidst the movement of carriages, wagons and engines, an environment considered far too hazardous for 'the fair sex'. By 1914, there were just 214 women carriage cleaners in Britain, all of whom worked only from station platforms. They earned about 15s a week. Men – who could work in sidings, yards or platforms and climb onto train roofs – earned about 21s. Women were forbidden to clean locomotives. This was a specialist job, carried out by young men as part of their apprenticeship to become firemen, from which they would, eventually, be promoted to engine driver.

During the early 20th century a few women worked on board trains. The GWR employed nursing attendants on trains to Fishguard that connected with Cunard steamers. From 1905 maids were employed on the Cornish Riviera Express that ran between Paddington and Plymouth. One was described as 'neatly attired in a black alpaca dress with white linen collar and cuffs, a Nurse's bonnet, fancy apron, and a badge in silver thread inscribed "GWR Lady's Attendant".'[23] From 1910 till 1915, typists worked in special compartments between Birmingham New Street and London Broad Street, LNWR, providing a secretarial service to passengers.

---

* The online transcription of the 1881 census lists Sarah Owen (b. 1835, in Neath) as a 'Railway Engine Driver' on the LNWR. In fact, her husband was the driver, which is clear when one sees the original.

Crossing Keepers

Level crossings were a liability to the companies: they raised no income but had to be attended (and by 'good and proper persons', according to the Highways Act of 1839). The railway companies, seeking to get the gates staffed as cheaply as possible, offered the jobs firstly to railwaymen who had lost limbs in service or who were otherwise disabled. They would accept a low wage because they were usually desperate, as there were no state benefits.* In the absence of an eligible disabled man the vacancy would be offered to the widow of the previous gatekeeper, or to a railwayman's wife or daughter, at an even lower rate of pay. A gateman's widow had doubtless helped him to operate the gates, needed little or no training and would be very thankful for the work:

> When employed by the Great Western company at Chard station, Mrs Hill's husband met with an accident in 1880. He was transferred to Leigh Wood crossing in the hope that he might the more speedily recover, but he was never again fit for duty. His wife pluckily undertook his work on the line and performed it so well that, ever since his death, which occurred in the following year, the company have allowed her to remain in charge of the crossing – an act of kindly consideration for which she is deeply grateful.[24]

The tenancy of a line-side cottage came with the job, enabling women to perform their domestic duties and attend to children in between trains. These benefits made the jobs highly sought-after and there was never a shortage of applicants.†

As early as 1856 there were already 2,044 gatekeepers (of both sexes) in Britain.‡ The identity of the first woman is not known but the 1851 Census shows that Elizabeth Peddlesden operated some gates near Bexhill, LBSCR, where she and her husband (a labourer) occupied the gatehouse.[25] In 1856, the Edinburgh, Perth & Dundee Railway hired Mrs Anderson at Larbert, at 2s a week. Also around mid-century 'Red Ellen' operated the gates, and one disc-and-bar signal, at Tag Lock Crossing between Brighouse and Elland, Lancashire & Yorkshire Railway (LYR):

> Before the introduction of signalling the LYR was run on the time interval system, and was controlled by a manually operated system of Disc and Crossbar Signalling at Mile Cabins. One of these was situated near where the River Calder made its closest approach to the railway and where a 'siding' from the Aire & Calder Canal was close at hand. This 'siding' was known as Tag Lock. Thus the crossing over the railway was similarly named, and was 'womanned' by Red Ellen. This Amazon was a rather powerful woman, a character in her own right who could hold her own with the stone delvers, wagon drivers and railwaymen.
>
> She had red hair and so was known as Red Ellen. My father used to tell me that as a young man he felt rather scared of Ellen and her broad north-country accent. Frequently during each day horse-drawn wagons came down with loads of stone from the quarries. Some of the stone, and especially the huge blocks, was loaded into railway wagons and carried to be loaded into barges at Tag Lock.

* Sometimes a small compensation payment was given to those whose accidents were the fault of the company, but it certainly would not have been enough to support them indefinitely; that would be promoting idleness.

† Before railways, women worked as toll-collectors and gatekeepers on turnpike roads.

‡ Of a total of 138,500 employees.

> was loaded into railway wagons and carried to be loaded into barges at Tag Lock. On the return journeys the teamsters would call on Red Ellen, ostensibly to give their horses a blow, though an equally important reason was to give themselves a rest and to receive a can of tea at her cottage before starting the long steep climb back up to the quarries.
>
> Ellen's single storey cottage contained two small rooms. There was a little yard at the rear, and alongside the railway was the sty in which she kept a pig. Amenities at the cottage were, of course, simple, the oil for her lamps and for the signal cabin was brought by train from Elland together with cans containing her water supply.
>
> There appeared to be a definite rivalry amongst Ellen's many visitors in bringing gifts, even poaching was not unknown. Rabbits and hares were caught in the woods and fish were taken from Tag Lock. Enginemen would throw nice lumps of coal as they passed, all in all it was a well arranged effort by her numerous friends. One day Ellen let it be known that she had suffered a grievous loss in the death of her pig. A score of helpful suggestions were put forward as the day wore on and in the afternoon when a goods train stopped, the tale was retold. After a little thought the train crew persuaded Ellen to retain the carcase for a day or two. This she did and a couple of days later another train stopped, one of its wagons held a consignment of pigs. A live pig was lifted out and Ellen's dead one substituted. The train proceeded on its way, leaving much happier Ellen.[26]

Crossing gates were operated according to local requirements: some were opened just a few times a day, others 50 times or more. It was usual for a gatekeeper to be on duty from the first train to the last, leaving only about six hours free of work before the next day's service began. If the gates were left closed against the road, drivers wishing to cross would wake the gatekeeper at any hour of the night. As well as opening and closing the gates, the gatekeeper also filled the gate lamps with oil, lit and extinguished them so that the gates were illuminated during the hours of darkness and in fog or falling snow, trimmed the wicks and polished the bull's eye lenses. At some crossings there were levers to pull to release and lock the gates.

Gatekeepers had to supervise vehicles using the crossing and be competent in emergencies. At Mrs Turner's (unnamed) crossing on the GCR, a cart's wheel became jammed in the crossing timbers just as a train was due. Mrs Turner seized her red flag and raced along the track, waving it furiously at the engine driver of the approaching train, who was unable to stop in time. Fortunately, no one was hurt in the collision.[27] Despite this and other displays of competence by gatewomen, there was a lack of confidence in them. The MR's instructions for the working of a royal train in 1904 ruled:

> At all Level Crossings which are in charge of Gatewomen, a competent man must be employed thereat, one hour before the Pilot Engine is due to pass until a quarter of an hour after the Royal Train has passed.[28]

Working in the vicinity of moving trains constitutes a danger to life and limb and requires constant vigilance. The aforementioned Elizabeth Peddlesden of Bexhill was killed operating her crossing, and Mary Haviland, keeper of Marston Crossing, died on 14th March 1870 in the following circumstances:

> SHOCKING RAILWAY ACCIDENT. On Monday afternoon an Inquest was held at the house adjoining the railway crossing between Marston-on-Dove and Rolleston, before Mr Joseph Sale, coroner, on the body of Mary Avelin*, aged 42. The evidence went to show that the deceased had attended to the gates of her crossing for about four years, her husband being employed as a night watchman on the North Stafford line at Egginton.
>
> On Saturday morning she was drying some clothes on the bridge next to the down line, and she crossed over the rails to attend to them at about twenty minutes past eleven o'clock, at which time the passenger train from Burton to Tutbury and the Macclesfield luggage train were due, and closely approaching the crossing. On her return, it is supposed, she was either discomfited by the boisterous wind, or her attention attracted towards the passenger train, for she was knocked down in the four foot† by the luggage train, run over, and her body literally cut in two. The husband, who was working a few yards away in his garden, hurried up to render his unfortunate wife assistance, but only got there in time to find her a corpse, and her mangled body lying — one part in the six-foot, and the other part in the four-foot. Verdict: Accidental death.[29]

Another press report, this time from 1912, describes how a gatewoman lost her life while trying to save the gates from demolition by some runaway trucks:

> The woman keeper of a level-crossing at Limeston Hall, Millom, Cumberland, was killed last Friday night while courageously attending to her duties. A portion of a goods train became detached a few miles out of Millom, and when the first portion reached the crossing the woman, an elderly widow named Raynes, let it through and, thinking it complete, turned the gates across the metals to allow the passage of a horse and cart. Then the uncoupled trucks came rushing along and Mrs Raynes ran in front and endeavoured to reclose the gates. She was knocked down and killed.[30]

The isolated position of level crossings made gatekeepers vulnerable. In 1861, 72-year-old Jane Emmerson was found beaten to death at Botcherby Crossing, Newcastle and Carlisle Railway. She was the widow of the previous gatekeeper, and had performed his duties while he was ill and for six years since his death. Her married daughter and two grandchildren lived with her, but they were away. The motive was robbery: silver spoons, linen sheets, 25s put aside for the quarterly rent, and a sum of between £5 and £10 saved for her funeral were missing. A reward of £150 was offered jointly by the directors of the railway and the Home Office. William Charlton, a 35-year-old engine driver, was charged, found guilty, and publicly hanged before a crowd of six to eight thousand onlookers.

Crossing keepers' pay was assessed by taking into account the hours of attendance, the frequency of traffic and the gender of the incumbent. In the 19th century a woman could earn as much as 20s a week and as little as zero. To earn 20s was exceedingly rare; typical wages were 3s to 10s. Mrs Corbett, at Craven Arms, GWR, earned 5s when appointed in 1872 and in 1911 Mrs Kemp at Arundel, LBSCR, was paid 5s 6d and lived in a rent-free cottage

---

* The newspaper misspelled her name.

† The 'four foot' is the space between the two running rails – it is a contraction of 4ft 8 1/2 inches, the standard gauge; the 'six foot' is the space between two sets of running rails.

worth 3s a week. In some cases the rent-free cottage was the sole remuneration.

Wives of station masters on the NBR were automatically employed as crossing keepers wherever their husbands were posted. For example, between 1898 and 1909 Kingsbarns in Fife was run by a succession of four couples. The husband's salary was £55 to £70 per annum, the wife's just 1/20th of this: 1s 3d a week – the price of a dozen eggs!

It sounds bizarre today, but a woman crossing-keeper's pay was reduced if she was married to a railwayman, and sometimes it was linked to her husband's grade: the more he earned, the less she did. For example, NBR gatekeepers who were married to station masters were paid 1s 3d, while the wives of trackmen received 2s 6d for the same work.

Sometimes a man held the post of gatekeeper as well as that of a porter or platelayer. In such cases his wife ostensibly minded the gates for him while he was at work. A railwayman's day lasted at least 12 hours, plus travelling time to and from his workplace, and he may have stopped off at a public house for a well-earned drink or three. He'd arrive home exhausted – maybe drunk – and in no fit state to operate a level crossing. And so, in practice, the wife as likely as not operated the gates full-time. Not being employees such women were not on the payroll; any wages went to the husband. In 1857 the GNR raised the pay of the station master at Manston & Cross Gates by 2s to 40s a week in respect of his wife's operating the gates 'in his absence'.[31] In 1911 women on the Thirsk and Malton branch of the NER were dissatisfied with operating their crossings from 6 a.m. till 5 p.m. for nothing but a rent-free cottage. A year's campaign resulted in a 1s rise for the husbands, leaving the women still unremunerated and without employee status.[32] Paying a husband for his wife's work was not viewed with the outrage such a practice would arouse today because, till 1870, a married woman's earnings belonged in law to her husband, in any case. Some railways continued the tradition long after the law was changed: the NER, for example, observed the custom till 1922.

Once a crossing job was obtained, a woman would hold on to it with tenacity. The turnover of gatekeepers was lower than that of any other grade; for example the LBSCR reported in 1858 that it was 6% compared with 21% for porters.[33] It was rare for a woman to resign or retire; she normally left only because her husband was transferred to another location or because of her failing health. If possible she would endeavour to pass on the job to her daughter or some other female relation.

Some female gatekeepers completed very long service. Miss Rough was at Rosemount, Caledonian Railway (later, LMS) from 1904 till 1927; Ann Tweddle worked at Bardon Mill, NER, from 1890 till 1927;[34] Mrs Critchley operated Finney Lane Crossing, LYR, from 1902 till 1946.[35] Alice Tubbs worked at Durley Crossing, LSWR, for 48 years, having taken it over from her father in 1906. Mrs Jane Cherry (listed in the 1901 Census as a 'Farmer and Rly Gatekeeper') was employed on 9th June 1862 at Waitby Gate, between Appleby and Kirkby Stephen, NER, and retained her post for 54 years till she died in service, aged 90, on 28th September 1916.[36] But even this impressive record was surpassed. In 1892 Mrs Cockshott took over Niffany Crossing, near Skipton, MR, and the tenancy of the cottage in which she was born, from her mother, who had worked there for 22 years. Fifty-six years later she told her employer, by then British Railways, that she intended to remain 'indefinitely'.[37] It is not known when she ceased to work for BR but between them she and her mother operated the crossing for at least 78 years.

Because crossing keepers worked in the public eye they were not as shrouded in obscurity as other railwaywomen; it is therefore odd that the trade journal *Railway Magazine*, presumably an authority on the industry, claimed in 1913:

> Abroad women are often employed as crossing keepers, and occasionally have control of a small roadside signal cabin as well; but in this country there are only a few instances where level crossings are in the charge of females.[38]

In fact, there were 437. Women comprised 13% of Britain's 3,453 gatekeepers but the greatest concentration was on the GWR, where they operated 40% of all crossings.

Women residential gatekeepers had the lowest wages, the worst hours and the poorest status of any railway workers. They had no promotional prospects; they didn't even get a uniform. Usually in isolated, rural locations, they had no workmates. The popularity of the occupation reveals much about the poor state of women's employment outside of railways. In comparison with typical 'women's work', which would require childcare to be arranged and paid for, and journeys to be made to and from the workplace, it was a convenient job for a wife and mother, enabling her to provide her family with — at the very least — a house and, usually, a small income as well. Despite being in the lowest grade, a gatewoman was entitled to feel that her job was an important and responsible one, and that she was contributing to the safe running of Britain's railways.

Shipping

Railways operated a large number of shipping services from 1846 until 1984 and also opened their own docks. The year in which women first worked in the railways' marine divisions is not known, nor are their exact numbers, grades and duties. The GCR portmaster's staff list for 1914 shows ten female employees but does not reveal the positions they held. They were likely to have been in the area of ticket sales and catering, although some may have been stewardesses on board steamships. There are no records relating to the employment of ships' stewardesses, but at least two — Miss Ada Preston and Mary Ann Rogers — worked for the LSWR aboard the SS *Stella*, which operated between Southampton and St Peter Port, Guernsey. Their names are known because they were both killed in service.

Senior Stewardess Rogers was a 44-year-old widow. In 1883 her husband, a seaman, had been washed overboard from a LSWR ferry, at which time she had a four-year-old daughter, was expecting another child, and had an elderly father to support. Annie Bryans, who travelled on the *Stella* four times in early 1899, said:

> I was fortunate to be tended by Mrs Rogers. From the first I was struck by her cheery, bright, capable ways: and on my last voyage with her I was in great sorrow, and her kindness was so cheering that I could not help specially thanking her, and this drew her own sad story. Some sixteen years ago her husband was killed at sea. She had then one girl and her boy was born soon after. To bring them up and educate them well became her first object in life and she obtained the situation of stewardess. She told me that it was five years before she lost her own sea-sickness, and during all that time she struggled on attending to others and sticking to her post for her children's sake.
>
> She found that on foggy nights people were sometimes nervous, and then she would look round to reassure those who were not sleeping. In speaking of her children she drew herself up, happily saying, 'Any mother might be proud of them, they are so good. I hope soon, when my son has finished his apprenticeship, to retire from sea life'.[39]

That day, alas, was never to come, for on 30th March 1899 the SS *Stella* was wrecked after striking the Casquets (a mass of rock) in thick fog. Of her passengers and crew 105 were lost and 112 saved. Most women on board survived, but both stewardesses perished.

On 10th April an unattributed, third-hand account of how Mary Ann Rogers sacrificed her life to save others appeared in *The Times.* Seizing upon this, women's rights campaigner Frances Power Cobbe wrote a letter to the editor for publication, eulogising Mrs Rogers as 'One of the most sublime figures in our Island story' and offering £25 towards a memorial fund. Annie Bryans founded one, and contributions were obtained from 519 people. A canopied drinking fountain was built and unveiled in 1901 opposite Southampton Pier. The inscription was written by Frances Power Cobbe herself:

> In memory of the heroic death of Mary Ann Rogers, Stewardess of the 'Stella', who on the night of the 30 March, 1899 amid the terror of shipwreck aided all the women under her charge to quit the vessel in safety, giving up her own life-belt to one who was unprotected. Urged by the sailors to make sure her escape she refused lest she might endanger the heavily-laden boat. Cheering the departing crew with the friendly cry of 'good-bye, good-bye.' She was seen a few moments later as the 'Stella' went down lifting her arms upwards with the prayer 'Lord have me' then sank in the waters with the sinking ship.

When, in 1900, the Memorial of Heroic Deeds was opened in Postman's Park in the City of London to commemorate people whose selfless actions saved the lives of others, it incorporated a tablet inscribed to Mrs Rogers. In 1908, the committee of the new Liverpool Anglican Cathedral included her in a group of 21 notable women depicted in the Staircase Window in the Lady Chapel.

Jake Simpkin, a local historian based in Southampton, points out that although the inquiry expresses the 'greatest admiration' for all the crew, including both stewardesses, it did not single out Mary Ann Rogers for special mention. Undoubtedly she lost her life in the course of duty; however, he suspects that the description of her last moments may be a little embroidered.[40]

Senior Stewardess Rogers

COURTESY OF GUERNSEY MUSEUM

Dyeing carriage window blinds at Stratford Works, 1911. GER MAGAZINE

Sewing machinists at Stratford Works, 1911. GER MAGAZINE

Workshops

Railway workshops supplied an extraordinarily wide range of items needed to run the industry, from steam engines to window blinds, and staff were employed in dozens of tasks, many of them highly skilled. Women were engaged as early as 1840 but were not accepted into apprenticeships; instead they were restricted to certain tasks thought suitable for their gender. Seamstresses were probably first hired when train seats began to be upholstered in the mid-19th century. This task was performed in the trimming shops, where the insides of carriages were fitted. From the 1870s women were engaged as sewing machinists, upholsterers and blind-dyers, while others were employed to knit the string netting for overhead luggage racks, to French-polish carriage panelling and to paint small cast-iron objects, such as the multicoloured coats of arms that ornamented engines and carriages. Women also mended sacks; for example, in the late 1880s the MR employed 12 needlewomen to keep their 450,000 sacks in good repair. Storeswomen were sometimes employed to issue items as needed; this was a highly responsible job given only to the most honest and trustworthy individuals. Most commonly, women staffed the workshop canteens and the tea trolleys.

Wolverton carriage and wagon works, the principal workshops of the LNWR, employed women soon after it opened in 1836, although in what capacity is not known. In 1906 it was noted that 40 were engaged in French polishing and a further 24 worked in the laundry. A further 60 worked in the cutting out room as sewers and trimmers, with ten more being engaged by 1914.[41]

The GER employed women at Stratford Works in east London from 1894. By 1911 there were nearly 60, the majority of whom, it was noted, were orphans of railwaymen.[42] *The Great Eastern Railway Magazine* published photographs of three grades: blind dyers, French polishers and machinists. Their workplace appears light and spacious, and the women look neat and conscientious. As well as the manufacture of new blinds, the carriage department undertook the cleaning, dyeing and repair of 30,000 blinds each year.

Women were also employed in railway-owned printing workshops. One of them, Charlotte Hoskins, was a book folder-and-sewer at the GER Printing Works at Stratford from 1864 till her death at the age of 71 in 1913, a total of 39 years' service, during which time she raised three children.[43] Her colleague Mrs Attridge was engaged in 1862 and, almost 30 years later, gained promotion to forewoman of the female section. She eventually completed over 50 years' service.[44] Another long serving workshopwoman was Margaret Scott, Forewoman Storekeeper at St Rollox, Glasgow & South Western Railway (GSWR), from 1904. She issued such items as flags, boiler suits, horses' nosebags and wagon covers. Later, she supervised a group of 104 cleaners till her retirement in 1953, at which time she had completed 49 years in railway service.[45]

By 1914, over 850 women were employed in railway workshops. Of these, 43 were classed as labourers, but unfortunately neither their exact duties nor the classification of the other 814 were recorded.

Clerks-in-Charge/Station Mistresses

Among the first women employed on Britain's railways were those universally known as 'station mistresses' but who were, in fact, the female equivalent of a clerk-in-charge (or porter-in-charge), a railwayman who sold tickets and performed administrative work at a small station or halt. As the sole member of staff, the clerk-in-charge also performed the duty of crossing keeper (where applicable) and of porter (weighing and handling parcels, attending to trains and passengers, lighting signal and station lamps, etc). If the station had a siding, there might have been a ground frame of points levers to operate. Very few women filled these posts; they were usually daughters, wives and widows of railwaymen and were engaged only at quiet, rural stations, purely at the whim of local management. Their titles were various and included station agent, lady station master, halt attendant and station mistress, the term most railwaymen, passengers, journalists and other observers used to describe them and which, therefore, will be used henceforth.

The first female railway employee whose name is recorded was described as a station mistress. Mary Argyle, a working wife, had charge of Merry Lees, Leicester & Swannington Railway (which was later absorbed into the MR) for nearly 39 years, from its opening on 17th July 1832 till its closure on 28th February 1871.[46] She performed all the duties of porter, booking clerk and crossing keeper and assisted when wagons were shunted into the siding. Her weekly pay was 2s 6d, raised to 3s 6d in 1847. Stretton, historian of the MR, wrote that he had often watched her climb 'up the ladder of the home-signal and light the lamps as well as any man'.[47] Her employer built a station house in 1839, which she occupied with her husband, a platelayer.[48]

There were isolated instances of station mistresses all over Victorian Britain. In 1849 they were recorded at Thornley and at Hesleden, on the Hartlepool Railway and Docks; at Elrington, NER;[49] Rosemount, Caledonian Railway and Braceborough Spa Halt, GNR.[50] St Harmon's Halt, Cambrian Railway, boasted at least two. In his diary for Thursday, 4th May 1876, Kilvert described Station Mistress Sarah Jones as 'A handsome, pleasant-faced woman, very stout, who lives in a cottage on the line.' At the turn of the century Mrs E. J. Bebb was described as St Harmon's 'Station mistress Gatekeeper' at a wage of 10s a week. Miss Anne Jenkins was listed as the 'agent' at Dolwen.[51] The incumbent at Langford, GER, was featured on a postcard in 1910 bearing the claim that she was the only station mistress in Britain.[52] From the 1890s till 1926 Harriet James ran two stations on the Ffestiniog to Bala line with her husband Robert, formerly the station master at Bala. They occupied the station house at Trawsfynedd and Mrs James regularly cycled nearly five miles uphill to operate Trawsfynedd crossing gates and, from 1902, a halt at Cwm Prysor, a lonely and mountainous spot by Tryweryn Lake, 1,200 feet above sea level. It was said that the latter task 'required considerable pluck and determination'. While pursuing her railway career Mrs James raised three daughters. On her retirement at age 65 the managers presented her with an armchair.[53]

On the LBSCR, Miss Robinson took over Woodgate* on her father's death in 1862 till her marriage the following year and, about the turn of the century, Nellie Piggot was the station mistress at Ockley.[54] The London & South Western Railway (LSWR) also had at least

* Woodgate comprised a halt and a level crossing. It closed in 1864.

A WOMAN STATION-MASTER

WHIPPINGHAM STATION

Flag Signalling and Shunting.

as Signalman.

Lamplighter & Trimmer Hoisting Light on Signal-Post.

as Billposter.

Without railways, Christmas, as we know it to-day, would be impossible. There would be none of those happy family re-unions in the old home which have become so characteristic of this gladsome festive season; it would be almost impossible to send Christmas greetings to friends at a distance; and the good things which we depend upon to grace our tables at this season of good fellowship and good fare could never reach us. So, as we go our journeys and send our messages over the iron road this Christmastide, let us give a thought to the great army of railway workers who will be toiling for the common good even while we are merrymaking. Mrs. Merwood, of Whippingham, is the only lady station-mistress in the country who has so many novel duties to perform. Mrs. Merwood is naturally busiest in the holiday season, but at Christmas time as well she has plenty to do.

Photos: Cribb, Southsea.

Mrs Jenkyn in 1910, with her niece and nephew, their father and some railway workers.
She is standing next to her 'request-stop' signal post. Anita Nicholls

Station mistress Sarah Jenkyn, Latchley

Mrs Jenkyn's house, which she is facing in the above photo.
The level crossing is in the foreground, this side of the cattle-grid and just out of shot. Anita Nicholls

Alverstone station, Isle of Wight. Mrs Young's house and the crossing gates she operated. ORIGIN UNKNOWN

STATION MISTRESS FANNY YOUNG, ALVERSTONE

Cranking the handle to hoist the signal up the post and pulling a lever of the ground frame. ISLAND RAIL NEWS

Cwm Prysor, c1902. The woman nearest the platform edge is Station Mistress Harriet James. Her husband is standing alongside her. COURTESY OF LINDA COLLINS

one: Mrs Jenkyn — born Sarah Jane Thomas in 1890 — grew up in a house opposite Latchley Halt, on a goods line in Cornwall.[*] When the line was opened to passenger traffic in 1908 she was invited to be station mistress. According to a Board of Trade Inspection Report, 'There is a home signal in each direction worked from the platform whenever it is required to stop a train'. Although she married and raised four children she stayed in her post till the line closed in 1966. In connection with her 48-year railway career, Mrs Jenkyn has been mentioned in several local history books and in later life appeared twice on television. She died in 1979.[55]

At least four station mistresses are known to have worked on the Isle of Wight prior to 1915. About 1900 Emily Merwood took over Whippingham from her father-in-law. The station, on the Newport to Ryde line, had been built to serve Queen Victoria's home, Osborne House, though it was later opened to the general public. In 1908 a full-page feature about Mrs Merwood was published in *Horner's Weekly* with photographs showing her pulling levers, posting bills and flag-signalling (see page 21). She retired in 1912, aged 69.[56] Mrs Prouten worked at the private station of Watchingwell, on the Freshwater line, for at least ten years.[†] Alverstone's station mistresses included Mary Ann Buckett,[‡] who was noted as being there in 1899, and her successor Frances Young, who was interviewed by Ethel Hargrove about 1913:

[*] Latchley Halt was opened in 1872 as Cox's Park, on the Callington branch of the East Cornwall Mineral Railway, which was taken over by the Plymouth, Devonport and South Western Junction Railway, which later amalgamated with the LSWR.

[†] The exact dates of Mrs Prouten's service are unknown. She was recorded as working at Watchingwell in 1923, and Mrs Young mentioned her in 1913.

[‡] John Buckett — possibly Mary's father — was at Sandown in 1864. Malcolm Buckett, - possibly her son — was stationmaster at Ryde in 1931.

What a kind station-mistress she was, for nothing would satisfy her less than my having a good rest in her comfortable parlour, where a fire was burning brightly, much to the satisfaction of a sleepy black and white cat.

Mrs Young informed me that she had occupied her present position for over twelve years, adding proudly 'It's in the family'. Seeing my look of surprise she informed me that her husband was a platelayer on the line, her two elder sons clerks, her two brothers, crane and engine drivers, her uncle a fireman on the engine, and she concluded proudly — 'Even my brother-in-law is a crane driver!'

I sat down in the pretty room; the wall-paper was a bright terra-cotta, and an extra door led into Mrs Young's office, for she has her accounts to do. 'In addition to my other work,' she laughed, 'I issue tickets, manage all the signalling, open the gates, wind up the lamps. I am provided with cardboard tickets available as far as Ryde Pier Head. If folks wish to travel beyond the Island I have to write them out paper ones. In the winter I am not so busy as in the summer, as the trains are less frequent. I go on duty for twelve and a half hours, but I am not overworked, as it is not constant.'

'What do you do when you are off duty?' I inquired. 'I am very fond of travelling to other parts of the Isle of Wight,' admitted Mrs Young, 'but I have never gone far on the other side of the water. I have only once been in the train there, as far as Chichester. I have not had much opportunity for reading, as the house keeping takes up much of my spare time. I am glad to say that I have enjoyed very good health, in fact I have never once had the doctor in all my life!' Mrs Young then told me she was a thorough 'Islander', having been born within a mile of Alverstone, at Borthwood, and married eighteen years ago at Newport, the Island capital.

'I love my work,' she exclaimed, 'and I have always found it to be quite suitable in every way. I do not see why other women should not take it up, and it is certainly more full of interest and variety than most other occupations'.[57]

Abbotsford Ferry, NBR, was in the hands of just two station mistresses for the whole of its 85-year existence. Jane Stubbs (b.1830), the wife of a platelayer, was in charge from 1856 till 1885 when her daughter Jane Ann (b.1861) — whose married name was Elder — took over. It is notable that Mrs Elder completed 46 years' service and said she would have remained even longer had the station not closed in 1931.[58]

Braystones was run by four successive women between 1849 and 1928. It was recorded as being in female hands when it was opened by the Whitehaven and Furness Junction Railway in 1849. On 29th December 1873 Mrs Caldwell, aged 28, was appointed 'Clerk in Charge' at 7s 6d a week, but she resigned after six months and was replaced by 41-year-old widow Maria McGill, whose husband had been station master at Seascale. Her title was 'Agent and Clerk in Charge' and her 10s a week wage, together with the tenancy of the station house were doubtless extremely welcome as she had six children to support, aged 14, 13, ten, eight, six and four. Mrs McGill was much respected in seafaring circles for the help she gave to seamen wrecked on the nearby shore. Her descendants still own a bible given to her by the captain of a ship.[59] She was described as a 'Station master' in 1889 and again in the Census of 1901. Mrs McGill was nominally station mistress at Braystones till she was 74, but her youngest child Catherine ('Kit') was doing most of the work by that time and in 1907 she took over officially. Mrs McGill died in 1912 and Miss Kit retained the post till her retirement at age 58, ostensibly through ill health, in 1928. (The real reason was her resentment towards the LMS for taking over the Whitehaven and Furness company: in fact, she was in fine health and reached the age of 97.) There was speculation in the press as to whether she was the last station mistress in England.[60]

Cumbria boasted a number of other station mistresses. Sarah Parker was at Calthwaite (recorded in 1864), Mrs Ashworth was at Papcastle (1891), and Mrs Gasgaith was at the private station of Dovenby (1894). The latter's successor was Elizabeth Davidson who, it was recorded, issued and collected tickets, managed the signals and did every other duty in connection with the service. Mrs N. Carty was noted as station mistress at Linefoot in 1909 and at Papcastle in 1919, and Mrs Dixon was recorded at Rampside in 1911. These were all tiny stations, and — except in two cases — the incumbent was the sole member of staff.[61]

Station mistresses earned between 2s and 6s a week, while their male equivalent, a clerk-in-charge, received between 25s and 45s (in 1870) and even the lowest paid men, such as crossing keepers, earned 17s. In most cases a cottage or house was provided for the station mistress, either gratis or at a very low rent.

Maria McGill, station mistress at Braystones 1874-1912.

D. Ravenswood

Salaried Grades

'Salaried' is a blanket term used to describe railway workers employed in administrative or booking offices, in technical departments and as supervisors and managers of clerical or wages grade staff. As in other industries, this kind of work was a male preserve, with a few isolated exceptions.

The first report of women in railway booking offices appeared in The Times in 1858:

> In taking a ticket the other day at the Edinburgh station of the Edinburgh, Perth and Dundee Railway, we were pleasantly surprised on being waited upon by a blooming and bonnie lassie, who, along with an activity quite equal to, exhibited a politeness very rare in, railway clerks of the literally ruder sex. We observed that the department was entirely occupied by women, there being another giving out tickets, and a third telegraphing. This innovation thus far north is rather startling; but, instead of objecting to it, we think it highly commendable, and hope to see the employment of women in light occupations rapidly extended. The only inconvenience we can see is that good-looking and intelligent girls like those ... will not book many passengers before they are booked themselves for the life-long journey of matrimony, so that the company will soon lose their services. We wish them for that journey first-class tickets.[62]

They set no precedent, however, and for the remainder of the 19th century few women worked in ticket offices. In the 1880s a few were employed by the LSWR at Honiton, Axminster, Sidmouth and Crewkerne.[63] The LBSCR at one time employed about 20, including Miss Alice Strevett at Hailsham, Miss Harris at Partridge Green, Nellie Piggot at Ockley, May Martin at Mitcham and Jane Piper at Bramley.[64] Julia Sparks worked at Cheam from 1892 to 1894 when, aged 18, she was married.[65] The 1881 Census lists Miss Frances M. Roach, aged 16, the station master's daughter, as 'Railway Telegraph and Booking Clerk' at Plumpton. One source explained that as their places fell vacant the LBSCR replaced all its female booking clerks with men, but at least one remained: Miss Strevett was still working at Hailsham 20 years later.

In 1907 the managers of the London Underground calculated that large sums could be saved by replacing men with women in its booking offices. *The Railway Gazette* remarked: 'Girl clerks will be experimentally engaged at the Charing Cross Tube Station, and the adoption of the plan on a more extensive scale will be dependent on the results obtained here.'[66] Two weeks later the *Gazette* reported 'several objections' to hiring girls:

> Such an innovation has obviously only one raison d'être, that of economy, and as the company is already paying its male clerks very small salaries, ranging, in fact, from 13s. to 18s. a week, it is difficult to see the possibility of much more substantial reductions ... Women do not give such particular satisfaction in this capacity, which demands more knowledge and experience than are necessary for the duties of an ordinary cash-desk assistant, who has merely to receive payments and give change. This is especially the case on the London tube lines, where so many alternative through routes, with through tickets, are now available. It is significant that in Scotland, where the girl booking clerk has been tried in isolated and special instances, the original number of the appointments has practically never undergone an increase ... We believe, however, that the Underground Company has reconsidered its decision, and that women clerks are not to be employed, at least for the present.[67]

'Red Ellen' at the gateway of her cottage at Tag Lock Crossing. Her disc and crossbar signal can be seen far left. F. Prince

Left: Refreshment room staff at Wolverton. Origin unknown

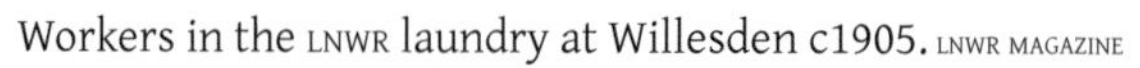

Workers in the LNWR laundry at Willesden c1905. LNWR magazine

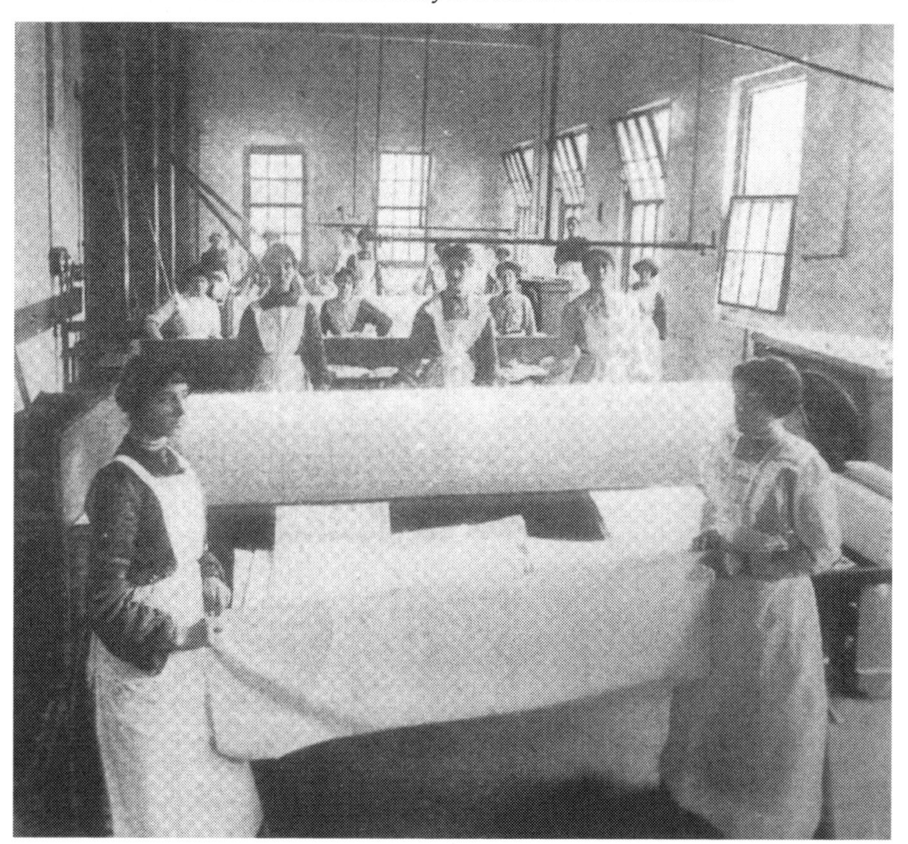

Administrative clerks

On railways, as in wider industry, the transfer of simple clerical work from men to women began in the last quarter of the 19th century. Women clerks in administrative posts were placed in 'female sections' supervised by other women and performed routine work only. In the early 1870s, for example, a group was engaged to sort used tickets in the NER accountant's department at Newcastle[68] and, in 1875, the LNWR's accountant tentatively employed 15 women as an experiment before recruiting a further 180 in the 1890s. They were judged 'fairly successful both on the score of economy and efficiency'.[69]

The introduction of free universal schooling from the 1870s extended education in the 'Three Rs' to the working classes and by the 1880s many more girls were sufficiently literate to be employed in clerical work. By the late 1890s all the larger railway offices employed women and some sustained long service. Miss L. J. Rieder joined the accounts department at Camden LNWR in 1888 and worked there for 50 years, during which time she gained promotion to supervisor. Twelve were engaged at King's Cross, London, in March 1900, provoking considerable discussion amongst RCA members, because they were paid only 12s a week, far less than the men. In 1902 women were engaged in York's Traffic Statistics Office on low salaries (between £48 and £90 per annum.) The Metropolitan Railway replaced men ticket sorters with women in 1913 and, in 1914, twelve girls were hired as diagram tracers in the GWR draughtsmen's office. When typewriters came into common use they quickly became a female monopoly and, although the work was skilled, it came to be seen as women's work and a low value was placed in it. By 1911 there were 1,120 women railway clerks in England and Wales compared with 84,802 men.[70]

The last male bastion to fall was the Railway Clearing House (RCH)* which maintained an all-male workforce from its founding in 1842 till 1912, when 27 female relatives of the male staff were employed. One of the men wrote a poem about them (reproduced overleaf).[71] Two years later the RCH had a staff of 180 women and 2,300 men.[72]

New areas of work were opened to women for two reasons: they were cheap, and they were considered to be more compliant than men. They were kept to routine tasks without responsibility or autonomy, partly because it was believed that women were weak mentally as well as physically and would crumble under stress. A railway clerk's wife reflected this belief when she wrote in 1900 that many clerical positions on the railway were 'impossible for a woman to fill' because 'she is not constituted to bear the worry and mental strain of particular railway clerical work.'[73] Some RCA members, including a number on its Executive Committee, went even further by opposing women's performing clerical work at all. One wrote to *The Railway Clerk*:

> Every effort should be made by the Association to convince the railway companies not to employ them, as female labour is a false economy and it takes several years of service and intelligent application to become that mysterious entity, a good railwayman.[74]

Such men were swimming against the tide. As the Edwardian era began, an increasing number of women were employed in railway offices. A good many served for several years, applied themselves intelligently and became 'good railwaymen'.

---

* The RCH, based at Euston, apportioned profits from fares to each company. It disbanded in 1963.

THE ADVENT OF THE SKIRT

The introduction of girl clerks into the Railway Clearing House has inspired the following :—

The years go by, and time and change,
Have altered our conditions;
And one by one, our old ideals,
Have gone with old traditions.
We know not what each day may bring,
Or who will be our neighbour,
The whole place is disorganized,
Because of cheaper labour.

Now, girls have come to swell our ranks,
The scheme at last has ripened;
And "22/6" per week,
Is quite a handsome stipend.
So! fathers, send your daughters up,
For they, at varying ages,
May reach this splendid maximum,
By very easy stages.

Perchance! this money-saving scheme,
May make their saving double;
And yet, it's clear to everyone,
They're only seeking trouble.
For, when a woman will, she will,
All other rules forgetting,
And Seymour Street, like Westminster,
May see some Suffragetting.

The sanctity of inner rooms,
That keeps men at a distance,
Will have no terror for the girls,
Or stem their bold resistance.
And, claiming by a woman's right,
Without a shade of pity,
They'll worry Heads, and Heads of D,
And way-lay the Committee.

Methinks! the staff have had enough,
Of shocks and sad surprises;
And men are waiting wearily,
Anticipating rises.
And now the girls are coming in
To make all this commotion;
The work will never get ahead,
And neither will promotion.

A spoof of *The Song of the Shirt*, written by a member of the Railway Clearing House staff, 1912.

THE RAILWAY CLERK

COMMUNICATIONS

The growth of communications technology opened a fresh source of employment to women. Telegraphing and operating a switchboard were dead-end jobs, which made them unattractive to men, and so they were offered to women on lower rates of pay.

The first woman railway telegraphist was employed by the Edinburgh, Perth and Dundee Railway at Edinburgh Waverley in 1858. Mrs Annie Bond appears in the 1861 Census as the telegraph clerk at Eastbourne, LBSCR, and in 1872 Miss E. Ashcroft was engaged at Edinburgh Waverley (by then under the auspices of the NBR). At Yeovil, LSWR, two sisters — daughters of Locomotive Superintendent Rouse — were employed in 1884.[75] In the 1890s Miss Bishop was the telegraphist at Sutton, LBSCR.[76]

Gradually telegraph work at many larger stations was transferred to women on lower pay than the men they replaced. In 1900 managers at Edinburgh Waverley recruited 40 women who were soon sending over 4,000 messages every day.[77] The following year the NER engaged six at York, and paid them 7s 6d each a week, as compared with a GNR junior male clerk's wage of about 11s (in 1904). In 1909 the GWR employed 13 learners and a supervisor at Paddington and six learners and a senior operator at Bristol. *The Great Western Railway Magazine* remarked:

> In the new school, sounder and single needle circuits have been erected, representing, for example, Paddington-Birmingham, Paddington-Cardiff, and as soon as the learners have mastered the alphabet they are given actual messages to signal under the rules and regulations obtaining in a telegraph office. At Paddington, a lady supervisor, having considerable experience of railway telegraph work, has been appointed, which augurs well for future success.
>
> It is generally known that the duties of a telegraph operator are arduous and exacting, but there is no reason to suppose the ladies will be found wanting, and it will then be possible for the male operators to be drafted into positions where there is greater scope for promotion in the service. This experiment will be watched with interest, and will, it is hoped, meet with success.[78]

Among those watching 'with interest' was the RCA, a member of which wrote in shocked tones to his union's newspaper that 'girls are being appointed at about half the salary!'[79]

As well as threatening to displace men by accepting lower wages, women were rostered the most sociable hours, in consequence of which men had to work more late and night duties. It is hardly surprising, therefore, that the employment of women was reported to be 'creating bitter feeling right through the department.' The cure: 'Needless to say we are in favour of sex equality all round' declared one avant-garde RCA member in 1912.[80]

Telephony was a later development and companies made switchboard operating available to women from the outset. Among the first were six engaged by the LBSCR at London Bridge in 1912 at 15s to 16s a week. All had been trained by, and had previously worked for, the General Post Office. Rules were strict and working conditions poor for both sexes. The GWR's contract of employment forbade telegraphists and telephonists from resigning in order to work for another company till they had completed three years' service.* The ten-hour day was regularly exceeded and little — if any — attention was

---

* Presumably this was enforced by the company's refusal to give references.

given to the provision of mess-rooms or toilets. Furthermore, the heating, lighting and ventilation in offices were usually inadequate. Two articles in the RCA newspaper of 1911 and 1912 reveal railwaywomen's working conditions. The first, *Poor Girl!*, pitied the unfortunate switchboard operator at Leicester Goods, MR:

> From 9 a.m. to 6 p.m.; less 1½ hours for dinner, she is inside a box within the chief clerk's office. This in itself is bad enough, the number of calls being sufficient to kill a horse, let alone a woman or a man; but there is not a peg for her clothes and no lavatory accommodation! [81]

The second revealed how two 'lady telegraphists' were being overworked by the LNWR:

> In less than three months both these operators had completely broken down, and one of them after several weeks' illness has resigned in disgust. The other has recommenced, but the strain has been so great that she is still undergoing medical treatment ... The ladies received no payment whatever during their absence through sickness, whereas a male operator would have received half pay, and this is a serious matter for them, as in addition to the loss of pay they have had to meet heavy doctors' bills.[82]

In contrast to their lack of concern for physical welfare the companies fretted over the moral welfare of women staff. Not only were they segregated and watched over by matronly female supervisors, but also their doors were locked to keep men out. The GNR insisted that all female clerks must reside with parents or relatives till the age of 21. The GWR was more lax: it merely demanded that women living away from home prove that they were 'suitably lodged'.

Clerks' Pay and Prospects

There were no national conditions of service, and so wages, leave, free travel and sick pay were different in each company. Generally, a woman clerk could expect at least one free return rail ticket, free travel between home and work, a number of reduced rate tickets, 12 to 15 days' annual leave and four weeks' sick pay per annum. Companies varied in relation to superannuation or pension schemes. The NER admitted women to its fund from its inception in 1882 and, in 1907, to its pension society. In error the company at one time was paying some women higher pensions than they had paid them in wages.[83] In contrast, the MR still had not admitted women clerks to its superannuation fund by 1918.

Remuneration was linked to length of service. Women's pay was generally 5s to 20s a week, while the few female supervisors earned 25s to 40s. As a rule of thumb, women were paid two-thirds of the male rate. However, by an oversight, one group of GWR women clerks was inadvertently placed on a scale that paid them 30s after 11 years' service, while the maximum for male clerks' was 29s after 23 years' service. Furthermore, the women had annual leave and sick pay not extended to their male counterparts. Although this was the sole instance in the whole of Britain's railways of women being paid more than men, rather than vice-versa, men objected strongly and raised the matter at the 1913 RCA annual conference.[84]

Railway companies did not want ambitious career women or dynamic, innovative individualists. Their ideal scenario was to recruit groups of hardworking and, above all, obedient girls aged 14 to 15 to carry out vast amounts of tedious, routine work without complaint and at lower rates than men. After five to ten years of faultless service the majority should leave to get married, leaving behind one or two mature spinsters to train and supervise their successors. Rigid policies, assisted by external social values, were very successful in channelling female staff into this pattern of behaviour. Dorothy R. Dalton B.A. explained that a woman railway clerk was employed 'solely to work under dictation', and 'neither expected or was offered anything but an inferior position; consequently she was not fit for a superior one'. As there were plenty of men to fill vacant posts, she continued, 'women were never even considered for the higher paid, responsible positions.' [85]

Managerial positions were closed to women and, unlike women in wages grades, female clerks were dismissed on marriage. The best a career woman could hope for was a one-step-up promotion to supervisor of a female section; that is to say, a typing pool or telephone exchange. From this point no further promotion was possible and a supervisor would remain at her post until retirement, suspending the ambitions of her subordinates for a good many years. This state of affairs suited male railway clerks perfectly: they were spared much of the dull, routine work and enjoyed promotional opportunities free from female competition.

The scarcity of prospects, the lack of support from male clerks and the marriage bar curbed women's interest in fighting for better pay or conditions, which in turn reinforced the stereotype of the woman clerk as docile. The promotional prospects of many hardworking, dedicated individuals were obstructed by the belief that all women were temporary and unambitious. It is ironic that the marriage bar inflicted the greatest damage upon those who never married: the assumption that they would do so led companies to treat them as temporary, in some cases for 30 or 40 years. The women could do nothing but carry on, seizing what training they could, sitting examinations in subjects such as railway accountancy, while entreating the RCA to get them a better deal. Though denied vertical promotion some women managed to obtain a sideways transfer to head offices in London, where the wages were higher and the work more prestigious. Many diverted their thwarted managerial talents into social, educational, and political pursuits. They organised sports teams and events, first-aid classes and amateur dramatics groups, and a good many became involved in trade union activity.

Although the system discouraged them, there have always been career women on the railways, even among the earliest recruits. The aforementioned Miss Ashcroft, engaged as a telegraphist at Edinburgh Waverley in 1872, held the post for 48 years. Similarly Miss L. J. Rieder joined the NER accounts office at Camden in 1888 and completed 50 years' service. The 'concrete ceiling' ensured that even in a career spanning half a century, women could advance no further than one grade.

Documents relating to groups of women railway clerks are rare, but a near-complete record can be inspected at the National Archives, relating to the staff of Swindon locomotive office, GWR. It provides an interesting example of women's service histories. Grace Buckland, aged 14, and Bessie Flew, 15, were employed in December, 1910, and three more 15-year-olds were engaged three weeks later. They were supervised by new recruit Gladys Noble, aged 19. The girls were paid 7s, raised to 8s after six months, and a shilling was added every year. Miss Noble earned 10s, raised to 14s after six months, and by 1914 she was earning 24s. The shortest period of employment among the clerks was seven years; one remained for 12 years, another for at least 16 years, while her colleague completed 25 years' service. In 1915 seven temporary war-workers were engaged in the same office, but only three left at the end of the war; the others remained for five, nine, 17 and 25 years. Miss Noble worked till ill health forced her early retirement in 1944, after 34 years' service.[86] The length of service completed by this group was comparable with that of men.

Freda and Irene Dening also joined the GWR at Swindon, in 1911 and 1914 respectively, at the age of 14. Keen to learn as much as they could about their chosen career, they travelled to London after work to attend railway-related courses in accountancy and office skills at the London School of Economics. For gaining consistently high marks throughout their three years' study, they became the first women to gain (in 1921 and 1922) the Brunel Silver Medal. Freda was promoted to supervisor of the typists' office while Irene became personal assistant to the stores manager. Both sisters made full use of their free train passes, travelling throughout Europe together. After 43 years' service, Freda resigned at the age of 57 to care for her elderly parents, while Irene retired aged 60 after 46 years.[87] They had both thoroughly enjoyed their work; Freda remarked that the railway was 'a fascinating place.'[88]

The Dening sisters' long service was by no means unique. Many other railwaywomen completed 30 or even 40 years' service. However, they passed into that obscurity which so often seems to engulf women who contravene stereotypical behaviour and, regardless of evidence to the contrary, the belief continued that all women railway clerks were transient.

Trades Unions

The poor conditions, long hours, lack of welfare and high accident rate among railway staff, as well as the rise of the trades union and labour movements contributed to the formation of five railway unions by 1911. They functioned — without the employers' recognition — in whatever ways they could. Before 1914, only the District Railway and the NER recognised the unions, which could act only as pressure-groups in their dealings with all the other companies.

It is not surprising that the Associated Society of Locomotive Engineers and Firemen (ASLEF), formed IN 1880, did not admit women, as they were barred from every grade it represented: driver, fireman and engine cleaner. Nor did the United Pointsmen's and Signalmen's Society (UPSS) admit them, for the same reason. But women were also excluded from the largest union: the Amalgamated Society of Railway Servants (ASRS), which was formed in 1871 and boasted 150,000 members by 1911.

Only two railway unions were open to women before 1915. The Railway Clerks' Association (RCA), formed in 1897, welcomed women from 1907 but the first, Miss C. Greenlees, of the Caledonian Telegraph Office, did not join till 1910. The 24,000-strong General Railway Workers Union admitted wages grade staff of both sexes. There is no record of the number of female members; perhaps some of its 10,000 workshop members were women.

By 1907 only 7% of railway servants enjoyed an eight-hour day while over 25% worked more than 12 hours. The ASRS demanded an eight-hour day for traffic grades, ten hours for other grades, a nine-hour rest period between shifts, a guaranteed week and unsociable hours payments. Demonstrations and mass-meetings were followed by strike threats and, under government pressure, the companies agreed to a conciliation scheme under which representatives from the companies and the workforce would meet to discuss pay and conditions. By 1911 so little had changed that railwaymen all over the country took action. Eventually, 200,000 were on strike and although there was no explicit recognition of the ASRS the companies subsequently allowed union officers to help settle disputes.

At that time the industry's five trades unions had a total membership of over 300,000 — about half the railway workforce. The UPSS, GRWU and ASRS discussed forming one union that would recruit all railway employees, regardless of grade. At a joint meeting, Mr Lowth, General Secretary of the GRWU, which recruited women, challenged the proposed title of the new union, 'The National Union of Railwaymen'. He wanted it amended to 'Railway Workers' because the companies employed over 12,000 women and the new union would want to recruit them. Mr Bellamy, for the ASRS, replied that an imminent change in British law would mean that the term 'man' would soon include women, anyway, and so there was no need to change the name.* Mr Bellamy stated clearly that the word 'railwaymen' was chosen only because the possible alternatives, i.e. 'workers' or 'servants', already featured in the titles of the existing unions and they wanted to avoid giving the impression that one union was swallowing up the others. He emphasised: 'That was the sole reason. It is not to limit membership.' After being given this absolute guarantee that women could join the new union, Mr Lowth withdrew his objection to the title.[89]

The National Union of Railwaymen (NUR) was born on 29th March 1913 with 180,000 members. Eighteen months later membership had reached 273,000. As Mr Lowth had predicted, the name caused problems. Although the amalgamation discussion quoted above was published in 1912, it seems that many branch officers did not read it, because they were unsure if the term 'railwaymen' included women. Because of this, in 1912 and 1913 at least three attempts were made at national level to clarify women's eligibility. To put an end to the ambiguity, some branches proposed a change of title to 'The National Union of Railway Workers' but they were outvoted.[90] However, there was no need to change the title because the union's rulebook made it quite clear that women could join; it stated: 'Any person employed on any railway or in connection with any railway in the United Kingdom shall be eligible for membership.' Women may not be 'railwaymen' but they are, unquestionably, 'persons'.

Women in all industries were keen to join trade unions and by 1913, 433,000 were members, an increase of 300% since 1892.[91] But when women applied to join the NUR their applications were declined.[92] Contradicting the union's rulebook and reneging on the promise given to Mr Lowth, General Secretary J. E. Williams decreed that women were not eligible for membership. Mr Bellamy, who had guaranteed women's inclusion less than two years before, was by then president of the NUR; yet he, and the rest of the EC, agreed with the general secretary. In this they were breaking not only the promise they had made to the GRWU, but also two sections of the rulebook. As well as the aforementioned clause on eligibility, Rule 1, clause 4 (a) decreed that the union intended to recruit: 'All workers employed on or in connection with any railway.'

Six years later, in 1919, Mr Williams' successor as general secretary, Jimmy Thomas, was economical with the truth when he told a government committee:

---

* Mr Bellamy believed that women would soon to win the vote. This did not happen for another six years.

> My union in 1914 did not cater for women. Prior to the war, except in the railway shops and one isolated grade of carriage cleaner, practically no women were engaged upon the railways, that is to say, defining the railways as the manipulation of traffic, not dealing with the office or the clerical side. The result was that women not being engaged, we as a union did not cater for them.[93]

This was nonsense. The NUR had never defined railway work as narrowly as 'the manipulation of traffic'. It welcomed all grades of men, from hotel bartenders to the drivers of horse-drawn vans and the men who trained Jack Russell terriers to catch rats. Only in relation to women was the proviso of 'railway operating' deemed to be an issue. Thomas's glib claim that women were 'not engaged' by railway companies beggars belief: nearly 13,000 were employed. There were over 400 women crossing keepers in 1914, undeniably a job concerned with 'the manipulation of traffic' and yet even they were barred from the NUR. Thomas mentioned the existence of workshopwomen and female carriage cleaners but failed to explain why they were not admitted to the union when, at the same time, their male colleagues were enthusiastically enrolled.* The NUR leaders were building the greatest union in the country, why did they turn down the opportunity of recruiting thousands of members?

This shameful episode in the history of the NUR has been buried. Even the union's historian, Philip Bagwell, claimed in 1982: 'Throughout its history the NUR has sought to organise men and women employed in station restaurants, train restaurant cars and buffets and railway hotels.'[94] This statement is simply not true in relation to women. Mr Thomas's remark seems even more odd when compared with one made by a later NUR leader, John Benstead, who said in 1945 that 'catering is as much an integral part of railway working as is the running of the trains and the operation of the signalboxes'.

In contrast the RCA did not discriminate between the sexes in respect of membership, rules or benefits. By 1914 it had 100 women among its 29,394 members and had developed a coherent plan of action to scupper the companies' scheme to exploit women as cheap labour and displace male clerks. The strategy was to recruit all women to the union, demand equal pay for them, and to persuade even the transient ones to consider the harm they inflicted on the permanent staff by accepting low wages – even if they as individuals did not mind being exploited as cheap labour. The RCA suggested that, since clerks in government, railways, banks and commerce were used by their employers as precedents for each other (that is to say, the level of their wages was kept on a par with each other across the various employers), a woman's acceptance of poor wages could result in her later having less money for housekeeping, for she might one day marry a government or bank clerk.[95]

Individual RCA members were frequently seen to occupy an ambiguous position with regard to their female colleagues. At the 1913 annual conference a delegate proposing equal pay for women clerks first assured members that his resolution 'was not directed against women labour' but later contradicted this by suggesting that equality of pay would 'weed out the females'.[96] Moving an amendment, another delegate at first demanded that women work the same shifts as men – nights, evenings and Sundays – but later opined that girls could not be expected to work evenings or to walk home alone at night. Curiously, both the resolution and the amendment were carried.

---

* According to Bagwell, one woman was in fact enrolled in the NUR in error, as she had the unisex name of 'Jesse'.

SUMMARY

As has been amply described by Bagwell, Kingsford and McKenna,[97] conditions for railwaymen were harsh, but the evidence presented in this chapter shows that railwaywomen were treated even more shoddily. They were earmarked for the lowest-status jobs with almost no hope of advancement, and at half to two-thirds the wages of men. Women's exclusion from the NUR meant that railwaymen's status might be improved while railwaywomen were left behind, or perhaps even further exploited as they became the weakest link in the chain of the labour movement.

There was nothing unusual about women's inferior role on the Victorian railways; it mirrored their poor status outside, both in work and in society. Women's struggles to improve their position as employees were often fruitless because men held all the power on both the bosses' and the unions' side, and in every other area of society.

Despite everything, women did establish a place for themselves on the railways of Victorian and Edwardian Britain, They were indispensable as ladies' waiting room attendants and ships' stewardesses, and they proved their worth as seamstresses, painters, French polishers, bookbinders and laundresses. Many, working as crossing keepers, were entrusted with the safety of both rail and road users, while a few were placed in sole charge of a station.

The admission of women into railway offices, though intended to exploit their economic vulnerability, was nevertheless beneficial to them. Clerical work offered women the opportunity to demonstrate that their labour was valuable, and gave some of them access, through membership of the RCA, to the labour and trades union movements.

Railwaywomen gradually increased in number between 1830 and 1914. While the majority, especially in the clerical grades, worked only until marriage when, owing to social expectations and, in the case of salaried staff, a marriage bar, they were obliged to resign, some amassed long service, in some cases as much as 40 and even 50 years, which belied the belief that every woman worker was short term.

In wider society, women made significant progress between 1870 and 1914. As well as the right to retain their property and wages after marriage, those who met certain qualifications gained the municipal vote, and some were admitted to higher education and to certain professions. Women in New Zealand, Australia and in many American states had won the parliamentary vote and, by 1914, with the suffragettes making headline news on a daily basis, the British campaign appeared to be on the brink of victory.

Some women felt that being allowed to vote would lead to their gaining higher positions on the railways. In 1894 one railway author told his readers:

> It was suggested that in this country [women] should 'man' the entire railway system. One female thought that 'when the equal citizenship of women was recognised by the possession of the parliamentary vote, they would be able to bring railway manners and customs up to date,' and contended that there ought to be women officials on all our lines.[98]

However, at the time this chapter closes, women had not won the vote. Moreover, they continued to be restricted to the most menial work at the lowest rates of pay, on railways and in every other workplace, till an event entirely unconnected with the women's rights movement revolutionised their employment on Britain's railways.

Appendices to Chapter One

Women Employed on Britain's Railways, July 1914	
Cooks, waitresses & attendants (for passengers)	6,272
Clerical workers	2,341
Cooks, waitresses & attendants (for staff)	1,239
Workshops	814
Painters, cleaners and charwomen	698
Signalwomen* and crossing keepers	437
Labourers	420
Telegraph and telephone operators	369
Carriage cleaners	214
Booking office clerks	152
Machinists and mechanics (in workshops)	44
Workshop labourers	43
Porters and checkers	3
TOTAL	13, 046

The Distribution of 9,374 Women Employed by Eleven Railway Companies, July 1914			
London & North Western	2,123	Glasgow & South Western	442
North Eastern	1,575	Great Central	342
Midland	1,396	North British	119
Great Western	1,371	London, Brighton & Sth Coast	99
Lancashire & Yorkshire	1,057	Caledonian	80
Great Eastern	770	TOTAL	9,374

The Distribution of Women Within Two Railway Companies, July 1914			
Great Western		*Great Central*	
Clerks	328	Accountant's Department	37
Tracers	5	Superintendents' Staff:	
Learners	7	Traffic, clerical	14
Crossing keepers	51	Other †	62
Charwomen	221	Portmaster's Staff: clerical	7
Carriage cleaners	6	Other	10
Miscellaneous wages grades	762	Hotels: clerical	8
		Other	204
TOTAL	1371	TOTAL	342

*There may have been no signalwomen, or one (Mrs Town) or more.
†Probably all crossing keepers.

LNWR Euston linen room circa 1900. ORIGIN UNKNOWN

References

1. Bennett, G, et al, (1990) *A Fighting Trade: Rail Transport in Tyne Coal 1600-1800* (Portcullis Press).
2. Coleman, T. (1965) *The Railway Navvies* (Hutchinson).
3. Ibid. p197.
4. NRM picture reference 10319169.
5. *The Times* 23 August 1858.
6. Philip Bagwell, in Simmons, J & Biddle, G. (Eds) (1997) *The Oxford Companion to British Railway History* (OUP) p24.
7. Bagwell, P. (1963) *The Railwaymen* (George Allen & Unwin) p20.
8. Cole, G.D.H. and Page Arnot, R. (1917) *Trade Unionism on the Railways: its history and problems* (Fabian Research Dept).
9. Census 1911.
10. Rolt, L.T.C. (1966) *Red For Danger* (Pan) pp207-215.
11. National Union of Railwaymen, Executive Committee Minutes 1915.
12. *North Eastern Express* August 1988, p57.
13. Wheelwright, J. (1989) *Amazons and Military Maids* (Pandora) pp83-84; *Morning Star* 13 March 1868.
14. MacDermot, E. T. (1964) *History of the Great Western Railway* volume one (Methuen) p337.
15. See Wojtczak, H. (2003) *Women of Victorian Sussex* (Hastings Press) for a study of women's work in the early Victorian era.
16. LNWR *Society Journal* March 2002. Courtesy of the Society.
17. *Great Eastern Magazine* December 1912, p66.

[18] Head, F. B. (1849) *Stokers and Pokers* (reprinted 1988, David & Charles) p85.
[19] Earnshaw, A. (1991) *Trains in Trouble* (Atlantic) p13.
[20] *British Railways Magazine* Western Region, 1955, p156.
[21] *British Railways Magazine* North Eastern Region, 1956. Retirements.
[22] *Railway Magazine* October 1913.
[23] *Railway Magazine* 1905.
[24] *Railway Magazine* October 1913.
[25] 1851 Census.
[26] Prince, F. (no date) *Tag Lock Crossing.* Mr Prince's father knew Red Ellen. A photograph of her appears in his book.
[27] *Great Central Railway Journal* June 1916.
[28] Midland Railway *Special Train Notice of Royal Train from Wolverton to Rowsley.*
[29] *Derby Mercury* 28 March 1870. Thanks to Dave Harris for publishing it at <http://www.derby-signalling.org.uk>.
[30] *Railway Gazette* 18 October 1912.
[31] Williams, B. (1987) *The Railway Industry* (Batsford) p14.
[32] *North Eastern Express* August 1988, p57.
[33] P. W. Kingsford, (1970) *Victorian Railwaymen* (Frank Cass) p38.
[34] Ibid.
[35] *Carry On* December 1946.
[36] *North Eastern Express* August 1988, p58.
[37] *Carry On* June 1948.
[38] *Railway Magazine* October 1913.
[39] Letter to *The Times* 13 April 1899.
[40] <http://homepages.tcp.co.uk/~jakesimpkin/StellaMemorial.html>.
[41] Thanks to Soujanya Guddanti for publicising McCorquodale's 1906 *Description of an L.N.W.R Carriage Works at Wolverton.*
[42] *Great Eastern Magazine* September 1911, p280.
[43] *Great Eastern Magazine* May 1913 and 1881 Census.
[44] *Railway Magazine* 1912, p66.
[45] *British Railways Magazine* Scottish Region 1953.
[46] Stretton, C. (1901) *The History of the Midland Railway* (Methuen) p31.
[47] It was the world's third public railway, and later became part of the Midland Railway.
[48] Clinker, C.R. (1977) *The Leicester & Swannington Railway* (Avon Anglia) p27.
[49] *North Eastern Express* August 1988, p57.
[50] *North Eastern Magazine* November 1919.
[51] <http://www.cheshire.gov.uk/recoff/railways/home.htm>.
[52] *Railway Gazette* 7 July 1915.
[53] <http://babylon6.homeip.net/>. Many thanks to Linda Collins for her help.
[54] *British Railways Magazine,* Southern Edition, 1954.
[55] Thanks to Bruce Hunt, Pat Cutts and Anita Nicholls for photos and information.
[56] *Horner's Weekly* 21 November 1908, reprinted in the *Island Rail News,* May-July 2002. The Hulton Deutsch Collection has a photograph of Mrs Merwood.
[57] Hargrove, E. (1913) *Wanderings on the Isle of Wight* (Melrose). *Island Rail News* Feb-April 2002. I am indebted to Roger MacDonald.

[58] *Daily Herald* 18 May 1930. This information conflicts with that given in the NER *Magazine,* March 1919, which gives the mother's service as 1868-1898; the daughter's, 1898-1919 (still in service at that date).

[59] <www.stbees.org.uk>

[60] Thanks to Dorothy Ravenswood, Maria McGill's great-granddaughter.

[61] Thanks to Peter Robinson for information on Cumbria.

[62] *The Times* 16 December 1858.

[63] *British Railways Magazine* SR Edition, June 1954, letters page.

[64] *British Railways Magazine* SR Edition, August 1954, letters page.

[65] *British Railways Magazine* SR Edition, September 1954, letters page.

[66] *Railway Gazette* 13 December 1907.

[67] *Railway Gazette* 27 December 1907.

[68] *North Eastern Express* August 1988, p56.

[69] Findlay, G. (1899*) The Working and Management of an English Railway* (EP Publishing, 1976) p71.

[70] Walkden, A.G. (1915) *A Word to Women* (RCA booklet).

[71] *The Railway Clerk* 15 February 1912, p26.

[72] Bagwell, P.S. (1968) *The Railway Clearing House* (Allen & Unwin) p153.

[73] *Railway Herald* 28 July 1900.

[74] *Railway Herald* 21 April 1900. Quoted in Wallace, M (1997) *Single or Return? The Official History of the TSSA* (TSSA)

[75] *British Railways Magazine* SR Edition, August 1954, Letters page.

[76] Ibid.

[77] *Railway Magazine* 1900, p129.

[78] *Great Western Magazine* 1909, p62.

[79] *The Railway Clerk* 15 September 1912, p226.

[80] Ibid.

[81] *The Railway Clerk* 15 April 1912, p90.

[82] *The Railway Clerk* 15 November 1912, p264.

[83] *North Eastern Express* August 1988, p57.

[84] *The Railway Clerk* 15 June 1913, p141.

[85] *Great Western Magazine* 1917, p178.

[86] National Archives RAIL 264/261.

[87] Thanks to Dr Barbara Carter, the Dening sisters' niece, for this information.

[88] *Swindon Evening Advertiser*, n.d. 1984.

[89] *Conference on the Fusion of Forces, 1911* (1912) (NUR booklet).

[90] NUR EC minutes 1913.

[91] Lewenhak, S. (1977) *Women and the Trade Unions* (Ernest Benn), p96.

[92] NUR EC Minutes September 1913.

[93] War Cabinet Committee, *Report on Women in Industry* 1919.

[94] Bagwell, P.S. (1982) *The Railwaymen* volume two, p316.

[95] Walkden, A.G. (1915) *A Word to Women* (RCA booklet).

[96] *The Railway Clerk* 15 June 1913.

[97] Bagwell P. S. (1963) *The Railwaymen* volume one (Allen & Unwin); Bagwell P. S. (1982) *The Railwaymen* volume two (Allen & Unwin); Kingsford, P. W. (1970) *Victorian Railwaymen* (Frank Cass); and McKenna, F. (1980) *The Railwayworkers 1840-1970* (Faber & Faber).

[98] Pendleton, J. (1894) *Our Railways* (Cassell).

Ticket collectors at London's Waterloo station c1917. Courtesy of the NRM ref 10446705

2: The First World War

> It must be clearly understood that any woman who by working helps to relieve a man or equip a man for fighting does national war service.
>
> Records of Railway Interests in the War, Part II, 1915

On August 4th 1914, Britain joined the European war. Railways were essential for transporting troops and war supplies and so the government took control of most* of the industry via a Railway Executive Committee (REC) comprised of the managers of the leading companies and chaired nominally by Sir Walter Runciman, President of the Board of Trade, but in practice by Herbert Walker, General Manager of the LSWR. The railway staff of 625,559 shrank rapidly as thousands of men joined the forces, shifting an impossibly heavy workload onto those remaining. To make matters worse the movement of troops and war supplies increased railway traffic considerably. The LSWR shouldered the greatest burden because it owned the railways and docks at Southampton, the main embarkation point for the British Expeditionary Force. Thousands of troops passed through, putting immense pressure on the workforce, and temporary staff were recruited to help in locations with the most taxing workload. One of them, Miss G. E. Cooper, was engaged to help operate the docks' telephone exchange for three weeks but the mammoth operation continued – seven million troops passed through in four years – and she remained throughout the war and beyond (eventually completing 41 years' service).

In the weeks following the outbreak of war, so many railwaymen joined the forces that the conveyance of troops and war supplies was threatened. At the same time, many women were losing their jobs as manufacturing and domestic service were curtailed. They overwhelmed the labour exchanges and, by April 1915, 47,000 had registered for war-work. By that time, women were already making kits and uniforms for the forces and had started to replace men in many jobs, such as window cleaning and as shop-keepers' delivery 'lads', for example. The Factories Acts that had banned women from night-work were suspended. In industry and engineering, unskilled men and women were engaged to supplement the skilled staff and perform the routine work, a practice known as 'dilution'.[1] Women became 'Munitionettes' (making ammunition) and joined the First Aid Nursing Yeomanry, the Land Army, the Women's Army Auxiliary Corps and other organisations. They took over men's jobs driving vans, both horse-drawn and motorised, and working for the bus and tram companies as clerks, timekeepers and conductresses.

Three factors – the staff shortage, the availability of female labour and the precedent of women replacing men in other industries – provoked debate about whether women could substitute for men on the railways, particularly in grades from which they had always been barred. The REC discussed it with Lord Kitchener, Secretary for War, and a sub-committee was appointed. After much deliberation, it recommended the employment of women in some male wages grades.

* Of the 178 railway companies, 130 came under state control.

Reactions and Objections

Many railwaymen were shocked at the mere suggestion that women might replace men in uniformed station grades such as porter and ticket collector. The dominant beliefs about women's correct sphere in life were coupled with the conviction that women were, as individuals, incapable of performing such work. Those outside of the industry felt uneasy and wondered if the 'weaker sex' was capable of shouldering the sort of responsibilities faced by railwaymen; after all, in some circumstances, passengers entrusted their very lives to them. The companies, although becoming desperate, were nevertheless tentative about putting women into men's jobs, as REC chairman Herbert Walker revealed:

> It has to be admitted that the subject was approached with a considerable amount of trepidation. The companies had little or no previous experience as to the suitability of women for the work, and it was questionable whether their strength and endurance would not be too severely tested.[2]

There was never any doubt in men's minds that women would want to work in railway operating. Indeed, many managers took the attitude that, like over-excited children, women had to be protected from their own zeal. It was also taken for granted that men alone had the right to determine women's occupational limitations.

While the REC gave careful consideration to the question of how war-workers might be utilised, journalists working for railway and union newspapers and magazines made instant and emphatic pronouncements about which jobs women could not perform. The *Great Western Magazine* declared that women were 'unsuitable for most railway duties',[3] while *The Railway Gazette* decreed that women could not be drivers, firemen, shunters or signalmen, or hold 'higher offices'.[4] The NUR's weekly paper, *The Railway Review*, extended that list to include motormen, cleaners, guards (goods and passenger), examiners, track maintenance platelayers and 'several other heavy grades.' It also warned that women could not be expected to uncouple engines, shunt wagons, climb ladders to reach signal lamps, or perform 'any of the more hazardous duties.'[5] It took many years to qualify as an engine driver, making it inappropriate to place temporary war-workers on the bottom rung of that particular promotional ladder, but the sweeping exclusion of women from the other grades cited was motivated by prejudice, as will be shown.

The Railway Review continued its commentary on the notion of 'female railwaymen' through the summer of 1915 by publishing a series of satirical cartoons depicting women in male wages grades. The humour derived from the belief that it was ludicrous for 'the fair sex' to perform certain work. One cartoon showed a pretty signalwoman being approached by several love-struck railwaymen, racing each other to the signalbox to comply with Rule 55.* Later the paper suggested that there were many women amongst railwaymen's families 'sufficiently intellectual enough' [sic] to memorise signalling regulations, and suggested that Rule 55 might have to be suspended if signalwomen were engaged, because it would place a woman and a man alone together.[6] Another depicted male passengers entreating a female guard to look after them — a hilarious reversal of sex roles. But behind this facade of humour lay a grave concern: women represented a huge threat to railwaymen's hard-won pay and conditions.

---

* Rule 55 decreed that a member of the train crew had to report in person to the signalbox if his train was delayed.

The use of women to their detriment weighed heavily upon railwaymen's minds during the first half of 1915 and a close watch was kept on developments. Across Britain, men aired their worries at union meetings and passed many resolutions demanding restrictions on women's labour and guarantees from the companies that any women employed would be temporary.

Men's objections fell into three categories: chauvinistic, economic, and protective of fellow railwaymen who had joined the forces. The chauvinistic objections centred on women's supposed inability to perform the work. It was deeply ingrained in society that women were mentally and physically inferior to men, and their reproductive processes supposedly rendered them too delicate to perform the kinds of tasks required of railway workers. Some men alleged that women were not 'the right sort' of persons to entrust with public safety because they lacked the requisite mental strength. Women were not even thought fit to judge the scope of their own abilities; that, too, would be decided by men. NUR EC member Jimmy Thomas told railwaymen: 'You have got to face this fact, that female labour has come to stop. Therefore, we have to make up our minds what grades it will be dangerous for women to work in.'[7] His intention to impose paternalistic restrictions on women was later put into effect: he successfully prevented them from working in several grades — without consulting women. *

While chauvinistic objections were grounded in prejudice, railwaymen's economic objections were based upon fact. Women had been manoeuvred over many years into a position in which they were forced to accept lower wages than men, and the companies had realised very quickly the potential to increase profits by replacing men with cheaper female labour. Segregation meant that undercutting by women had never before been a problem on the railways; now, conditions for it were ripe. This put men in a dilemma: male pride was adamant that women were not worth the same wage as men, yet the only way to protect male rates was to insist that women receive equal pay.

The third objection to women's replacing men was born out of concern for railwaymen who had joined the forces. Would all women be dismissed to make way for them after the war? If employers got the work done more cheaply, would they reinstate returning soldiers at lower rates? Or would they retain the women and consign the brave ex-soldiers to the dole queue? The NUR EC demanded that the companies acknowledge their moral responsibility to re-employ the men on their return. This was agreed, but when the union asked the REC to promise that women would be employed only for the duration of the war, it refused. The chairman remarked of the NUR's objection: 'It is only the higher paid grades; they do not mind women being put into the lower-paid grades.'[8]

There is no doubt that the NUR leaders appeared misogynistic (even against the background of a generally sexist society), so much so that Jimmy Thomas admitted to the REC: 'It is true to say that at one stage an anti-woman view was held', but he assured them that the NUR leadership had removed it.

Some members of the REC believed that the NUR was using women as an excuse to make conflict. During confidential discussions and correspondence between the Board of Trade and the general managers, Brother E. Charles of the NUR EC was repeatedly called a 'troublemaker'. Charles had tried to get Mr Potter of the GWR to agree that all women would be sacked at the end of the war; 'In other words', remarked Potter, 'that they should dictate whether the Railway Companies should employ women'. Similarly, when the NUR

* A potted biography of Jimmy Thomas is posted at www.railwaywomen.co.uk/jimmythomas.html

accused him of treating female ticket collectors as permanent staff, Sir William Forbes of the LBSCR asked the Board of Trade: 'Has the railway a right to employ women permanently or not, in such positions as they may be considered qualified for?'[9]

In April 1915 an agreement was finally reached between the NUR and the REC, dealing with the three key issues. First, women's war work would not be regarded as setting a precedent regarding their employment in peacetime; secondly, railwaymen serving in the forces were guaranteed reinstatement; and, thirdly, women substituting for men would receive no less than the minimum male rate.[10] The union was not concerned with getting a good deal for women; its intention was to protect male rates, therefore the EC agreed that women should not receive yearly pay increments.* All three parts of the agreement were to be bones of contention for several years.

The NUR also agreed that women would receive no war bonus. This bonus, paid to men from February 1915, was intended to compensate working people for the massive increase in the cost of living. It was set initially at 3s (2s for men earning over 30s), and was increased several times over the next few years. The Government reimbursed the companies 75% of the cost of the war bonus.

The war had deposited an unexpected, unprecedented and unwarranted amount of power into the laps of the NUR EC. In just 25 years, the union had transformed itself from a feeble association that had managed to recruit only 12% of railway workers† and was not recognised by the companies, into a body that had more power than any other trades union – or, indeed, any railway company and the managers did not doubt that the NUR EC would flex its muscles. Just three years previously it had called a successful national strike that brought almost the entire service to a standstill, led to rioting and looting and culminated in two bystanders being shot dead by the military.[11]

In a document marked 'confidential', Mr Potter of the GWR remarked that the NUR would leap on any perceived breach of the tripartite agreement on female labour because, 'It is an attempt on their part to let us taste the quality of their power in the circumstances that exist today'.[12] The President of the Board of Trade agreed, adding: 'There is no shutting our eyes to the fact that ... if [the NUR EC] were so minded ... they would bring you and us to our knees; they have the power to do it.'[13]

Wanted: Female Railwaymen

As soon as the bar against women's being appointed to male railway positions was lifted, in the spring of 1915, the companies were inundated with applications. At Sheffield, 100 women signed up as engine cleaners in 14 days, while a Manchester station master reported receiving 'scores and scores' of requests for work as carriage cleaners.[14] When men vacated their arduous posts as goods porters, appeals for women to come forward 'met with a hearty response and women from all walks of life presented themselves.'[15] Women were recruited as passenger and goods porters at an average rate of 125 a month for 16 months until, by August 1916, there were over 2,000 in the two grades. The LBSCR attracted 30 to 35 women applicants per vacancy and the employment correspondent of *The Daily Express* reported receiving 'continuous requests' from domestic servants seeking advice on obtaining railway work. The number of applicants was so great that managers

* Almost a century later the NUR would boast that it had fought for women's equality 'since the First World War'.

† 48,000 of a potential membership of 381,000.

began to select women according to their personal attractiveness, and it was even said of one station that 'The four ticket collectors might honour the front row of the chorus.'[16]

It is a common myth that the majority of war workers were housewives without gainful employment; in fact women already comprised 29% of the British workforce — nearly six million — when war broke out. This figure rose by 1,345,000 in wartime. On the railways, many war-workers were wives or daughters of railwaymen serving in the forces; some of those who became clerks were middle-class girls with no previous occupation; others were war-widows unable to support their families on the government allowance; indeed, the GWR gave preference to the latter. But the majority were already in the workforce and had resigned from 'women's jobs' to do war-work, or had lost their livelihood owing to the war. A few were already employed by the railways in female grades, such as Mrs Joy, a GWR nursing attendant who became a ticket collector at Acton. She wasn't the first woman ticket collector on the railways; that honour went to 33-year-old Vera George, who wrote to the GWR from her home in Malvern Link, in April 1915:

> SIR, — If you would care to engage me as a ticket collector here, or at any of the smaller stations on the line, and so release a man for more important work, I should be very willing to undertake the duty. I have earned my own living for 10 years, but am now 'unemployed' owing to the war. It struck me that a woman could be a 'ticket collector' as well as a man.

Women's eagerness to take up men's work is indicative of their discontent with the monotonous and ill-paid tasks assigned to their sex. In comparison, even the lowest-grade railway work was preferable. One newspaper reported:

> Some of the women who have taken up these men's jobs disappeared quite suddenly from their old places of employment. A young woman had failed to show up at the works, and enquiries showed that she had been engaged as a porter ... the pay for this work was 20s as compared to 14s in her former position.[17]

One tailoress-turned-goods porter declared that she would never return to the 'stuffy, steam-saturated atmosphere of a tailoring workroom and the cramped posture of that occupation at any price'.[18] Londoner Louie Weaver resigned her job as a highly-skilled West End dressmaker and was soon earning five times her pre-war wage by working on the Metropolitan Railway.[19]

Among the first women to be engaged to substitute for men were carriage cleaners and clerks. These were simple and obvious choices, as both were increasingly being considered suitable for women. Temporary female clerks replacing men were often given tasks formerly the sole province of men; for example, calculating engine mileage. At the end of 1914 the LNWR began to train groups of women to be booking clerks, and in the spring of 1915 the LBSCR, LNWR and the Mersey Railway followed suit. As well as ticketing, the women were taught telegraphy, parcel regulations, the rudiments of signalling, railway operating and bylaws. When they began working in busy, main-line booking offices under the direction of male supervisors the public and the press initially showed great curiosity, but this was short-lived for their attention was soon drawn to more sensational developments: women were to take men's places in uniformed grades.

Women in Men's Jobs

As 'that section of the field of labour hitherto regarded as the exclusive property of men' was 'rapidly invaded by women',[20] the press swarmed to watch them perform men's work in the public eye. A woman 'manning' a ticket barrier was newsworthy; one shifting heavy luggage, a sensation. A wealth of photographs accompanied the texts.

The courage of these early substitutes cannot be overstated. For women raised in the late Victorian era, working in the public eye on railways was an extraordinary task to undertake. They had first to overcome their deeply ingrained gender-role conditioning. Many had come straight from a life of domestic service, where they were inculcated to be modest, self effacing and – above all – as invisible as possible. Such a background ill prepared them for the blaze of publicity they received. How self-conscious they must have felt as their first faltering steps in their new jobs – performing work for which women were considered unsuitable – were taken under the intense and incessant scrutiny of passengers, managers, railwaymen and their union officers, reporters and photographers! To make matters worse, both union and company newspapers had predicted women's failure. At last the managers, unions and even the Board of Trade found something to agree upon. For example, a writer in the NUR's *Railway Review* remarked:

> The ticket collector is often exposed to the calumnies of a rough element which passes through the ticket gates, and this is the objectionable part of the position, unsuitable to the fair sex.[21]

while *The Railway Gazette* believed that 'A woman ticket collector ... can never be so successful as a man. She cannot deal with an obstreperous passenger nor get passengers to show expedition.'[22] Sir Walter Runciman, President of the Board of Trade, stated that female ticket collectors 'are not capable of doing the same work as men ... in handling unruly people she is usually at a great disadvantage'. NUR President A. Bellamy disagreed: 'She is really at a great advantage, because an unruly person would not hit a woman,' to which Sir Walter retorted, 'I think you place the chivalry of an unruly man too high.'[23]

Women were employed as ticket collectors on every major station, and a small number examined tickets on board trains. The first three companies to recruit them had engaged 169 between April and July 1915, of whom 78 were put to work at Paddington. Because of the minimum rate agreement, they were paid just 3s less than men. The GWR's general manager was aghast:

> 24s a week ... and a uniform for a woman who has never done a stroke of work before in her life seems to be absurdly generous! The labour of these women is not worth 24s a week.[24]

Lord Aberconway, Director of the Metropolitan, disagreed, saying that his 'lady' collectors did 'much better work than the men that occupied the positions before the war,' and stated that it was impossible for anyone to pass the barrier without a ticket.[25] The press flocked to stare; one journalist enjoyed contrasting the women with their male predecessors: 'In place of the stern gentleman ... a charming lady will be pleased to punch your ticket for you';[26] while another said that the women had 'cultivated instinctively a severely official manner'. Describing them as 'lynx-eyed in the detection of irregularities in the use of tickets', he warned that they 'rigidly enforce the rules of the companies'.[27]

This contrasts starkly with the predictions made – or, rather, prejudices aired – on the subject both by the NUR and the companies. No doubt many war-workers strove to prove themselves at least as competent as men and for this reason they may have been overly conscientious. Praise boosted morale among war-workers and served to encourage more women to volunteer their services.

The first dispute regarding the tripartite agreement arose within three months: the LBSCR admitted 28 female ticket collectors into its pension fund,* allegedly because General Manager Sir William Forbes 'seemed to fear that Mrs Pankhurst would take the matter up warmly on behalf of the women'.† The NUR's objection was that letting war workers join a pension scheme contradicted the agreement that they be treated as temporary. In August 1915 the Board of Trade told Sir William: 'It is of importance that the company should not appear to have taken women into their permanent employment' because of the trouble this would cause with the NUR. The problem affected only the LBSCR because other companies allowed only clerks to join their pension fund. Sir William consulted a solicitor, who assured him that the women had a legal right to remain as members of the fund. He then telephoned the Board of Trade and said that if admitting women to the fund was going to cause industrial unrest he would dismiss them all, then re-employ them 'on the understanding that they are not eligible for the fund'. Whether he did, in fact, take this course is not recorded. [28]

In 18 months, 706 female ticket collectors had been recruited. One on the Central London Railway was observed 'Perched on the examiner's box, with legs crossed, and her uniform hat at a rakish angle' playing *Till the Boys Come Home* on a harmonica.[29]

Women faced the same problems as their male counterparts. For example, when one ticket collector prevented a reckless lady from boarding a moving train, the ungrateful passenger slapped her face and lodged a complaint of 'obstruction'.[30] In another incident, William Lucas was fined £8 with £10.10s costs for 'outrageous conduct in a railway carriage' including 'obscene, abusive, and offensive language' towards Roslyn Gill, a travelling ticket examiner.[31] Those working on the ticket barriers took fares from passengers arriving without tickets, and it is recorded that one woman succumbed to temptation and kept some of the money for her own use. She was dismissed from Bushey, LNWR, in September 1915.

Another male province 'invaded' by women was portering, for which they earned 17s to 25s,‡ augmented in the case of station staff by tips. A writer in the companies' *Railway Gazette* opined:

> The woman porter is hardly likely to become general at the great termini, or even at country stations on the main line, where heavy loads have to be shifted.[32]

However, women worked in both city and rural locations. At Marylebone, the first London terminus to engage them, press attention was excessive and *The Railway Review* commented that the women resented it. 'PORTER IN SKIRTS' yelled the *Daily Mirror*, 'Wears a man's cap' it told readers, before recounting that Mrs Lloyd 'shouldered a couple of heavy

* The company allowed waiting room attendants to join the fund, and 30 were paying contributions in 1916.

† Emmeline Pankhurst was leader of the militant suffragette movement.

‡ Girls aged 15 earned 15s rising by 2s yearly until reaching this maximum.

bags' while their owner looked on 'in amazement.'[33] A male porter was spotted staring 'in helpless astonishment' at his female counterpart shifting heavy luggage.[34] Even a Scottish newspaper carried a report about them, commenting that, 'Their education is complete even down to the give-me-my-tip expression so well known to Londoners'.[35] After women had performed the work for a few weeks, *The Railway Gazette* relented on its former negativity and even thought that, in some ways, women porters were preferable to men:

> The employment of women on work for which their physique does not unfit them, is preferable to engaging the services of hobbledehoys.* And the women do not smoke five-a-penny cigarettes.[36]

Predictably, women porters were reported to excel at cleaning waiting rooms, but journalists were surprised to find them eager to perform the entire range of duties expected of male staff:

> If permitted she would climb signal posts, or take her turn at shunting, for Elsie is never happier than when she is proving that her strength is equal to that of the male employees.[37]

It was reported that women were adamant that their labour was equal to that of men and that they did not request special treatment; nonetheless in May 1915 the REC asked passengers to limit the weight of their luggage and from 1917 it imposed a maximum of 100lbs per item. Opposition to women porters was mainly confined to disapproval of their calling station names aloud, which was considered unfeminine. They received some good-natured banter from railwaymen but little open hostility. Some men complained that they performed most of the heavy labour when working alongside women; others were appalled to see women demolishing the myth of female incapability by carrying heavy luggage. There were also many instances of kindness from railwaymen on the 'shop floor': some vacated their messrooms for women's use while others made pacts to curb their swearing to make the working environment more congenial for 'the ladies'.

Closing train doors and giving the ready-to-start hand signal to guards provoked little controversy until a horrific accident occurred at Holland Park on the Central London Railway at midnight on 4th August 1915. After handing a letter to the guard, Porter Alice Dixon merrily rode on his step-board as the train moved out of the platform. She slipped, fell backwards, and her long skirts became caught on the carriage, dragging her into the tunnel, where she died of dreadful injuries. It was clearly Miss Dixon's individual foolishness, exacerbated by her clothing, that led to her death yet some people cited the case as 'proof' of the unsuitability of all women for railway operating work. However, one level-headed journalist reminded readers that women 'are less inclined to foolhardiness than the male porters, among whom accidents are frequent'.[38] Although by 1915 women had discarded crinolines, bustles and the multiple layers of underskirts worn in the Victorian era, corsets were still worn universally and skirts had not risen above ankle level. For some railway jobs this was impractical and for a few, dangerous. Concern for women's safety led to some shocking innovations, as will be seen.

* Hobbledehoy: an awkward, bad-mannered adolescent boy.

Women were proud of their railway work and some were later to recount it in detail to their children and grandchildren. Ethel Wright's daughter remembers her mother's anecdotes about life as a porter for the GER at Fairlop:

> Her uniform was heavy and ugly, of navy serge trimmed with leather on skirt hems and jacket, tightly buttoned up to the neck winter and summer. Black leather boots and a leather belt cinching a tiny waist. A peaked cap, too large, that would keep falling over her nose, completed the ensemble. Her railway duties were arduous and the hours long: 12 hour shifts. She was responsible for the care and safety of passengers and luggage, keeping the platforms and waiting rooms and station-master's office clean, polishing and trimming lamps, pushing heavy sack barrows, humping Royal Mail bags into trains and, at times, washing down carriages that had been shunted into sidings for that purpose.
>
> Livestock was held in the goods yard ready for transportation to Ilford cattle market. On one occasion Bill the signalman handed her a pail and asked her to milk one of the cows as he had a fancy for a glass of the stuff. Gingerly she moved to one of the beasts that was laying down. Suddenly it got to its feet – it was a large bull. Dropping the pail Ethel took to her heels; laughter and jeers following her. There was a lot of laughter, jokes and banter with the staff, especially the girl porters and Margery, the booking clerk. One day the sky-larking got a bit out of hand resulting in a sack barrow being pushed off a platform and landing on the track.
>
> She still lived with her parents, as unmarried girls did in those days. Her social life was practically nil, her little free time taken up with washing and ironing her clothes and keeping her room clean. Diversions did occur nonetheless with the appearance, at times, of the men from the Naval Air Barracks who were stationed at Forest Road.
>
> In April 1916 Zeppelins raided London and Fairlop was hit by bombs. The station master's house was wrecked, Ethel's house lost its windows and her precious china collection was smashed. In September 1916 Ethel watched as a Zeppelin was trapped in the cross beams of searchlights. Then a tiny little aeroplane strafed the monster till it caught fire, cremating the crew. That image stayed with her for the rest of her life.[39]

Women also replaced men in the railways' enormous and busy goods departments. By October 1916, 900 women nationally were working as goods porters. At Portsmouth and Southampton, LSWR, women proudly wheeled heavily-laden trucks, and 'would never admit that men could do any work better than they could do it themselves'.[40] At Manchester, LNWR, women loaded one-hundredweight sacks of grain onto barges for nine hours a day. At Somers Town,* MR, several hundred women shifted goods between wagons and drays, overseen by two 'matrons'. The work was so heavy that the company gave illustrated lectures on safe lifting practices.

Women were also engaged to perform various other tasks connected with the trans-shipment of goods; for example, Edwin Pratt was appalled to see women load-recorders at Southampton Docks working on an open quay in all weathers until late at night. At the South Eastern & Chatham's (SECR) Bricklayer's Arms depot over 100 were employed as van washers, weighbridge attendants, checkers and horse-van drivers and as porters to load

* The site that once housed Somers Town goods depot is now occupied by the British Library.

and unload goods and war supplies. One said the job 'braced them up wonderfully'.[41] Goods Superintendent Frederick West declared that three untrained but physically fit girls could do the same work that two strong, experienced men performed before the war. He observed that any muscular shortcomings were amply compensated by their abundant enthusiasm[42] and the *Railway Gazette* commented:

> It is not surprising that women should be able to fill the places of men drawn into the Army from offices or shops, but that they should successfully undertake work calling for such severe physical endurances as the work of the porters in railway goods sheds is a possibility which would have been simply derided three years ago.[43]

Women drove horse-vans, cleaned the stables and cared for the horses, despite considerable male opposition. At Chalk Farm for example, a meeting of 130 railwaymen opposed the employment of women in the goods yard and stables. They asserted: 'we are not female-haters' and claimed that their motive was to 'save women from tasks so unwomanly.'[44] The LNWR retained the women but agreed to recruit no more unless it was unavoidable. Women drove motor-lorries to deliver goods from stations to customers and some of them were also trained to maintain their vehicles. One of them, Miss Edwards, explained:

> I do everything to my car and I can refer you to the officials of Paddington who now hold a letter from my garage commending me upon the conduct of my car and the perfect running of the mechanism and the oiling. I loaded my own van – and I have had packages of up to one hundredweight. I got no help. I did exactly the same as a man. I have had as much as 5½ cwt* and I had no crane to do it with ... From 1st October to 6th ... the exact number of parcels that passed through my hands was 1,170, and if there is any man on the Great Western who can handle more than that, he must be a jolly smart fellow.[45]

Cleaning

Carriage cleaning – 'an occupation well-suited to those belonging to the working classes'[46] – required 'the constitution of a horse'.[47] But, because cleaning was – according to the *Manchester Courier* – 'woman's particular vocation',[48] there was little controversy when, by October 1916, 2,173 women were so employed, a tenfold increase in two years. While some station masters put women to work on the full range of duties, others barred them from vacuum-cleaning trains or from cleaning the ends of coaches or between the buffers.

Before the war, women had never worn trousers in public, but the long skirts and corsets universally worn by Edwardian women made the work difficult and dangerous, if not impossible, as women had to climb up into carriages from the track, using ladders and footboards, and globe cleaners had to negotiate narrow steps on the back of carriages to climb onto the roofs. Women at Wimbledon Park, LSWR, were the first carriage cleaners to tackle the clothing problem. They loosened or removed their corsets, shortened their

* Cwt = a hundredweight, an imperial measurement equivalent to just over 50 kilos.

skirts and then, in a revolutionary move, donned men's breeches! This daring innovation spread rapidly and soon trousers were officially approved and issued to female carriage cleaners by the companies. Some women were shocked by their colleagues' brazenness and retained the traditional mode of feminine dress.*

Cleaning engines was strenuous, filthy, and had never before been performed by women. The first were hired in March 1916 and in six months 587 had been recruited; in two years, over 3,000. The press called them 'Our heroines in overalls' and 'Ladies' Maids to Locomotives'. At Sheffield's Rutland Bridge, women earned £1 for a 53-hour week:

> Their suits consisting of trouser overalls, coat and cap in blue 'galatea'† are natty and workmanlike, and amply protective from grease and dirt. A spacious mess-room with whitewashed walls has been provided for the use of the women only. ... They [have] half an hour for breakfast and an hour for dinner.[49]

Those at York were said to cause 'no small stir as they took their after-dinner walk along Leeman Road'.[50] One widow with five children to support found her new post 'more congenial, and more profitable, as well as healthier' than her former work as a laundress.[51]

Workshops

Women swiftly filled the vacancies left by men in railway workshops. They assisted in many mechanical processes alongside the skilled men, and themselves learned many new skills; for example, as early as 1916 the London Electric Railways taught women to make and repair all parts of their trains and trams. Elsewhere, workshopwomen made and repaired sacking for grain-bags and wagon covers. The number employed as workshop labourers increased from 43 in 1914 to 2,547 in 1918 — they tackled portering, sweeping, storekeeping, cleaning and sorting waste-paper gathered for war economy.

In order to placate the NUR, workshopwomen had to be graded as temporary. This was acknowledged in a letter from the LNWR to the President of the Board of Trade in 1916, which stated that the Chief Mechanical Engineer at Crewe had promised the unions that within a year of the declaration of peace no female labour would be employed 'that will prejudice the position of ... men now serving with the Colours, or sons of Crewe Works men eligible to be taken on ... under ordinary conditions'. If more staff were needed and men were not available, 'supplementary female labour will be obtained by employing widows of former employees in the Locomotive Department, daughters or sisters of men employed in the Works'.

As the women were unchaperoned, managers were warned not to allow the sexes to take lunch together, fearing that such familiarity might encourage immorality:

> Rigid discipline as to conduct should be established from the very start, and carelessness on the part of either sex in relation to the other should not be tolerated for a moment. So far as possible women should be worked in groups and be segregated from the men.[52]

* The mid-19th-century proposal that they might wear Turkish-style loose pantaloons under flared knee-length skirts (known as the Bloomer Costume) was ridiculed so mercilessly that it never caught on.

† A durable, striped cotton fabric usually used for children's sailor suits. From the *Galatea*, a warship.

CLEANING

These photographs show clearly how dissimilar carriage cleaning was to domestic work. Women climbed up onto buffers, down into pits and handled heavy, greasy couplings and pipes.

This particular group worked in the vicinity of the current-carrying conductor rails at Wimbledon Park depot, LSWR (a conductor rail can be seen clearly in the photograph below; it is the largest of the three rails and carried between 600-700 volts.) In latter years railwayworkers were under strict instructions never to place a foot between the conductor rail and the running rail.

Left: In the pit. © IWM

Below: A group of carriage cleaners with their inspector. COURTESY OF THE NRM REF 10446701

Wimbledon Park Depot, LSWR, c1917. One woman sits on the buffer above the conductor rail and cleans, while her colleague applies grease with a brush onto the screw coupling, having used the coupling hook to hang up the grease pot. The carriage was one of 84 built in 1915, and among the first electric trains in Britain.

COURTESY OF THE NRM REF 10446712

The heavy and cumbersome cast iron vacuum cleaners in use in the early 20th century. © IWM 109879

Carriage cleaners at London Bridge in 1918. COURTESY OF THE NRM REF 10446647

Women van washers at the SECR Bricklayer's Arms Depot. ORIGIN UNKNOWN

To clean or refill the gas or paraffin lamps in carriages, globe cleaners climbed up a set of steps attached to the end of a carriage, walked or crawled along the roof, opened the lids and cleaned the lights from above.

Woman glober climbing onto the roof.
COURTESY OF THE NRM REF RAIL 343/725

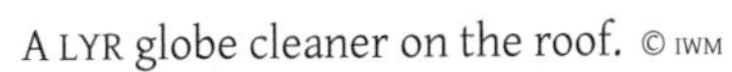

A LYR globe cleaner on the roof. © IWM

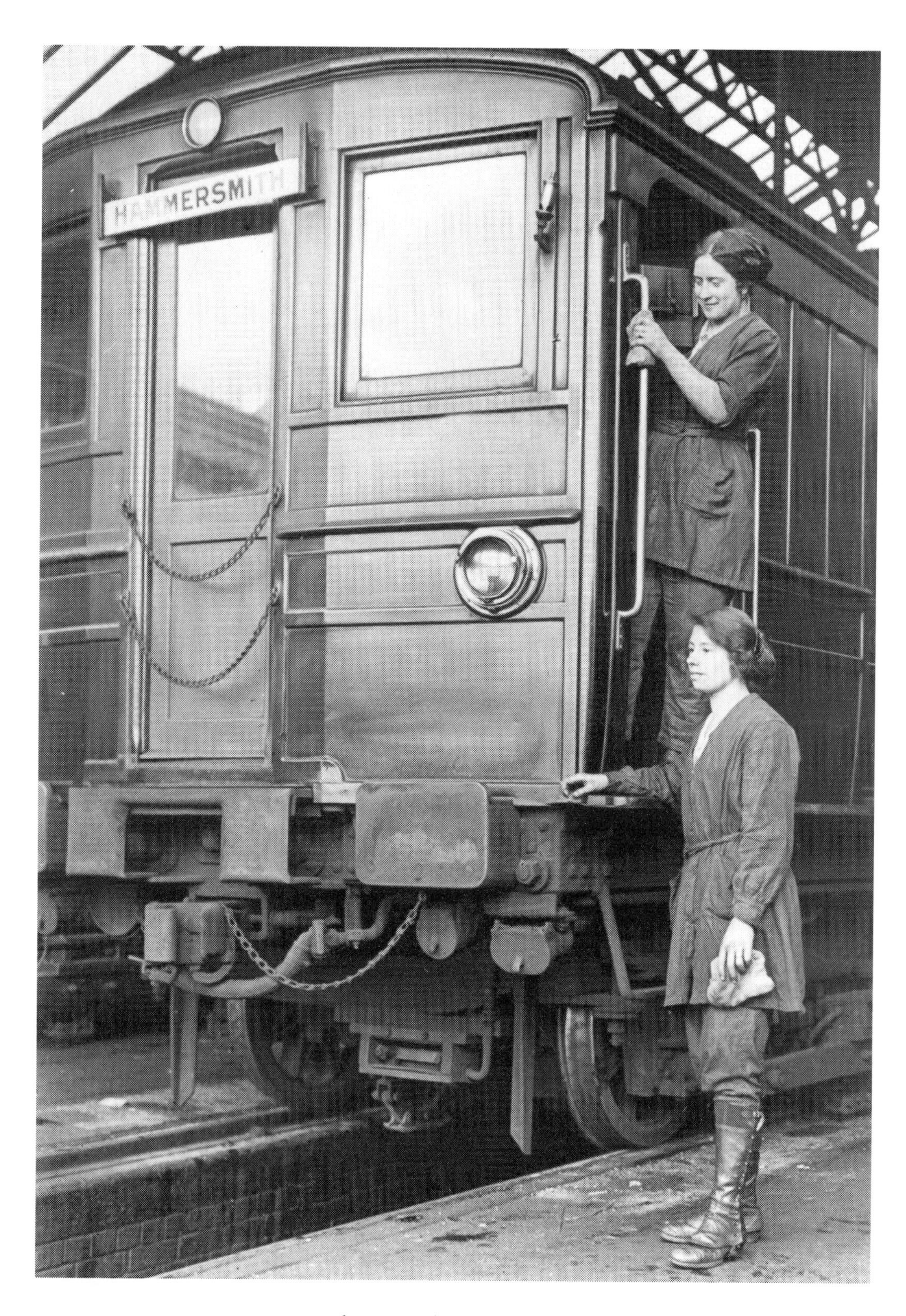

Car cleaners on the underground. © TFL

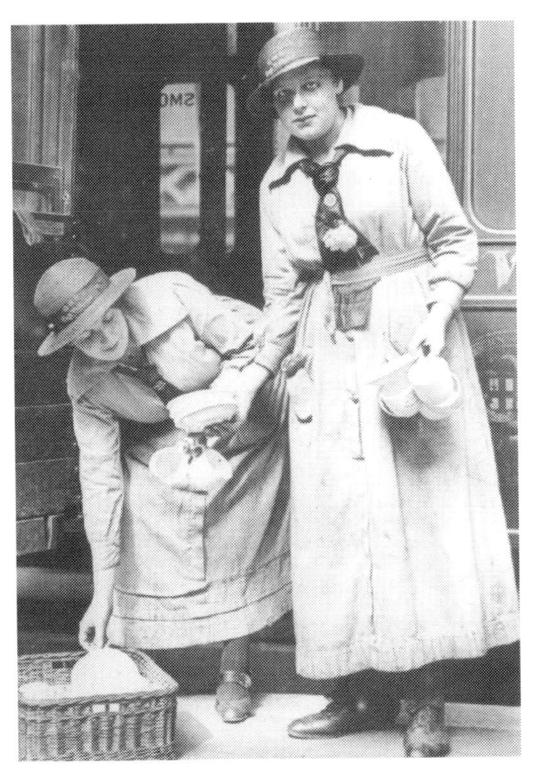

Catering employees. The words GWR CUP COLLECTOR are embroidered on their hat bands. © IWM.

Edith Addison, the first woman on the GCR to receive a bravery award. Courtesy of L. Biddulph

Women coal shovellers working for the LYR, 3rd May 1917. Courtesy of the NRM ref 10445320

A GER parcels porter driving a Railodok electric trolley. © IWM

Goods porters at Paddington shifting hundredweight sacks.
Vaughan/Kenning Collection

Three porters at Belper, MR. COURTESY OF GLYNN WAITE

A 'charming lady' at Taunton, with a flower in her buttonhole. © IWM

With all the able-bodied adult men enlisted in the forces, female porters often had to work with lads. Elmton & Cresswell, MR. COURTESY OF GLYNN WAITE

Police

In the 19th century, railway policemen on undercover detective work on stations occasionally brought their wives along to appear less conspicuous, and this would have led to the women giving evidence in court. However, no woman was on the payroll until about 1915. In 1914 Margaret Damer Dawson saw men at a station attempting to recruit Belgian women to prostitution, an event that led her to organise the Women Police Volunteers. Later, both the Home Office and the railway companies employed and trained women police officers. The first worked for the GER, followed closely by the NER, the GCR and the London Electric (which employed 13). There were at least six at Liverpool Street, including a sergeant. Unfortunately, details of the numbers of women officers, the crimes they dealt with and the arrests they made, and a host of other interesting facts and figures, have been lost.[53]

WPC Ruth Bryant, Great Eastern Railway. BTP

SHIPPING

Women were employed as ticket clerks and refreshment room assistants at all the ports used by railway-owned shipping services. They were also engaged as stewardesses by the NBR on its Clyde, Forth Ferry, and Wemyss Bay to Rothesay steamer services, by the GWR on services to Ireland, and by the GER on its cross-channel steamships.

During the war the GER maintained its services to the Netherlands, although the coasts of Belgium and France were occupied by German naval forces. One of its steamships, the *Brussels*, was sailing from Hoek van Holland to Harwich in June 1916 under the command of Captain Charles Fryatt, carrying a valuable cargo of foodstuffs and parcels, and refugees from Belgium. At 1.30 a.m. on 23rd it was captured by the enemy and taken to Zeebrugge. Five stewardesses were on board.

> The stewardesses were kept busy for some five hours serving the Germans and comforting the unfortunate weeping refugees whom they provided, as soon as the alarm came, with abundance of biscuits and bread. ... Two nights were passed at the Bruges Town hall, the stewardesses being locked in an upper room icily cold. ... Black bread and ersatz coffee was served but they could not touch it. Refugees who had white bread from the ship insisted upon giving it to them – the stewardesses had provided themselves with a few biscuits only.
>
> They went in a cattle truck to Ghent and there spent a night in a slimy damp cellar. ...They stood all night. In the early morning, they were made to walk with their baggage about a mile down the railway line and entrained there in a German fourth-class carriage [to Cologne]. Captain Fryatt assured them it could only mean some days' detention for them and for the men, at the worst, detention during the war.
>
> Without opportunity to say farewell they were then separated from the 'Brussels' men and passed on ... to Holzminden, where they had to march two miles with their luggage to the camp. There they suffered bad accommodation, verminous and damp bedding, rations inadequate and uneatable, unpleasant company, and all that lack of liberty means. They were not molested in any way by the Germans they came into contact with. ...The stewardesses wore their blue uniform with brass buttons and Germans took them for fighting women.[54]

Captain Fryatt was falsely accused of sinking a German submarine in 1915 and was murdered, showing that 'the enemy had overthrown the last vestiges of principle in their warfare'[55] and giving rise to fears for the lives of the stewardesses. Their fate remained in jeopardy until the intervention of the Secretary of State for Foreign Affairs, whose request that the women be repatriated led to their liberation. They arrived in England to be lauded as heroines:

> It was indeed a pleasure and a relief to see again the released stewardesses of the 'S.S. Brussels'. Mrs Elwood, Miss Elwood, Mrs Stalker, Miss Bobby and Miss Smith have passed through a most trying experience and have done so in a manner of which G.E.R. women can be proud. The Germans who boarded the 'Brussels' wondered at their calmness and asked if they were not afraid of being shot. 'We are Englishwomen' was considered sufficient reply.[56]

SALARIED STAFF

The localised, controlled and gradual introduction of women into railway offices throughout the late nineteenth century was revolutionised by the outbreak of war. Since the first woman was employed in a railway office, it had taken more than 50 years for the female complement to reach just 2,431. Four years of war swelled this to over 20,000.

Railway clerks worked in a wide range of different workplaces. Some were in administration buildings, surrounded by dozens or hundreds of others like themselves. Others worked alongside wages-grade staff in goods depots and on stations, either selling tickets, keeping accounts or providing clerical services to station or yard masters.

In May 1915, a month after she turned 14, Miss Clowser joined her station master father as his clerk at Waldron & Horeham Road, LBSCR, which served an agricultural area and handled considerable goods traffic. The station was understaffed and Miss Clowser soon found herself a 'Jill of all trades': she had to learn the Morse code for the telegraph and how to operate the signal box in emergencies.[57]

Ada Bryant started work as a teenager in Bournemouth West booking office. Among other duties she operated the telegraph and carried the day's takings to the bank. The cash bag was very heavy and she carried it on the front of her bicycle. One day she was riding down Poole Hill when she caught her bicycle wheel in a tram rail. She and the cash bag were thrown off the bike and the coins scattered down a very steep hill. Passers-by ran to help and between them they scooped it all back into the case (mud and all). When it was later counted by the bank she hadn't lost a penny.[58] Miss Bryant stayed on after the war and continued working until 1928 when, like all female clerks, she had to resign because she married. May Atkinson joined Middlesbrough goods office, NER, in 1915:

> I was well received in the goods station office, but after a spell I was transferred to Porters' Accounts. The man who had to train me had held the job for over twenty years and did not take kindly to a girl of twenty taking over, so I didn't have it so good for the first week. But I didn't complain or weep as some girls did. In time he was quite friendly and told me to consult him if I had any difficulties. There was a lot of adding up to do, and no adding machines, either. We didn't have a staff room; just a cloakroom and toilet and one cold water tap. No coffee or tea breaks: if we were going to the station we used to sneak down a spiral staircase to the porters' room [for tea.][59]

The NER paid Miss Atkinson 9s 6d a week, but the MR paid considerably more: 23s (26s in London) and granted seven days' annual leave and four free passes, including one for other companies' lines. Both sexes received compensatory leave for working bank holidays and free travel to work if they earned less than 17s a week. Their wages were stopped if they were absent through illness, except if they were off sick only part of a day.[60] The NER's temporary women clerks were not entitled to sick pay but, in an example of almost impenetrable euphemism, managers explained that they might still be paid if their absence was caused by menstruation:

> The concession as to payment, at the descretion [sic] of the Head of Department, for odd days was made in order to meet the cases of females who, peculiar to themselves, it has been found are liable to be away from the Office odd days periodically.[61]

Although women were still restricted to certain jobs and had much lower status than men clerks, some opportunities were opened to them that had hitherto been closed. One of them was formal training in various areas of railway working. Exams were held and certificates given to those with the highest marks. In 1918 women were admitted to station accountancy classes for the first time, and the newcomers immediately began to outshine the men: all but two of the certificates were won by women. Miss Spooner, of the Chief Goods Manager's Office, Paddington, took first place in her mixed class with 365 marks out of a possible 375.

The hostility induced by the swift and large 'invasion' of female staff to a male workplace aggravated the existing frosty relationship between the men and women of the permanent staff. Some war workers were placed alongside male clerks who had never before worked with 'females' and who had a poor opinion of them. Men's antagonism was vented in staff journals and at union meetings as well as in the offices. Whereas women in railway wages grades rarely responded to male derision, women clerks fought back. Perhaps their superior education supplied the eloquence to counter male criticism, and the prospect (or at least the possibility) of permanence provided a more secure base from which to retaliate. Responding to men's accusations that women were inferior workers, one woman commented incisively on men's office habits:

> The female clerk can contentedly ply her art at the type-writer until her last letter is written, without feeling obliged to break off occasionally to stand with her back to the fire and talk about sport, politics, or the conduct of the war.[62]

Another objected to the term 'female labour', asserting: 'We are more than mere females ... we are women.'[63] When a man complained that women were 'less amenable' to discipline and disliked criticism and sharp tones being used, Alice Redsull replied: 'It is quite an erroneous idea to suppose that work is done any better when a truculent and aggressive manner is adopted towards us.'[64] When the same man cited the stereotype of unambitious women clerks who would soon leave to 'fulfil their proper destiny', Miss Redsull replied:

> We do consider that we are entitled to equal opportunities of advancement with our male colleagues. ... Give us the chance of getting on, and there will be no question of us rising to the occasion.[65]

One RCA member's criticisms were unusually comprehensive: they put women firmly in the wrong no matter what they did. He complained that women were not worth training because they left on marriage. Then he denounced them for not pursuing careers, but mocked any one who did by calling her a 'dessicated [sic], morally hybridised female of sufficient austerity, to desire no other lot than an office career'.[66]

Staff accommodation caused trouble. In 1915 men at Hereford Great Eastern Goods complained to the RCA that their toilet had been given to female war-workers and they were expected to use one that was 'dilapidated, damp, the plaster falls off the roof and gives one a shower-bath of dust at times, the water flush works sometimes but more often than not flushes the floor, and the smell is beastly'.[67] Such comments are wonderfully evocative of the standard of railway staff accommodation at that time.

There were also men who were friendly to their women colleagues and cared for their welfare. A writer in *The Railway Clerk* asked pointedly whether it was reasonable that a 'lady' in one North-Eastern office 'has to work from 4.45 a.m. until 1 p.m., and from 1 p.m. until 12.10 a.m., alternate weeks, without meal-times, having to proceed to and from home in total darkness'.[68]

During the war there was an increase in the number of female clerks-in-charge, or station mistresses. As early as 1915, Jimmy Thomas remarked: 'A large number of halts that had one man now have one woman'.[69] One of them, railwayman's daughter Alice Lidster, was appointed at Troedyrhiw on the joint GWR and Rhymney Railway on 15th April 1915. After explaining that, if permitted, she would have joined the forces, she declared that running the station was one of the tasks a woman ought to be able to do just as well as a man'. Her daily hours were from 8 a.m. to 7 p.m.[70] The first station – apart from single-manned halts – to have an all-female staff was Maida Vale on the Bakerloo Line. In June 1916, *The Railway Gazette* quipped: 'Not even an odd-job boy disturbs this Adamless Eden.'[71] Beaconsfield Golf Links (now Seer Green) was also run by a woman, and a station mistress and two women porters took over Irlams O' Th' Heights station in Salford, LYR, in December 1917. A report of a near-miss on the Glasgow Subway reveals that at least one station mistress worked there, and that she had control of the signals. On 26th April 1917, owing to a misinterpretation of a telephone message between Hillhead Station Mistress Miss Webster and the station master at Partick Cross, two trains were sent on a collision course. Both were found partly to blame, along with the train driver, who was a boy of just 17. When the Watford extension of the Bakerloo Line opened in April 1917 all staff on the line were female.

Clerk Miss Clowser with her station master father (seated, centre) and the staff at Waldron & Horeham Rd, LBSCR. Courtesy of Ann Shah

The station mistress (centre) and her staff at Irlams O' Th' Heights, Salford. © IWM

An unnamed station mistress lighting the oil lamp at Beaconsfield Golf Links station (the name of which changed to Seer Green in 1918) on the joint GWR/GCR line. © Getty Images.

Mileage clerks on the GWR, 1916. Freda Dening is in the second row, third from the right. Courtesy of B. Carter

Teenagers learning their railway duties under the tutelage of female instructors at the East Croydon Training School, LBSCR, in 1915. On the table on the far left a model railway is laid out, no doubt to instruct students in signalling and general railway operating. The girls on the far right are learning how to operate the telegraph system. The only woman whose name is known is Eva May Robbins, seated centre front, nearest the camera. Courtesy of J.Hayes

Two women fitters' assistants with spanners engaged in routine maintenance of the axle boxes and suspension of a carriage on the LYR, c1918. The same pair adjusting or replacing the cast iron brake shoes on a carriage.

A railwaywoman cleaning and obscuring lamps in accordance with air raid precautions.
LYR, 1917. © IWM

Engine cleaners at Stafford locomotive sheds.
Courtesy of Edward Talbot

A gatewoman on the underground c1916. © TFL

A trio of goods porters wearing their specially-made dustcoats. The tallest one reveals that they wore knickerbockers tucked into leggings. The shape of women's legs had never before been seen in public or in the workplace. © IWM

Goods porters shifting 17-gallon milk churns. Vaughan/Kenning Collection

A group of happy painters working for the London Underground railways. © TFL

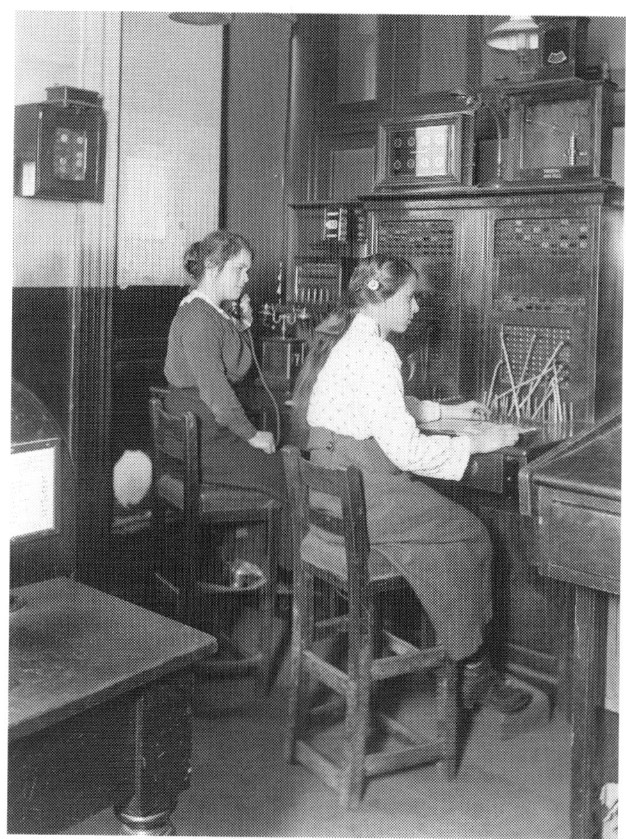

Telephone operators at Horwich Works, LYR, May, 1917. COURTESY OF THE NRM REF 10444124

A clerk in the mineral audit office at Doncaster Works, 1916. The office recorded mineral traffic carried on freight trains and issued invoices to customers.
COURTESY OF THE NRM REF 10446147

Woman operating a mobile crane to lift locomotive wheels in the wheelshop. ORIGIN UNKNOWN

GER goods porter driving a 'Railodok' electric trolley along a platform, 1918. © IWM

Two views of a pointswoman in action at Marylebone, GCR. © IWM

LBSCR goods porter handling calves in sacks, 1917 © IWM

Goods porter (location unknown) driving an electric trolley along a platform. © IWM

Carriage cleaners posing in front of an H-class locomotive, somewhere on the SECR. ORIGIN UNKNOWN

A carter at the SECR goods department, Bricklayer's Arms Depot, London, c1918. © IWM

UNIFORM

There was no uniform for female staff in 1915 other than that issued to ladies' waiting room inspectresses. While waiting for the matter to be decided the railway companies issued makeshift identifying items to the first women who worked in the public eye; for example, those on the ticket barriers at Paddington, GWR, were distinguished by white armbands embroidered TICKET COLLECTOR. Later, a drab skirt-suit of thick, dark serge was issued. These outfits were very heavy, and were made more so by the addition of leather trimming along the hems of some porters' jackets and skirts, to make the garments more durable. The uniform was completed with either a fashionable, wide-brimmed hat or a railwayman's peaked cap.

The MR invited its first female goods porters at Somers Town to choose a suitable outfit for themselves. They opted for a long jacket and, rather daringly, breeches, which the manager described as 'unorthodox'.[72] Trousers became the official issue, but only to those in work for which skirts were impractical; women working on stations in the public eye were never permitted to wear trousers.

The MR's women porters' and ticket collectors' uniform in 1917 comprised a serge skirt, a coat (to last two winters), a black tie, a hat, and two muslin collars. Half-yearly an extra hat and tie were issued and porters received an extra skirt. Van drivers were given breeches and spring-sided leather leggings instead of the skirt, and a mackintosh (to last two winters). In the summer the station staff wore crush frock coats and straw hats, while the van drivers wore cream crush jumper blouses, straw hats and breeches.[73]

The GER policewomen's uniform consisted of a long, dark blue skirt, an open necked belted jacket, a white shirt, a black tie and a flat peaked cap with a white top. On the left sleeve they wore a striped armlet bearing the letters GER. On the lapels they wore the same collar dog as their male counterparts, consisting of a bat's wing device from the company's coat of arms. The cap badge consisted of the same device enclosed within a laurel wreath. The jacket buttons were in nickel with the device in the centre and THE GREAT EASTERN RAILWAY around the edge. Constables carried white gloves, while those of women sergeants were of brown kidskin.[74]

The smartest uniforms without doubt were those made for the Metropolitan's women guards. Many decades after she wore it, Louie Weaver still remembered every detail:

> It was navy blue cloth with a skirt, which came just below the knee to allow for movement, and a jacket buttoned to the neck with a collar and brass buttons all the way down. The collar and cuffs had a blue band with gold braid trimming. The job involved leaping on to the train after the 'all clear' signal had been given. Special knickers were provided to preserve decency! They ensured that no tempting flashes of female leg were revealed to the passengers. They were navy blue and came down below the knees where they were tucked into long, black leather boots. To complete this very smart outfit was a peaked cap with a blue band and more braid.[75]

Their counterparts on Berlin's railways were banned from wearing knickerbockers and had to wear men's uniforms.[76] Clerical staff did not have a uniform. Male clerks were often referred to as 'black coats', and some managers wanted women to adopt a similar mode of dress: 'high-necked white blouses, and a dark or black neck bow or tie strings, long dark grey or black skirts, black stockings with tie up or strapped shoes to match.'[77]

The Railway Unions

The RCA

The influx of women clerks gave a colossal boost to the RCA. Just before the war it had only 100 female members; by 1918 there were 13,655. They were not universally welcomed, even by RCA General Secretary Walkden,* who admitted in a letter to a member that he recognised 'the weakness of our position in any attempt which might be made to take up an attitude of absolute opposition to the introduction of female clerk labour'.[78]

Railwayman's daughter Mamie (Mary Elizabeth) Thompson was one of the RCA's first female activists. Born in Waterloo, Lancashire, in 1895 she joined the LYR in 1911 as a ledger clerk at Oldham Mumps. A suffragette, she soon became active in the RCA and, in 1915, at the age of 21, became the first woman delegated to an annual conference of any railway union:

> The Dublin conference was more to me than I imagined then. I was proud of being the first woman delegate, yet nervous about my fitness for such a position of trust for the branch. In addition to all that, the Lusitania† was torpedoed the week before we sailed, and we realised what that might mean. The tenseness of the journey will never be forgotten by any of us, but when we reached Ireland, what a welcome we received!

To mark the historic occasion, the hosts presented her with a gold bracelet. However, her attendance was not universally celebrated:

> Some men within her branch had made a determined effort to stop her going. Thompson had already made a significant contribution to the RCA as a Divisional Council Organiser for Women but some men simply refused to co-operate with her for no other reason than their distaste of being represented by a girl.[79]

Miss Thompson later organised petitions to demand for women the war bonuses that had been given to men. She was passionately dedicated to her mission, which took her all over Britain:

> By mastering timetables, sleeping in railway carriages instead of getting home to bed, we were able to get north, south, east and west to take the message to the lukewarm or the unconverted.[80]

Writing in *The Railway Clerk* she revealed her logical approach to women's rights, maintaining 'there are no differences shown between men and women [clerks] until it comes to pay-day'[81] and asked: 'Why should a woman ... take a less wage than a man and give the difference to her employer?'[82]

---

* Later, Lord Walkden of Great Bookham.

† The Lusitania was a British passenger ship en route from New York to Liverpool that was attacked and sunk by a German submarine off the Irish coast in May, 1915, killing 1,153 people.

By 1916 Miss Thompson, for unknown reasons, had transferred to the NUR, but another woman managed to get delegated to the RCA annual conference: Miss H. M. Knighton, of Weymouth branch, an activist on the union's Western Divisional Council. At this time the RCA boasted over 49,000 members, of whom 3,378 were women, and was the largest union of office workers in the world.[83] In 1917, when railwaywomen were almost at the peak of their numerical strength, 20 women attended the conference but by 1919 this had decreased to nine and by the early 1920s (when all the war-workers had left) to a mere three. Not until 1930 did the number of female delegates again reach double figures.

The RCA inaugurated women's conferences in 1916. The first was at Leeds in July and it was a great success: 93 delegates attended, representing 46 branches, and employed by 17 companies. There were lively discussions about special meetings for 'lady' clerks and concerning women's participation in union activism. The delegates requested that a full page in each issue of *The Railway Clerk* be dedicated to matters affecting women, and that a special pamphlet be issued as soon as possible. This was duly printed and distributed under the title *An Open Letter to a Lady Clerk*. RCA women's conferences continued to be held annually until 1938.

A couple of unpleasant incidents occurred concerning women and the RCA. Some clerks employed at Eastleigh, LSWR, and Marylebone, GCR, had been obliged to sign an undertaking not to join any society or association. The companies had claimed that this was to prevent their employees becoming suffragettes,* but managers later claimed that it also encompassed unions. A few shorthand typists at Marylebone were considering joining the RCA, but their manager warned them of the consequences and told them not to attend any branch meetings. When later brought in for questioning they admitted being at a meeting and joining the RCA. They were asked to resign from the union and, when they refused, were moved to different work, suffering a pay cut of 10s a week. General Manager Sir Sam Fay denied victimisation, saying he had always banned confidential clerks from joining unions.

The RCA leader Alexander Walkden told Sir Sam that his managers had exceeded their duties and requested that the typists be reinstated to their former jobs. He expected a positive response from Sir Sam because the latter was, as a Liberal, supposedly a supporter of the rights of the working classes. But Sir Sam ignored him, so Walkden contacted the President of the Board of Trade. A union-sponsored MP called George Wardle raised the matter in the House of Commons in December, 1915. The Parliamentary Secretary to the Board of Trade, Captain Pretyman, replied that the GCR did not object to clerks' joining trade unions unless they were in confidential positions at head offices. Sir Sam wrote to all MPs, criticising the RCA for wasting time and energy that ought to be directed towards defeating the Germans. George Wardle raised the subject again, and the President of the Board of Trade said that if the policy of banning confidential clerks from joining unions had existed prior to the war, the current matter should be dropped until peacetime, but if the rule had been instituted during the war, he would ask the company to withdraw it. The RCA argued that the matter was one of principle. The rule not only directly affected over 1,000 clerks but thousands more whose promotional prospects might be blighted. Eventually, the ban on staff in head and district offices joining the RCA was lifted.

* The suffragettes had committed over 40 attacks on railway property as part of their militant campaign against the government. Between 1912 and 1914 three stations were completely destroyed by fire.

Just a few months later, hostilities again flared up between the RCA and the GCR in a matter concerning female staff. A typist at Manchester enquired whether women could obtain the war bonus as given to men. Her manager, Albert Leigh, Chief Assistant to the Audit Accountant, explained that men had agitated for it, provoking her to retort that women could agitate, too. The manager warned her that the company didn't want agitators, and that women did not need bonuses – but husbands! William Stott, writing in the RCA's journal *The Railway Clerk*, claimed that Albert Leigh summonsed the typist and:

> After bullying her he said he had a good mind to give them all a week's notice and get a fresh lot of girls in at half their wages as he had 150 on his books waiting for positions. The girl ... was in tears when he had finished with her.[84]

Mr Leigh, backed by Sir Sam Fay and the GCR, sued Stott, the RCA, the publisher and even the printer for libel. The typist, possibly under threat of losing her job, testified that the conversation had been 'jocular' and Leigh was awarded a massive £600 in damages.

ASLEF AND THE NUR

Women's organisations urged trades unions in all industries to enrol war-workers, but this was not a simple issue. The NUR and ASLEF worried that admitting women would introduce struggles that might conflict with those of men. Nor did they relish wasting time and energy fighting battles for an enormous number of temporary workers who would be leaving the moment the war ended. But excluding women was even more hazardous: it was difficult to monitor the minimum-rate agreement without women's co-operation and, in the worst-case scenario, non-unionised women might be used as a 'scab army' in the event of a strike.

The engine drivers' union ASLEF, which had 36,000 members by 1917, enrolled male but not female engine cleaners, insisting that the job was 'unsuitable' for women and holding stubbornly to that belief even when, by 1918, more than 3,000 women were successfully performing the work.

For the NUR the matter of female membership came to a head in the summer of 1915, when 25 branches asked the union's AGM to admit women. The delegates' vote was 33 for and 23 against. As explained earlier, according to the NUR rulebook women were eligible to join anyway, so the vote was a farce. In fact it actually reduced women's equality, for they were to be confined to Scale D, which was for temporary staff; this covered strike pay, legal assistance, and representation in cases of unjust dismissal.* Although allowed full voting rights, women could not serve on committees.

Women's admittance was widely acknowledged. The front page of *Votes for Women*, a suffragette weekly paper, depicted a railwayman welcoming a woman on the threshold of the union's HQ with the headline 'Bravo NUR!'[85] *The Railway Review* published a cartoon in which the words 'and Women' were being appended to 'National Union of Railwaymen' on the HQ's nameplate.[86] In reality, attempts to change the union's name continued to be met with a negative response from the NUR EC.

---

* Other scales provided unemployment allowance, accident cover, incapacity allowance and provision for orphaned children.

The first woman to join the NUR was Jennie Burden, a 19-year-old carriage cleaner who joined Brighton 3 branch on 2nd July. The second was porter Lucy Heale of Poole. Women's names were entered in the union's register in red ink, in contrast to the usual black. Over 2,000 enrolled in the first six months and soon they began to attend branch meetings, where sometimes a group of women was able to pass a resolution in favour of their own sex, only to see it later retracted by their branch officers, or overturned by the NUR EC. At one time 161 branches voted to alter the union's title from 'Railwaymen' to 'Railway Workers', but the AGM soon put a stop to it by voting 15 for, 44 against.

Finding little support at branch meetings, in AGM resolutions, or EC decisions, the new member might turn for solace to the pages of her union's newspaper, *The Railway Review.* Here she would be confronted with a barrage of hostility towards women in editorials, readers' letters and branch reports. One article claimed that women were 'a menace to all established working conditions', and:

> They threaten to lower the standard of living. They threaten to lengthen the hours of labour. And they threaten the continuity of employment as far as men are concerned.[87]

The new member could be forgiven for discarding the publication after reading such a tirade, but if she could bring herself to continue she would discover that employers' greed and opportunism were (eventually) blamed, and that women were merely pawns in the struggle for power between capital and (male) labour.

It would have been unfortunate if women turned away from *The Railway Review* because, in later months, it published articles preaching sex-equality from a socialist perspective. Some railwaymen thought that women should be excluded from the union because they took no interest in union affairs,* but one explained:

> You cannot keep a dog in a cellar all its life without dwarfing its powers. When we remember the thousands of years that woman has been confined to the domicile of her lord and master, specialised to child-rearing and house cleaning, it is not to be wondered at if her mental outlook is limited by the backyard fence or the front doorstep.[88]

Another railwayman thought his colleagues inconsistent in their attitude to women:

> No man, who has taken unto himself a wife, or who contemplates doing so, has any right to object to one of her sex being included amongst the members of his Trade Union.[89]

Brother Dix of Bromley branch was unhappy with the AGM decision to admit women, and demanded a ballot of the entire NUR membership, believing that the majority would vote against it. He intended to reject all applications from women and urged others to do the same, not because he was a misogynist but because he feared a conflict of interest:

* The same circular argument was used in relation to the parliamentary vote: women had no vote and consequently most took little interest in politics. This lack of interest was then cited by some men as a reason to deny them the vote.

> What in the name of justice are we going to do for our soldier brothers at the Front[?] By admitting women to our union they are entitled to the identical privileges as the men we have got to get reinstated. How we are to do this and act honourably to our female members is beyond me.[90]

Although the NUR accepted women into membership it did not support their campaign for the vote. In 1916 the London Society for Women's Suffrage asked all trades unions to send a resolution to the government in support of votes for women, but the NUR EC refused, saying it had 'no opinion on the subject' — yet the union had 15,000 female members.[91]

Some individual activists, however, did support women's occupational, political and social equality. The most notable of the NUR's early female officials was Mamie Thompson (mentioned earlier in connection with the RCA). A passionate crusader for women's equality, she rallied colleagues with slogans such as 'No men workers, and no women workers, but all workers in the railway service!' She was a leading proponent of the amalgamation of the RCA and the NUR* and in 1916 *The Railway Review* reported that she was the first woman NUR branch secretary, at Ashton-Under-Lyne No. 1, which she represented at Manchester NUR District Council.[92] It is hard to argue with the source; *The Railway Review* was, after all, the NUR's own newspaper; but attempts at verification have proved inconclusive. A list of branch Secretaries shows 'J. Thomas' as secretary of Ashton-Under-Lyne in 1916.†

Women's Pay

The issue of war workers' pay was complex and gave rise to comments and arguments that were often illogical and hypocritical. Before the war, railwaymen and their three unions were entirely unconcerned about the inequality of pay between the sexes, but when women began to replace men the unions feared they would accept lower wages and thereby either displace men or bring down male rates. This threat depended upon women being capable of performing men's work, so there was a tendency for the companies to stress women's competence and for the unions to cast doubt upon it. Simultaneously, the bosses wanted to pay women as little as possible, while the unions sought to protect male minimum rates by demanding men's pay for women. Therefore both sides held paradoxical positions: the companies argued that women were competent but should be paid less than men; the unions contended that women were not as capable as men, but wanted them to get equal pay.

To add to the controversy, some women were against equal pay. They feared that if employers had to pay the same to each sex, men would be favoured and women left without work — 'half a loaf', they believed, was 'better than no bread at all'. Other women demanded equal pay on principle. Men, too, were not of one mind: some criticised women for accepting lower pay (because they were undercutting men, which might lead to men

* A campaign that to this day has not borne fruit.

† Mamie Thompson left the railway in July 1918 to become an organiser for the Labour Party. In 1919 she married railway clerk Frank Anderson, who was later to become the Labour MP for Whitehaven (1935-1959). She attended RCA conferences as an observer for many years.

Girls in Railway Offices.—A correspondent writes :—The advent of girls into railway offices has been variously regarded. In one respect, though, there would appear to be something approaching to unanimity of opinion. It is the general view that some at least of the girls would be well advised in their own interests were they to dress as though they were going to business and not to a garden party. The writer has in mind a particular girl whose vagaries in this respect are the subject of much amused comment in certain office circles. And here let it be said that the girl in question is thoroughly capable and satisfactory as regards her work. There is no fault to be found with her on that head. Indeed, she is quite aware of the fact, and would be much astonished to find herself a subject for adverse criticism in any way. This was amusingly illustrated by her artless reply on an occasion when she was asked whether a particularly startling hat she was wearing was a new one. "New," she exclaimed, "Good gracious, no, I've had it nearly a week!"

SIR,—I was much moved to answer the article in your last issue under a title superficially resembling the above, but essentially different. I am one of those new importations labelled "the female clerk," and speak not only for myself but for others who have expressed a detestation for that term. Regarded critically it makes one wonder whether the writer knew what we were, of what animal we are the "female" kind, or even whether we are bipeds or quadrupeds—or does he, perchance, think the Company, in its need, has hunted round and discovered the feminine form of the missing link, some more advanced type of the anthropoid ape? On further consideration one concludes he really must know we belong to the highest order of creatures, that of reasoning, intellectual beings (though but of the feminine sex) and that consequently we are more than mere females: we are *women*. And if an alternative form to the term "women clerks" is needed from literary necessity—it cannot be from any other—then courtesy would suggest the word "lady"—a not exorbitant demand to make, as the custom has been well formed in the case of "women students" and "lady students." One has even heard of the "char-lady," but never of the "female char."

Some examples of the abundant articles and letters regarding the influx of women into railway offices.

Top: A man commenting on the way his girl colleagues dressed. *The Railway Clerk*, 21st September 1917.

Left: A clerk objects to being called a 'female'. *GWR Magazine*, 1916.

Below: Sympathy for a lady at Dinting. *The Railway Clerk*, 15th December 1917.

Drudgery at Dinting.

There is reason to believe that some time ago an enquiry was made into the conditions of the lady clerk at Dinting, G.C., but as nothing has been done we think it well to publish a few details. This clerk works from 8 a.m. to 8 p.m., less 1½ hours for meals, six days each week, and is also on duty every third Sunday. She is in sole charge of the Booking Office, and does booking, coaching accounts, parcels traffic, telegraphy, and receives and transmits telegraph messages for Glossop and Old Dinting Goods. All this was done by the man whose place she fills, and who had much more money, and as porters book before 8 a.m. and after 8 p.m., there is obviously room for another clerk. By the wa wey, understand this is only a sample of what exists at other G.C. stations in the district.

Cartoon in the *Railway Review*, July 1915, suggesting that the NUR might change its name to reflect the admission of women. COURTESY OF THE RMT

The War Paper for Women

VOTES FOR WOMEN

OFFICIAL ORGAN OF THE UNITED SUFFRAGISTS

VOL. VIII. (Third Series), No. [illegible] FRIDAY, JULY 2, 1915. Price 1d. Weekly

BRAVO, N.U.R.!

Right: A women's rights newspaper celebrates the NUR's momentous decision. *Votes for Women* 2ND JULY 1915

A cartoon in the NUR's newspaper depicting the comical notion of a female guard. *Railway Review*, March 1915. COURTESY OF THE RMT

losing work); others condemned them for expecting the same pay as a man when, clearly, they were the inferior sex. Traditional myths were aired, based on the belief that all working men were married with children while all working women were spinsters. An example of the prevailing ideology was vocalised in 1915 when the Postmaster General said: 'If you pay a single woman the same wage as you pay a family man, you are giving her a much higher standard of comfort than you are giving him.' Men were never paid according to how much money they were deemed to need for their living expenses; this question was only ever raised in relation to women's pay.

The companies' dilemma was aired in *The Railway Gazette*. Paying war-workers too little 'may create a bad impression'; that is, it might be construed as exploiting either the war or the women. On the other hand, equal pay was described as 'a waste of money' and 'unjustifiable'. The companies finally settled on the stance that women war-workers' wages were 'correctly assessed on a somewhat lower basis than those of men.' It is intriguing that the author of that statement expected 'any attempt to foment trouble' to be 'promptly suppressed by the Trades Unions'.[93]

There were no national pay scales; each grade within each railway company had its own rate of pay, negotiated by the conciliation boards. After being engaged at a minimum rate, men were commonly awarded a 1s increment per annum, reaching the maximum in five years. Temporary staff received only the minimum with no increments. In April 1915 the REC and NUR agreed that women war-workers should be paid as temporary staff. No one expected the war to last four years; many predicted it would be 'over by Christmas', so labelling them as 'temporary' was reasonable under the circumstances. Some NUR District Councils demanded increments for women, but the EC was finding it difficult enough to force companies to comply even with the minimum-rate agreement.

As complaints increased *The Railway Gazette* declared: 'To talk of the companies "exploiting their fellow country-women" in order to reduce expense is not only unjust but absurd.'[94] However, the transgressions continued and on 31st July the NUR EC threatened to cancel its wartime truce if the REC did not honour the minimum-rate agreement within 14 days. Nothing was heard until 10th August, when Sir Sam Fay promised that the ten companies he represented would henceforth pay the minimum and the Board of Trade promised to take action if the others did not comply.

Being denied yearly increments and being excluded from the war bonus scheme meant that women in men's jobs earned 2s to 8s a week less than their male counterparts. Indeed, a woman's wages became more unequal the longer she remained employed, since only men received yearly increments. They were hardly going to complain, however, because a woman in a man's job was still far better paid than her colleague in traditional women's work. A young woman porter, for example, earned about 20s a week, double the wage of, say, a ladies' waiting room attendant with 30 years' service. This discrepancy arose because only women replacing men in male wages grades were included in the minimum-rate agreement. Women in female grades were excluded because the purpose of the agreement was to protect the rates of men, not to improve the pay of women.

Because they, too, were excluded from the agreement, women in jobs performed by both sexes continued to earn less than their male colleagues on identical work. Miss Smedley, a French polisher on the MR, revealed that women's piece-rate was 8d and men's, 2s; therefore women had to polish three times as many items as their male counterparts to obtain the same pay. Crossing keepers fared even worse — after all, they did not have the option of working faster to make up some of the difference between their wage and that of a man. The NER paid the woman gatekeeper at Barnard Castle just 8s for a 144-hour week, while another, at Garforth, earned just 3s 6d for 84 hours. In contrast, male crossing keepers earned 20s to 25s for 58 to 60 hours.

The NUR's determination to ensure that women replacing men were paid the male rate sometimes encountered difficulties: if a woman was newly recruited to a job performed by both sexes was she in a female grade (and thus not eligible for equal pay), or was she employed in a male grade and entitled to the male rate for the job? Controversy erupted in 1915 over carriage cleaners on the LNWR at Euston. To comply with the NUR's minimum rate agreement the LNWR increased the women's hours from 47 a week to 57 to match those of men. The women, most of whom were married with children and had sole responsibility for running a home, strongly objected to this increase in hours and asked to be returned to their old contracts. The company not only acceded to their request but gave the women an 8d an hour increase. This put their hourly rate exactly on a par with that of their male colleagues. (Female carriage cleaners at the other LNWR cleaning depots did not object to the 57-hour week.)[95] A similar problem occurred at Old Oak Common, GWR, where women's hours were increased from nine to ten per day to comply with the minimum rate agreement. This resulted in the first ever strike of railwaywomen, when all 48 of them walked out on 30th August 1915. The GWR and NUR agreed to let the women continue to work their 48-hour week.[96]

More trouble arose when the GSWR claimed to have employed female carriage cleaners at Bellahouston depot 'to a very considerable extent' before the war, while the NUR argued that there had been only four. The company wanted to pay new recruits at women's rates; the NUR insisted the women were replacing men. The squabble was eventually settled thus: of the 100 female carriage cleaners, 35 were deemed to be replacing men and were paid the minimum rate (21s) while 65 were designated as being in a female grade and were paid only 12s plus 3s war bonus. It is not known whether the women managed to work together without resentment being vocalised.

Clerks were excluded from the agreement to pay women the minimum male rate for the job, leaving the way open for the companies to cut their wage bills quite substantially by employing women to replace men. The following examples from the NER illustrate some of the remarkable savings made. The Chief Mechanical and Electrical Engineer replaced 148 male clerks, whose total pay was £11,467 per annum, with 196 women war-workers whose pay totalled just £6,391. In the same way the locomotive accounts department at Darlington reduced its wage bill from £340 to £146 per annum. These cases challenge the employers' claims that they were exploiting neither the war nor the women. It is interesting to note that while Sir Herbert Walker of the LSWR stated that his female clerks 'do as much work as men as a rule and in abstracting they do more',[97] he felt no embarrassment in paying them less than men.

The RCA president, W. E. Williams, was acutely aware of the poor position of working women and openly condemned it. At the 1917 annual conference he described the history of women in modern industry as 'the history of tragedy' and remarked that they 'have too often been exploited by employers in a manner which is entirely reprehensible'. Other members of his union thought women as much to blame as the companies. A writer in *The Railway clerk* commented:

> Ye ancient city of Loidis [Leeds] is the latest citadel to fall into the hands of the ladies. Two cashiers and half a dozen collectors have fled, leaving their domicile to the advancing wave of modern feminism. ... The picture of old railway veterans, 50 to 60 years of age, with their £3 per week and upwards, making way for 15-year-old girls, with 6s 11d per week was, to say the least, significant of

> much. ... the clerks whose positions are being usurped are the individuals deputed to teach the ... girls their work. To have your bread and butter purloined or endangered is surely bad enough, but to have to teach the culprit how to eat it after she has got it is something akin to adding insult to injury.[98]

It is interesting that the writer felt that it was men and not women who were being injured and insulted, although it was women who were being paid less for the same work.

Pay inequality was often exacerbated by disparities in the provision of leave and free travel. At best, a woman could expect just three days' holiday per annum and a train pass for herself and her children, but not for her husband or for any 'illegitimate' offspring.

The War Bonus

A 5s rise in men's war bonus in October 1915 prompted railwaywomen to demand the bonus for themselves. By January 1916 their claim was in the hands of the NUR EC, the majority of which supported it, with seven against. But the companies refused to pay, claiming that some women had fathers or husbands who received the war bonus, that others received government separation allowances in respect of their breadwinners serving in the forces and that, in any case, women did not have the same financial responsibilities as men. The women disagreed: some were spinsters, others war-widows, a number had children wholly dependent on them, a few supported elderly parents or grandparents. Their protests mounted until militancy erupted in April 1916, when seven carriage cleaners at Old Oak Common, GWR, went on strike for equal pay. Their colleagues raised £73 for a strike fund – equivalent to about 70 weeks' wages – to help them to stay out, but their claim was declined by the company and they returned to work defeated. Later a more general group of railwaywomen managed to initiate an NUR-backed application to the GWR for the war bonus. This was refused, and the matter was referred to the Committee on Production in July 1916, which decided:

> No case has been made. ... From statistics it would appear that the majority of railwaywomen replacing men are (1) Wives and daughters of railwaymen (2) wives and daughters of men drawing wages (3) unmarried women. [The war bonus] was intended to be given to the head of the family.[99]

The war bonus was not subjected to any such bogus means-testing before it was given to railwaymen, plenty of whom were bachelors living with their parents.

Despite the ruling, railwaywomen did not give up. When men's war bonus was again increased, in September 1916, deep feelings of grievance led women to initiate a campaign which, after eight weeks, resulted in a partial victory. Some companies agreed to give them the bonus; only the GCR, GNR, NER, all Scottish companies and the Barry, Brecon and Merthyr Railway continued to withhold it. Railwaymen's bonus was at that time 5s, but women were granted only 3s. The employers' justification was that women's labour was only three-fifths as productive as men's. The NUR asked how this could apply to women ticket collectors, but the companies declined to reply. In fact, the question of whether women's labour was equal to that of men was irrelevant; the bonus when given to men was not linked to productivity; its sole purpose was to compensate for the increased cost of living. As retailers, landlords, utility companies and even bus conductors charged women the same as men, their bonus surely should have been the same. During the negotiations, men's bonus was doubled to 10s, making the 3s given to women seem even more derisory. In April 1917 women's bonus was raised by only 2s 6d while men's increased by 5s. Even the men complained that their bonus was inadequate: food prices had increased 95% since 1914 while their bonus had increased less than 40%.

From August 1917 the bonus was consolidated into the basic rate and re-named the 'war-wage'. The change increased the disparity between men's and women's pay, since men performed more overtime. This incited even more railwaywomen to join the equal pay campaign. The issue gained momentum and came to a head in 1918. That year many NUR women, weary of the union's failure to represent them, began to organise their own meetings to protest against unequal pay. At one rally 500 women gathered at the Euston Theatre, King's Cross, on 17th February 1918, (by which time women's war wage was 8s 6d compared to men's 21s). Mrs Mason, president of the Railway Women's Guild (a charitable, fund-raising body) asserted that women would get equal pay or strike, while Mamie Thompson criticised the NUR EC for accepting a lower rate for women, and demanded it re-open negotiations at once.

NUR leaders prevaricated throughout the war on the issue of equal pay for women, each pronouncement contradicting the previous one. Even women's increased militancy in 1918 failed to stabilise the EC: it supported equal war wages in March, then in May passed a resolution not to fight for them. In June, under pressure from women members, the NUR AGM again put it to the vote. The outcome was one man for and 51 against. Despite this overwhelming defeat, just two months later NUR leader Jimmy Thomas lied to women, saying that the union supported their claim for equal pay. Four months later he lied again, this time to a War Cabinet Committee,* saying that the NUR 'strongly' upheld women's claim to equal pay, adding that they were 'entitled to it because of their work.'[100]

By the summer of 1918 women bus and tram workers had reached the end of their tether. In London, where women comprised 45% of transport workers, over 17,000 bus and tram women went on strike on 18th August, demanding equal pay. Many men walked out in solidarity with their soldier brothers at the Front, as they did not want to see rates of pay reduced or women being kept on after the war because they were cheaper. Pickets persuaded about 100 women working for the London Electric Railway to walk out, too, but the only main line railway affected was the GWR: about 200 women at Paddington and Old Oak Common joined the strike on the 23rd. Jimmy Thomas asked those who were NUR members to return to work and let the NUR settle the matter for them but the women — by then justifiably mistrustful of the EC — resolved to continue. The women road transport employees were promised an immediate hearing by the Committee on Production, but railway wages could be negotiated only between the REC and the NUR.

Doubting that the NUR EC would champion their cause, women working for the London Underground also took industrial action without NUR approval. To the exasperation of London's travelling public, when the bus and tram women returned to work on 24th August, a thousand women and men working for the capital's underground railways met at the King's Hall, Walworth, and resolved to cease work until women received a 12s 6d rise in their war wages, the amount needed to give them parity with men. Thousands went on strike, in defiance of the NUR. Their actions caused considerable inconvenience to

* Female bus conductors received equal pay with men, yet were denied a 5s increase in pay granted to men in July 1918. They went on strike and the men joined them. The women won, and the incident led to the appointment of the War Cabinet Committee on Women in Industry.

Londoners: it was reported that most underground trains were late, overcrowded or cancelled. A deputation of women attended the NUR HQ on 26th August, where the EC told them that the union supported equal war wages (when in fact the AGM had voted overwhelmingly against this just a few weeks before) but that it was unable to begin negotiations unless the women returned to work.

A mass meeting was held at *The Ring* public house, Blackfriars. After some communal singing those present roundly lambasted the NUR EC. Mabel Edwards, a motor-driver of Paddington, GWR, 'denounced Mr J. H. Thomas in the most trenchant manner'. Mr F. Beale declared that the strikers 'had done more to bring the principle of equal pay ... before the railway authorities than the Union had done in its whole existence'. He pointed out that the strikers operated not only without the machinery, the funds, or the assistance of the NUR leadership, but 'in spite of its most bitter and efficient opposition.'[101]

The strike committee intended to bypass the NUR EC if necessary and indeed an agreement was reached with the Ministry of Labour to the effect that, if the NUR EC should continue to fail to help its female members, the minister himself would intervene and try to conduct negotiations directly with the employers on the women's behalf. This promise motivated the women to return to work but, such was their mood of triumph, they declared the next day an impromptu holiday and did not resume duty until 28th. The companies agreed to reinstate all the strikers and the strike committee warned that the truce would be abandoned unless progress was made.

On 30th August the companies conceded equal war wage increments, which arrangement gave men a war wage of 28s while women had to make do with just 15s 6d. This inequality led to more protests and threats of further strikes;[102] however, militancy died down and women decided to accept what they were given. Equality was never achieved: the final rise in the war wage was 5s for each sex, this meant that men's total war bonus was 33s, while women received just 20s 6d.

Another way to reduce pay disparity between the sexes was proposed by Swadlincote NUR branch: it asked the EC to negotiate yearly increments for women. The EC refused because temporary staff did not receive increments and they wanted to make certain that nothing altered women's status from that of temporary workers. This ruling, plus the inequalities in the war wage, together with the practice of favouring men for any overtime that was available, meant that by 1918 the average pay for a woman working in a male railway grade and supposedly enjoying 'equal pay' was, in practice, just two-thirds that of her male counterpart.

A War Cabinet Committee on Women in Industry investigated women's pay in 1918. The RCA leader Alexander Walkden, Mr W. E. Hill and four women members (C. Greenlees, I. Moore, K. Ralph and E. Peters) gave evidence on behalf of female clerks, machine operators and telegraph and telephone operators. Several wages-grade railwaywomen gave evidence revealing that a good number of them supported elderly parents, widowed mothers, invalids or dependent children. A widow who was raising six children solely on her earnings as an engine cleaner declared, 'We should receive the same, if not more, than the men ... We do as much and more in the time.' Miss Edwards, a GWR motor-lorry driver, declared emphatically: 'Every particle that a man can do in the grade I do myself', yet she earned 46s 6d compared with her male colleagues' 66s. She asserted:

> I think I am entitled to the same war wages as the men owing to the fact that they were granted to meet the high cost of commodities, and seeing I have

> someone dependent upon me and I have to pay the same as a man, I see no reason why there should be any distinction made.[103]

Miss Edwards's statement summed up succinctly the essence of women's claim to equal pay. However, by the time the report was published the war had ended, and the movement for equal pay on the railways lost momentum as women were no longer going to perform 'men's work'.

Women in the Higher Grades

By 1916 over 33,000 women were employed on railways, comprising 7% of the industry's workforce. This was not a uniform percentage; for example, the Mersey Railway had the greatest proportion, while the Midland & South Western employed none. In no company did they exceed 10% and in some Scottish companies they were only 1% of the staff.

From January 1916 men were conscripted into the forces, and more women had to be recruited to replace them. By December there were over 46,000 women working in 135 grades, of whom more than 34,000 were performing work that had previously been considered suitable only for men. As the war continued into 1917, more and more men were needed for the forces, so the companies had to reassess women's capabilities. Their competence in the lower wages grades led managers to consider offering them higher-grade railway operating work. Women were very receptive to these proposals, which promised higher pay and status and hinted at the possibility of permanence. A small handful was already working in signalboxes; among the earliest was a porter-signalwoman at Netherton, LYR. Mrs Flintcrof of Wingate, NER, had taken such an interest in her signalman husband's work that, when he was killed in action, she was found to be proficient to take over his job without formal instruction.

The NUR — both rank-and-file and leadership — was against women taking up higher grade work, despite Jimmy Thomas's comment at a meeting of Middlesbrough railwaymen two years earlier:

> It must not be assumed that the employment of women is not more fully developed because of the objections of men. It is far more the fault of the employers than employés.

In fact, the opposite was true: the companies wanted to extend women's employment and it was railwaymen, their union officers and the NUR EC who stopped them. They did not want women in track maintenance or in shunting, signalling or guarding trains, hiding their complex motives behind the simple plea that the work was 'too hazardous for the fair sex'. The Home Secretary acknowledged that railwaywomen were 'naturally anxious to do their part', to which Jimmy Thomas replied 'We quite recognise the spirit of the women, but we do not want them to be killed by their work.' The Home Secretary agreed:

> The women must be protected as much as possible. There is an obligation on our part not to let them overdo it or be carried away by their goodwill to the point of physical suffering.[104]

As soon as the companies began negotiating with the NUR EC about the employment of women in the higher operating grades objections and protests arose from the men, who used every means at their disposal to obstruct the plan. Vociferous mass-meetings were held, and branches sent resolutions to the EC and the AGM. Railwaymen demanded that the Board of Trade intervene to stop women being trained for skilled operating grades. The posts that most incensed men were those of guard, shunter and – above all – signalwoman, but Jimmy Thomas also prevented women from being trained as platelayers (i.e. trackworkers), because they would have to take their turn at fog-signalling which, he argued, was 'the most undesirable work ... the mortality is about one in 24'.[105]

The first railway to employ women in an on-board train operating role had been the London Electric, which employed gatewomen from December 1916. They travelled on a platform at the ends of the cars, each gatewoman (or man) operating four sets of bi-fold lattice-gates for passengers.* A six-car train might have five gatemen or gatewomen and one guard. Only the latter could give the starting signal to the driver; having done so, he would board the train as it moved away, and managers on the London Electric believed this made the guard's job too dangerous for women. The Metropolitan Railway's managers disagreed: they thought it was women's clothing, rather than anything inherent in being female, that made the job unsuitable for them, and so the company ordered a bespoke, tailored suit (with a scandalously short skirt!) for each woman it trained as a guard.

The London Electric relented in February 1917, employing female guards on its Baker Street to Waterloo section. The LSWR was the first mainline railway company to follow suit; however, women were restricted to its short, electrified underground link, the Waterloo and City line. In 1918 the Metropolitan reported that its female guards joined moving trains 'safely and gracefully' and performed their duties 'more thoroughly and attentively' than did their male predecessors.[106]

Louie Weaver was among the first on the Metropolitan. She was engaged as a gatewoman in 1916 when she was 18 and was later promoted to guard. The job paid five times as much as her previous, highly skilled occupation as a court dressmaker in Bond Street. Every day for two years she walked from Knightsbridge to Hammersmith in time to start work at 4 a.m., then worked a split shift comprising four hours each morning and four each evening, with four hours (unpaid) break in between. Her route, from Hammersmith to New Cross, was partly over-ground and passed through areas of London that were bombed.

While Miss Weaver found the men at her NUR branch (Chiswick) supportive, guards at Newcastle branch passed a unanimous resolution against women being trained in their grade. They demanded that the Board of Trade ban women because: 'It would be dangerous to themselves, other railway employees and the general public, and practically impossible for them to perform the duty.'[107] In 1918 guards on the SECR passed a resolution 'emphatically' protesting against the proposed introduction of women, citing the safety of the public, the safety of the women, and the unsuitability of women for the work.[108] In Edinburgh, a special meeting of guards was called to oppose women entering their ranks, from which was appointed a deputation to state their objection to the district superintendent. Men of all grades at the local NUR branch (Edinburgh 1) supported the guards' objections. Before the deputation left, an addendum asking that 'no obstacle be placed in the way of women' was put forth, but was rejected by 11 votes to two.[109] Despite the resistance, the GWR, LNWR, NER and NBR employed women as guards. The Great North of

* There were no air-operated doors on the underground until 1919.

Scotland placed them on local trains in the Aberdeen district, while the Caledonian engaged 21 women as full-time guards and trained 16 female porters to be stand-in guards. Elizabeth Anderson Crighton was the first on the Caledonian, working on the Cathcart Circle line. It has been said that the male passengers became very fond of her: 'She was often presented with roses or other flowers, which passengers would produce from their hats as she went past.' [110]

In several locations women were trained as shunters and pointswomen. Again, railwaymen fought to block them: protests were raised at both branch and national levels. The most vociferous opponents were those on the GCR and at Brent, MR. The latter emphasised that they were concerned only about women being exposed to the hazards involved in manipulating moving vehicles. In September 1917 the NUR EC passed a resolution against the employment of women shunters. Jimmy Thomas said that this was because 'The rate of mortality amongst men shunters is 1 in 19 killed or injured and the risk is altogether too great.[111] Indeed, records reveal how common it was for shunters to be run over or crushed between buffers. The number of women who became shunters was not recorded, but there was at least one on the NBR. The IWM owns two photographs of what appears to be a pointswoman at Marylebone (see page 76).

Guard Crighton, Caledonian Railway
COURTESY OF GLASGOW MUSEUM

By citing the dangers of jobs that placed workers in the vicinity of moving vehicles, railwaymen could claim to be motivated only by concern for women's safety and avoid being labelled as anti-female, but when managers suggested that women be trained in signalling, mostly an indoor job which was less hazardous even than carriage cleaning, men's objections were forced to take a different tack. All remaining euphemism and false gallantry were set aside as railwaymen launched a blatant attack on women, calling them 'irresponsible' and 'incompetent'.

The burden of responsibility shouldered by signalmen and the dreadful consequences of a small mistake were firmly in the forefront of railwaymen's minds in 1917 because, only two years earlier, signalmen's errors had caused two catastrophic collisions. At Quintinshill — still the worst rail disaster in British history — 227 were killed and 246 injured in a four-train collision, and 19 were killed and 82 injured in a crash near Jarrow.[112]

The whole female sex was subjected to insult and condemnation as railwaymen tried to get rid of signalwomen and to prevent any more being trained. The hostility exploded the boundaries of the railway press and was soon being featured and discussed in local and national newspapers:

> The railway signal box is now being invaded by women ... 'The members of the sex,' said an experienced railwayman, 'are so apt to lose their heads even over relatively small matters, that they hardly appear to be the right persons to entrust with work on which the safety of so much life and property depends.'[113]

Some railwaymen thought women would make as good signallers as men; however, their voices were drowned in a sea of anti-female vilification. At Rotherham, GCR, signalmen 'emphatically protested' against women entering their profession.[114] The NUR EC supported its rank-and-file by passing a unanimous resolution against signalwomen. In London a mass protest meeting of male delegates from 30 NUR branches, representing 10,000 men employed by the SECR, was held in July 1917. Elsewhere men asserted: 'Women are not fitted for the strain of signalmen's work ... neither is lever-pulling good for women's delicate constitution.'[115] (No such objection was raised against women goods porters shifting sacks weighing a hundredweight or carriage cleaners lifting heavy equipment.) On the GCR, men were opposed even to women working as train register recorders ('box girls') who performed clerical work in signalboxes but took no part in signalling. The 1918 Conference of Railway Signalmen passed a resolution demanding the instant removal of all signalwomen, whom they accused of being 'constitutionally unfitted' for signalling work, and 'a danger to the travelling public'.[116]

The employers did not agree. The companies' magazine, *The Railway Gazette*, asserted:

> [Signalling] requires foresight, decision and some little determination ... To find that women are capable of safely and satisfactorily meeting all the emergencies that a signal-box creates and furnishes is a great compliment to her sex.[117]

Unfortunately, surviving evidence of the opinions of the women concerned is nonexistent except for a letter in *The Railway Review* from four signalwomen (members of Market Rasen NUR branch) who refused to stay silent any longer. After their union 'brothers' had passed a branch resolution against their employment they wrote: 'We would like to know what our membership in the union stands for? Apparently we are contributing to our own downfall. If this is the spirit of trade unionism the sooner we are out of it the better.'[118] The women — S. Burr, E. Ellis, A. Key and S. Michael — threatened to leave the NUR unless the resolution was rescinded. It was not, and so, presumably, they did so. *The Railway Review* published several anti-female letters in the following issues. One man insisted that members of the 'weaker sex' should not be employed in signalling because they lacked the 'clear-sightedness' and 'level-headedness' which, he claimed, 'nature' had bestowed solely upon men. Woman, he argued, was 'neither physically nor mentally capable of accepting responsibilities'.[119]

In addition, railwaymen had been increasingly provoked with each new territory entered by women and this was the final straw. Signalling was a specialised railway skill, which gave it connotations of permanence.

GCR signalwoman flagging to an engine driver. Name and location unknown. © IWM

GCR signalwoman pulling a lever at a box somewhere in Birmingham. © IWM

BRITAIN'S FIRST FEMALE GUARDS

Many photographs were taken of the female guards at Neasden, Metropolitan Railway. Their tailor-made uniforms consisted of a skirt that was scandalouly short for 1917, but safety was paramount and outweighed any other consideration. To safeguard women's modesty, knee-length knickerbockers were worn and tucked into leather leggings, which covered their heeled shoes like spats.

Above: © TFL Following page: a group of of nine, c1917. © TFL

WELFARE AND SOCIAL ACTIVITIES

Women war-workers on the railways entered an industry with a 98% male workforce and a 100% male management. Some complained of 'harsh treatment' from male supervisors, most of whom had never worked with women and had no notion of how to deal with them. Some were opposed to 'females' being engaged at all, and treated them accordingly; others were disconcerted by feminine company and their discomposure led to some inconsistent behaviour. Some men coped by simply treating the newcomers as though they were men, raising objections from women.

Many women were not accustomed to the rigid discipline demanded by railway companies and had never worked with large numbers of the general public. Not did any of them have previous experience of the transport industry. Their working days were sometimes very stressful, especially when managers, union officials, the public, railwaymen and the press kept them under scrutiny, much of it hostile. When railway duty ended many had sole responsibility for the care of children and the burden of heavy shopping and domestic chores fell to them – something most railwaymen were spared. Without labour-saving appliances, laundry took a whole day's backbreaking labour and women trudged by foot from shop to shop for this was an age in which mass car-ownership and supermarkets were unknown.

From 1916 some companies engaged women's welfare supervisors to liaise between female staff and male managers, attend to any problems, and monitor the health and safety of female employees. For example, one investigated a complaint from carriage cleaners that train-cleaning acid made their nails split and their fingers bleed. They also inspected staff accommodation, checking that there were adequate toilet facilities at each location, and kept an eye on women doing 'male' work, to ensure that they were not overstrained. There were few problems of this nature; indeed, the aforementioned War Cabinet Committee found that 'heavy domestic work, especially the household washing, is often far more fatiguing and liable to cause injury than an industrial occupation.'[120] It had been feared that women's health would suffer if they performed 'men's work' but, as one authority pointed out, 'a great many industrial women before the War were so ill-paid as to be habitually undernourished.'[121] War-work gave women strenuous labour and higher wages than they were accustomed to, a combination that made them stronger, fitter and better fed.

The first convalescent home for railwaywomen was opened at Lavenham, Suffolk, in 1916. The Princess Royal* presented a property known as the Old Wool Hall to Mrs E. Bruce Culver, wife of the Secretary of the Railwaymen's Convalescent Homes.† Lavenham had only 24 beds, but later a 57-bed home at Leasowe Castle, Cheshire, was given to railwaywomen, and in 1927 Shottendane was opened at Margate, with 45 beds. Any railwaywoman or wife of a railwayman, could pay a penny a week subscription and spend up to two weeks there convalescing from illness. Potential users were promised that 'wireless, piano and games are provided'.

Women also took advantage of the other benefits of railway employment, such as dining, social and sports facilities. In December 1916 a new club for the 4,000 women on

* Princess Louise (1867-1931), a daughter of Edward VII.

† The first convalescent home for railwaymen was opened in 1901. British Rail closed most homes by the 1970s.

the administrative staff of London's underground railways was opened. Entered from Earl's Court Station, the building consisted of five storeys and a kitchen in the basement capable of producing 200 meals a day. There were also rest rooms and club rooms, and dining halls that could seat over 100 women. Railwaymen had for many years organised their own sports and social clubs and first aid teams. Although many women were hampered by their domestic responsibilities, a large number did participate.

An unusual event took place on 29th June 1918 when 50 railwaywomen from 11 companies were treated to a gala lunch at the Euston Hotel before being conveyed by a fleet of omnibuses to Hyde Park where, led by Miss N. Page, an electric trolley operator at Liverpool Street, GER, they joined a procession of homage to the King and Queen.

Bombs, Accidents and Fatalities

Railway work was much more demanding during wartime. The industry was under immense strain because of the movement of troops and supplies; some areas suffered air raids and work was sometimes performed in partial blackout. Enemy air attacks began on Christmas Day, 1914, when the line was bombed near Stanford-le-Hope, and continued until the middle of 1918, damaging King's Lynn, Grimsby, Croydon, Derby, Cannon Street, Immingham, Streatham, Liverpool Street, Stratford and many other locations. During the war 24 railway staff were killed by enemy action while at work, of whom eight died in a single incident when St Pancras was bombed on 17th February, 1918, killing 20 people.

As well as the special dangers occasioned by the war, women shared with men the hazards peculiar to railway work; for example, venturing into dimly lit yards where wagons and engines were shunted about. Women climbed tall ladders and shifted heavy parcels, luggage and goods. The safety of the public became their concern, and in some cases their capabilities were tested to the limit. For example, in June 1916, GCR porter Edith Addison of Fairfield, Manchester, became the first woman to receive the GCR's bravery award. She had rescued a passenger whose coat became shut in the door of a train which then moved off, dragging her along and causing her to fall down between the carriage and the platform.[122] At Robin Hood's Bay, LYR, a 16-year-old girl booking clerk saved three women from drowning in the sea close to the station.[123]

Accidents were common among railway workers, and women in male grades sustained the same kinds of injuries as men: crushed fingers, fractures, back strain etc. The NUR EC's success in keeping women out of occupations with the highest mortality rate no doubt contributed to women accounting for only 2% of fatalities even when they comprised 16% of the workforce (1918 statistics). The exact number of women killed on railway duty is not known. The only surviving records are those of NUR members, 24 of whom lost their lives while on duty between 1915 and 1920.

In one fatal accident, Mrs Monroe and Mrs Nelson, carriage cleaners at Glasgow Queen Street, were knocked down by the same train; in another, Alice Golding, a glober for the LYR at Manchester Victoria, was on the roof of a carriage, cleaning its gas lamps, when she was struck and thrown onto the tracks by a large and heavy basket. The basket was part of an electrically-powered overhead carrier that was suspended from two rails running high in the air and was used to transport parcels across the station. It was being driven in reverse by a 17-year-old lad. After Miss Golding's death, the LYR had the carrier adjusted so that the driver always faced the direction of travel, and warned globers to keep a look out for the basket and to lie flat on the carriage roof if they saw it motoring towards them.[124]

A LYR globe cleaner at Manchester Victoria in March 1919, less than a month after her colleague was killed by being knocked off a train roof by the basket of the overhead parcel carrier. COURTESY OF THE NRM REF 10444185

WOMEN NUR MEMBERS KILLED ON DUTY 1915-1920

Date	*Name*	*Grade*	*Railway*	*Location*	*Cause*
14 08 15	Alice Dixon	Porter	Central London	Holland Park	Fell under a train
26 02 16	Mrs Roberts	Goods porter	LYR	Oldham	Killed during shunting
14 07 16	Amelia Crewel	Porter	Caledonian	Hamilton	Struck by a train
27 07 16	Mrs Nelson	Carriage cleaner	NBR	Glasgow Queen St	Knocked down by a train
27 07 16	Mrs Monroe	Carriage cleaner	NBR	Glasgow Queen St	Knocked down by a train
23 08 16	Mabel Dexter	Cook	Midland	N/A	Knocked down by a train
23 03 17	C. Willard	Porter	GCR	Leicester	Crushed between wagons
23 04 17	Mrs Lofts	Guard	NER	Wheaten	Run over by a train
30 09 17	Mrs Hazlehurst	Porter	GNR	Leeds	Slipped with a barrow
14 11 17	Ms Rushden	Engine cleaner	Midland	N/A	Run over
08 03 18	(Not listed)	Carwoman	LNWR	Birmingham	Crushed against a wall
25 03 18	Emily Ackland	Motor conductor	GWR	Pontypool Crane St	Cut hand: blood poisoning
23 04 18	Mrs R. Hall	Carriage cleaner	LBSCR	London, Victoria	Fell between carriages
14 05 18	Jane Rowland	Carriage cleaner	GCR	Chester	Knocked down by a train
23 08 18	Mrs McCormack	Porter	Caledonian	Micalder	Hit by an express train
19 09 18	Margaret Barclay	Distiller	NBR	Cameron Bridge	Run over by an engine
03 02 19	Mrs Lockwood	Telephone operator	LNWR	Camden loco shed	Clothes caught fire
07 02 19	Anne Moule	Porter	GER	Enfield Dock	Knocked down by a train
27 02 19	Alice Golding	Carriage glober	LYR	Manchester Vic.	Knocked off carriage roof
27 02 19	Frances Dillon	Clerk	LSWR	Guildford Street	Knocked down
28 02 19	Mrs Fenwick	Lampwoman	NER	N/A	Knocked down
07 03 19	Jesse Cooper	Guard	GWR	Dudley	Knocked down
08 10 19	Miss L Parker	Motor conductor	Midland	N/A	Fractured leg; blood poisoning
14 04 20	Mary A Mort	Passenger guard	LNWR	Colborne	Fell between train & platform

Source: NUR EC *Committee Minutes 1915-1920.* (Information on non-members is not available.)

Hayward's Heath, 1918. A group of ticket collectors, porters and booking clerks. Ticket Collector Grace Kent (standing, far left) was the 21-year-old daughter of a guard. (She lived to be almost 101.) COURTESY OF MURIEL KENT

Cannon Street, 1918. Ticket Collector Violet Cecilia White (1895-1983) is the third seated person from the right in this group of 13 female station staff posing with nine male colleagues and an engine crew. Miss White worked there for four years and was known as The Walking Timetable. At the age of 88 she could still recite all the stations down the line. COURTESY OF JOY NEWMAN

Lathe operators using capstan lathes at Horwich workshops, LYR, May 1917. They appear to be machining parts for the valves laid out on the right. COURTESY OF THE NRM REF 10444132

Women in clogs working in Horwich telegraph workshops, LYR, May 1917. Those on the right are winding coils while the one on the left is operating a small fly-press. COURTESY OF THE NRM REF 10444125

Post-War Commentary

Despite women's magnificent war effort, an attitude of antipathy towards them began to emerge after the war. This was evidently absorbed by Edwin Pratt (1860-1922), a journalist on *The Times* who wrote various pamphlets and books, including one about railways in wartime. He noted that women's railway service tended to be short, but the reasons he gave blamed only women's shortcomings: he offered no mitigating circumstances. He alleged that women 'either soon wearied of the work or else realised their physical unfitness for it', but neglected to cite the many other reasons for leaving. He did not mention that over 100,000 women had taken up railway work, nor did he point out that it is inevitable that a percentage found it unsuitable, as (of course) did a percentage of men. He omitted to describe the atmosphere of suspicion and hostility from male colleagues that often made the railways a stressful workplace for women. He also failed to mention that, in many cases, 'permanent' railwaymen were as transitory as 'temporary' women war-workers and that persons of either sex, if happy in their work, will show their satisfaction by remaining in service. Comparative data is rare, but a SECR staff register held at the National Archives shows that of 34 permanent men and 34 temporary women employed as ticket collectors at London Victoria between 1915 and 1918, 26 of the women and 27 of the men were still on the payroll at the end of 1918.

Edwin Pratt's criticism was illogical as well as unfair; for example, he accused railwaywomen of having no ambition:

> The lack of desire for training in higher branches of railway work was especially characteristic of women employed in the manual grades. These women were almost invariably content to follow instructions in regard to the work to which they were put and did not aspire to anything better.[125]

In saying this, Pratt withheld a rather vital piece of information from his readers: there were two reasons why there was no point in women having ambition. First, they had been told that they were short-term, temporary workers who would lose their jobs as soon as the war ended; secondly, railwaymen and NUR officials had made it perfectly clear that, while they tolerated women in the lower grades as a war emergency, every attempt to train them in higher grade work would be (and was) opposed.

Pratt complained that lateness, absenteeism and illness were higher among women than men, but failed to mention the wider social issues. While devoting a paragraph to cold statistics he omitted to explain that many women had sole responsibility for childcare, domestic chores and shopping, while most of their male counterparts were free of such burdens, as their wives or mothers took care of their needs.

Pratt's biased and unfair assessment of wartime railwaywomen was published in 1921 in *British Railways and the Great War*, his third and final railway book. Unfortunately, this has long been the standard reference book on the subject and has been described by as 'a solid and careful account'.[126]

Alan Earnshaw, in his 1990 book *Britain's Railways at War*, was more generous towards war workers. He referred to the 'extreme prejudice' they faced before pointing out that almost two-thirds of new female recruits left railway service within three months, and gave several reasons why so many resigned so soon, citing the NUR's insistence that they be classed as temporary and the lure of munitions work paying £11 a week. He stated that women's railway labour was of 'immense value' and concluded his comments by remarking that, in many ways, 'they excelled in their new careers'.[127]

Such praise was not in evidence when J. A. B. Hamilton published his brief and inaccurate précis of women's war work in his 1967 book *Britain's Railways in World War I*:

> Of course there were limitations. Driving and firing were out of the question. Women porters were employed ... but their lack of strength was one reason for the reduction in the weight allowed for passengers' luggage. Nor could women porters be called upon, as men could, to act in an emergency as guards. Women signalmen were tried in a few quiet boxes, but their men colleagues didn't like it, alleging that the women would not accept responsibility.

Anyone reading that paragraph would be excused for believing that there weren't many women employed and that the few who were weren't of much use. Hamilton created the impression that female porters could not lift even a large suitcase, that women did not work as guards, that a small handful of signalwomen were engaged without success and were withdrawn as unsuitable. In fact photographic and written evidence shows that female porters lifted very heavy items such as milk churns, one-hundredweight sacks, beer crates and barrels. Women did work as guards and in over 100 other grades that Hamilton chose not to mention. Signalwomen were found to be as competent as men and many held their posts for several years, some continuing after the war. Hamilton's final remark is a misinterpretation of a comment made by Edwin Pratt[128] in which he (Pratt) stated that 'they' (meaning signalmen) would not take responsibility for signalwomen in the boxes adjoining theirs.

Hamilton was not entirely antipathetic; later, he defended railwaywomen, countering Pratt's accusation that they were not ambitious: 'What, it may be asked, could be expected of employees who knew they were going to be sacked when the war was over?'

Summary

During the war, hundreds of thousands of women proved to themselves and to others that they were capable of performing 'men's work' in diverse fields of labour. Their contribution to the war effort is indisputable. They provided three-quarters of the food for Europe, manufactured most of the munitions and staffed the hospitals, transport systems, auxiliary forces and factories. A War Cabinet Committee reported that performing 'men's work' had not harmed women's health but improved it, and acknowledged that incapability was not the real reason women were barred from certain jobs. Comments made at the end of the war illustrate the prevailing feeling of optimism. For example, Ray Strachey remarked that 'the success of women's war work, and the great publicity that attended it, startled men of all kinds into forming a more favourable judgement of the female sex.'[129]

In common with the constraints placed on women in all other areas of life, their pre-war exclusion from 'male' railway work did not have to be justified. Women were expected to accept the status quo and not to question it. Explanations of women's exclusion were not given until the wartime staff shortage sparked discussion on the subject. When the reasons for it were vocalised they proved to be fallacious. It was thought that women would not want the work, yet thousands applied. It was argued that they could not mentally or physically manage the work, yet thousands did throughout the war and many would have stayed on afterwards if permitted. It was said that women would 'go to pieces' in emergencies, but when they were put to the test they proved the assertion untrue. It was feared that they would undercut men's rates and be a 'scab' army in the event of a strike, yet many of them campaigned long and loud, and some even struck work, for equal pay.

While railway managers were impressed by women's success, the same cannot be said of the unions. Throughout the war, ASLEF never wavered from the belief that women should not clean engines, while the mere notion of women firing or driving locomotives was risible. The NUR's attitude to women was ambivalent. Before the war things were simple: women were kept out of men's jobs and excluded from the union, despite the pre-amalgamation promise to include them. During the war they became union 'sisters' but simultaneously a threat to hard-won rates of pay. The union discharged its duty to absent members by guaranteeing the reinstatement of every railwayman who had served in the forces, but the list of those killed and disabled — published weekly in *The Railway Review* — made it clear that hundreds would not be returning to reclaim their jobs. With thousands of women becoming experienced and skilled in railway work, the NUR had every reason to suspect that companies would attempt to retain them after the war.

Railway bosses, and outside agencies who were invited to intervene in disputes about pay or war bonuses, always put forth the argument that women needed less money to live upon, either because they were spinsters, or because their household had other income. This sloppy attempt at rough-and-ready means-testing was never applied to male staff. Nor was it applied fairly: women were assessed not individually but collectively: all women were treated as though they had other income and no one but themselves to support, whether or not this was true.

The proportion of female staff increased from 2% in July 1914 to 16% four years later. During this period, the number in wages grades rose from 9,135 to 36,984, in clerical grades from 3,000 to 22,598, and in workshop grades from 857 to 6,305. Altogether there were 65,887 female railway employees in mid-1918, at which time the total number of railwaymen released to the forces was 190,000, or 29% of the total male staff. By the end of the war women were working in hundreds of capacities.

Three-quarters of ticket collectors were female and nearly 10,000 became porters. For the first time, a few women (for example a cartage forewoman) were put in charge of men. These women presented a challenge to their male critics by demonstrating competence and endurance in their new occupations. The final words in this chapter are from a man writing in *The Railway Review*, summing up the results of the experiment of 'female railwaymen':

> 'You could never put women on railways,' someone once said in the early days of the war. 'They would lose their heads in an emergency. A sudden rush and they would be lost.' Well, there have been rumours of raids, with nervous people wanting to dash in or out of the trains. ... But the women have not lost their calm common-sense. The sense of responsibility, the desire to prove their worth, and the sense that their fellow workers are depending on them for efficiency has rendered them equal to all the little mishaps and difficulties.[130]

Appendices

The information included here is inconsistent, because companies recorded statistics in varying ways and presented them differently. Some companies' statistics are not available. Pre-war figures refer to July 1914; wartime figures refer to August 1918 except as shown.

Caledonian Railway

Pre-war: 80 (unspecified). Wartime: 1911 distributed thus:

Line Superintendent's Dept	1105	Porter-signalwomen	20
Goods Department	455	Signalwomen	16
Locomotive Department	232	Wagon painters	10
Engineering Department	119	Engine coalers	8
Clerks and typists	387	Engine tube cleaners	4
Parcel and booking clerks	281	Workshopwomen	46
Porters	239	Guards	21
Carriage cleaners	204	Parcel porters	89
Workshop labourers	120	Screwers and turners, machine workers and drillers	24
Ticket collectors	106		

Furness Railway

Pre-war, unknown; wartime, 113.

Glasgow & South Western Railway

Pre-war: 442 comprising 243 hotel workers and 199 in other departments.
Wartime: 1282 comprising 571 in clerical grades and 711 in wages grades.

Great Central Railway

Pre-war: 342 (unspecified). Wartime:

Date	*Year*	*Clerks*	*Wages Grades*	*Total*
August	1914	67	350	417
June	1915	632	560	1192
December	1915	1053	733	1785
December	1916	1933	2043	3975
December	1917	2206	3228	5434
December	1918	2314	3081	5395
May	1919	1729	1904	3633

Details of the December 1917 figures:

Porters	454	Signal cleaners	55
Carriage cleaners	186	Booking clerks	783
Ticket collectors	18	Male grades	1732
Clerks, shorthand typists, abstractors, telephone operators			2206

Great Eastern Railway

Pre-war: 18 clerical; 770 wages workers. Wartime: 2,000 distributed thus:

Operating & Locomotive Depts: 1148 in male grades.

Commercial Dept: 698 clerical; 439 wages workers.

Secretary & Comptroller's Dept: 70 in male clerical grades.

Chief Mechanical Engineer's Dept: 130 railway and 400 munitions workers.

General Engineer's Dept: 42 in male grades and 6 in munitions.

Printing Works: 23 male grades (readers, layers-on, ticket printers & clerks).

Stores Dept: unknown number in male grades, making and repairing wagon covers and grain sacks, cleaning, and gathering waste paper for war economy.

Great Western Railway

Pre-war: 1371, comprising 497 in railway operating; 874 in unspecified grades.
Wartime: 6345, distributed thus:

Clerks	2905	Cleaners	31
Goods porters	616	Tracers	23
Carriage cleaners	594	Callers-off	20
Charwomen	437	Numbertakers	17
Porters	346	Cloakroom porters	14
Ticket collectors	323	Storewomen	11
Crossing keepers	143	Porters (miscellaneous)	9
Messengers	111	Platform/halt attendants	7
Parcel porters	92	District examiners	6
Carwomen (goods)	53	Lamp cleaners/trimmers	6
Carwomen (parcels)	38	Lampwomen	2
Rail motor conductors	32	Motor drivers	1
Miscellaneous	508		

Lancashire & Yorkshire Railway

Pre-war: 1057.
Wartime: 1121 in female grades plus the following in male grades:
1915 - 943. 1916 - 2265. 1917 - 3249. 1918 (Nov) – 3338.

London & North Western Railway

Pre-war: 2123. Wartime: 9154.

London Brighton & South Coast Railway
Pre-war: 99. Wartime: 683.

London Electric Railway
Pre-War: unknown. Wartime: 1819, distributed thus:
Travelling ticket examiners 16; police women 13; porters159; car cleaners 160; unspecified 1471.

London Underground
Pre-war: unknown. Wartime (in 1917): porters 238; ticket collectors 115; liftwomen 98; booking clerks 360; gatewomen on trains 64.

Metropolitan Railway
Pre-war: unknown. Wartime: 543 (in 1916).

Midland Railway
Pre-war: 1396. Wartime: 9000 (in 1917), of whom:
Clerical grades 2500; Carriage & Wagon and Locomotive Departments 2500; wages grades 4000, of whom: carriage cleaners, 480; engine cleaners 475, labourers 37, workshop labourers 226.

North British Railway
Pre-war: 119 (mainly crossing keepers). Wartime: 950, distributed thus:

Operating	*women*	*men*	Workshops	
Porters	393	(378)	Labourers	101
Ticket collectors	118	(37)	Lifters	34
Crossing keepers	117	(69)	Sheet dressers	25
Goods porters	78	(464)	Sewing machinists	8
Telegraphists	62	(67)	Sweepers	6
Office cleaners	43	(1)	Wood machinists	5
Messengers	22	(2)	Strikers	4
Temporary telegraphists	21	(28)	Drillers	3
Signalwomen/men	21	(1451)	Messengers	3
Goods checkers	18	(194)		
Luggage & cloakroom att'nts (Glasgow)	18	(8)	**Marine**	
Signal lampwomen/men	15	(52)	Clyde steamer stewardess	6
Cloakroom attendants (Edinburgh)	9	(4)	Clyde ticket girl	1
Carriage Lampwomen/men	8	(38)	Clyde tea room staff	16
Lads [sic]	7	(4)	Forth Ferry steamer stewardess	1
Excess luggage weighers	4	(2)		
Charwomen	4	(0)		
Numbertakers	3	(94)		
Weighers	2	(56)		
Electric truck operators	2	(0)		
Forewomen/men porters	1	(77)		
Pilot guard	1	(9)		

NBR DUNDEE & ARBROATH LINE
Crossing keepers 1 (3 men) Ticket collectors 3 (1 man).

NBR DUMBARTON & BALLOCH JOINT LINE
Ticket collectors 6 (3 men).

NBR KILSYTH & BONNYBRIDGE JOINT LINE
Porters 17 (28 men) various grades 3.

NORTH EASTERN RAILWAY
Pre-war: 1470. Wartime: 7885 (1000 more worked in munitions in railway workshops).

NORTH STAFFORDSHIRE RAILWAY
Pre-war: unknown. Wartime: 147 (in 1917).

SOUTH EASTERN & CHATHAM RAILWAY
Pre-war: unknown. Wartime: 1300 (in 1917).

Sources: Various companies' documents. Pratt, E. (1921) *British Railways and the Great War.*

AVERAGE PAY OF RAILWAYMEN AND WOMEN, 1919		
Grade	*Men*	*Women*
	s. d.	*s. d.*
Clerks	83 0	40 6
Ticket collectors	64 5	46 9
Rail Motor Conductors	59 7	48 1
Porters (Passenger)	53 1	43 11
(Parcels)	60 3	42 6
(Goods)	59 5	46 9
Carmen/carwomen	65 1	42 5
Checkers	66 9	45 3
Timekeepers	-	41 6
Carriage cleaners	60 11	40 10
Lamptrimmers, etc.	63 9	41 7
Storemen/storewomen	60 4	40 1
Charwomen	-	14 7
Messengers	69 11	40 4
Source: War Cabinet Committee Report on Women in Industry, 1919		

References

[1] See Braybon, G. (1984) *Women Workers in the First World War.* Croom Helm.
[2] Imperial War Museum 32/2. Letter from the REC to IWM, 28 April 1919.
[3] *Great Western Magazine* May 1915.
[4] *The Railway Gazette* May 1915.
[5] *The Railway Review* 9 July 1915.
[6] *The Railway Review* 21 May 1915.
[7] *The Railway Review* 27 June 1915.
[8] National Archives document MT6 2454/12.
[9] Ibid.
[10] NUR EC Minutes April 1915.
[11] Edwards, J. (1988) *Remembrance of a Riot* (Llanelli Borough Council).
[12] National Archives document MT6 2454/12.
[13] Ibid.
[14] *Sheffield Independent* 18 May 1915 and *Manchester Guardian* 10 April 1915.
[15] *The Railway Gazette* 8 June 1917.
[16] *Daily News & Leader,* 23 November 1916.
[17] *Daily Despatch* 27 April 1915.
[18] *Sunday Chronicle* 16 May 1915.
[19] Letter from Louie Weaver's daughter, 1990.
[20] *The Times* 7 March 1915.
[21] *The Railway Review* 12 June 1915.
[22] *The Railway Gazette* 14 May 1915.
[23] National Archives document MT6 2454/12.
[24] National Archives document MT6 2454/12.
[25] Ibid.
[26] *Evening Express* 6 May 1915.
[27] *Birmingham Post* 4 August 1915.
[28] National Archives document MT6 2454/12.
[29] *The Railway Review* 9 July 1915.
[30] *Daily News & Leader* 23 November 1916.
[31] *The Times* 27 September 1918.
[32] *The Railway Gazette* 11 June 1916.
[33] *Daily Mirror* 9 April 1915.
[34] *Northern Echo* 8 April 1915.
[35] *Aberdeen Daily Journal* 8 April 1916.
[36] *The Railway Gazette* 11 June 1915.
[37] *Great Central Railway Journal* April 1915. The report concerns Porter Elsie Bridham of Meadowhall Station, near Sheffield.
[38] *The Yorkshire Post* 20 August 1915.
[39] Letter from Dawn Hellman-Birch (Ethel's daughter), 2005.
[40] Pratt, E. (1921) *British Railways and the Great War.* (Selwyn & Blount) p1029.
[41] *Sunday Chronicle* 16 May 1915.
[42] *Daily Telegraph* 12 October 1915.
[43] *The Railway Gazette* 8 June 1917.
[44] *The Railway Review* 1 December 1916.

[45] War Cabinet Committee (1919) *Report on Women in Industry.*
[46] Pratt (1921) *op. cit.* p1028.
[47] *The Railway Review* 6 August 1915.
[48] *Manchester Courier* 9 April 1915.
[49] *Sheffield Independent* 17 June 1916.
[50] *North Eastern Magazine* December 1916.
[51] Ibid.
[52] *The Railway Gazette* 7 March 1915.
[53] Thanks to BT PC Kevin Gordon and Steve Daly.
[54] *Great Eastern Railway Magazine,* November 1916, pp. 273-4. Many thanks to the Institute of Railway Studies for bringing this story to my attention.
[55] *Great Eastern Railway Magazine,* September 1916, pp. 218-226.
[56] Ibid.
[57] Letter from Ann Shah, 2005
[58] Thanks to Brenda Glover, Ada's daughter.
[59] Letter from May Atkinson, 1989.
[60] *Midland Railway* General Superintendent's Office, Derby, November 1916.
[61] *North Eastern Magazine* Volume 27 August 1988, p56.
[62] *Great Western Magazine* January 1916.
[63] Ibid.
[64] *Great Western Magazine* 1917, p137.
[65] Ibid. p166.
[66] *The Railway Clerk* 14 April 1916.
[67] *The Railway Clerk* 15 September 1915.
[68] *The Railway Gazette* 15 November 1915.
[69] National Archives document MT6 2454/12.
[70] *The Globe* 20 April 1915.
[71] *The Railway Gazette* 19 October 1917.
[72] *The Railway Gazette* 8 June 1917.
[73] Bakewell Station memorandum book, Jan-Jun 1917. Quoted in *Midland Railway Society Journal* No. 13.
[74] Thanks to BT PC Kevin Gordon and Steve Daly.
[75] Correspondence with Evelyn Amos, Louie Weaver's daughter, 1992.
[76] *Railway Gazette* 4 August 1916.
[77] Peck, A.S. (1983) *The Great Western at Swindon Works,* Oxford.
[78] Letter from A. G. Walkden to Mr Bevan 21 February 1914. Modern Records Centre, Warwick University. MSS.55B/3/WEH3.i. Quoted in Wallace, M., (1997) *Single or Return? The Official History of the* TSSA.
[79] Wallace, M., (1997) *Single or Return? The Official History of the* TSSA. Mr Wallace interviewed Joyce Husbands, a former RCA member and friend of Miss Thompson, in 1994.
[80] *The Railway Service Journal* November 1928.
[81] *The Railway Clerk* 15 Dec 1916.
[82] *The Railway Clerk* 15 July 1916.
[83] Wallace, M., (1997) *Single or Return? The Official History of the* TSSA (TSSA).
[84] *The Railway Clerk* 14 April 1916 and its Special Supplement.
[85] *Votes for Women* 2 July 1915.
[86] *The Railway Review* 2 July 1915.
[87] *The Railway Review* 13 August 1915.

[88] *The Railway Review* 2 July 1915.
[89] *The Railway Review* 15 April 1915.
[90] *The Railway Review* 27 June 1915.
[91] NUR EC Minutes 1916.
[92] *The Railway Review* 2 August 1916 and *The Railway Clerk* 22 February 1918.
[93] *The Railway Gazette* 5 May 1915.
[94] *The Railway Gazette* 7 March 1915.
[95] National Archives document MT6 2454/12.
[96] Ibid.
[97] Ibid.
[98] *The Railway Clerk* 15 January 1915.
[99] National Archives document MT6 2454/12.
[100] War Cabinet Committee (1919) op. cit.
[101] *The Times* 27 August 1918.
[102] *The Times* 9 September 1918.
[103] War Cabinet Committee (1919) op. cit.
[104] TUC Parliamentary Committee Meeting. September 1917.
[105] War Cabinet Committee (1919) op. cit.
[106] *Sussex Weekly News* 7 September 1918.
[107] *The Railway Review* 8 December 1916.
[108] *The Railway Gazette* 5 July 1918.
[109] Holford, J. (1988) *Reshaping labour: organisation, work and politics - Edinburgh in the Great War and after*, p83 and NUR Edinburgh No 1 Branch minutes 26 May 1918.
[110] <www.theglasgowstory.com>
[111] War Cabinet Committee (1919) op. cit.
[112] Rolt, L.T.C (1966), *Red for Danger.* (Pan) pp207-13 & 214.
[113] *Camberwell and Peckham Times* 8 September 1917.
[114] *The Railway Review* 2 August 1918.
[115] *The Railway Review* 16 August 1918.
[116] *Daily News* 22 August 1918.
[117] *The Railway Gazette* 10 August 1917.
[118] *The Railway Review* 16 April 1918.
[119] *The Railway Review* 18 October 1918.
[120] War Cabinet Committee (1919) op. cit.
[121] Blainey, J. (1924) *The Women Worker and Restrictive Legislation* (Arrowsmith) p10.
[122] *Great Central Railway Journal* June 1916. Her certificate of bravery is held at the NRM.
[123] *The Railway Gazette* 25 August 1916.
[124] TNA 343/901.
[125] Pratt. *Op. Cit.* p481.
[126] Michael Robbins in Simmons, J & Biddle, G. (1997) *The Oxford Companion to British Railway History* (OUP) p393.
[127] Earnshaw, A. (1990) *Britain's Railways at War* (Atlantic) p35.
[128] Pratt, E. (1921) *British Railways and the Great War* (Selwyn & Blount).
[129] Strachey, R. (1928) *The Cause* (reprinted 1978, Virago) p389.
[130] *The Railway Review* 18 October 1918.

3: Between the Wars

> Always in the back of a certain type of brain there lurks the idea that women can 'go back to the home' as conveniently as a gramophone can be put in a cupboard when one is tired of hearing it play.
>
> *Manchester Despatch*, 20 September 1919

The war ended in November 1918. In common with other industries, the railway companies unequivocally commended the women workers who had replaced men over the previous four years. Sir Herbert Walker, chairman of the REC, who had in 1915 approached the idea of women replacing railwaymen 'with a considerable amount of trepidation', said:

> Since the cessation of hostilities many glowing tributes have been paid to the efficient conduct of the railways during the war, and it may be truly said that no small measure of the credit is due to the women. The part played by women in the national effort which resulted in bringing the war to a successful issue has received many eulogies, and I venture to say that in no instance is the praise more well-deserved than in the case of the railway women.[1]

Although many others echoed his sentiments, Edwin Pratt saw women's most important role as facilitating the release of 184,475 railwaymen to the forces:

> The value of the services rendered by so considerable a body of women in enabling many more railwaymen to join the Colours ... is beyond all question, and the women are deserving of the gratitude of the country, and are entitled to think that they, also, helped to win the war.[2]

During their years in the railway industry, women had accumulated specialised knowledge and experience, which led them to cease thinking of themselves as laundresses or housemaids doing war work but as railwaywomen. Some hoped that their male replacement would not arrive too soon, because traditional women's work held no attractions for them.

Of the 36,000 women working in male railway grades in 1918, only about 30% resigned in the weeks following the Armistice. Many of those remaining were dismissed rather hastily. Metropolitan guard Louie Weaver and her colleagues were given just one week's notice and:

> Poor Louie was forced back into dressmaking, a bitter pill to swallow. Rescue came three years later when she met and married her husband, a member of a great railway family.'[3]

Thousands of spinsters, having tasted the relative personal freedom, shorter hours and, above all, higher wages of railway work, refused to return to domestic service. A large number of married women had lost their breadwinner and needed to earn a 'man's wage' themselves, especially as the cost of living had rocketed; by November 1920, prices were 176% above 1914 figures.

In some cases, employers raised women's hopes. For example, in late 1918 gatewomen on the Bakerloo line were heartened when the company ordered their uniforms for the following spring, but they were all dismissed within the next six months. The London Railway Women Workers' Committee* requested that women in the higher-skilled grades be offered the option to remain. This was declined, even though heavy war casualties meant that 20,000 railwaymen would never return to their jobs.

The transport unions were well aware of how much women enjoyed their war work and how reluctant they would be to leave it. The TUC even passed a resolution demanding that all tram- and bus-women's licences be revoked as soon as the war ended, to make certain that women could not stay on.

Railwaymen were concerned that if women were not promptly expelled when the war ended they might stake a claim to permanency. However, attempts by the railway unions to have women's temporary status enshrined in the companies' national agreements had produced only the response that the employment of war-workers set no precedent regarding the jobs women would perform in peacetime.

The NUR leader had remarked in 1916 that anyone who believed that women would all quietly disappear after the war was living 'in a fool's paradise'.[4] He was right. Attempts to evict them began just days after the Armistice and, over the next two years, bitterness arose that almost turned into a sex war. In July 1919 the NUR EC pledged that women would leave the railway 'automatically' to make way for men returning from the forces – a clear message to its female members that any attempt to retain their jobs would be unsupported by their union. There was less anti-woman feeling within the RCA; however, it was still the policy of the RCA that women should resign when the men returned from the forces, and a few members called for women clerks to give up their jobs to any man. As RCA historian Malcolm Wallace has pointed out, 'The fact that some railway women had also joined the services was never considered by those who voiced such opinions.'[5]

In the wake of wartime praise and compliments and post-war applause came a mass of defamatory comments about women war workers in all industries, and no grumble was too petty to vocalise. It was claimed that women were less punctual, less reliable, less efficient, more easily fatigued and clumsier than men – and even that they wore out their uniforms faster. 'Heroine mothers' were now denounced for allowing a child's illness to keep them from work. These attacks generated attitudes that would help to exclude women from men's jobs permanently and force them back into women's work.

When *Woman Worker* magazine interviewed women in February 1919, 65% stated that they would never return to domestic service, regardless of their situation. Five per cent said that they would, but only on their terms: £40 a year, 2.5 days a week off and to choose their own clothes (unless the employer paid for them).

---

* Alas, no other references to this committee came to light during research.

The passage of the Restoration of Pre-war Practices Act‡ in 1919 and the Employment of Women, Young Persons and Children Act in 1920, together with a proliferation of feature articles, letters and editorials in newspapers and magazines demanding that women vacate 'men's jobs', bear witness that not all war workers resigned voluntarily. Massive social pressure was placed on women to 'make way for the men'. The National Federation of Demobilised Sailors and Soldiers demanded that all females vacate 'men's jobs' and 'get back to the home'.[6] Women were labelled 'unnatural' if they did not meekly yield the jobs men wanted; these were, of course, the best-paid and highest-status jobs: there was no campaign to oust women from jobs involving domestic-style drudgery. Women were entreated to be 'patriotic' and were told that they ought to have a 'natural, womanly feeling' to reward fighting men for their heroism and sacrifice by relinquishing their jobs.

Women's heroism and sacrifice, however, were to be rewarded with a return to ill-paid, menial, women's work, or by a place in the dole queue. At first, they were expected to surrender their jobs to the men they had replaced; then to any ex-serviceman. Finally, it was demanded that every woman give up her job to any man who wanted it, even to those who had never served in the forces. The campaign was an overwhelming success, much to the disappointment of feminists such as Winifred Holtby, who wrote:

> Women had been excluded from the more highly-skilled and better-paid industrial posts [and] told that certain processes were beyond their power. It was a lie. During the war they had proved it to be so, by their own skill and efficiency. Why surrender without a word opportunities closed to them by fraud and falsehood? ... Why then pretend that they were intruders in a world which was as much their own as their brothers?[7]

Working women, especially those performing traditionally-male jobs, were subjected to unpleasant remarks, as a woman journalist writing in the *Manchester Despatch* observed:

> Every day one comes across evidence of it — now in some minor discourtesy of some man towards working woman, again in some savage public demand that women should give up their jobs and 'go home'.[8]

It is possible that such discourtesy was responsible for an incident that provoked the following intriguing announcement on the front page of *The Railway Review*:

> Apology: I, Horace Bird ... lately a foreman in the employ of the SECR hereby unconditionally apologise to Miss Jessie Jordan ... ticket examiner at the Strood station ... and unreservedly apologise and withdraw the statements I then made concerning her character and reputation, and very much regret ever having made such assault upon her person and character.[9]

After the war women NUR members experienced an increase in hostility from their union 'brothers'. In mid-1919 a correspondent to *The Railway Review* described the

‡ This Act forced women back into unskilled low paid jobs by making it illegal to retain war-workers in jobs formerly reserved for skilled craftsmen.

retention of 120 women in the sheet repair workshop as 'monstrous'. He and his colleagues were furious because the managers had not only refused to dismiss the women, but were so satisfied with their work that they considered engaging more.[10] Similarly, Manchester railwaymen complained bitterly that women had not yet been ousted from the parcels office, while those on the NBR called for all signalwomen to be sacked, purely because of their gender. Men at Plaistow and Radcliffe NUR branches took things even further: they demanded that all women be withdrawn from railways. The NUR EC, however, said the union had no objection to women being retained, provided they were paid male rates. Like most people at that time, they believed that employers would prefer to hire a man if they had to pay a man's wage. More of a problem were those women who were paid less than men. In 1921 a correspondent to *The Railway Review* remarked: 'There does not seem to be any considerable anxiety on the part of the companies to dispense with ... [female labour]'. The writer felt that 'the matter will need careful watching or we shall find women permanently installed at lower rates'.[11]

It seems that the NUR used the atmosphere of hostility to women to take retaliatory action against two signalwomen who worked during a strike in 1919. They wanted Maud Hewitt and May Basnett, of Spath Crossing Box, North Staffordshire Railway,* to be replaced by men. The company refused to dismiss the women, who had five and six years' service, instead, it casually consented to move them to female grades 'when the opportunity arose'.[12]

Many railway war-workers gave in to the pressure to return to traditional female jobs, while those who remained were subjected to workplace hostility that became unbearable. In addition, women's welfare departments were closed, and women who remained in male grades saw their working conditions deteriorate and their isolation increase as their female colleagues left. By 1920 only a few hundred women war workers remained on the railways and by 1922 almost all had vacated male grades.

One way to remain in railway service was to transfer to a female grade. After four years as a guard on the Caledonian at Glasgow, Margaret Johnson was downgraded to carriage cleaner. Margaret M'Geehen, Chief Purser on the Wemyss Bay to Rothesay Steamer from 1916 to 1920, was demoted and confined to shore. The resulting decrease in status and pay was preferable to unemployment or domestic service, but it must have been demoralising for women who had enjoyed men's work and men's wages. However, these women were fortunate compared to those who had been discharged and were living on 25s unemployment allowance until they were forced into menial work paying 15s; refusal meant forfeiting the 'dole'. The NUR leader Jimmy Thomas (by this time MP for Derby) told the House of Commons he knew of 'scores and scores' of such cases.[13]

The crusade to return women to their pre-war position in the labour market continued into the 1920s. The Employment of Women, Young Persons and Children Act (operative from 1922) reimposed the pre-war ban on women's working between 10 p.m. and 5 a.m. This caused some panic among railway managers, because 12 companies employed between them about 1,000 women who were required to work night shifts, and most of them were indispensable. Ladies' toilets and waiting rooms could not close at night,

* This box was equipped with a ten-lever frame. The four interlocking crossing gates were worked from a wheel in the box. In 1961 Spath Crossing became the first automatic level crossing in Britain.

particularly at stations where boat trains arrived and departed at all hours. It was essential for the LBSCR to employ a woman at Newhaven Harbour because it would have been improper for a foreign lady to be detained overnight without the presence of a female member of staff as chaperone. The Caledonian's female police officers were needed at night to search female suspects and, obviously, hostel matrons could not work day shifts.

The companies dearly hoped that the 450 female crossing keepers they employed would be exempt. To replace them with men would cost a small fortune, because men were paid so much more. For example, the GWR employed 199, of whom 165 worked nights, and the company calculated that replacing them with men would add £10,000 to the annual wage bill. The GER worried that the new law might even make it illegal for gatemen's wives to operate the gates in their husbands' occasional absence.

The companies were able to breathe a collective sigh of relief: crossing keepers were among those for whom exemption was granted. Some railwaywomen had their hours altered but hundreds were abruptly dismissed, in many cases after years of loyal service.[14] Some were war widows with a family to support; others were self-dependent spinsters, and yet they were thrown into unemployment purely for being female.

The 1920s and 1930s

The 20s promised great advances for women. Their image had changed dramatically since the turn of the century: the pre-war militant suffragette campaign, followed by women's war work, revealed a side of womanhood very different from the Victorian stereotype of reticent and weak persons who were content with the status quo and who were unsuited to anything other than drudgery or idleness, depending on their social class.

Women over 30 were granted the vote in 1918 and a step towards professional equality was taken when the Sex Disqualification (Removal) Act was passed in 1919. This ruled that women were no longer disqualified by sex or marriage from practising any profession or from holding any public office. It seemed that women had at last triumphed, but it later became apparent that not being disqualified did not mean that women had any right to such positions and, furthermore, this act applied only to the qualified, white collar professions and had no effect whatever on the prospects of the vast majority of working women. It also seemed that women were soon to be paid the same as men for the same work: after the war Britain was signatory to Part 13 of the 1920 Treaty of Versailles, which required equal pay for women; however, it was not implemented.

The post war years saw great changes for railways and their staff. The unions revived their pre-war campaigns; the companies finally recognised ASLEF and the RCA, industrial unrest led to a nine-day strike in 1919; and railway workers (except crossing keepers) won the eight-hour day. Negotiations between the unions and the companies were hampered by the existence of over 500 grades of staff working for scores of railway companies, which paid varying rates and gave different titles to persons performing identical work. The solution was to standardise grades and rates of pay, a scheme that was completed in 1921. Gatewomen were the only railway servants excluded from the standardisation.

There was to be no return to the pre-war, fragmented railway system. Although the unions favoured nationalisation, the 1921 Railways Act amalgamated most railways into four large companies. This is known as the 'Grouping' and it created the 'Big Four': the Southern (SR), the London and North Eastern (LNER), the London, Midland & Scottish (LMS) and the Great Western (GWR). In 1933 the London Passenger Transport Board (LPTB) took over the five London railways under the collective title London Underground.*

The economic slump of the late 1920s and the 1930s adversely affected the railway industry. Prices fell and companies initially reduced the war wage, and then cut pay. Much of the duplication generated by the scores of small railway companies was eradicated by the Grouping, so fewer staff were needed, and competition from road vehicles – together with a decline in production – reduced railway traffic, leading to redundancies.

Railway workers joined the 1926 General Strike and women played their part. A letter from an NUR officer at Wimbledon exhorted branch Secretaries to 'Keep your members busy, by organising Concerts, Football matches, Games, etc. Also meetings for WOMEN ONLY. OUR WOMEN MUST NOT BE NEGLECTED.'[15] Aristocratic 'scabs' tried to keep the railways running, among them well-to-do young ladies, who acted as volunteer engine cleaners. The few surviving photographs show their elegant patent leather shoes peeping from beneath oily blue overalls. Online photographic libraries Getty Images and Corbis have some photographs of what the captions claim to be 'lady' engine drivers, but they are incorrect. It took many years to train a locomotive driver and the strike lasted only a few days.[16]

After the strike some railway workers suffered repercussions; for example, the GWR refused to pay a marriage dowry to women RCA members who had taken part.[17]

Wages Grades

At the start of the 1920s, wages-grade railwaywomen fell into four categories: former war-workers in male wages grades, women in former male grades now deemed to be fit for females, women in mixed-sex grades and women in female grades.

War workers in male grades were scattered across the country in tiny numbers. National figures for 1921 (when the railways employed almost a quarter of a million staff) show just 88 female messengers, 50 station porters, 31 goods porters, 26 ticket collectors, 13 carriage oilers, 12 signalwomen, ten station mistresses, four crane operators, four engine cleaners and one shunter (she worked for the NBR). In many cases, women had endured much hostility in order to retain these jobs. The financial rewards were high, but were offset by the constant insecurity of waiting for the axe of dismissal to fall.

The highest-paid women in non-supervisory positions were those still filling male grades; for example, a signalwoman earned about 40s a week, while women in the lower female grades earned between 9s and 18s. Hostel matrons working for the NBR earned 20s for 72 hours and received free accommodation, coal and electric light, six days' leave and six local train passes per annum. The LBSCR's 'lady alien attendant' earned 30s a week plus 10s for each occasion she was required to chaperon a 'lady alien' overnight. Higher up the scale, ladies' waiting room supervisors earned 35s to 45s. The highest paid woman on any railway was the GER's senior women's welfare supervisor, who earned 86s 4d a week. In addition to these basic rates, all women received a war wage of 29s.

The number of railway workers of both sexes decreased throughout the 1920s. In number and distribution, the position of railwaywomen began to resemble that of 1914. By 1929 there were only 4,356 in female grades, 5,198 in hotels and catering, and 197 in the

* These five were: the District, Central London, Metropolitan, City and South London, and London Electric (which was made up of the Bakerloo, Piccadilly, and Hampstead and Highgate lines). The LPTB also controlled all of London's buses and trams.

shipping and ports divisions.* In 1921 there were 1,038 female mechanics and artisans in railway workshops. Two years later only 699 remained, but from then the number increased until by 1929 there were 1,047. This pattern of fluctuation was caused by the expulsion of war-workers on male rates of pay and the recruitment of more women to female and unisex grades, such as (sewing) machinists, French polishers, lining-makers, blind-makers and dyers, painters and trimmers on female rates. Women were also engaged in armature coil winding: tedious, laborious work requiring a good deal of manual dexterity. Miss K. Fagan worked at Swindon Carriage & Wagon depot, GWR, for 25 years, retiring as forewoman of the lining-sewers and axle-box pad makers. Elsie Cook joined Doncaster trimming shop in 1920, when there were 72 women upholsterers, who were strictly segregated from the men, and went on to complete 42 years' service.[18]

Women in male operating grades once again became rarities whose very existence was deemed newsworthy. Mrs Joy, who had been a nursing attendant on board GWR trains from 1908, became a ticket collector at Acton in 1918 and managed to retain the job for 20 years till 1938. *The Daily Herald* reported in 1928 that Mrs Wharton of Meols, LMS, was the only signalwoman in Britain. Her length of service is not recorded, but a photograph dated 1938 establishes that she was still employed. However, in the photograph she was a crossing keeper, so either the newspaper was wrong — which they frequently were in relation to railway matters — or she had been demoted. David Williams of Eltham, London, recalled his astonishment when, visiting Minehead signalbox as a boy of ten in 1935, he found it 'manned' by a woman.[19]

Between the wars, carriage cleaning edged slightly closer to being thought of as 'women's work'. Only 214 women had been employed in 1914, but by 1939 there were 739 (and 5,748 men). Because it was considered 'morally undesirable' for the sexes to work together, women were usually placed in an all-female gang. However, at Dundee this strategy failed to protect them; in 1928 the station foreman indecently exposed himself to the whole group.[20]

Railway companies at this time were very concerned about the sexual morality of their staff and tried to exercise control over their lives even when off-duty. Managers were primarily concerned that sexual activity took place only within marriage; anything else was labelled 'immoral' and, if detected, could lead to dismissal. In 1932 the LNER sacked a (male) porter for having 'immoral relations' with a signalman's wife, while a carriage-cleaning forewoman suffered the same punishment for having 'immoral relations with a coal merchant'. This rash act also rendered her homeless, for she was evicted from her railway house.[21]

Crossing Keepers

The longstanding grievances of female crossing keepers surfaced many times during the inter-war period, usually in the form of a branch request to the NUR EC to take up their case. Many were not union members — and who can blame them? Throughout its history, the NUR had not won a single improvement in their conditions. Those who did join found that constant gate attendance made it difficult — if not impossible — to attend branch meetings, and those who managed to get someone to mind the gates and travel to a meeting often lacked the self-confidence to vocalise their grievances to a roomful of men

* In 1934 Britain's railways were reported to be, collectively, the world's largest hotel owners, with 79 establishments, and also the largest dock owners in the world. Between them they owned 147 steamships.

who at best did not view them as 'real' railway workers and at worst treated them as a bit of a joke. Having no common workplace they were isolated from each other and unable to present a united front. Perhaps the greatest obstacle to progress was the timeworn image of the female crossing keeper as a 'non-employee'. This had its roots in the tradition of wives operating gates only as their husbands' helpmates. Although it was illogical, this entrenched attitude continued even when the crossing keeper was a single woman or widow.

The habit of excluding gatewomen from negotiations and agreements to improve working conditions continued. In 1921 only gatemen were included in the standardisation and also in the newly-negotiated national conditions of service. Under these arrangements, men earned 59s to 60s a week for 24-hour daily attendance of a crossing, and 40s to 59s for 16 hrs. Women earned appreciably less. At Wilstrop, Leeds, for example, a woman earned just 4s 6d (plus the rent-free cottage) for a 90-hour week. She was also required to supervise wagon unloading, and to issue and collect tickets on Saturdays. To add insult to injury, her sex disqualified her from night-rate, annual leave and free travel.

Although the new conditions of service excluded gatewomen they sometimes affected their work. At many residential crossings, the arrangement was that the wife was supposed to mind the gates only when her husband was doing his day job on the railway. The NUR EC pointed out to the SR that a man operating the gates after his day's work would be in breach of his new conditions of service, which guaranteed him 12 hours' free time between shifts. This forced the SR to retort that the wife was in charge the whole 24 hours, which admission highlighted the company's exploitation of women.

Evelyn Hobden, gatewoman at Fotherby Halt, near Louth. © Northgate Studios

Crossing keepers married to railwaymen were affronted in 1919 when six days' paid annual leave was granted to their husbands but withheld from them, meaning that the couple could never take a holiday together. One pressure group successfully persuaded the employer to concede six days' leave to them too, despite the fact that they were unpaid except for 6s war wage and a rent-free cottage.[22]

Excluding gatewomen from the standardisation caused men to lose jobs. Men's new conditions of service made them more expensive to employ, so companies began replacing men with women when the opportunity arose. In 1923 there were 1,417 gatewomen* and 1,568 gatemen. Four years later women had gained 106 crossings and men had lost 97. By 1929 men had lost 81 posts through redundancy, while women had lost only five,[23] but this disparity was attributable to the busier, male-operated crossings being replaced with overbridges.

Gatewomen were dissatisfied with repeatedly being left out when pay and conditions were improved and from time to time individuals complained, but their efforts always came to nought. The keeper of Eyton Crossing, Baschurch, earned only 25s for working 144 hours per week, while railwaymen's average pay was 67s for 40 hours. She complained to the GWR and to the NUR and finally, getting no satisfaction from either, to the Minister of Labour:

> I have been in charge of a level crossing for twenty years which crosses the Shrewsbury to Birkenhead main line working 24 hours a day with no fixed arrangement for relief. The crossing is very busy, gates are opened on average 40 times a day, plus the working of five ground frame levers, four of which control signals on the up & down line. I get 4s 2d a day for 6 days and 3d per hour on Sundays. That is my total remuneration and does not include house.

The Minister declined to comment and referred her to her employer and union.

In the late 30s there were a few more failed attempts to get gatewomen included in the standardisation. In 1936 the NUR's Leeds and York District Council asked the EC to reopen negotiations, but the general secretary admitted that they had given up, and could only suggest that grievances be dealt with locally and referred to the EC only if no progress was made. This was far from adequate and women continued to appeal. The EC again tried to negotiate nationally but the companies failed to reply. In 1938 the companies at last agreed to consider the women's longstanding grievances, but gave advance warning that equal pay with men was not even to be placed on the agenda for discussion. The outcome of negotiations was, predictably, failure to agree, and the dispute was subsequently discussed by a Railway Staff Conference, which decreed that standardisation was impracticable because they had no staff available to visit the 1,467 female-operated crossings in order to collect the necessary data. The EC was dissatisfied with this, and passed the matter to a Traffic Sub-Committee. The negotiations dragged on. To the exasperation of the long-suffering women, the outbreak of another war in 1939 provided the companies with a perfect excuse to return the issue to the back-burner indefinitely.

* LNER: 647. LMS: 347. GWR: 199. SR: 129. Midland: 67. Colne Valley: 6. Freshwater, Yarmouth & Newport: 5. Mid-Suffolk Light Railway: 5. Sixteen more were distributed between a handful of even smaller companies.

Above: Miss Rough was the crossing keeper at Rosemount, LMS, for 23 years. Origin unknown

Top left: Crossing Keeper Wharton of Meols, LMS, with her daughter, February 1938. The box protected the dials and levers from the elements. © Getty images

Left: GWR female ticket collector's uniform, c1930. Origin unknown

Below: Station Mistress Brown seeing to the signal lamps at Raglan Rd Crossing. *Daily Herald* 29th January 1937

Clerks-in-Charge/Station mistresses

Station mistresses continued to be employed throughout the inter-war period, but they were few and far between and worked only at halts, mainly in rural Wales and Scotland. At Deadwater LNER, which straddled the English/Scottish border, Margaret Wylie's duties in the early 1920s included operating a two-lever ground frame that controlled points and signals for shunting trains in and out of the sidings. Twenty-five years later the LNER revealed that Deadwater was still being run by a woman (who was not named – perhaps it was still Miss Wylie).[24] According to a women's magazine, twelve station mistresses employed by the LMS were 'treated in every way as if they were men', including their remuneration.[25] At Abbotsford Ferry, Mrs Elder was photographed with her levers to celebrate her retirement in 1930 after 45 years' service.[26] Other Scottish stations in female hands included Lamancha, Macbie Hill, Beasdale and Gordon. In 1928 Margaret Cochrane 'inherited' the post at Eddleston, LNER, from her father, station master there for 48 years. In 1931 the LNER said that the number of station mistresses was dwindling, that most had long service, and that all were widows or daughters of station masters who had taken over on his death; the company revealed that it did not engage station mistresses in any other circumstances. In the mid to late 30s its station mistresses included Mrs Ethel Cummings, in charge of Brinkburn around the mid 30s (designated a 'station attendant', she earned only 7s 6d per week); Mrs Scott, who worked successively at Gilmerton, Invergarry and Lundin Links; Miss L. Smith, who ran Locheilside; and Miss Amy Wearmouth at Smardale Halt, near Kirkby Stephen. The existence of the latter three came to light because they won prizes in 'Best Kept Station' competitions. [27] Mrs Margaret Potts ran Thorneyburn from March 1938 (it closed in 1956) and Mrs Mary Laing was appointed 'sub-station mistress' at Thornielee, near Galashiels, in January 1939.

Kit McGill, station mistress at Braystones 1907-1928, on her leaving day. D. Ravenswood

Miss Smith, station mistress at Locheilside, hands a letter to a guard. 1930s. Railway Magazine

Tan-y-Bwlch station mistress Bessie Jones, who gained worldwide fame for working in Welsh national costume. Here she is handing the single line token to a member of the engine crew, enabling his train to go forward into the single line towards Porthmadog, and receiving the token for the section it has just vacated. December 1936.
© Getty Images

Mrs Brown undertook all the duties of station mistress, signalwoman, booking clerk and crossing keeper at Raglan Road Crossing, GWR.[28] Pathé News filmed her in 1934 attending to her signal lamps at the single-line, one-platform halt, her peaked railway cap contrasting curiously with her fashionable, fur-collared coat.[29]

At Dol-Y-Gaer, Brecon Mountain Railway, a station mistress was sighted in 1929 unloading milk churns and parcels 'with greater alacrity than is frequently displayed by the male'.[30] Photographs taken in the 1930s of Beddgelert, terminus of the North Wales Narrow Gauge railway, frequently feature Miriam Jones and claim she was a station mistress but she was simply a local girl who dressed in Welsh costume for the benefit of tourists; she was not on the payroll. However, Bessie Jones, station mistress at Tan-y-Bwlch, Ffestiniog Railway was a bona fide employee. A much-photographed celebrity who also wore traditional Welsh dress, she was depicted in the film *The Phantom Light,* in which she was played by Louie Emery. Four years later, in September 1939, Mrs Jones lost her job when the station closed.

In England, station mistresses were either scarcer or attracted less publicity. Pathé has a silent newsreel about Mrs Watkins, the 'lady-stationmaster' at Maesbrook halt, six miles south of Oswestry on the Shropshire and Montgomery Light Railway.* Filmed in 1928, she is seen shifting a heavy basket with a barrow, turning the 'request-stop' signal to 'stop' and giving the start signal to the driver of a petrol-driven railcar (which had no guard).[31]

When her father, the station master at Waldron & Horeham Road, LBSCR, died in 1922, clerk Miss Clowser was allowed to take over as station mistress, but only until a replacement man was found. When a new incumbent was appointed, she and her mother were rendered not only unemployed but homeless, as they were told to vacate the station house. Luckily, Mrs Clowser found a job as a residential crossing keeper at Tidemills, while Miss Clowser obtained a post as a clerk, first at Seaford and then at Newhaven goods, where she worked until her marriage at the age of 38. To commemorate her 24 years of service, her colleagues presented her with an inscribed canteen of cutlery. But for sex discrimination, she might have spent 18 of those years as station mistress.[32]

Police

Several railway companies retained women police after the war. The Caledonian's had no powers of arrest; they patrolled the platforms and ladies' rooms at night. The GER's woman sergeant, on the other hand, detected female pickpockets, searched female suspects and had full powers of arrest. The Metropolitan WPC's sole duty was to prevent soliciting (euphemistically called 'objectionable female loitering') in the booking hall at Piccadilly Circus.

The number of railway policewomen declined gradually until, by 1923, there were only six, compared with 2,767 men. After the Grouping, each of the Big Four had its own police and all employed a small number of female officers. The London Transport Police was formed in 1933 and a year later two women detective constables and one woman uniform constable were among its 95 officers. On 29th May 1924 Ada Atherton started work at Waterloo station as the first 'Female Detective' and went on to complete 25 years' service.

* A 20-mile standard gauge, privately-owned light railway between Shrewsbury and Llanymynech.

Booking Clerk Olive Robbins and Porter-Signalman Brooker at Rowfant, LBSCR, 1926. © Bluebell Archives

'Works outing' of some typists working for the GWR.
The lady on the far right is Typing Supervisor Freda Dening. Courtesy of B. Carter

The RCA used poems and cartoons in its atttempts to recruit women.

Railway Service Journal, 1928

Workshopwomen at Stratford making blinds for carriage windows. Note the leather window straps piled up on the near left. Courtesy of the NRM

GWR worker with her refreshment trolley, 1921. Courtesy of the NRM ref 10442496

The NUR

Railwaymen and their unions had a very tough time in the inter-war years. The total workforce decreased from 736,000 in 1921 to 677,000 in 1928, mainly owing to road transport competition and the Grouping. After 1923 receipts fell and from 1925 the companies and unions became embroiled in a long and bitter struggle over pay cuts. This battle preoccupied NUR activists and officers and it is not surprising that problems specific to women fell by the wayside.

Women were a tiny minority within the NUR: in 1920 they comprised just 0.75% of the membership (3,442 of 458,000). Even in the branch with the highest proportion of women – Manchester 5 – they were little more than one-tenth (139 of 1201). The union excluded women from all decision-making processes by banning them from holding any union office or from attending conferences. One of the decisions made without female input was to make women ineligible to join the union's Provident Fund.

The NUR EC's attitude towards women is clearly illustrated by its behaviour when the TUC inaugurated the Annual Conference of Unions Catering for Women Workers (ACUCWW – now called the TUC Women's Conference) in 1931. Although the NUR was entitled to send two delegates it sent only one – and that was a man! It was seven years before the EC decided to allow a female member (Jane Maguire of Birmingham 15) to accompany him, and even then, one EC member voted against sending a woman to a women's conference.

An incident in 1936 illustrates the attitude of the NUR rank-and-file to their 'sisters'. Having been persuaded to join the NUR by the union's recruitment officers, two female carriage cleaners at Slateford, Edinburgh, subsequently had their applications declined by the local branch officials, who believed that women were not eligible for membership.. When the EC confirmed that they were, a discussion was provoked that led to the men passing a resolution demanding the dismissal of all women carriage cleaners on the LMS. The men were particularly incensed at the dismissal of 34 male cleaners whose places were subsequently taken by females on lower rates. Nothing could be done. As was the case with crossing keepers, the EC had agreed to women being paid less than men, and this led to men losing jobs. This incident reveals, of course, that Slateford branch had no female members.[33]

Salaried Staff

The wartime substitution of women in clerical work was considered an unmitigated success. In 1919 *The Railway Gazette* opined that 'Women railway clerks have given every satisfaction, as is the case with other grades of women railway employees'. The writers believed that this was 'due to the way in which the companies concerned have endeavoured to arrange the most pleasant and favourable working conditions' for women. He cited an office at Curzon Street goods, Birmingham, where the LNWR 'went out of its way to study the psychology of the girl worker':

> Flowers were placed on their desks, a few minutes interval for tea was enforced in the middle of the afternoon, and office routine was diversified by the institution of such attractions as horticultural shows with concerts and costume tableaux. Furthermore, the rule was rigidly laid down that no girl should work more than 41 hours a week, and regular intervals were arranged for meals, while

> the day's work was timed to end promptly at 5 p.m. A holiday programme is also arranged at the beginning of the year, and each girl is allowed a free pass to any part of the British Isles, and is given a choice of date as to when she will take her holiday.
>
> The girl workers are given a practical insight into the work of other departments by means of station and goods yard visits, &c., to show how their duties link up with outside work, and with all these facilities one can understand that they have proved themselves to be very intelligent and adaptable employees. The places of very many have now been filled by demobilised men, but there are certain departments of 'railroading' in which the girl clerk, who is by no means an innovation of the war, will no doubt continue to be employed.[34]

The pay of male and female clerks continued to be unequal and became more so as women clocked up more service and thus more skills and experience. At the age of 22, for example, men earned 28s to women's 25s, but with promotion men could obtain as much as 38s.

Between the wars all routine railway administration came to be seen as 'women's work'. Thousands performed adding, abstracting, typing, shorthand and tracing and as telephone and telegraph operators, women predominated.

Conditions of employment varied enormously between companies. For example, the GWR contract reveals that women had to satisfy the company that they were 'suitably lodged', furnish three testimonials and pass exams in orthography, handwriting, arithmetic, composition and (where applicable) shorthand and typing. Applicants had to undergo a medical examination to establish that they were 'organically sound'. The physician was asked to comment on the candidate's sight and hearing, to examine her for varicose veins and to discover whether she had ever been an inmate of a lunatic asylum. If she passed and was employed, the 5s doctor's fee was deducted from her first week's wage.

Mrs K. Odell of Derby completed 39 years in railway service. After leaving school aged 16 in 1938, her father wanted her to go on the railway. 'Looking back, I've few regrets that I took his advice', she said.

> There was an entrance examination and then a medical. I passed and started work in the offices at Derby Loco. Hours were from 9 to 5 weekdays and 9 to 12 on Saturdays, and we had to clock in and out, morning and afternoon. The bridge reverberated to many a running footstep as starting time drew near, and if you had clocked in yourself but could see a colleague on the way, you would get her card from the rack and in the machine, ready for her to do the actual deed.
>
> The Nursing Sisters and the ladies with the tea-trolleys went into the works, of course, but the only time I, and indeed most of my colleagues, were in the workshops was at the Christmas concert. This was held in the Erecting Shop and we sat there surrounded by locomotives in various stages of construction – quite novel surroundings for a concert. I learned later that the men had been warned that there were to be no questionable jokes (as a naïve 16-year-old, they would probably have gone over my head anyway), and no bad language.
>
> At 18 I took the exam which all clerical staff were required to take: English and maths, and also questions which involved naming so many stations within a radius of certain towns or naming the stations on a route which could be anywhere on the system. On the strength of it I was transferred to the HQ of the

> Chief Mechanical Engineer's Department at Nelson Street.
>
> The next two or three years I spent in the Typing Bureau. There I learnt my trade as a shorthand typist. I learnt to type on a machine with a blank keyboard so that it was necessary to memorise where each letter and number came on the keyboard. As my shorthand improved I started to take dictation which led to my getting a secretarial job in the Staff Office.[35]

Despite the 1919 Sex Disqualification (Removal) Act's ruling that women would no longer be disqualified by marriage from holding any post, all female clerks continued to be dismissed when they wed. Most companies gave them a wedding dowry, to qualify for which the GER and NER required women to have entered their service prior to 1915, ensuring that the many who joined as war workers could not claim it. The GNR required five years' service, as did the MR, which granted £10 to £20 according to length of employment. The GWR paid £5 to £10, but required entry before 1920. There was also considerable variation between companies regarding sick leave. For example, the NER paid up to 12 weeks' sick pay per annum, while the MR and the SECR paid none.

Reductions in traffic and receipts, together with the elimination of duplication concomitant with the 1923 Grouping, forced railways to reduce staff. Because it was mainly routine work that decreased, from 1922 to 1923 men lost 200 jobs while women lost 370. However, over the decade, clerical work expanded and by 1929 there were 9,774 female clerks. One of them, Muriel Mose, described the conditions:

> The office was drab, with a large black fireplace and brown lino. On a wet day the smoke blew straight back down the chimney and we sat coughing in a sooty blue haze. Some of us wore coat overalls to protect our clothes but our white underwear was always grey. In 1933 we had a new bureau with central heating.
>
> My first shock was being confronted with an old typewriter with a double keyboard – one for capitals and one for small letters. There were two solid wood fixed benches, where four typists sat each side, and a large desk raised up on a dais where a lady supervisor sat overlooking us. The men at the ledger office sat or stood at high wooden desks. When one of them wanted a typist to take shorthand one of us was called on to go.
>
> We had half an hour for lunch and 10 minutes before lunch to wash, and 10 minutes p.m. There were no tea breaks; a tea lady came twice a day.
>
> There was a railway handbook with 32 Rules, and for the efficiency exam we had to quote two. I learnt the whole 32 by heart. For passing the exam at age 18 we received a rise of 9s per week, after which we received annual rises of 2s until reaching the age of 31. A woman could not earn more without promotion, which was rare. Women's pay seemed reasonable at that time. There was a superannuation fund, which provided a pension on retirement or a lump sum on marriage. It was necessary to know all the stations on the two main lines: St Pancras to Thurso and Euston to Glasgow, and the names of places within a 20-mile radius of large towns. On the whole I liked the job, which taught me the geography of the British Isles.

Ethel, May and Olive Robbins, daughters of a LBSCR railwayman, joined the company as teenagers. Ethel and May attended East Croydon Training School around 1915, after which Ethel worked in the local rates section at London Bridge, leaving in 1924 to get married. May was booking clerk at Horley before moving to the superintendent's office at London

Bridge until her own marriage in 1924. Olive joined her sister at Horley before moving to Three Bridges, where her father was the station inspector. In 1920 she was sent to Rowfant station, where, four months later, porter-signalman George Baldwin arrived. The two 18-year-olds worked on the isolated little station together and romance blossomed. Olive's career came to an end when she married George in 1928.

Miss E. L. Winterton began work in 1915 as a tracer in the signal engineer's office at Reading, GWR and qualified as a draughtswoman two years later. She made wiring diagrams for signalling appliances in connection with track circuits, signals and points. She studied maths, physics, machine construction and drawing, electricity, magnetism and applied mechanics at University College, Reading, winning the College Prize for Machine Construction in 1919-20 and the Wells Prize for Science in 1922. In 1923 she became the first woman Associate Member of the Institution of Railway Signal Engineers.

A few women filled special posts: for example Audrey Shirtliff — 'an experienced traveller ... and accomplished linguist' — marketed excursions on the GWR to women's organisations, factories and mothers' unions.[36] The highest grades (those of welfare officer and personal secretary) were reserved for graduates or for women holding professional qualifications. These were the highest-paid railwaywomen, earning about 154s a week.

Although men labelled them 'unambitious', women complained long and loud about their lack of prospects throughout the 30s. Hundreds spent their whole working lives in railway service without being promoted even one grade. Very few rose through the ranks. As was the case prior to the war, the only supervisory posts open to them were in 'women's sectors' (typing pools, telephone exchanges, etc). Competition for such positions was fierce and, once installed, the supervisor — having no prospect of further advancement — became a permanent fixture until her retirement.

In 1930 a journalist suggested that women be appointed to the Board of Directors of the SR. However, this was merely to extend their domestic role to the workplace: the writer thought women could improve the passengers' accommodation and the tea rooms, which, he claimed, had 'dingy lace curtains and an array of veteran snacks'.[37]

The RCA and Equal Pay

The pay of female railway clerks in 1920 was about 17-18s a week at age 16, rising over time to a maximum of 70s a week for the small handful who gained promotion to Class 1. The average pay of an established female clerk was about 34s a week. Their male counterparts started at 20s a week and could reach a maximum of 134s a week, though the average male clerk earned about 80s. The war bonus increased the inequality: until August 1918 a woman's bonus was half that of a man, and by the end of the war, women received only 20s 3d compared with the 33s paid to men. A 48-hour week was standard for both sexes.

Women in the lower grades conducted a year-long campaign for improvements in pay. Those on the LYR and NBR were particularly vociferous and demanded complete equality with men. However, a committee of managers and a Railway Wages Tribunal (both all-male) decreed that women's work was not equal to men's and that women deserved to get lower pay. Improvements were offered following a meeting between the RCA and the Standing Committee of General Managers, but they fell far short of equality. The RCA EC held a special conference of women at Birmingham in 1920, at which the 130 delegates unanimously rejected the companies' offer. A consultative sub-committee of seven women was elected to help the EC to fight for a better deal for women, and further negotiations took place, resulting in substantial improvements and the first Women's Agreement.

The RCA EC at this time did not support its female members' demands for equal pay and opportunity. General Secretary Alexander Walkden had supported women's campaign for the vote, and had claimed equal pay for them when they had replaced men during the war but, by the 1930s, he refused to discuss it, saying that he feared it would 'open a door that it was desirable to keep shut at the moment.' By then, women's increased confidence and growing numerical strength had combined to produce a body of workers who asserted their demands so vigorously that the union leadership could not ignore them.

At the height of the war, 20 women had attended the RCA annual conference, but in 1919 only nine attended. During the early 1920s the number of female delegates dropped to just three and did not return to double figures until 1930 (see table on page 141). A small number of women in the RCA had suggested in 1918 that there be a guaranteed seat for a woman on the National Executive, but the majority of women rejected this. When seats were reserved for certain grade representatives, however, the idea began to gain favour and in 1927 the 80 delegates at the RCA women's conference recommended it. In addition they requested that each Divisional Council have a women's committee. A special conference in November 1929 changed RCA rules to enable a woman to be elected to the Executive. The following year Elsie Orman* of King's Cross branch became the first, and she served for three years. Not until 1938 was a place on the RCA EC reserved for a woman.

Miss Orman expressed her feminist views frankly, believing that women 'should definitely repudiate the mischievous doctrine that "woman is the lesser man" '.[38] Another leading activist was shorthand typist Margaret Gamble, who proudly announced that she was a descendant of a Tolpuddle Martyr. She was particularly keen that middle-class girls working as railway clerks should not regard themselves as 'above' trade union membership. Her writings, published in *The Railway Service Journal*, included the assertion, 'Eve was a later model than Adam, therefore she should be an improvement, more modern, more advanced.'[39]

At the 1933 RCA conference a resolution for equal pay incited 'eloquent pleas' from Mary Keenan, a clerk at Manchester Oldham Road, notable for having attended Oxford University, where she gained the highest honour a woman could obtain at that time: a Diploma with Distinction in Economics and Political Science. (Oxford University did not at that time award degrees to women graduates.) Miss Keenan argued that there was no justification for pay inequality 'on ethical, economic, or any other grounds.' She was followed by Miss Cocker, who asked her union brothers: 'Do you think you would like to tell your wives that they were of less value than you?' The women were outvoted by male delegates and the equal pay resolution was lost.[40] Far from advancing equality, the following year's conference passed a resolution against the employment of female clerks on night shifts.

Women railway clerks were still campaigning fruitlessly for equality when the Second World War broke out in 1939.

---

* Miss Orman was educated at London College and joined the NER accountant's department in 1907. She enrolled in the RCA in 1918 and was a delegate to the National Labour Women and Standing Joint Committee of Women's Industrial Organisations, a member of the Great Northern Salaries Movement Committee and a national representative in negotiations that secured the 1920 Women's Agreement.

Women's Right to Work

The 20s and 30s were decades of economic depression and job losses. Many people openly vocalised the belief that men had more right than women to paid work. The press exploited this zeitgeist with headlines such as 'Down with women in industry' and 'Are women displacing men?' Contemporary observer Winifred Holtby remarked:

> The bitterness began that has lasted ever since — the women keeping jobs and men resenting it — the men regaining the jobs and the women resenting it.[41]

It was widely argued that all women should be supported by their husbands. Quite apart from the issue of women's rights, this naïve demand was impossible to fulfil. The war had created a large number of widows, who needed to earn a living; many wives supported war-wounded or shell-shocked husbands; and a huge number of single women would never marry, because their potential spouses had been killed in the war. Women had won the vote and had helped to win a war. Their desire to take their place in public and professional life had never been greater.

Married women, especially, were blamed for pitching men into unemployment. Working men wanted their wives to stay at home, because of the many benefits this gave them. Not only would they get a full-time housekeeper to cater to their every need, but also they could use her financial dependence to bolster their demand that every man's wage ought to be sufficiently high to support two people at the very least, and ought to take into account the children that would inevitably come along.

The railway companies, along with similar employers, did not employ married women in salaried grades. Only spinsters were recruited and those who subsequently married had to resign. (Of course, it is possible that some may have kept their marriage a secret in order to retain their income for a little longer.) The reason for the marriage bar, as the practice was termed, is unclear. One may speculate that perhaps the companies felt that 'a woman's place is in the home', but that does not explain why the marriage bar did not apply to railwaywomen in wages grades. During the 20s this bar was relaxed slightly, and in 1927 Manchester 3 RCA branch asked the Executive to make it union policy that women clerks must resign upon marriage. It did not become policy, but the bar was back in operation again by the 1930s.

In 1929 Jimmy Thomas, general secretary of the NUR, caused a furore by accusing married women of working only for 'pin money'. The aftermath filled the press for seven days. Many indignant journalists, union officials, women's organisations, writers and working women were provoked sufficiently to respond. Lady Rhondda, herself a businesswoman, accused Thomas of 'advocating idleness' and of having 'very little knowledge of economics'. She remarked that male-led unions (like his) were to blame for undercutting because they had failed to secure equal pay for women.[42] Others challenged his claim to be a socialist, and some labelled him a hypocrite. One woman described his statement as 'simply scandalous' and asked: 'Why does he not ask MPs who have another job besides that in the House to give up one of them?'[43] This was another personal attack: as well as leading the NUR, Thomas was MP for Derby and Minister for Unemployment. Men, too, criticised him: one wrote: 'It is most disquieting to hear from one of His Majesty's Ministers that it is better to be idle than to work.'[44]

As well as offending and annoying many working people of both sexes, Thomas found himself out of step with the TUC, which in 1935 passed a resolution (moved by the General and Municipal Workers Union) asserting that the problems of unemployment could not be solved by transferring available work from one group of workers to another. It opposed the idea that the unemployment problem could be solved simply by dismissing wives from their jobs.

Malcolm Wallace, historian of the RCA, states that the RCA leadership 'played a progressive role in defending a woman's right to work';[45] unfortunately, there is no record of what they thought of their fellow trade unionist's attitude.

Women's right to work continued to be a hot topic throughout the decade. In November 1936, the GWR Lecture and Debating Society invited Betty Gardner, the (non-earning) wife of a railwayman to read her paper 'Women's Place in Business. Should it be extended or curtailed?' It was noted that she was the first woman ever to address the society and that a large number of railwaywomen had attended because the speaker was of their own sex.

Mrs Gardner began by making a series of provocative comments such as: 'For generations man has striven to keep woman in her proper place', and she predicted that 'man will go on exploiting woman in all sorts of ways for generations to come'. However, she then brought forth hackneyed stereotypes that antagonised female attendees:

> The vast majority of young women hope to get married, and quite a large amount of their thoughts and energy is centred around this. Even if a girl is not all the time thinking of the boy she is going to meet after work she is most likely cogitating about the clothes she will don in order to fascinate him.

None of the railwaywomen in the audience appears to have agreed with her. One asserted: 'Some girls do not come to business with the idea of just waiting to get married, but they take an interest in their work.' Another said: 'There are many women on the railways who are forced to work because they have no mothers or fathers, and they have to work to keep homes together.' It also became clear that what most concerned railwaywomen was the lack of equal opportunity. One railwaywoman remarked:

> You ... cannot get any farther because you are a woman — only got a woman's brain, cannot take responsibility. ... A girl is merely expected to type — perhaps for twenty or thirty years. Then, at the age of fifty, a young fellow dictates letters to her.

Mrs Gardner said that such women should be offered early retirement. Her view on married women workers echoed that which was 'doing the rounds' in every public bar:

> It seems manifestly unfair that a married woman, without children ... whose husband is drawing an income sufficient to keep two people in comfort, should add another income to his, and so deprive a single girl or young man of employment.

Finally, Mrs Gardner suggested 'prohibiting women from doing work which is too great a physical strain' and 'restricting the married woman ... from taking part in business and commerce'. Her proposals received no support from the audience.[46]

Summary

Women experienced both gains and losses during the inter-war period. The parliamentary vote had been conceded (after half a century of campaigning) and the war had given them the opportunity to prove that their exclusion from 'male' work was attributable not to female disinclination or incompetence, but to male prejudice and jealousy. Yet, after the war, they failed to consolidate their occupational advances or to make much progress with equal pay. In 1906 women had earned 44% of male earnings; by 1931 this had risen to 48%.

There was a shift back to the pre-war position, with a distinction being drawn once again between men's jobs and women's jobs. The powerful but invisible force of social expectation was the main factor responsible for this, bolstered by overt pressure from men's organisations, including trades unions. While it may be argued that war-work raised women's status, it also inflamed much anti-woman feeling after the war and the campaign to oust women from 'men's jobs' triumphed because, as one contemporary observer remarked:

> The women themselves acquiesced. ... They did not want to stand in the way of the returned soldiers, and, far from being the selfish creatures the Press described, they were only too meek and yielding.[47]

On the railways, the 35,000 women filling male wages grades in November 1918 had dwindled to fewer than 200 in five years. By the mid-1920s men had successfully repossessed all their former 'territory' and women were again relegated to the worst-paid, lowest-status work. Between the wars women gained more low-grade jobs as companies resumed their pre-war plans to exploit cheaper female labour by replacing men with women on lower rates of pay. Men were powerless to prevent it, because their union leaders had agreed to lower rates for women. Tension and resentment grew as women gained from men over 7,000 clerical positions, nearly 700 jobs as carriage cleaners and about 100 crossing keepers' posts — in which occupation women outnumbered men for the first time by the year 1926. Women also gained more than 200 jobs in the marine division.

Although the NUR and the RCA differed in their attitude to railwaywomen between the wars, neither upheld women's claim to equal pay or equal opportunity. ASLEF allowed women to join only its Women's Guild, a social and fund-raising body founded in 1924. Its membership ban had no practical consequence, in any case; since the last wartime woman engine cleaner was 'dispensed with', there were no women in any of the grades ASLEF represented (i.e. driver, fireman, engine cleaner, or motorman*).

By 1939 there were 25,260 women railway employees. Of these, 11,565 were salaried staff† and 6,900 were in hotels and catering. Of the remaining 6,795, nearly all worked in female wages grades.

---

* Motorman was the name given to the driver of an electric train, as opposed to a steam engine.

† According to Malcolm Wallace, 13,655 railwaywomen were members of the RCA.

APPENDICES

WOMEN EMPLOYED BY BRITAIN'S RAILWAYS IN THE 1920S						
	1923		*1926*		*1929*	
	Women	*Men*	*Women*	*Men*	*Women*	*Men*
Clerks	8,536	71,772	9,927		9,774	
Carriage cleaners	882	6,829	641	7,128	675	6,801
Crossing keepers	1,417	1,568	1,531	1,497	1,518	1,390
Waiting/messroom att's			744		663	
Workshop/artisans			1,320		1,047	
Cleaners/chars			3,407		3,121	
Hotel/catering/laundry			6,083		5,705	
Marine department			121		197	
Miscellaneous			438		453	
Checkers	4	11,689				
Labourers	37	35,709				
Messengers	21	641				
Police	6	2,767				
Goods porters	14	19,430				
Passenger porters	22	22,996				
Signal (wo)men	2	29,256				
Yard and station masters	10	7,673				
Ticket collectors	11	5,287				
Engine cleaners	2	10,023				
Inspectors	11	7,748				

AVERAGE PAY, GWR, 1929	
Male clerk	70s 10d
Male wages grades	54s 9d
Female clerk	34s 0d
Messenger	34s 0d
Waiting room attendant	25s 6d
Halt attendant	22s 0d
Crossing keeper	12s 5d
Charwoman	10s 8d

Distribution of women staff by company, 1921			
North Eastern	3,635	London & South Western	666
London & North Western	3,534	Glasgow & South Western	663
Great Western	3,245	London, Brighton & Sth Coast	330
Midland	2,665	Great North of Scotland	263
Lancashire & Yorkshire	2,204	Metropolitan	195
Great Eastern	1,607	Railway Clearing House	183
Caledonian	1,586	Highland	148
Great Central	1,447	Metropolitan District	145
North British	762	North Staffordshire	125
South Eastern & Chatham	759	Midland & Gt Northern Joint	100
		Subtotal	22,706
Women employed by companies with fewer than 100 female staff			1,120
Total number of women employed by railway companies			23,826

Distribution of women employed by the GWR, 1929					
Traffic department		*Clerical staff*		*Hotel & catering*	
Crossing keepers	178	Women	185	Women & girls	594
Charwomen	151	Girls	146		
Waiting room att'nts	86				
Carriage cleaners	19	*Printing*		*Carriage & wagon*	
Pneumatic tube att'ts	4	Printer's assistant	6	Charwomen	65
Gatekeepers	3	Ticket checkers	5	Polishers	38
Halt attendant	1	Ticket cutters	2	Laundresses	35
Messenger	1	Ticket backer	1	Seamstresses	25
		Bookbinder's ass'nt	1	Axle pad makers	14
Docks department				Stores women	6
Charwomen	9			Messroom att'ts	2
Stewardesses	7			Workshop superv.	1

DELEGATES TO RCA CONFERENCES 1927-1940		
Year	*Delegates*	*Women*
1927	455	9
1928	461	5
1929	447	7
1930	494	10
1931	512	9
1932	503	4
1933	508	6
1934	509	10
1935	509	5
1936	512	8
1937	501	9
1938	519	9
1939	539	13

Women Stationmasters Are Most Tidy

Two L.N.E.R. stations—Deadwater (Northumberland) and Gordon (Berwickshire)—which have women stationmasters, have received awards in the company's 1938 Best Kept Station Competition.

Special class prizes, the highest awards, have been given to Appleby (Lincolnshire), Bealings (Suffolk), Bellingham (Northumberland), Egton (Yorkshire), Helensburgh (Dumbarton), Hessle (Yorkshire), Leadenham (Lincolnshire), Newham (Northumberland), and St. Monance (Fife).

Points were given among other things for general tidiness and the cultivation of gardens and shrubs.

Tidy stationmasters. *Evening Standard*, 2nd September 1938.
Mrs Scott. *Evening Standard*, 10th July 1931.

MRS. SCOTT, OF THE L.N.E.R.

HER NEW POST.

How many people know that there are station-mistresses on British railways?

The L.N.E.R. have just announced that Mrs. Scott, stationmistress at Gilmerton, has been appointed stationmistress at Invergarry.

An L.N.E.R. official told the "Evening Standard" to-day that the company have a number of stationmistresses in Scotland, but their numbers are gradually dwindling.

"Most of these women," he said, "have been in the company's service many years. They are either the widows or daughters of stationmasters and became so used to the duty that they were able to take it over on the death of their relative.

"It is not the policy of the company to appoint stationmistresses except in cases in which a man relative has occupied the post."

There are no stationmistresses in England, but there is one in Wales.

RCA MEMBERSHIP 1912-1923		
Year	*Men*	*Women*
1912	19,121	30
1913	25,741	50
1914	29,294	100
1915	41,723	931
1916	45,458	3,378
1917	49,890	8,771
1918	57,786	13,655
1919	74,742	9,565
1920	78,171	8,883
1921	55,620	4,644
1922	48,156	2,981
1923	54,504	2,978

References

[1] Imperial War Museum, Reading Room documents. EMP 32/4.
[2] Pratt, E.A. (1921) *British Railways and the Great War* (Selwyn & Blount) p479.
[3] Letter from Evelyn Amos, Louie's daughter. 1992.
[4] *Railway Review* 29 September 1916.
[5] Wallace, M. (1997) *Single or Return?* (TSSA).
[6] *The Times* 8 October 1920.
[7] Holtby, W. (1934) *Woman and a Changing Civilisation* (Douglas) p113.
[8] *Manchester Despatch* 20 September 1919.
[9] *The Railway Review* 20 June 1919.
[10] NUR EC Minutes June 1919.
[11] *The Railway Review* 4 July 1921.
[12] Letter from NUR EC to Mr Wheeler of the Negotiating Committee of General Managers. March 1921.
[13] Braybon, G. (1984) *Women Workers in the First World* War (Croom Helm).
[14] National Archives. Correspondence between the companies and the Railway Staff and Labour Committee, 1921-22.
[15] University of Warwick, Modern Records Centre. MSS 127x/NU/IN/15ii.
[16] <www.gettyimages.com>. Images 254716, 3254191 and 3289639.
[17] Wallace, M. (1997) *Single or Return?* (TSSA).
[18] *British Railways Magazine* Eastern Region Edition1962.
[19] Letter to the author, 2005.
[20] Scottish Record Office. NBR 15/60.
[21] Ibid.
[22] NUR EC Minutes 1919.
[23] National Archives. Census of Railway Staff 1923, 1927, 1929.
[24] *British Railways Magazine* NE Edition June 1953 p107.
[25] *Women's Leader* 3 October 1928.
[26] *Daily Herald* 17 January 1928 and 8 May 1930.
[27] *Evening Standard* 2 September 1938.
[28] *Daily Herald* 29 January 1937.
[29] Pathé News (1934), *Caught by the Camera 6*. Available at <www.itnarchive.com/britishpathe>.
[30] *Railway Magazine* August 1929.
[31] Pathé News. *Eve's Film Review* issue 350, 1928; *Railway Magazine* December 1926.
[32] Letter from Ann Shah, 2005.
[33] NUR EC Minutes 1936.
[34] *Railway Gazette* 6 June 1919.
[35] Letter to the author, 2005.
[36] *Great Western Magazine* August 1936.
[37] *Manchester Guardian* 28 September 1938.
[38] *The Railway Service Journal* July 1930, p271.
[39] *The Railway Service Journal* September 1934 p358.
[40] RCA 1933 Conference Report.
[41] Holtby, W. (1934) *Woman and a Changing Civilisation* (Douglas) p113.
[42] *Evening Standard* 29 November 1929.
[43] *Manchester Guardian* 29 November 1929.
[44] *Daily News* 29 November 1929.
[45] Wallace, M. (1997) *Single or Return?* (TSSA).
[46] *Proceedings of the* GWR *Lecture and Debating Society*, Session 1936-7. Many thanks to Terry Hewitt.
[47] Strachey, R. (1928) *The Cause* (Reprinted 1978, Virago) p371.

4: THE SECOND WORLD WAR

> We never created about anything; we just got on with the job. The men had to go and fight for this country of ours, and the women got on with the work.
>
> ANNIE BROWN

When the Second World War began in September 1939, the precedent had already been set of men joining the forces and being replaced 'for the duration' by women, so the organisation of war-work was swifter and less tentative than it had been in 1914-1915. Furthermore, from 1941 the Ministry of Labour could compel employers to recruit women and they could also be conscripted into the services, civil defence and essential industries. By 1943 over two million additional women had entered the workforce.*

At the outbreak of war, 563,264 men and boys and 25,253 women and girls were working on the railways. Over the next six years, over 98,000 railwaymen (17.5%) joined the forces, civil defence and essential industries. Over 4,000 (16%) of the female staff enlisted, too: 3,129 joined the forces, 397 worked in civil defence and 680 transferred to other essential industries.[1] A few railwaywomen held commissions: 11 in the Auxiliary Territorial Service and one in the Women's Royal Naval Service.

The Railway Executive Committee (REC), which had been placed in charge of railways for the duration of the war, talked with the unions, predominantly the NUR, about women replacing the 12,000 railwaymen who had already enlisted. Union negotiators were less hostile to women war-workers than they had been in 1915; perhaps because — despite fears to the contrary — women had been easily ejected when railwaymen returned after 1918. Nevertheless the NUR was taking no chances and again strove for tight control over women's employment; for example, in June 1940 the union agreed to the employment of women lift attendants on the Underground only if they would never be expected to 'attempt to interfere with the mechanism of the machine rooms in case of failures'.[2]

Negotiations were sometimes complex and protracted. In mid-1940 London Underground needed 90 female car cleaners to replace the male staff who had enlisted. The NUR had agreed before the war to women being paid 37% less than men; now it demanded the male rate for new recruits and insisted that women deal solely with the interiors and windows, leaving the exteriors to the remaining men. London Underground refused but, when the staff shortage reached 185 in early 1941, it was forced to capitulate. The NUR then demanded that rates be re-negotiated if women were in the future expected to clean the exteriors.[3]

---

* In 1939, the total UK workforce consisted of 13 million men and 4.8 million women; in 1945 the figures were 10 million and 6.2 million respectively.

In a repeat of 1915, women applied eagerly for railway work. Many responded to newspaper advertisements – one in Bristol asking for porters drew 250 applicants – others saw recruitment posters or blackboards at stations, or heard of vacancies from friends or family. Many a railwayman entreated his daughter to join the railways rather than risk her being conscripted and sent away from home. Some women were directed to railway work under the Essential Works Order and, while a few did not like it, many preferred it to other industries such as munitions manufacture. For a few it was the realisation of a lifelong dream. Engine driver's daughter Marjorie Smeaton recalled 'I used to wish I was a boy, so that I could go "on the railway", too.' She became a signalwoman.[4] For Mrs Sprigg, it was almost inevitable:

> My father was a signalman for over 50 years. We lived in a railway cottage next to his signal box, so I grew up going in and out of the signalbox. My eldest brother went into a signalbox. My father came home from work one day and said: 'They want women to train for signalling so I have sent your name forward.' As I had grown up with signal boxes it just seemed natural.[5]

Some women were apprehensive: Joan Levick, who became a guard, revealed, 'I did not think I could do a man's job, but I proved myself wrong.'[6] Women's temporary status was made clear to them. Gwynneth Dixon, who applied to be a porter, explained: 'We were made to understand, before being given the job, that we would not be required after the war.'[7]

Railway war-workers' previous occupations were extraordinarily diverse. One woman was formerly an ichthyologist at Buckingham Palace; a LMS gas fitter had been a cow girl in Mexico; a policewoman had trained as an opera singer; a GWR guard had once worked as a cook-housekeeper at Windsor Castle; a woman operating a four-ton steam hammer was a former egg-packer; an inspector of tyres had once planted rubber in Malaya; a goods porter had previously worked for a chocolate firm – and she had 'never been so pleased to say farewell to one job and hail to another'.[8]

Women were recruited swiftly into the starting grades and soon began to replace men in higher grades, such as guard and signalman. This pattern was echoed in other railway undertakings such as workshops and shipping.* By May 1942, so many railwaymen had joined the forces that the REC told the Ministry of Transport that its operating department was 'dangerously weak' on manpower. It was decided that no man would be taken into the forces without his company's consent and that, as far as possible, men would be switched to work deemed 'unsuitable' for women, and their posts filled by women.

By the spring of 1943, 88,464 women were working on the railways, of whom over 65,000 were replacing men in railway operating, workshops, goods and cartage, clerical work and shipping. Of those replacing men, the SR employed 8,000; the LNER, 10,000; the GWR, 11,500; the LMS, 24,000; and London Transport, 12,000. The vast majority were in the lower grades. A few were promoted to forewoman of female gangs, but supervisory and managerial positions remained closed to them, as did workshop apprenticeships.

Some women found themselves repeatedly switched to different jobs and locations. Mabel Fairbrass began in 1942 at Par, GWR, in a track-laying gang of six men and four women. They were moved to points-oiling duty, then on to station painting at Lostwithiel, then Par. Next, she was sent to Penmere Halt as booking clerk and 'general lackey'. Miss

* Britain's railways owned 130 steamships in 1939.

Fairbrass later moved house to Plymouth, re-applied to the GWR and became a guard. [9]

The USSR boasted that women filled all grades on its railways. By 1943 it had 56 women engine drivers, 2,900 drivers' assistants and numerous motorwomen (drivers of electric trains).[10] Zinaida Troitskaya, its first woman steam-engine driver, was now Line Superintendent. A delegate to the NUR's 1942 AGM, Mr E. Bowers of Barking branch, proclaimed that if Soviet women drove trains, British women should, too. This so alarmed the general secretaries of both the NUR and ASLEF that they publicly repudiated the suggestion. The latter asserted:

> Work on the Russian railways is very different from that involved in our complicated system, and the physical and mental strain of footplate work here is enormously greater. There is also the fact that years of experience are essential to qualify for work on our railways. So, even setting aside the question of physical and mental strain, no women would be qualified before the war ended.[11]

Indeed, no woman fired a steam engine or drove any train on the railways of Britain throughout the war.

The Railways in Wartime

Railways were crucial to the war effort. They moved civilian evacuees to safer areas, played a central role in the Dunkirk* and D-Day operations and carried wounded and deceased servicemen. The pre-war average passenger mileage doubled: petrol shortages caused more passengers and goods to go by rail and trains were utilised to convey military and food supplies. They were also used to mobilise forces' and auxiliary personnel: the SR alone carried 9.3 million during the six years of war.

Wartime railway work was considerably more stressful and demanding than in peacetime. The enemy inflicted considerable damage on stations, yards, engines and rolling stock, and maintenance routines were severely disrupted. By the winter of 1942-3, there were 1,000 to 1,500 cancellations a week and stations often swarmed with delayed passengers, already disgruntled because reservations had been abolished, restaurant cars withdrawn and fares raised threefold.

In addition to these extra stresses, railway workers were burdened with a multitude of additional wartime duties and had to memorise a large number of extra rules and regulations. Signalwoman Annie Hodgeon was instructed that, if the Germans invaded, she had to disable her signalbox by pulling out all of its wires.[12] Station announcers were given special messages to broadcast, such as: 'Guard your conversation – careless talk costs lives.' Even office staff had special wartime rules: at Euston all work had to be cleared every day, 'which meant working late most evenings, as no papers were to be left overnight on the premises in case the station was bombed, thankfully it never was'.[13]

Staff at 79 London Underground stations accommodated up to 160,000 people at a time, seeking refuge from the Blitz in 1940.[14] Hundreds of thousands of extra trains were provided for the government to carry evacuees, troops, casualties, food and a wide range of war supplies. In 1944, for example, 178,000 such trains were run and, by that year, 1,000 carriages had been converted for use as ambulance trains.

---

* 620 special trains were run in just 16 days to collect the Dunkirk evacuees.

Enemy bombs were deliberately aimed at railways and special arrangements were implemented. Signalmen, engine crews and guards were told to keep trains moving during air raids. At first, other staff were told to stop work and take cover immediately; later they had to continue working until the danger was imminent. Emergency instructions were posted at every station, shelters were constructed in workshops and in some locations glass was removed from station roofs. Stations within 20 miles of the coast had their nameplates removed; elsewhere, tiny signs had letters no more than 3 inches high.[15] Over 308,000 railway men and women served in the National Fire Guard, over 170,000 were trained in civil defence, and railway workers' Home Guard units patrolled bridges, viaducts and tunnels while off-duty.

Railway workers put enormous effort into maintaining the blackout, so that the Luftwaffe could not see any train or structure at night. This involved ensuring that lamps were fitted with hoods and that station lights were kept dimmed and shielded. Black borders were painted around the edges of carriage windows in case the blinds did not completely cover them. The blackout had to be strictly observed at crossing keepers' cottages, too, since they often had the only lights in the vicinity of a railway line, making them extremely vulnerable. Some crossing keepers received a one-person metal air-raid shelter resembling a large safe.

Working in the blackout brought many additional dangers. For example, in 1943, 145 passengers were killed in accidents involving the movement of rail vehicles, compared with the pre-war average of 69. There was also a large increase in the number of passengers falling from platforms and out of trains. An order was given to paint white lines along all platform edges in an attempt to remedy this.

The London Underground being used as a shelter during the Blitz.

In blacked-out marshalling yards, railwaymen's peacetime familiarity with the walkways, track layout, points handles and other equipment and structures provided them with a mental map of the site, which proved invaluable in the darkness. But women war-workers had no such resource, as Lennoxtown guard Isabella Anderson discovered:

> The blackout was so horrible – not knowing where one was. Going into strange yards, and listening to trains moving, and not seeing them, not knowing where the points are, and nobody to ask, is very alarming.[16]

Guard Anna Wolsey also found the blackout challenging:

> My first job was on the single line railway up to Blaenau Ffestiniog. There was complete black-out. I was supposed to throw out the mailbags at their destinations but I did not know on which side of the line the platforms were. At one point I saw a little light and as I threw the mailbags out the light went flying up in the air: I had hit the station master's cigarette straight out of his mouth.[17]

During the war there was an increase in the number of railway staff killed in accidents not attributable to enemy action; no doubt the blackout, stress and overwork were contributory factors. In 1943 of the total staff of 544,700 men and 105,700 women, 296 staff (of whom 15 were women) were killed in accidents, compared with an average of 228 for the years 1935-9.

The railways were subjected to substantial bombing. In May 1941 London's Waterloo, Victoria, Cannon Street, London Bridge, King's Cross and St Pancras stations were all closed owing to enemy action. The SR suffered the most bombing incidents by far – 3,637, or 170 per route mile.* One short section of track – from Waterloo to Queenstown Road – was hit 92 times in the eight months beginning September 1940. Waterloo itself sustained 66 hits, and 42 flying bombs hit SR property. Mary Davies was a porter at London Bridge, SR, when nearby Docklands suffered a devastating aerial attack. She recalled:

> I never thought I'd see my home that night, I honestly didn't. Everywhere you looked was in flames! And the glass [roof] was all coming in on the station. We didn't know where to go ... we just hid where we could on the station. I can never forget that night so long as I live.[18]

Between July 1940 and September 1943, there were 58 attacks on SR trains, during which 142 carriages were destroyed. Altogether, 170 SR staff were killed,† and 687 male and 59 female employees were injured by enemy action. Former guard Louisa Jupp recalled:

> We were given a little metal badge. On the back was a number. I said, 'What's this in aid of?' 'Well, if you do get blown up on a train, we know who you are.'[19]

Her colleague on the SR, Edie Winser (now Mrs Rowe) was based at Ore depot in Hastings:

---

* The GWR sustained 1202 (33 per route mile); the LMS, 1939 (29 p.r.m); the LNER, 1737 (28 p.r.m.) Bernard Darwin, (1946) *War on the Line* p107.

† Not separately enumerated by sex.

> It was a very dangerous job. One night we stopped at Winchelsea and we were stuck there while we watched these flying bombs go over, hundreds of them. Once they thought it was clear enough we were allowed to go on.[20]

Mary Davies, evidently undeterred by her experiences at London Bridge, became a guard and was based at Beckenham. On two occasions, stations were bombed just after her train had departed. But her luck ran out:

> I got caught once — at Herne Hill. There was a great big block of flats there. They bombed that and it caught my train right the way across. You never see so many cut faces and everything in all your life. Ooh, it was a slaughter. Well, we could only get the First Aid to them. Our train was a wreck — every window had gone. I was very frightened; I was shaking from head to foot, actually. I got three days off for shock.[21]

Air raids were not confined to the south. Coventry suffered 600 hits in November 1940, of which 122 were on LMS property. Clydebank was devastated by a bombing raid in March 1941, when guard Isabella Anderson was taking out her first train alone. Fifty years later she remembered her disorientation clearly:

> Our usual station was bombed. We went into another station. We then had to shunt up the line. I'll never forget, when I had to get out of the brakevan to change the tail lamp, there was hardly anything there but rubble. I did not know where I was. I had the greatest desire to run, but there was no place to run.[22]

Altogether, there were 9,239 bombing incidents on railway property. In these, over 24,000 goods wagons and 14,000 of the railways' 40,000 passenger vehicles were damaged or destroyed. Enemy action injured 2,444 staff, and killed 395 staff and 498 passengers on railway premises. In comparison, just under 1,500 railwaymen were killed serving in the forces. In 1942 LPTB revealed that, since the outbreak of war, more of its staff had been killed while on duty than while serving in the forces: 142 compared with 138.[23] In total, 181 LPTB employees were killed on duty during the war, and 1,867 were injured. The RCA noted that, by May 1942, 25 of their members had died in the forces and 22 (of whom 3 were women) had been killed during bombing raids.

Some areas of Britain sustained no enemy attack, but working on the railway brought distressing reminders of the war. Doreen Spackman (now Mrs Stevens), who was a porter and later a signalwoman on the GWR, recalled, 'Living in the countryside the bombing and mayhem seemed so far way, until we saw the hospital trains bringing the injured back from the coast after D-Day.'[24] Cardiff Guard Mary Marchant remembered going to Whitchurch Halt with a train of wounded soldiers evacuated from Dunkirk: 'It really upset me. I just couldn't get them out of my mind — some of them were only boys of eighteen.'[25] Mary Davies had another bad experience when working as a porter at London Bridge:

> I remember one night we were unloading a train that had come up from Dover. Oh my God, I opened the door and I had the fright of my life. There was nothing but coffins, every door, and they were all draped with the British flag, every one of them, the whole train. Some of our boys being sent back. Oh, it was awful, seeing it at dead of night, you know.[26]

The challenge of working on railways in wartime brought out the best in railway workers and damaged structures were usually repaired immediately. In one case, a 68-lever signalbox destroyed in an air raid was replaced within a day. In the East End of London, a gang of women set to work directly after a bombing incident to repair and rejoin damaged multi-core and telephone cables.

Passengers soon came to expect staff to treat bombings almost as part of their daily routine and would tolerate only minimal disruption to services. Catering assistant Renée Parsons remembered the day she was serving in the refreshment room at Ashford (Kent), SR, when a bomb blew out the back of the building: her customers still demanded tea.

Although it became commonplace for railwaywomen to carry on working under such difficult and dangerous circumstances, there were some acts of particularly outstanding bravery that merit special mention. Miss Haster, a ticket collector at Hull Paragon, remained at her barrier directing passengers to the shelter while bombs were falling on the station. Alice Steckhahn — a 'five foot high girl porter' — single-handedly extinguished a shower of incendiary bombs with sand and water.[27] After her station 'somewhere in the North of England' was bombed at 1 a.m., LMS porter Mrs B. Kelly laboured from 3 a.m. until 3 p.m. to clear the debris and reopen the station. She was commended for her 'high sense of duty, gallantry and determination'.[28]

At Walsden, LMS, a 77-year-old man fell from the platform when a train was due. Porter Nellie Bentley grabbed her lamp and dashed along the line waving a red light at the engine driver. The train stopped just eight yards short of where the man had fallen.[29] Porter Violet Wisdom of witnessed an air raid on 16th December 1942. A train from Guildford to Horsham was bombed and machine-gunned near her station at Bramley, SR. Although shocked and frightened, she had the presence of mind to lock the booking office before running along the track toward the train. There she found a horrific scene: the driver and guard had been killed, eight passengers were dead or dying, and the rest were injured. She and the fireman, William Fairey, later received meritorious certificates for the way that they handled the situation. Miss Wisdom was especially commended for her 'great courage and resource directly the bombs had fallen'.[30] Although her contribution was well-publicised at the time, when railway historian Bernard Darwin gave an account of this incident in his 1946 book *War on the Line* he stated that Fairey 'single-handedly attended the injured' and 'was unaided in his rescue work,' until six soldiers arrived. Miss Wisdom was not even mentioned.[31]

In addition to the troubles and traumas of working on a bombing target, there were of course the usual railway incidents and accidents, among them several in which railwaywomen risked their lives to save others. At Rushden, LMS, a six-year-old boy fell onto the track and lay, bleeding and unconscious, with his head on a rail. It was too late to stop an approaching train, which was only 200 yards away, so porter Violet Wilson jumped on to the track and 'snatched him from death'.[32] Even ticket office clerks sometimes faced danger, and sometimes death. Ida Luff, booking clerk at Carshalton, SR, was on duty when a boy fell onto the electrified line. After telephoning the signalbox, Mrs Luff seized some special rubber insulation gloves, went onto the track, ran 100 yards to where the boy lay on the live rail and dragged him off by the legs. Unfortunately, he was already dead.[33] Mrs Wright, ticket office clerk at Elephant and Castle, SR, bravely fended off armed robbers.[34]

Accident reports — usually devoid of female names — also bear witness to the presence of railwaywomen. For example, at an enquiry into a collision at Northwood, London Underground, in 1945, in which two trains collided in fog and three passengers died from smoke inhalation from the resultant fire, among those who gave evidence were Porters Mrs L. M. Sparkes and Miss Vi Ryder and Assistant Train Fitter Miss Atkins, based at Neasden, who was responsible for putting fire extinguishers on trains.[35]

As if railway workers had not enough to cope with in wartime, to cap it all, from 1940 to 1943 Britain suffered three winters of unusual severity, which highlighted the susceptibility of railways to bad weather. The workforce had to carry on regardless and deal with the aftermath: snow blocks, fallen telegraph poles, and frozen points, rods, brakes, points levers and signal wires. Even axle grease froze in some locations. In the 'big freeze' of January 1942, railwaywomen joined troops to clear snowdrifts and free thousands of pairs of frozen points. The winter of 1946-7 was the coldest ever recorded and was followed by floods. Telegraphist Eileen Bridges remembered Colchester station:

> This had one of the longest platforms, the end of which was likened to Siberia. During one very cold winter, could have been 1947, our dear station inspector, a very tall gentleman, was feeling the cold, so a nose-cover was knitted by his 'fans' in the telegraph office. This was held on by elastic, to keep his poor nose from becoming a beacon. It was greeted by much laughter and, dare we say, gratitude. A trivial incident, but one which held us together.[36]

The press, politicians and railway managers applauded railway workers for their hard work in difficult circumstances. Many received honours for their wartime railway service, including a number of female staff who maintained communications instead of taking shelter during air raids. Other honours were awarded for dealing with secret documents. A complete list of railwaywomen who won awards is not available, but the following came to light during this research:

Some who were awarded the British Empire Medal (BEM):

- Miss C. Davenport, Clerk-in-Charge, Telephone Enquiry Bureau. (GWR)
- Miss M.C. Steward, Paddington Telephone Exchange Supervisor. (GWR)
- Miss E. E. Barratt, York Telephone Exchange Supervisor. (LNER)
- Miss G.E. Cooper, Southampton Telephone Exchange Supervisor. (SR)
- Miss G. Kallender, Telephone Exchange Supervisor. (SR)

Some who were made Members of the Order of the British Empire (OBE):

- Miss D. Thompson, Personal Clerk to the Chairman of the REC.
- Miss Helen Catto, Chief Welfare Superintendent. (LMS)
- Miss E. E. Smith, Lord Stamp's Private Secretary. (LMS)
- Miss Pearl Wadham, Personal Clerk to the Divisional General Manager. (SR)

Railway telephone operators contributed to the war effort by relaying warnings to other staff. One of them, Joan Evans, worked at Hastings, a heavily-bombed town:

> I worked in shifts, one week early, one week late and as I used to live a distance from the station I used to cycle. It was not safe to walk when it was dark, too many drunken soldiers about. My office was just off the main station entrance and was supposed to be bomb-proof. We were very busy as besides our public train time service we had all the military calls for soldiers going on leave,

working out routes for them. A lot of Canadians were billeted in the countryside and on my early shift I used to find them sleeping on benches in the ladies'. They had missed their trains the night before and would be woken up and given a cup of tea so they would be able to catch the 6.30 a.m. milk train.

One morning every month we had to work the switchboard with our gas masks on. This was very difficult and very unpleasant, but it was a drill that had to be done. Our main job was sending air raid warnings, we had a special phone which used to ring to tell us of an impending raid. First, yellow to be alert, then the red alert, which meant the enemy were close, then it was all systems go. When we received the yellow, we had to notify all signal boxes and small stations to Ashford, Eastbourne and Tunbridge. The last three had their own operators to pass the warning on. The red usually followed, and we had to do it all again: 'warning, red'. The codes for all the signal boxes all had to be remembered, you couldn't afford to make a mistake, as the signal boxes somehow managed to warn a moving train which would reduce speed to a crawl.

During raids I had to stay at the board and, if it was a bad one, I would get very frightened. We all left a key open and sang songs; our favourite was *Apple Blossom Time.* When the 'all clear' came through we had to ring everyone again and we heaved a sigh of relief. We all became very friendly over the years.[37]

Another switchboard operator, Molly Eagle, witnessed the London Blitz from Oxford:

One night I was on the switchboard talking to the telephone operator at Paddington Station and she said to me, 'Can you hear the noise?' As I listened I could hear the noise of bombs banging and whining as they fell and exploded. She told me that there was a terrific air raid going on at that very moment over London. I think she was very brave and frightened as she stuck to her post.[38]

On 6th July 1945 a convoy of US army lorries carrying 'cluster' bombs in wooden cases was using Drake's Lane Crossing at Earsham, Suffolk, when some cases fell on the track. When the driver of the following lorry braked sharply to avoid them, cases of bombs fell from his lorry, too, into the path of an approaching train. The American servicemen begged her to run to safety, but Crossing Keeper V. M. Hewitt risked her life rather than let a train collide with the bombs. She darted to her cottage, seized her emergency equipment, ran along the track towards the train (pausing only to lay three detonators on the rail in accordance with the regulations) and waved her red flag to the engine driver. The train came to a halt just 175 yards short of the obstruction. Mrs Hewitt was awarded the LNER Medal for outstanding courage and resource — the first woman to receive it.[39]

On Friday 13th June 1941, the Great Western steamer *St Patrick* was dive-bombed en route to Rosslare, killing the captain, 18 crew members and 11 passengers. It sank in just six minutes. The steerage stewardess, Elizabeth May Owen, repeatedly swam into submerged cabins and saved the lives of several passengers. She was awarded the George Medal and the Lloyd's Medal for bravery — the only woman railway employee ever to be awarded such accolades.* It is most odd that Stewardess Owen was not even mentioned in the report of the loss of the St Patrick published in the *Great Western Magazine.*

* During the war, the following were awarded to railway staff: George Cross — 3; George Medal — 28; MBE — 9; BEM — 76; Commendation — 127.

The railway offices at Paddington station after being hit by a bomb. © IWM

A scene of devastation at Middlesbrough after being bombed. © IWM

Women attaching chairs to wooden sleepers; the chairs hold the rails. Courtesy of the NRM

Blacksmith's hammer striker, Gateshead, April 1944. COURTESY OF THE NRM

'Rivet-hotter' heating up rivets for the fitter. COURTESY OF SWINDON RAILWAY MUSEUM

Fitting a bogie onto a London Transport underground train. © TFL

Shovelling wet concrete into moulds to make sleepers. COURTESY OF THE NRM

A woman fitter mending a GWR motor bus.

A points oiler and her lookout, Middlesbrough, 1942.

Freda Jenkins at Loftus signalbox, LNER , 1942.

ALL PHOTOS COURTESY OF THE NRM

Above: Cartoon from *SR Magazine*

A public notice asking passengers to limit the weight of their parcels, September 1941. RAILWAY GAZETTE

Below left: NUR joke about the supposed incompetence of female guards. COURTESY OF THE RMT

Below: NUR recruitment cartoon. COURTESY OF THE RMT

Doris Winn, guard at Wrexham. LNER MAGAZINE

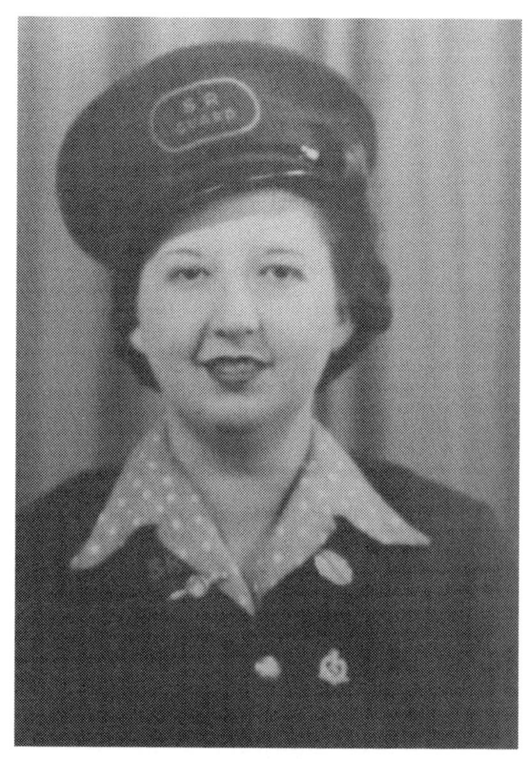

Guard Edith Rowe of Hastings depot. E. ROWE

A fitter's assistant at Cowlairs attaching or tightening a running board. COURTESY OF THE NRM

Station mistress Bertha Allan sticking a 'save gas' poster to a hoarding at Padbury. GRIGG, TOWN OF TRAINS

Violet May Holah, signalwoman at Speeton, near Filey, LNER, with her husband Fred and colleague John Tennyson, 1942. COURTESY OF THE NRM AND JOHN HINSON

Porter Joyce Watson shackling a ferry at Hull Corporation Pier. ORIGIN UNKNOWN

Porter-in-Charge Joan Long loading an oil drum at Hammerton, LNER. COURTESY OF THE NRM

Wartime Railwaywomen and Their Work

Workshops

Railway workshops were at their busiest in wartime, doubling their staff and trebling their workload. War workers were needed urgently. In 1940 the REC reached the following agreement with the unions to dilute skilled workshopmen with female staff: no woman would be employed on skilled work (unless no semi-skilled man wanted it) and all women were to be classed as temporary. For eight weeks they would be paid female rates, then awarded increments until, after 32 weeks, they received male rates – provided they could perform a man's work without supervision or assistance. It was emphasised that women's employment must not affect the range of work open to them or their pay structure after the war. The pay agreement differed from that which applied to other wages-grade women war-workers because there were 37 unions covering the shop grades – 'with sometimes 37 policies and views', grumbled one NUR official.[40]

Many women qualified for their work more quickly than their employers expected, leading the NUR to request that they receive the male rate sooner. In some cases, when her 32-week, low-paid training period was completed, a woman was sent to learn another job, thus staying on the low rate for another 32 weeks. After many complaints the matter was rectified by the NUR. However, individual cases arose which confused the issue; for example, a newly employed fitter's assistant at Stewart's Lane, SR, was a skilled driller and spot-welder, having previously held a similar post in another industry. The NUR demanded that she be paid the male rate from the outset.[41]

When the war began, just 635 women had been employed in railway workshops, all in female grades. By June 1942 this number had risen to 3,892, and an additional 10,899 were replacing men. They performed an enormous variety of tasks, becoming mechanics and operating and servicing forges, lathes and radial drills. They were steam-hammer drivers, oxy-gas flame cutters, oxy-acetylene welders, fitters, blacksmiths, electricians and shot-blasters. Some made concrete sleepers and coping posts, others assisted in building, wiring and painting new steam engines and repairing old ones. Women helped convert engines from coal to oil power, and helped to build steel-framed wagons for the USSR. They were riveters, rivet heaters, tube welders and jig-borers. Some were drop-stamp 'hammer-girls', working with red-hot steel and furnaces in the smithy. Others operated machines that shaped wooden sleepers to hold crossovers and points.

Some workshop tasks were intricate, such as assembling electrical equipment and repairing signal apparatus, as Mrs Wileman explained:

> On receiving the instruments, my job is to take them to pieces, which entails taking off nuts, terminals, coils, bolts, and numerous other parts which I thoroughly clean. ... I am frequently called upon to accompany a skilled man ... in carrying out repairs to instruments in signal boxes, etc, where I get an opportunity of appreciating how the safe working of the railways depends on our work in the Shops being of first-class order.[42]

In stark contrast to such delicate work, at Redbridge, SR, Bernard Darwin watched as 'Amazons' fashioned and creosoted sleepers:

> A sleeper weighs 1½ cwt, and two women lift it and keep on lifting it. A 'chair' weighs 46lbs and one woman lifts 1,600 chairs a day. ... They look wonderfully strong and fit, but strength is not all, for they are in charge of machines of precision which need brain and nerve as well.[43]

Darwin saw women 'whisking chains about as if they were as light as air', and remarked:

> The only occasion on which women showed any signs of discontent was when they were not allowed to work as hard as they wanted to, as hard as the men. They worked long hours, very often in all sorts of weather, and in many places under dangerous conditions from bombing attacks.[44]

By the end of his visit, Darwin felt 'particularly puny and helpless and full of admiration'.

Emma Vine lifting two chairs, each weighing 46 lbs, 22nd February 1943. BR

POLICE

The railways increased the number of policewomen they employed, and the BTP archives have details of over 100 paid Women Special Constables. A much-reproduced photograph shows a policewoman assisting evacuees on the London Underground. In 1942 the number of female officers on three of the railway police forces was given as: LNER — 28; GWR — three; SR — eight. Unfortunately, further information about these women has proved elusive. One that did gain publicity did so because of tragic circumstances: WPC Lillian Gale was run over and killed by an engine in Plymouth docks, GWR, in 1944.[45]

Porter-shunter Dale uncoupling a carriage at Connah's Quay. COURTESY OF GLYNN WAITE

STATION STAFF

There was an increase in the number of station mistresses and porters- or clerks-in-charge during the war, all of them at single-staffed stations. Among them were Joan Long at Hammerton, LNER; Dolly Palmer at Althorne, LNER; Mrs Moore at Bishopstone, SR; Mrs Gittins at Wortley, LNER; and Mrs Allan at Padbury, LMS.* Pathé News made short newsreels about Mrs Moore and Mrs Gittins.[46] Emma Harding was working as a goods porter at the LNER's Marsh Lane depot, Leeds. One day she was crossing a bridge when she saw a small station below. She remarked to her husband and fellow railway worker that she would love to work at a place like that. When the man in charge was called up, she applied and became station mistress of Penda's Way, a job she held to the end of the war.[47]

From mid-1940, applications were invited for the post of woman porter – also known as 'porterwoman', 'portress' or 'porterette' – and within two years the Big Four had engaged 6,000.† A large proportion was married, which scandalised one newspaperman, who declared: 'Mrs Smith and Mrs Jones ... [are] forced by this wicked man to give up their household duties.'[48] (The writer was, presumably, referring to Hitler and not to the Minister of Labour.) Railway magazines implored passengers to limit the weight of their luggage and parcels because 'the women are willing, but even a willing horse can be overloaded'.[49] Another reporter explained: 'The plea is based on gallantry to those of the weaker sex.'[50] It is ironic that, while such journalists sat indoors at their desks writing such condescending remarks, the 'weaker sex' was outdoors in all weathers, at all hours of the day and night, mooring ferries, coupling trains, heaving mailbags, loading hundredweight sacks of grain and dodging bombs.

A porter's work was very diverse, and women were expected to undertake whatever duties their particular location required. Marjorie Currie recalled: 'I had to get on my hands and knees and scrub the wooden floors, with just hard soap and the water from the engine.'[51] Lighting the station gas lamps often involved a long walk carrying a lighted rag on a pole, and when the air-raid warning sounded women hastily retraced their steps, extinguishing each light. Joyce Watson was a porter at Hull Corporation Pier:

> I stand on the edge of a floating pontoon, catch and haul ashore a heavy mooring rope. This is quite simple when the weather is calm, but the Humber can be very rough indeed. At these times the pontoon heaves up and down like a boat, and of course the ferry is doing likewise. Catching ropes under these conditions is no easy job, especially if you are feeling very seasick.[52]

Despite railwaymen's attempts to prevent women from performing shunter's duties, women such as Porter-Shunter Dale and her colleagues coupled and uncoupled trains on a daily basis, and without any difficulty, at Connah's Quay, a busy junction linking the LNER and LMS:

---

* Information has been received that Mrs Allan held her job until 1964, while raising six children.

† Women porters are depicted in paintings by William Roberts, now at the Imperial War Museum, and in several sketches by Helen Mackie, held at the National Railway Museum.

> After assisting with passengers, parcels, carriage doors, etc I have to attend to the uncoupling of the engine, running round of train. ... At first this work was approached with a little nervousness, but dealing with screw-shackles, vacuum brake and steam heating pipes have become almost second nature to the women porters employed here. Enginemen have become well acquainted with our requests from between their engine and vehicles to 'ease up'; 'go over the top', or 'round 'em'.[53]

Some porters handled livestock, including homing pigeons, which they had to release. Anything not in a cage could prove awkward, as Rose Eastwood found. She was leading a tethered goat through the subway at Stockport when an engine's whistle blew:

> This caused the goat to panic, and it made off like a greyhound, dragging me along with it. I dare not let it go even though I was frantic. It reminded me of a saying that was prominent amongst porters: 'Stop that dog - it's a parcel'.[54]

And, it seems, if they weren't running, they were refusing to move at all. Mary Davies, a guard at Beckenham, recalled:

> They put a goat on my train. He was ever so good, he really was. I made a fuss of him all the way up, you know, he did behave hisself [sic]. But when it came to unloading him, do you think I could move him? He would not move. I've never known an animal be so stubborn. Course, there was a gang of men outside waiting for him and they were killing 'emselves a-laughing, and in the end I couldn't move for laughing. They had to come in the brakevan to get him out.[55]

Joan Percival found being a woman a drawback when dealing with a sheep:

> One day the signalman phoned to say that there was a sheep on the line near the station, and would I go and catch it. I took a rope and found a sheep eating grass at the side of the track. I was a bit scared, but I tied the rope around its neck, then I pulled and pulled, but it would not budge. By this time trains were stopped all over the place because of this sheep, and a fireman got off his engine and came to help. As soon as he pulled the rope, the sheep trotted after him. We locked the sheep in an empty waiting room and informed the police. The farmer came and the sheep trotted after him into the van. So I guess that sheep only liked men.[56]

Other women found that 'human livestock' caused them the greatest problems:

> One night Teresa (the ticket collector) told me there was some Yankee soldiers out cold with drink and they had to catch another train on another platform. We each had a heavy four wheel barrow. We manhandled these Yanks on to the barrow — we each had two. Took them to the lift, down to the subway, up the next lift and threw them into the other train. We deserved a medal for that.[57]

Engine cleaners. Courtesy of the NRM

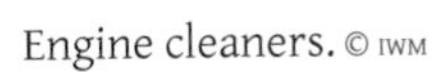

Engine cleaners. © IWM

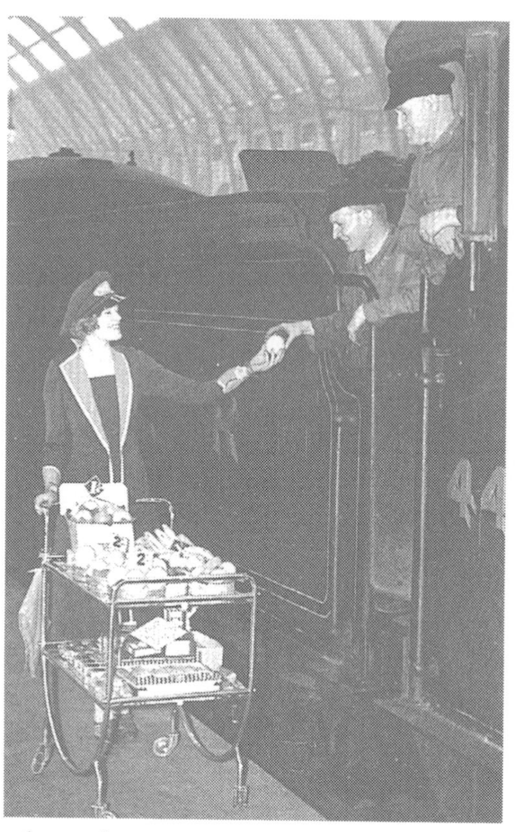

A fruit trolley assistant handing an orange to an engineman at King's Cross. ORIGIN UNKNOWN

LMS telephone operators demonstrate how they might work wearing gas masks. COURTESY OF THE NRM

Four grades of female staff at Waterloo. Left to right: guard, porter, carriage cleaner and ticket collector. ORIGIN UNKNOWN

A happy group of engine cleaners. BR

Lampwomen repairing, cleaning and filling lamps at Brighton depot, SR. The lamps had extra-long hoods to comply with wartime blackout regulations. Courtesy of the NRM

Station announcer using a megaphone.

Workshopwoman welding a motorcase.

SOME LONDON TRANSPORT STAFF

Women learning the technicalities of signalling at the LT training school. ALL PHOTOS © TFL

Goods, Cartage and Road Transport Workers

Railwaywomen handled goods, delivered them to customers, and drove and maintained the various types of road vehicle used for those purposes. Thousands drove luggage tractors, horse-drawn vans and two- and three-ton motor lorries and worked as vanguards, stablewomen, and chauffeuses to senior managers. Annie Hughes, for example, passed her Heavy Goods Vehicle Group 1 test and drove a two-ton lorry for the GWR:

> I worked seven days a week for six months without a break. I was very fit and muscular. Twice a week I used to deliver a full load of beer to two pubs. I had to get the barrels down off the lorry with a gantry, get them down to the cellars with two ropes, then stillage them. I delivered two tons of flour, each bag weighed 135lb. I carried each bag against my stomach. A Liverpool newspaper ran an article on me: 'Utility lady of North Wales: a young woman who could do any job a man could do.'[58]

Mrs Grace Healy of Sheffield drove a horse drawn van:

> With trepidation I went to the stables situated in arches below the station approach. The 'boss' there eyed me up – slim, 5'2', 'green as grass' – and asked me what experience I had, and was I used to horses? I replied 'Not really, but I love horses'. Was I scared of them? I faltered: 'N-n-no, not at all!' Eventually I became a fully fledged driver with a van lad at the back who was a foot taller than me, and somewhat resentful of my position.[59]

Kathleen White of Lancaster worked in a goods delivery office

> I was responsible for the carter's records. There were five horses and three motor-lorries to deal with. I made all the loads up when the details were brought from the warehouse. Of course it was a job previously done by a man and as a 16-year-old girl I quickly grew up.
>
> The men's work sheets were very detailed, giving the destination of each load, the approximate weight and the time taken. On the lorry sheets the petrol consumption was given, very important in those war-time days. All but two of the drivers were old enough to be my granddad, but when I told them they had to do a certain thing, they accepted the situation and I never had any swear words directed at me.
>
> We had many traumatic incidents whilst I was looking after the lorry drivers. The worst one was when five out of the seven horses were poisoned by sulphur that had been contaminated by arsenic from a local farm.[60]

Pressmen wrote articles in tones of amazed admiration for women goods porters, who performed extremely heavy work:

> They were working in gangs, four loaders to each vehicle. ... This legion of women raced their barrows backwards and forwards over the cobbles as if they were a nest of ants that had just been disturbed. Some of them sang in loud strong voices that echoed around the railway arches. They were well and they were happy. The work, they told me, kept them fit and gave them an appetite for food they had never known before. They're 'in the swim'. Because they are women of spirit that is where they want to be.[61]

Women were employed as numbertakers, recording the serial numbers of carriages and wagons as they came into goods' yards or stations. They operated cranes 40 feet above the ground, and with precise judgement they 'luffed' enormous loads onto barges or the landing-stages of tall warehouses. Operating 'Goliath' cranes, women lifted containers between trains, ships and lorries. Landing the containers perfectly was a source of great pride. A grandmother at Nine Elms, SR, changed wagon wheels using heavy jacks. Thousands of railwaywomen undertook this kind of heavy work for up to six years.

Mrs Russell, a widow with 15 children, returned to the job she had held during the First World War as a goods porter at Nottingham, LMS, and spent eight hours a day shifting bags of slate dust weighing 140 lbs. She told journalists:

> Am I tired when I finish work? Not a bit of it. I start at eight and finish at five. When I get home, there is time to do a good wash. A job like this will add ten years to my life.[62]

Of course, grumblers would not have seen their names in the paper the next day. Quotes like this acted as propaganda to ensure that replacements would be available should such women succumb to exhaustion. Speaking long after the war, some former railwaywomen related quite a different story:

> It was a struggle lugging heavy mail-bags, milk churns, enormous wooden packages, bicycles, pieces of machinery, perishables, and livestock. The barrows were very difficult to push and manoeuvre especially backing them up to the guards' vans. We worked 18 different shifts, eight to 12 hours, commencing at different times, like 2 or 3 a.m. The changeover was often only 8 to 10 hours, in which time we ate, slept, washed, and went back on duty, having walked miles.[63]

> I was 19 and had only ever done shop-work. I was the youngest of 110 women employed in the goods at Leeds. We were in the throes of a bad winter; the weather was atrocious, with heavy snow. When I was given a shovel to clear snow off the tarpaulin covering some wagons I nearly crumbled. However, five o' clock came (I never thought it would). I had to walk home about a mile, wet through, cold, stiff and bent double — and fed up. I hated it at first, it was so very hard. A little bit different from handling bread and groceries to ten stone sacks of flour, wheat, sheaves of leather, crates, barrels of wine, shell cases, ammunition boxes, brass ingots and asbestos. We worked outside all the time. It was rough, and after handling pig iron my hands and fingers were red raw and cut to shreds, even wearing gloves didn't help. However, they did eventually harden up and felt like rhinoceros skin.[64]

> Very heavy work but we got used to it. At London Bridge we used to have to unload all the mailbags, and my knuckles used to be raw where we used to pull them across, and we used to have to heave them up onto the platform, that was the hardest job of the lot. That's partly why I went out as a guard. I thought 'Well it can't be no harder than it is up here'.[65]

Maintenance workers

Women were employed in civil, mechanical and electrical engineers' departments all over Britain, maintaining the whole range of railway structures and equipment, from the track to the clocks. Mrs E. Robinson, the first woman rubber-tyre inspector, was given responsibility for 924 vehicles and 885 trailers spread across 40 LMS depots. At the age of 52, Mrs Lovsey became a points oiler at Woodford, LNER. Her domain comprised four marshalling yards and huge, complicated junctions with the LMS and GWR. It included about 300 sets of points over 90 acres, which she traversed all day carrying an oval oil bucket and a long-handled brush.[66] Ellen Bevan dug holes by the lineside to take cables and lighting poles, while former hairdresser Mary Causebrook was a chainman in the engineering department at Northampton, LMS:

> Starting work at 7.30 a.m., I was sent to a different location each day, usually with different draughtsmen. We surveyed bridges, sidings, goods yards, etc. We would be out all day, with sandwiches eaten sitting in the ganger's hut with tea out of his old black can. My job was to hold the staff for the draughtsman to read the level. Sometimes when doing the gauge of the track we had to stamp the cant with a metal stamp on the lead posts every 100 feet, so there was quite a bit of walking to do. In tunnels we also had to measure the height of the walls with a huge wooden gauge – often getting soaked with black water dripping off the roof. On the track we always had a lookout man to warn us of approaching trains – in tunnels we had one at each end. One had a whistle and the other a hooter to tell us which track the train was coming along. When this happened we had to shelter in the little alcoves until it passed. It's a funny feeling when two trains pass you in a tunnel: you feel 'drawn' towards them. On one occasion we had just rigged up the gauge when we heard the hooter and having no time to retrieve it we ran for an alcove and the express smashed the gauge to bits.[67]

Women worked in the signal & telegraph departments as linesman's labourers. They went underneath signalboxes, along the track, through tunnels and up signal ladders, checking the 'run' of the signalling wires. These would be freed if jammed, scraped of dirt and oiled.

For the first time, women were allowed to perform track maintenance, labour from which they had been barred even during the First World War. By 1944 over 2,000 were engaged in this work. Newsreel exists of them working with spades to prepare sleeper beds for the reception of ballast, carrying and placing the sleepers, and tightening the fishplates.[68] Photographs also bear witness to women's work on the track, tightening bolts, oiling points and spading weeds away. Emily Jones, who worked in a 20-woman gang based at Shotton, recalled an incident in which a manually operated rail trolley became derailed with the gang on board. Several women were injured and Mrs Jones broke her arm.[69] Women were also employed to clean tunnels on the London Underground. A reporter described the working life of a 'fluffer' in a tunnel under the Thames:

> Here a most efficient women's gang was at work as part of the permanent way staff. Their job is to clean the track. Sleepers and 'chairs' become caked with fluff and brake dust, and the women - 'fluffers', as they are called - remove the deposits with scrapers and stiff brushes ... These pleasant, happy-looking women work in pairs, collecting the dust into heaps, which are shovelled into containers and removed by special train. We left these cheerful women singing at their work and showing a fine team spirit.[70]

The first woman wheeltapper, Mrs Christina Axworthy, worked in Derby yard, LMS, from June 1943. Wheeltappers walked alongside slow-moving trains, tapping the wheels with a long-handled metal hammer and swiftly attaching report cards to those that did not ring 'true'. 1943 also saw the first women fog-signallers, work that the NUR had prevented women from performing during the First World War. When fog or falling snow was so thick that drivers could not see the signals, a railway worker would be detailed to sit alone in the fog, often on a lonely and remote piece of track, for many hours, often in freezing condition, in a hut at the base of a signal post, in order to place detonators on the rail to warn enginemen if the signal was at danger or at caution. The fog-signaller was not left unattended; the ganger looked after them with food and a hot drink in a thermos. There was a fire in a brazier outside each hut and this was kept supplied with coal by the ganger who brought it from the signalbox.

Women were also employed as gas fitters. One of them, Margaret Barnes, looked after all the lamps in signalboxes, sidings, goods yards and sheds from Yorkshire to the Scottish border. She said: 'I love an outdoor life. It's great fun — and thrilling at times — especially when I'm perched high on my ladder and an express whizzes by beneath me.'[71]

In the 1930s, carriage cleaning came to be seen as suitable work for women. Just before the war, 739 women were so employed (as were 5,748 male cleaners) and by mid-1942 there were 3,426. When Victoria Simpson took the job at London's Victoria station, she found a surprising number of tasks awaited her:

> Carriage cleaner? That was a laugh, you name it we did it, cleaning inside and outside trains and the brass handles, sweeping the platforms and forecourt, cleaning the signal lamps, tanking — which was climbing on to the roof of the trains with a hose pipe and filling the water tanks for the toilets and basins with water through a hole in the roof. We also filled up the tanks for the buffet cars on the 'Brighton Belle' and the NAAFI cars on troop trains. We cleaned all the trains for the evacuation of Dunkirk; they were returned to Dover in a couple of hours. We unloaded mail bags from luggage vans, put them on trolleys and loaded them onto Royal Mail vans for delivery to Mount Pleasant. Then we unloaded the vans with tomatoes and vegetables from Worthing and put them on lorries for Covent Garden.
>
> We used acid to clean the outside of the trains using a brush on a long stick — which we called Audrey — the acid stayed on for about one hour by which time we had covered an eight coach train. Then we had to wash it off, sometimes in the winter the acid and water froze on the windows and it was hard work, couldn't use hot water, the windows would have broke. The only hot water we had was an old copper that we kept going with coal from the engine drivers, and that was for scrubbing floors and sides. One lady went through with raw soap and a small Audrey and second would come along rinsing, bending down all the time right through the train, and a third to dry it up. We could get through a train in no time. We had our funny moments. Once we were cleaning a troop train and when we came to one carriage — it was just before Christmas — hanging from all the luggage racks the troops had blown up their Army issue of condoms and they were hanging like balloons all through the coach. Needless to say we were in hysterics.
>
> We all had children and our husbands were in the Forces. We only earned about £4 and we had to do shift work in between dodging the Doodlebugs and we had to train for fire fighting also. We often had to walk over the live lines. All in all we worked very hard. I stayed in the job for seven years.[72]

Engine cleaning was closed to women after the First World War; however, in March 1941 the unions agreed that women could, once again, perform the work, but only after strenuous efforts had been made to obtain male labour, and providing that no attempt was made to train women to fire or drive engines. By June 1942 the LNER and LMS employed 747 women; the other companies soon followed and, by 1944, there were 8,500.

> We worked in pairs. I had two long steel rods about three to four yards long, one had a screw end; one had a very pointed end. Wearing clogs, we had to climb upon the engine, walk round to the front, open the door to the smoke box, which contained lots of tubes reaching from the smoke box to the fire box. I then had to rod each tube, which was very hard if they were blocked with clinker. My mate then had to steam blow, fixing her pipe to the steam pipe on the side of the engine, then blow each tube. It was a very dirty job and we had to be very careful when it was raining or ice about when climbing the engine. It was also very dark we had a little can with cotton wool soaked in oil for a torch. We pulled the cotton wool through the spout, and lit it. The men were very good; we got on very well with them. We done shift work. 7.00 a.m. to 4.00 p.m., 1.00 p.m. to 10.00 p.m., 10.00 p.m. to 7.00 a.m. Some of the older men told us that women worked down the loco in the first war but they cleaned the outside of the engines. I was at Leicester loco shed for four years. I enjoyed working there but wouldn't like to do it again, as a lot of rats ran about and it was very cold working outside all the while in all weather. [73]

> At Cambridge we were given boiler suits and mob caps, a bundle of thick, oily cloths and a scraper for the wheels. Each engine had three girls working on it, cleaning the boiler, smoke stack, tender and wheels. This was where the scraper came in: thick, black grime and grease gathered there and this had to be scraped out, cleaned with the oily cloths and dried, so that the tappers could test the wheels for cracks. Getting clean at night was a nightmare. I remember using paraffin, Vim, Swarfega. Each time my mother put clean sheets and pillow cases on the bed they would be black in the morning. I used to have a piece of old cloth placed over my pillow.[74]

> The engines would come into Hither Green overnight and the firemen would clean their fires out over the pit. In the morning they would be red hot, so we cooled them down with a hosepipe and one woman would get in and shovel the ashes on to the edge of the pit. Then we would fetch two trucks, and four women would shovel the ash into the trucks. While we were doing this, the bombs were falling.[75]

Women scraping rust off a bridge, preparatory to repainting. Darwin

Twin sisters 'man' a platform refreshment trolley at Waterloo, SR. Origin unknown

Women hauling newly-made sleepers at Redbridge, SR. BR

A workshopwoman operating a power lathe.
COURTESY OF THE NRM

SR Porter Edna Pontifex.
COURTESY OF E. PONTIFEX

Four women and five men in a tracklaying gang, off to perform lifting and packing on the GWR.

COURTESY OF SWINDON RAILWAY MUSEUM

Women shifting heavy crates of Newcastle Brown Ale, Newcastle Forth Goods, October 1942.

COURTESY OF THE NRM

An electrician's assistant joining telephone wires by the side of the track.
COURTESY OF THE NRM

Porter Mary Jordan working as a pilotwoman on the five-mile single line from Newchurch to Risley, LNER. At 19 she was the youngest of four women porters in the area who, in an emergency, could be called upon to act as pilotwomen.
COURTESY OF FRED DARBYSHIRE

On-Train Staff

Women replaced men in all on-train catering roles. They also worked as train attendants, to maintain the blackout, help passengers and deal with infringements of the bylaws. Mary McCluskey worked as an attendant on the LNER main line from Manchester to London, stayed overnight and returned the following day. She felt her job had 'a grand future' (it was abolished after the war.)[76] Women were also employed as travelling porters, assisting the guard by dealing with parcel traffic en route.

The railways wanted to employ women as guards but this was not as simple as with other grades. Traditionally, guards worked on goods trains for a number of years before being promoted to passenger work. The duties of goods guards were not deemed suitable for women because the work involved heavy and dangerous tasks on a daily basis, such as coupling wagons, applying handbrakes, pulling points and walking on the track in the vicinity of moving vehicles. An additional problem was that goods trains moved slowly over long distances and had no toilet facilities. Passenger guards performed less heavy manual labour, worked fewer night shifts and had access to public toilets, so the companies decided it was best to recruit women straight into that grade. As this contravened union agreements on seniority and promotion, consent had to be obtained from the NUR EC, who agreed, provided the employment of female guards was kept to the smallest possible numbers, and no woman was to be placed in charge of a train if she could not carry out all the duties normally performed by a male guard.[77]

Some men resented women being allowed to bypass the promotional procedures; the more canny realised it guaranteed that women would be dispensed with at the end of the war, when all special wartime arrangements were rescinded. The situation led to some curious episodes; for example, at Aberbeeg the NUR challenged the recruitment of a new male recruit to a passenger guard's job, insisting that a woman replace him.[78]

Women were employed as guards by each of the Big Four companies between 1941 and 1947. The GWR engaged the first and by June 1942 it had 46. Although during the First World War the London underground railways had set the precedent of employing female guards, London Transport did not engage any during the Second World War.

The women were sent on intense training courses where they were inculcated with safety procedures, after which they had to pass a rigorous exam. Former guard Louisa Jupp recalled that at Brighton, SR:

> We did a month at school learning all the roads, all the routes, and what you do when you use the detonators, and what happens if there is an accident on the other line; about going to signalboxes — if you stand too long at one signal you've got to get down and find out, but remembering to pull the Westinghouse [brake handle] down otherwise the train's going to go without you. You had to know your signals — your semaphore, your colour light — the road. Then you had to know about the train, the butterflies†, and then you had to know the rules — what happens if there's an emergency. And you went through this day after day. Somebody came down from Redhill to examine us, then you had a week with a male guard, so that you got into the running of the things. And after a week that's it: you're on your own — and the best of British luck![79]

† External indicators on carriages that show where the communication cord has been pulled.

And they certainly needed it. At some depots a little difficulty was experienced when trying to obtain the necessary 'on the job' training with another guard, as Edie Winser (now Rowe) explained: 'Some said, "I want no women in with me", but the majority didn't mind'.[80] After the training, there were the enginemen to deal with, as former fireman Mr Reynolds recalled:

> You can imagine a man about 50 or more years, only ever worked with men, suddenly being told that he was booked with a woman guard. The ones I worked with were a miserable lot and would have been most upset – even to refusing to take out the train. Younger men were more tolerant. I think that the strains of the war, long hours, the bombing etc. took their toll.[81]

Most women enjoyed the work. Violet Ridler (now Lee) was based at Gloucester:

> I loved the job. When I clocked on duty, I'd have a chat with the fireman and driver, check the paraffin tail lamp, take the weight and description of each vehicle, and look to see that the emergency chains on each vehicle had not been pulled. I'd check the brakes were acting correctly, and give the tare weight to the driver, and enter it in my log book – also the engine number and the driver's name. I used to climb on the engine, have my egg and bacon cooked on the steel shovel in the firebox, also a brew of tea in my enamel pint can which I carried everywhere with me. We worked from Hereford to Gloucester at night. At halts in the middle of nowhere I would lean out of the guards' van window swinging a white light to help the driver know exactly where to stop, to let the country folk off.[82]

Many women guards wore men's caps and waistcoats with whistles and fob-watches on chains. Dressed like men, they copied men's habits, such as waving their green flags while standing on the platform, then boarding the train as it moved off. 'You liked to do the same as the men – be as cocky as them – and let them see you could do anything they could do,' said former Retford guard Clara Evans.[83]

Some railways trained female guards to couple and uncouple engines and carriages, which involved manhandling extremely heavy, greasy iron couplings and manipulating brake-pipes. Others banned them from such work. Gloucester guard Phyllis Mortimer was told that women could not do these tasks, because: 'It's in case you strain yourself, you see, and of course your bust would get in the way.'[84] She heard of one woman who coupled a carriage to her train – without difficulty or mishap – but when the District Inspector found out he was furious and sternly warned the others never to repeat such folly.

The emergency procedures drilled into women during their training were rarely put into practice, but they were not found wanting when a crisis did arise. Hastings guard Edie Winser (now Rowe) was the guard of a train that derailed late one night across the electrified lines at Willingdon Junction, Eastbourne. After protecting the train she led the passengers to safety, then had to stay on site all night until her train was re-railed. Eventually, she reached home at 6.30 a.m., after 16 hours on duty.[85] Her supervisor had sent a messenger to her parents to warn them that she would be out all night (in those days working-class homes did not have telephones).

Hair-raising as this incident was, Guard Winser was lucky compared with Florence Haden, who on 16th September 1946 was faced with every guard's worst nightmare. As her train, the 9.32 p.m. Hatfield to King's Cross, was braking for Potter's Bar, Guard Haden stood up and made towards her brakevan door in the usual way. Suddenly a violent jolt threw her to the floor: the train had derailed while changing tracks and crashed into the buffer stops. Carriages were skewed across the adjacent lines, where the 9.45 p.m. King's Cross to Edinburgh had immediately collided with them. Shocked and disorientated, Guard Haden stood up, went to her window and peered out into the darkness:

> I knew we were not at a station. I saw what appeared to be an obstruction. I got out and heard an up train approaching. I could not see it. I ran towards the approaching train shouting as I did so and showing a red light in my hand lamp. I noticed that the brakes were being applied to the up train, but the train passed me.

The driver of the third train, the 5 p.m. Bradford to King's Cross, had in fact seen Guard Haden's handlamp and also saw the signal ahead of him change to red. He quickly applied his brakes, colliding with the wreckage at a greatly reduced speed. Although between them the three trains carried 1,075 passengers, only two were killed. The Ministry of War Transport, commending all the staff involved, especially praised Mrs Haden's 'alertness and action'.[86]

SIGNALLING

Wartime railwaywomen worked in two different jobs in signalboxes: as train register recorders and as signalwomen. The former were known colloquially as 'box girls' because their predecessors were 'box lads'. It was their duty to keep a register of all manoeuvres made in relation to every train processed by the box. They were employed only in large, busy signalboxes; in small, single-manned boxes the signalman or woman had time to perform this task themselves.

Over 1,200 signalwomen were employed during the Second World War, mostly in single-manned boxes on branch lines.* Training took between two and four months and culminated in a rigorous examination. There were two teaching methods: classroom and box, or box-only. In-box training usually involved being alone with a man — often causing awkwardness on both sides and arousing concern from the trainees' parents and the signalmen's wives. Trainees were thoroughly inculcated and later examined on regulations and emergency procedures, and their responsibilities were clearly stated to them, as Phyllis Dewhurst of New Hey, LMS, recalled:

> I went to Manchester for my final exams. A man congratulated me and said I'd passed. I gave him a beaming smile which faded rapidly as he told me, 'Of course, you know you could be prosecuted or had up for manslaughter if something goes wrong.' After that he shook my hand, and I left.[87]

The hours worked were different from box to box, depending mainly on the amount of traffic. At Marlow, GWR, the box was manned from 5.20 a.m. until midnight, and the three signalwomen worked a three shift system: 5.20 a.m. till 1.20 p.m., 8 a.m. till 4 p.m. and 4 p.m. till midnight. The signalwoman on the 5.20 a.m. shift had to sell workmen's tickets until the booking office opened and light the signalbox fire. Whoever did the 8 a.m. shift

* There were 10,300 signalboxes in Britain in 1943.

cleaned the station, toilets and waiting rooms before taking over the box when the early shift signalwoman left at 1.20 p.m.

Most signalwomen worked in the smaller boxes, often in isolated locations in rural areas. Unauthorised visitors were strictly forbidden and an eight or 12 hour shift was often worked in complete solitude. In the small hours a signalbox could be an eerie place, full of rather unnerving noises caused by iron and steel creaking as they contracted and expanded with temperature changes — and the scuttling of mice and rats underneath the signalbox. However, compared to most pre-war 'women's work', signalling was highly responsible and much more worthwhile, as Doreen Stevens recalled:

> I was 16 when war was declared, working in domestic service — which I hated! This was not a reserved occupation so at 18 we would have to register for war work; instead I joined the GWR at Steventon in Berkshire as a Grade 2 porter. Sometimes I worked in the Causeway Crossing Box, relieving the crossing keepers on annual leave. This gave me a liking for Box work so when the District Signalling Inspector suggested I went to Collingbourne Signalbox I was delighted.

No woman interviewed said anything negative about signalbox work. Judy Gascoyne enjoyed her on-the-job training in Marlow box and 'longed to take it over'. She remarked, 'On the whole, I had a great time!' Some took enormous pride in their new status. Joan Percival, who worked at Warrington, LMS, recalled:

> Our box covered an eight-mile stretch of track in both directions, a high-level bridge and a station. It was a very busy line with double-headed crossover points and three sidings — one was half a mile away, another, one mile away. The training was very vigorous and I only knew three other signalwomen in the north west. You had to be at least 21, and special permission was sought for me as I was 19. I was the youngest ever placed in charge of a signalbox.[88]

Women found their strength greatly enhanced by the exertion of pulling signal levers: one remembered having 'muscles like duck-eggs'. Another found her biceps no longer fitted into the sleeves of her clothes. However, the belief that all women were physically inadequate for the work continued. In some cases a particularly heavy signal lever was too difficult for an individual woman to operate. In 1943, the signalwomen employed on the Burry Port & Gwendraeth Valley Section of the GWR found some levers too hard and their Divisional Superintendent asked the signals and telegraphs department to remedy this. After initial alterations he found that:

> Although Miss Melton can manage it fairly well, Miss Morgans, who is slightly built, has a little difficulty in doing so. I have no doubt that with a little practice, she could master this, but if something further can be done to ease the pulling operation, it would be a distinct advantage ... The lever has been more difficult to pull today after the sun had been shining on the spring and Miss Melton then failed to pull it over.

Further alterations were made until Miss Morgans could to operate the lever with ease.[89] It was by no means the case that all slightly-built women had trouble with heavy levers. When a signalling inspector watched Vera Perry — five feet tall and weighing seven and a half stone – operate her distant signal 1,750 yards away, he was astonished: 'Unless I saw you pull that lever,' he remarked, 'I would not believe you could do it.'[90] The timeworn male belief that women could not cope in emergencies was frequently aired, but signalwomen themselves strongly disagreed. As Joan Percival put it: 'Men and women face their responsibilities exactly the same: short of dying themselves, they would do their utmost to prevent a train crash.' So deeply were they ingrained that, 45 years after her training, Mrs Percival remembered the emergency procedures in detail:

> The signalling was done by cipher Morse code, the Morse code took too long, so it had to be cipher, that means you could tap a whole sentence with one or two dots and dashes. 1 tap = call attention; 2 taps = train approaching your section; 3 taps = is your line clear for an express passenger train? 3.2 = 3 taps, pause, 2 taps = is your line clear for a light engine? 6 taps = obstruction danger and upon receiving it you slam all signals back to 'stop' and put three detonators on the line, in double quick time to try to prevent a train crash being made worse by having further trains run into it.[91]

Unfortunately signalwomen suffered constant insults from their male colleagues, sometimes via their trade union newspaper, which published letters from men who assumed that signalwomen were not properly trained. One man claimed that examining signalwomen on the rules was 'a farce', and remarked: 'There's a telephone and a man at the box on each side, and trust in Providence'.[92]

Railway accidents are rare and only a tiny proportion of signallers are ever involved in an emergency. When an incident arose, signalwomen acted no differently to signalmen. Hilda Lund recalled working with a goods train that knocked down and killed a platelayer: 'I didn't panic; in fact I was praised at the inquest for my coolness in putting all my signals to danger once I had been told what happened'.[93]

One night in dense fog, Gracie Adamek was operating Long Eaton signalbox on the LMS. A combination of experience and sharp hearing made it possible for her to ascertain by sound alone that a train had passed a yellow signal too fast to stop at the next, which was red. The line ahead was occupied by another train, and Mrs Adamek realised that two trains were on a collision course:

> I had to run down the track as fast as possible and place detonators on the track and wave a red lamp. He did just overrun the signal but managed to stop a few yards short of the Attenburgh train, thus averting what would have been a terrific crash.[94]

Vera Perry, signalwoman at Collingbourne Ducis, GWR, noticed that a 28-van goods train had no tail lamp. Seconds later five 'runaway' vans, along with the guard's brakevan, flew past. Realising the train was divided in two, she immediately implemented the emergency procedures, averting a serious accident. Later, the guard involved paid her a call to thank her for saving the lives of three men: himself and two trackmen travelling in his brakevan.[95] LMS signalwoman Mrs R. Jago spotted some wagons running away on a gradient and reacted swiftly, pulling points to divert them off the running line and into a sand drag. She later received a commendation and an award for 'taking prompt and effective action to prevent injuries to staff'.[96]

Working Conditions and Welfare

Many women who joined the railways had little or no idea what to expect. The industry was more structured and its unions more powerful than was the case with most 'women's work'. This brought many benefits such as definitive job descriptions, demarcation, national pay scales and conditions of service, and strong union representation. The drawback was that all these structures were designed with a male workforce in mind.

All companies opened women's welfare departments because 'the substitution of women for men brought with it a host of welfare questions, which the male supervisors found themselves quite unable to tackle,' explained former LNER Women's Welfare Supervisor Kate Henderson.[97] Welfare officers undertook an enormous task; one of their duties was to place those women who had been directed to railways by the Ministry of Labour, another was to assist with domestic and childcare problems. In many cases, women wished to work on the railways but were unable to obtain childcare. Often, welfare officers were able to find vacancies in kindergartens and sometimes they could arrange alternative hours of duty to facilitate women's participation in railway work. They also investigated women's applications for release, in an attempt to reduce labour turnover. Another welfare office dealt with male staff.

Welfare officers were often matronly women with long service in other clerical grades who had a special interest in helping others. One of them, Miss Pattenden, had been first woman clerk in the GCR operating superintendent's office when she joined the railway service in 1915. During her career she gained promotion to personal secretary and qualified as a Sister of the Order of St John. By the Second World War she was in her 50s and was appointed Assistant Women's Welfare Supervisor at Marylebone. (She retired in 1953 with 38 years' service.)

Welfare officers were concerned about the arduous work carried out by women and usually tested tasks themselves to ensure they were within the 'average' woman's capacity. Sometimes, this didn't have quite the expected result. For example, after Bessie Ellinor had worked at Cheriton box for several months without any difficulty, the SR Women's Welfare Officer arrived to investigate whether the signal levers were suitable for women to operate – and found that she couldn't move them! They were particularly worried about goods porters, and were surprised that they were able to lift heavy crates, sacks, barrels and milk churns all day. However, many of them were quite burly before they joined the industry, as one clerk pointed out:

> Pre-war Lancashire women did not boast many labour saving devices in the home and they would have been used to lugging coal from outside; carrying dolly tubs for their washing, etc. Some of them were twice as big as the men, with terrific muscles.[98]

The influx of women highlighted the already poor working environment and the inadequate staff accommodation that had been endured by generations of railwaymen. In some offices working conditions had not changed since the last century. 'We sat on high stools at high, Dickensian-looking desks, working under gas mantles,' recalled Vera Williams.[99] Mess-rooms were usually grubby and sometimes infested with vermin. Audrey Brown recalled Wolverhampton guards' room:

> It was like something out of Dickens: gas lighting, dim. Everywhere was terribly grimy from the smoke. The majority of the guards' rooms were an absolute disgrace. Somebody would bring a broom, sweep them out, and the dust would go miles high.[100]

Responsibility for heating the workplace also fell to the staff. Susan Sallis, employed by the GWR as a shorthand typist, remembered: 'My most important job was to light the courtier stove each morning and fill the coal buckets for the day.'[101] The majority of railway workers accepted the poor environment but some locations were insufferable, causing staff to seek out more agreeable and salubrious surroundings in public houses.

Women tolerated piecemeal arrangements for toilet facilities in an industry built only for male staff. Most had to use the public WCs but one gang of porters secretly locked off a cubicle for their sole use, having discovered that the lock could be operated with a key from a sardine tin. Signalwomen used whatever had been provided for their male predecessors; however, at Marlow, where three signalwoman were employed, the GWR bowed to pressure from the NUR and had a special toilet built right outside the box.[102] Women's welfare officers checked up on toilet facilities. One rather dainty, middle class officer was appalled at the bucket-toilet provided at Cheriton, SR, for Signalwoman Ellinor – a country girl who had used them all her life.

Signalwomen had no mess-room and no meal breaks. They cooked on the stove provided and ate when they could, between trains. Other grades shared canteens and mess-rooms with men, who taught them to play cards and dominoes, and with whom they shared anecdotes and huge pots of strong tea. Mabel Watkinson, a wartime porter at Armley Goods, Leeds, remembered:

> Our mess-room had an old Yorkshire stone fireplace with an oven, and the fire never went out, it was roaring up the chimney. On the trivet was the largest iron kettle I had ever seen. It was heaven to get in there to eat our sandwiches and make tea in our pint pots, lifting the kettle off the hob – feet apart and with both hands, it was so heavy.[103]

The House of Commons heard complaints about the working conditions of railwaywomen several times. One case concerned Stratford, where 75 women were employed and up to 50 might be on duty at any time, and yet there were only two toilets and six washbasins. Railway premises were not covered by the 1937 Factories Act but, having suffered the humiliation of being criticised in Parliament, the LNER voluntarily added five toilets and six basins.

Another domestic problem discussed by politicians was the situation at Thornton Junction, LNER, where women porters had no mess-room. The station master had instructed them to use the ladies' waiting room but later, after a passenger had complained that wet clothing was draped about the room, he upbraided one of the porters. She protested to the NUR, which passed the matter to the local MP, who referred it to the Ministry of War Transport, which sent it the REC, which passed it back to the LNER, which denied the existence of any problem.[104]

Although some women raised complaints about the poor working environment, very few grumbled about their duties, although two women callers-up at Shrewsbury, LMS, said that they felt unsafe walking the dark streets all night to wake railway workers for duty. Their supervisors were happy to send them out in pairs, but management had insisted they go singly. The NUR supported the women and settled the case in their favour.[105]

Accidents were common on railways and thousands of women were injured in the course of their war-work. Most accidents were minor but some were very serious. In 1943 Newcastle goods porter Mrs E. McGuigan suffered injuries that led to premature labour and a still-born child. The LNER admitted liability and paid her 40s a week compensation. Trackwoman C. Brown of Basford was knocked down by some wagons and suffered the loss of a leg; in addition, she sustained such severe injuries to the foot of the other that it was later amputated. Miss Brown fought her case with the support of the legal department of the NUR (fortunately, she had joined the union just three days before the accident), which managed to prove that the LMS was at fault for failing to provide a lookout. She received £3,334 6s 2d compensation.[106] Another trackwoman lost both feet when she was run over by wagons at Whifflet, near Airdrie, LMS.[107] This accident was described in *The LMS at War*, which names the (male) ganger who saved her life but, curiously, not the unfortunate trackwoman who was the subject of the story.

One day in 1948 Lampwoman Edna Higgins was helping an electrician to trace a fuse when she fell through a glass roof which – for war precautions – had been painted. The Western Region of British Railways declined her claim for damages because the NUR could not prove that the electrician had specifically instructed her to climb upon the roof.[108]

The number of women war workers killed in the course of railway duty has not been recorded. From personal testimony it is known that Mrs A Hughes, a carter at Kentish Town, was killed in 1944, and that an unnamed woman died when a bomb hit the workshops at Ashford, (Kent), SR. Porter Doris Glindon was loading mailbags at Stockport, LMS, when she slipped and fell between the platform and a moving train, severing both legs. She died later in hospital.[109]

Pay and Perks

The railway companies' pay, bonus, and war wage arrangements, covering over half a million staff in diverse undertakings, were extremely complicated and changed constantly throughout the war. Generally, women war-workers were paid 4s less than the male rate for their first 12 weeks, then the male rate.

Just as during the First World War, a woman could not receive the same pay as her male counterpart. One reason was that the war wage (paid from January 1940) began at 3s for women and 4s for men (5s for workshopmen) and a differential was maintained with every increase. By mid-1943, when men's war wage had reached 20s 6d, women's was only 16s 6d (15s 6d for workshopwomen). The average pay at that time for women in male wages grades was 64s compared with men's 105s 5d. This was mainly due to men's performing more overtime, which was partly because supervisors gave preference to men, in the belief that they needed more money than women, and partly because many women had to hurry away to collect children from schools and nurseries and begin their second shift as housewives and mothers.

The majority of women accepted pay disparity; after all, they were earning more than they had in women's work. Signalwoman Judy Gascoyne recalled earning £5.10s a week after tax and deductions, a superb wage compared with the £1.10s she earned as a teacher. Elizabeth Cox earned £5 as a porter compared with £3 as a shop assistant before the war. Most women enjoyed railway life and were proud of working in an essential industry. Furthermore, this was national war service, so it was unpatriotic to complain. Former porter Rose Eastwood explained:

> The rate of pay for women was slightly less than for male personnel because women's rights was not in force until after the war. So we just grinned and carried out our work without any thoughts of discontent, etc.[110]

Not every woman was acquiescent; there was agitation throughout the war. The NUR did not ask for equal pay for women. It demanded only that those in male grades received male rates, to protect men from undercutting by women and to preserve the 'rate for the job'. The union was content for women in unisex jobs – clerks, carriage cleaners and crossing keepers – to receive lower rates than men, even when engaged in identical work, and for women in female grades to be paid less than men performing comparable work. Indeed, the notion of equal pay was considered a suitable topic for jokes in *The Railway Review*. One ran as follows: 'The time will come,' shouted the speaker, 'when women will get men's wages.' 'Yes,' interjected the little man, 'next Friday night.'[111]

The rank-and-file tried to progress matters but this proved impossible without support from the NUR leadership. For example, in 1942 Earl's Court NUR branch demanded equal war wages for women, but the EC unanimously opposed it. In contrast, RCA leaders supported equal pay for equal work, and women clerks' inter-war campaign was reawakened when many were transferred to men's work on women's rates; furthermore, the great influx of war-workers boosted the clerks' campaign by providing greater numerical strength.

The issue of railwaywomen's unequal pay was tackled by a Railway Staff Conference (RSC) in 1944. War-workers were omitted from consideration because they were temporary. Women in female grades were disregarded because they had no men with whom to claim equality. This left only unisex grades: clerks, carriage cleaners and crossing keepers. Companies paid women clerks 20% less than men, but the RSC agreed that this was a perfectly acceptable practice, because the Civil Service did the same. Carriage cleaners also earned 20% less than men but, as they did not climb on to the roofs to fill the water-tanks, their labour was not equal.* Women crossing keepers earned less than men, but that was because they were generally allocated the 'lighter' crossings. Once all these exceptions were omitted not one woman was granted equal pay with men.

The RSC observed that pay inequality was attributable to 'the consideration of the social obligations of men compared to women'; in other words, the belief that a typical man had a family to support while a typical woman did not. In cases where the reverse was true a man was still paid more. Even at 15 years of age boys were paid more than girls. The RSC warned that, if women were ever to win their fight for equal pay, all limitations on their labour would be removed and they would work on the same terms as men, without favours or leniency. What is more, in 'unisex' grades, if employers had to pay each sex the same, they would probably favour men and women would be left without jobs.

Many men believed that some women took more sick leave than most men because of menstruation and 'female troubles'. They thought that all women ought to be punished for this by forfeiting any claim to equal pay, meaning that women who never took a day off sick would be financially penalised just for being female. In any case, the RSC reported that 'gynaecological disturbances' were not responsible for women being unwell more frequently than men. It found that women were worn out by inadequate nutrition and by trying to hold down two jobs: paid work and running a household.

The 1944 Royal Commission on Equal Pay was inconclusive, but it revealed some deeply entrenched attitudes about women and work. It rejected the claim that equal pay

* And yet, as we have read, Victoria Simpson's female cleaning gang did fill these tanks.

should be granted on the grounds of human justice. It endorsed the idea of equal pay for professional women performing the same work as men, but felt that the general principle would put women out of work, as men would always be preferred by employers if both sexes cost the same. It recommended fixed pay scales for women's jobs and men's jobs, thus perpetuating sex segregation. Three of the four women on the Commission dissented from the view of the male majority; however, even they did not fully support equal pay; they simply felt that women were underpaid.

The landslide Labour victory in 1945 changed nothing for women campaigning for equal pay. Despite adopting the principle the TUC and the relevant union leaders were persuaded by the government to drop the matter on the grounds that it would cause inflation at a time of national austerity. Out of loyalty to the Labour Party they agreed, reneging on the TUC resolution to 'engage without delay in vigorous, co-ordinated activity to secure equal pay.'

Part of railway workers' remuneration took the form of free and reduced rate travel, and free uniform and protective clothing. Women were treated unfairly in the provision of both. Attempts to obtain parity in the provision of clothing were often long, drawn-out and, ultimately, futile, though most were not as absurd as the case of Mrs Davison's overcoat. The story began in 1945 when Crossing Keeper Davison of Bishopston Lane, Hartlepool, LNER, applied for a coat but was refused on the grounds that they were issued only to male staff. She pursued the matter, claiming that bitterly cold mornings affected both sexes equally. She began in the usual way, taking the matter to her local union representative, who presented it to West Hartlepool 1 NUR branch. The case was processed through increasingly high levels of the NUR, each of which met with a corresponding level of railway management, without success. The matter eventually reached the NUR EC, which discussed it on three occasions. In the meantime Mrs Davison approached her MP. The saga reached farcical proportions when the NUR EC met the Minister of Transport to discuss a crossing keeper's overcoat. The meeting was fruitless: no amount of negotiation or pressure could persuade the LNER to issue a coat to Mrs Davison. After two years the NUR gave up, blaming 'the obstinate attitude of the Company', which by then was in any case refusing further meetings on the subject. It is astonishing that the LNER preferred to spend dozens of man-hours and create reams of paperwork fighting the case rather than simply issue an overcoat out of the stores.[112]

While railwaymen could obtain free travel for their wives, a railwaywoman could obtain it for her husband only if he was incapable of any employment. There was further discrimination against single mothers. Vera Williams remembers one hard-working young woman who had three illegitimate children. When she applied for a very modest privilege ticket (quarter fare) for them she was, as a single woman, refused. 'A lot of us felt it was more than a little unfair'.[113]

Women were not admitted to the railways' superannuation schemes until 1st July 1941, when some grades were admitted to those of the GWR, SR, and LMS. Contributions were to be the same as men's and backdating terms were arranged. Many women were still omitted, however, by 1946 catering grades, for example, were still not in the scheme.

Many whose work involved handling goods were tempted to pilfer items in transit in the face of wartime shortages, queues, high prices and rationing. Some people thought it a perk of the job, but the punishments were severe: for example, two women goods porters at Sheffield were instantly dismissed for eating a few cherries from a barrel they were unloading. From 1941 war-workers were not subject to the usual railway disciplinary machinery but were dealt with under the Essential Work (Railway Undertakings) Order.

RAILWAYMEN

Railwaymen's reactions to women war-workers encompassed a wide range of attitudes, from camaraderie and friendship through flirtation and romance to prejudice, acrimony and resentment. Typical first-hand accounts describe a pattern of hostile reception followed by acceptance; sometimes grudging, at other times respectful.

Many men were shocked to see women in male grades. Annie Hodgeon recalled her first day in charge of Shaw North signalbox, LMS:

> It was 4:45 a.m., blacked out with curtains and only a gas light burning. I heard the driver of an engine outside the box, swearing, so I pulled a little of the blackout curtain back and looked out. Then I heard him shout to the fireman: 'It's a bloody woman!' Ten minutes later the signalman at Shaw South phoned to say the driver was very sorry. He didn't know women were taking over the signalboxes. That driver had an allotment, and afterwards he often used to hand me a shopping bag of potatoes, onions, veg, and sometimes flowers.[114]

Another woman porter found her male colleagues 'not very keen on us women at first. They didn't help us in any way'. After some time 'they realised we were as good as them and we got on very well.'[115] Another, the daughter of a well-liked station foreman, said she was treated with great respect: 'The staff in the parcels office were men of 50 years and over and were like fathers to me.'[116] A woman concreter recalled her male colleagues as 'rather abrupt, passing awful remarks',[117] while Signalwoman Hilda Lund discovered: 'The ones who objected were the signalmen — "no job for a woman".'[118] However, she and other signalwomen remembered very happy working relationships with men in other grades. Mrs Lund recalled that 'shunters who marshalled and sorted the various engines and wagons would come into our box for a friendly chat and to offer advice.' Similarly, Signalwoman Hodgeon remembered the kindness of engine crews:

> The early goods train used to pull up at Shaw station and I would get a lift to work. The fireman would shovel fire out of the engine's firebox and carry it to the fireplace in the signalbox. That way I would have a ready-made fire. [119]

Throughout the war, railwaymen raised grievances against women war-workers. One complaint was that women received 'preferential treatment'. For example, in 1943 male painters employed by the SR were indignant that women were given the lightest tasks, leaving them to do the heavier work.[120] Of course, it wasn't the women who were cherry-picking the easiest tasks; all decisions concerning the employment of women war-workers and the tasks they carried out were made between company managers and union officers — all of whom were men.

Another type of grievance originated from men's belief in women's inferiority. Echoing the sentiments of the First World War, women were accused of being temperamentally and physically unfitted for certain railway work. For example, at Norwich, LNER, motor drivers refused to train women, claiming the work was unsuitable for 'the fair sex'. The NUR EC informed them that women performed identical work elsewhere, and that the Ministry of Labour required railways to employ women in that capacity. Even when women were successfully performing 'men's work', disbelief continued in some quarters. For example, a correspondent to *The Railway Gazette* viewed 'with misgiving and apprehension' a photograph in a previous edition of a woman carrying a 56lb weight, calling it a 'travesty of truth'. The editor confirmed that the photograph was genuine, adding that railwaywomen dealt 'regularly and easily with weights in excess of 56lb' and were considered capable of lifting up to 112 lb.[121]

In contrast to the hate campaign being waged against signalwomen during the First World War, there were few official complaints from railwaymen, provided women were employed only in the lowest graded boxes — classes 5 and 4. Employing a woman in even a slightly higher graded post, say a class 3, would cause controversy.

This time, war-workers were more likely to defend themselves from male criticism than were their First World War predecessors. For example, during the 1943 NUR AGM one delegate accused railwaywomen of 'walking about dressed up like mannequins'. An indignant gang of women porters at nearby Carlisle sent their spokeswoman Pat Saunders to the conference hall to tackle the man in person. She told the press: 'Mannequins indeed. He should see us working in fish vans and manhandling boxes with ten stones* of fish in them, or unloading calves.'[122]

Women guards, more than any other grade, suffered male hostility. Before the first had even began her induction, some railwaymen assumed that none of them would be properly trained. W. Richards claimed: 'Enginemen are becoming nervy, as they feel it is too much of a strain to have an unqualified person in the rear of the train.' He asked if the GWR thought that 'A set of flags, a lamp, a kindly face and a way with children' were the only prerequisites for guards.[123] LMS guards objected when women were allocated the new, electric trains while men were 'demoted' to the old-fashioned, grimy steam trains.[124] In 1942 NUR branches at Hereford and Gloucester objected when the GWR advertised for women to guard goods trains from Gloucester to the Docks sidings. Elsewhere, men complained when minimum height requirements for guards were abolished by some companies to facilitate the recruitment of more women. Emily Price, a guard at Worcester, remembered that porters and other male staff 'appeared to resent the fact that we were getting paid the same as them'.[125] One man wrote to *The Railway Review* to criticise a woman guard for 'drawing money it takes a man years to attain'.[126]

Such attitudes were not confined to the rank-and-file; staff representatives and NUR officers joined in. One northern NUR District Council passed a resolution deploring the employment of women guards and signalwomen, especially when the men in those grades objected. Mr E. Godin, the staff representative for St Pancras guards, wrote:

> Our female members, before accepting the post of guard, should ask themselves: 'Am I prepared to carry out the full duties of a guard in all emergencies?' Take the use of the communication cord by passengers. This may be owing to attempted assault, rape, drunkenness, suicide, or any other extremity. ... Would she consider herself able to deal with the guard's part of such an emergency? I feel this is the one job they are liable to fall down on, and the risk is too great.[127]

One of the women he represented, 24-year-old Glaswegian Sally Knox, replied:

> On being selected I made myself cognisant with LMSR rules and regulations and was duly passed by a Company's official. ... May I remind him that women in this war have met and acquitted themselves very ably in far worse responsibilities than he quotes.[128]

---

* Ten stones = 140 pounds, or 63.5 kilos.

Brother Godin responded by accusing Knox of being 'a mouthpiece' for management.[129] Another of her male colleagues joined the attack by suggesting that when an emergency arose on a train guarded by a woman, 'someone else jumps into the breach.'[130] Knox, clearly weary of these insults, retorted sarcastically: 'Oh dear. I must have accepted the position ... with my eyes shut!'[131] Even the President of the 1944 Shunters and Guards Conference automatically assumed, without producing any supporting evidence, that women guards were incompetent:

> A passenger guard never knows when he is likely to be called upon in an emergency. ... Perhaps the brains trusts could tell us what action the female guard is to take. It would appear she will have to ask her passengers to volunteer.[132]

Of course these men were free to make such scurrilous accusations because of the infrequency of railway accidents. Women guards were rarely afforded opportunities to refute the unremitting allegations of incompetence. When incidents did arise, women's actions failed to support any of their critics' assertions, but no record has come to light of any apology being offered.

Guard Mary Davies had to tolerate many disparaging comments from her colleagues on the Southern:

> We used to have to go in their mess-room, down at Orpington, to get your tea and that, and they'd say, 'Oh blimey, here comes the women — let's get out'. You had to take a lot of stick, really, The men certainly didn't like us going into their ranks, that's dead certain. They were really quite nasty to us when we first went in. They used language on us: 'Bloody women coming in here, taking the bloody jobs! Pity they ain't got nothing else to do. Should stop at home and do their knitting.' Used to get all that, but they soon came round and on the whole were pretty good, really, when they'd got used to us, they used to treat us with respect. But some of the girls had quite a lot to put up with, I think, one way and another, with them. [133]

Guard Anna Wolsey also had a tough time at her depot on the LMS:

> The male guards at Mansfield did not like me. I had to cycle to the station for my shift and found several times that my bicycle tyres had been slashed. Men had to be 5 ft 10 inches to become a passenger guard and then a dwarf like me, only 5 ft 1½, was given that job. One of the senior guards was known to be very anti-feminist but after a while we had long conversations together and on payday he even took me to a pub and paid for my drink. When I had to leave (because I was pregnant) he gave me his guard's cap as a souvenir.[134]

It may seem surprising, but it appears that railwaymen were more afraid of being alone with women than vice versa. At the end of 1943, after 377 women guards and 230 signalwomen had qualified on the LMS, railwaymen working for that company suddenly refused to train unaccompanied women. The NUR supported the men, stating: 'where any party objects to working in isolation with one of the opposite sex, the women should be trained in pairs.' The company assured the worried men that the women were of 'known good character' and punishments of between one and six days' suspension were imposed upon men who refused to train them. The NUR EC managed to get all the punishments waived and secured the company's promise that in future, women would be trained in pairs or by other women.[135] Research revealed no evidence of a woman objecting to being trained by a lone signalman or guard, although there were certainly instances of what nowadays would be termed 'sexual harassment'. Edie Rowe recalled: 'One or two tried it on, yes, you got the odd one who it was a bit inclined to take advantage, but I dealt with it myself: slapped his hand.'. [136]

The Railway Review published letters from railwaymen who disagreed with the hostility meted out to war-workers. Union activist John Lilley of Hatfield remarked, 'The war has given women their chance, and they are taking it with both hands.'[137] Another declared:

> There is no job on the railway for which suitable 'physical' and 'mental' types in women cannot be found. There may be a disinclination to handle jobs involving grease and dirt, but to say that women are physically unfit is wrong. All women are not physically suited for a particular task. Some have made me shudder the way they have handled crates of fish and other heavy articles. But others, if on the railway long enough, may lose some of the more extreme feminine 'artifices'.[138]

Henry Powers reminded his railway colleagues that many women were relatives of railwaymen in the forces: 'What will the repercussions be when these lads return when they learn how some members have attacked their wives and daughters?'[139] The atmosphere was, apparently, quite different on London Transport, the management of which claimed that 'relations between the sexes in the various grades of railway service of the Board are excellent.'[140]

There was noticeably less formality between men and women staff than had been the case during the First World War. Women were no longer segregated, locked in their offices or placed under the watchful eye of stern matrons. Undercurrents of sexual attraction created an atmosphere of flirtation, which many enjoyed. There were romances, marriages and extramarital affairs. However, platonic friendships were the most common, especially as most of the remaining railwaymen were, as one former war-worker put it, 'Well past their sell-by date.' These paternal relationships were a source of much affection and joviality on both sides. Teenager Rose Bramley was 'mate' to an electrician, Joe, who was 'like a father' to her. 'A most kind and considerate man and very protective,' she recalled, adding: 'and I never heard him swear.' When her male colleagues heard she was getting married, 'they all came and sat with me in the corner and said did I want to know the facts of life? My colour rose.'[141] Evelyn Mack, former track labourer at Potter's Bar, LNER, recalled her colleagues as:

> A hard-swearing but also a hard-working gang. Some of them laughingly suggested that before I left the railway they would have me use swear words and have an intoxicating drink, but they never succeeded.[142]

Mrs Mack recalled that, when walking through tunnels, they took refuge in recesses while trains passed at speeds in excess of 100 mph, 'My linesman would put his arms outstretched in front of me to prevent me being sucked in by the rush of the coaches.' The signalmen were a jovial bunch; when Mrs Mack was up a signal ladder, they would waggle the mechanical signal arms up and down while she was trying to clean them. To make amends, later they would let her press the signal bells and pull the levers. The platelayers and linesmen always moderated their language in her presence. When hitching a lift on an engine, she was told to 'work her passage' by stoking the firebox. 'I did manage to use their huge shovel and toss some coal into the furnace.'

Firemen were in a reserved occupation and were often the only railwaymen in women war-workers' age group. Many of these muscular young men enjoyed gallantly assisting women guards with the very heavy tasks – such as releasing frozen handbrakes in winter. Many a light-hearted flirtation developed into romance. Audrey Brown eventually married a colleague:

> It was all romance. They were all railwaymen – you never had a chance to meet anybody else. It was lovely. Life was all romance.[143]

But sometimes it all went wrong. One Christmas a woman clerk bought a sprig of mistletoe and kissed all the men in the office:

> But one grumpy soul struggled, fell, and she stepped on his hand, breaking his wrist. His reason for a claim for compensation – 'She tried to kiss me' – did not go down well with the authorities.[144]

This kind of female forwardness was very rare; most of the unwanted attention was paid by males to females: a railwayman at Brighton, SR, for example, was formally reprimanded for 'persistently whistling at and calling after female employees'.[145] Worried parents felt the need to caution daughters who intended to work with men. Guard Clara Evans' mother warned her:

> 'Don't join in with the men if they're telling dirty jokes; just walk away, because if you do, and they take advantage of you, then they'd say that, well, you'd listened to all these mucky jokes, and they thought you was an easy partner'. I just used to walk off as soon as they started it, so I never got involved. Well I suppose they had to try it out and see what sort of person you were.[146]

Similarly, Guard Edie Winser's mother guided her on choosing her clothing:

> We were given a choice of a skirt or slacks. Well my mother thought – and you know what parents are like – that when you are bending, etc, that it was more decent to wear trousers when there are men about. So I had trousers.[147]

Signalwoman Hodgeon had an unnerving experience. She had just taken over from a woman colleague and was operating her levers as usual. Through the gaps where the levers went through the floor, she saw some technicians in the locking room, working on the equipment under the signalbox.

> I could hear them a-laughing underneath me, and I said, 'Let's all share it – what are you laughing at?' And they said, 'You're a damned spoilsport, you. You've got trousers on. Your mate had a skirt on – and she wears French knickers'.[148]

Lecherous behaviour was not confined to men in the wages grades. When the RCA investigated a case in which some managers objected to women clerks wearing slacks, it transpired that the company had no regulation requiring skirts to be worn; the managers simply wanted women's legs on display for their own enjoyment.[149]

Women in male grades were often put to work together in same-sex groups, and the comradeship that developed was a source of great strength. Many of those contacted recalled sharing the fun and the hardships. Photographs show them smiling and hugging each other and their reminiscences abound with fond memories of their former colleagues. Pat Foreman recalled the singing and laughing at Kentish Town engine shed: 'they worked hard, they shared the hazards of the men. They also shared their pastimes, a drink, a smoke, and a game of darts in the pub.'[150]

Women in gangs enjoyed ready-made allies in times of adversity, as former goods porter Kathleen Hadfield of Warrington Bank Quay, LMS, recalled: 'There were about six of us girls together and we never had a wrong word between us. We helped each other and we had some good laughs.'[151] Some of these friendships continued for decades after the war. Vera Perry, Doreen Stevens, Thelma Dursford and Gladys Kimber were all still in touch when they contacted me in the 1990s, as were Clara Evans and Joan Levick.

Women platelayers at Darlington, LNER. One lifts the rail; the other packs the ballast underneath.

COURTESY OF THE NRM

LOOK OUT

A guard in culottes attaching a paraffin tail lamp to the rear carriage of her train. COURTESY OF THE NRM

Overleaf: GWR trackwomen with oil cans and scrapers clearing and oiling points near Reading while a female lookout, equipped with two flags and a whistle, keeps watch for trains. COURTESY OF THE NRM

ASLEF AND THE NUR

ASLEF had no female members throughout the war.* There were no female drivers or firemen, and the union refused to enrol women engine cleaners even though 8,500 were performing the work by 1944.

Female membership of the NUR rose tenfold in the first two years of the war – from 1,722 in 1939 to over 17,000 by the end of 1941 – and then doubled over the next five years to 34,000 (of a total membership of 462,000).† The dramatic growth in female NUR membership is attributable partly to the efforts of its women activists. One of them, Sister Brookes of Crewe 1 branch, was presented with an inscribed medallion in 1942 for her great success in enrolling women.

During mid-1942 female membership of the NUR reached 30,000. This was a milestone, because it entitled the union to send six delegates to the Annual Conference of Unions Catering for Women Workers (ACUCWW, now the TUC Women's Conference). However, the NUR sent only two – and one was a man! Later the EC conceded that both delegates should be female. The women who attended the 1946 ACUCWW reported that the NUR's attitude to women still left much to be desired. Lily Yates of Crewe branch wrote:

> I wish all my brothers in the N.U.R could have heard delegates speaking on resolutions dealing with the 'rate for the job', women's wages and conditions, and equal pay for equal work. ... One delegate remarked that when dealing with the right of women to get paid the 'rate for the job' we found pockets of resistance in the most unexpected places. How right she was. Perhaps she had been talking to some of the male members of the N.U.R.

Her fellow delegate, Constance Meadows of Paddington branch, revealed other problems:

> Again we urge Head office to take this annual conference for women trade unionists seriously, and in the future arrange a preliminary meeting of the delegates in order that they can discuss the union's view of the agenda. ... But perhaps before next year we may have held a delegate conference of railwaywomen and perhaps our union will be called the National Union of Railwaymen and women. Who knows?[152]

Miss Meadows's suggestion for a women's NUR conference was pursued in 1946 by her branch and its District Council, but the EC unanimously rejected the request, seeing 'no purpose' in it.[153] Her suggestion to alter the union's title to include women was never adopted in the union's lifetime.

The chief vehicle for NUR propaganda was, of course, *The Railway Review*. During the First World War the paper's cartoons had mocked and ridiculed women; now they implored them to enrol. One depicted a 'voice from the battlefield' entreating the female porter who had taken his job to take his place in the union as well.

One full-page banner – 'A call to women on the railways' – appears at first to advertise magnificent, equal benefits for women members but on closer inspection its wording is remarkable for clouding the facts. Lines such as 'action – Initiation of

---

* ASLEF had 74,000 members by 1949.

† In 1944 there were 2.2 million women members of Britain trade unions.

negotiations immediately employment of women anticipated' suggests that such negotiations were for women's benefit, when in fact the intention was to protect male rates and male re-employment. The paper claimed: 'Women need advice and assistance on all phases of their employment' yet, as we have seen, NUR officers joined the rank-and-file in attacking women filling the higher male grades.

Although, as branch Secretary John Lilley of Hatfield remarked: 'The pogrom that threatened to develop against the entire woman membership has petered out',[154] women had little success in obtaining support for their causes. 'Most of the female labour are members of the Union. But what representative has the 'guts' to fight for equal conditions for females?'[155] asked one railwaywoman, while another asserted: 'The trades unions, and men in general, have been trumpeting about equality for years. Is it equality for men only and dictatorship for women?'[156] Yet the NUR could hardly fight for sexual equality when it blatantly treated its own female employees unfairly. In 1946 it advertised for six male clerks at a salary of £228 per annum and for 12 female clerks at £105.*

Off-Duty Life

War-workers joined the existing railway staff social clubs, allotment associations and ambulance teams, the last of which competed in first-aid competitions. (In March 1947 an all-woman team at Stirling beat the men to win the Allengrange Trophy.) Some war-workers joined women's sports teams organised by the permanent staff. Railwaywomen also spent some of their free time knitting articles of clothing for 'our boys' in the forces.

An annual 'Railway Queen' was customarily chosen from among railwaymen's daughters but, in 1947, for the first time, a member of staff was chosen. She was Greta Richards, a shorthand-typist at Victoria, SR. The queen's main duty was to visit a foreign country and obtain from its railwaymen a link shaped like a miniature train coupling; these were collected and added to her 'Chain of International Peace'.

Railwaywomen were well known to the public and often praised. As a gesture of his admiration one Blackpool businessman treated local railwaywomen to a tea party, followed by a show. He even repeated the event so that staff on both shifts could attend. A London society caterer offered a free wedding reception to the first railway couple to wed. A vanwoman who married a St Pancras goods porter claimed the prize. Some war-workers recalled that bus and tram conductors, seeing their railway uniform, would beckon railwaywomen to the front of the queue. The other passengers, recognising that the women worked in an essential industry, did not object. Such incidents served to bolster war-workers' sense of pride and emphasised how important they were to the war effort.

A great many railwaywomen were married with children and their off-duty hours were entirely devoted to domestic responsibilities. After a long, tiring day of manual railway work, they queued for their food rations and struggled with their shopping onto overcrowded, infrequent public transport. When they finally reached home there were children to take care of and cooking, cleaning and laundry to be done, and all without the modern labour-saving equipment that today we now take for granted.

* RCA office staff were also paid and treated unequally. During the war Mary Longhorn became the union's first female employee to receive equal pay when she was appointed LNER clerk at men's rate.

Women with children under 14 were exempt from conscription to war-work but many chose to join the workforce anyway. One railwaywoman, Mrs Dearsley, had 11 children: three toddlers, five of school-age, two in the forces and one working in the goods yard.[157]

Childcare was a huge problem during the war. More state nurseries were opened, but not nearly enough and, as a report in *The Times* on London Transport staff explained:

> Day nurseries do not meet the needs of transport workers with changing hours of duty, and ... only residential nurseries are satisfactory. [These are] too few ... and if the cost is 25s a week the charge for two children is more than a working woman's wage will bear.[158]

Even where available, nurseries were not always convenient, as engine cleaner Mrs Roberts had to get her two children – one nine months old; the other, five – ready at 6.30 a.m., then walk 25 minutes to catch a tram, leave the baby in a nursery while the boy went to school. Then a half-hour bus journey to Hither Green sidings, hopefully by 8 a.m. 'I was always late and they stopped my money'.[159] She, in common with so many other women, exhausted themselves trying to be housewives, mothers and full-time railway workers. A *Daily Telegraph* report on railway war workers explained that:

> Most of the women have young children. When they arrive home from their night's work they have breakfast to cook, housework to do, shopping to get in. They go to bed after lunch, and before they leave again for their night's work they have more meals to prepare, some have young children to put to bed, and all the other small things that make up a housewife's round.[160]

In most cases men were away in the forces, but some women had their husbands at home, such as this LMS station mistress:

> By 8 a.m., Bertha Allan has cooked breakfast for her husband and six children, tidied the house and cycled to [Padbury] station. She also cycles three miles during her luncheon time to do the family shopping.[161]

In common with many husbands, Mr Allan did nothing to help around the house. Railway clerk Kathrin Smith felt that the burden of this 'double shift' was holding women back:

> Whereas any man feels to have done his bit after a day's work and to be entitled to rest and recreation, many working women are doing two full-time jobs: their badly-paid jobs in offices and their unpaid jobs as housewives. We can never expect to raise the status of women as long as we allow this double-exploitation to go on.[162]

Some women were lucky: when Joan Percival's husband was demobbed he looked after the household and would bring the children to visit her in the signalbox.

Many railway workers spent some of their leisure time in civil defence work, as firewatchers and air-raid wardens. When railway workers' homes were destroyed by bombs, they would salvage what they could and then arrange alternative accommodation for themselves and their families before reporting for duty. This was so taxing that the REC allowed three days' emergency leave for staff in such circumstances.

Women in Female Grades.

With all the attention placed on women in male grades, it is easy to forget the thousands who laboured out of the limelight in dead-end, menial, women's jobs. When the war began there were 11,693 women in female wages grades (excluding workshop staff). During the war this figure hardly changed, as they were mainly domestic and catering workers mostly unaffected by wartime staffing fluctuations.

Some women were chagrined to find themselves working alongside others who, because they were substituting a man, received a man's wage. For example, skilled women ticket printers on the permanent staff earned between 32s and the maximum of 74s. Working alongside them were women war-workers who, after 12 weeks' probation, were paid only 4s less than the male rate, which was 85s to 110s (depending on age and length of service).

The massive wartime increase in passenger traffic made refreshment rooms crowded, stressful workplaces. The arrival of a troop train meant preparing an enormous amount of food and hot drinks at very short notice. There was considerable discontent among women in these grades when they saw that war-workers such as porters, ticket collectors and guards not only enjoyed their work and were applauded as national heroines, but also earned double the wage of a woman working in the catering department. Adding insult to injury, the war wage was withheld from all catering staff as they were assumed to receive tips. Many women became demoralised and looked instead for work of national importance. The inevitable result was that, as early as April 1940, there was a shortage of catering staff. The solution, reached in 1941, was to increase pay by 3s and bring the work within the Essential Work Order, ensuring that staff could not leave without permission. It also established that railway catering was an essential industry.[163]

After a pre-war NUR enquiry confirmed that hotel and catering staff worked long hours for low pay in bad conditions, in 1940 the union demanded for them a maximum ten-hour day, overtime payments and Sunday enhancements. The companies replied that meeting these conditions would make their hotels 'entirely unremunerative', thus substantiating the union's accusation that profits depended upon exploiting the workforce. However, the companies agreed to standardise the 68 refreshment room grades and the 45 female and 150 male hotel grades. Minimum wage scales were brought in, giving most women a rise of 1s or 2s. But women's pay was still far lower than that of men; for example, the average pay of hotel and catering staff employed by the GWR in 1946 was 57s 10d for its 807 women, and 112s 4d for its 602 men. *[164]

Women continued to work in their traditional jobs as ladies'- and waiting room attendants, office cleaners, hostel matrons and mess-room attendants throughout the war. They saw no improvement in their conditions or status; on the contrary, some felt their status had sunk in comparison to the war workers. In 1946 the pay for ladies' room attendants was just 41s 6d in London and 39s 6d in the provinces, plus 24s war wage.

Women taking a joint post with their husbands endured what was, perhaps, the most blatant unfairness. For example, Mr and Mrs Labrum were lodging house stewards at Burton-on-Trent. They both worked an identical, seven-day, 60-hour week on the same premises, performing the same tasks. However, LMS rules stated: 'Where a man and his wife are both employed, as Steward and Stewardess, the stewardess is to be dealt with separately, i.e. to be graded and paid as a mess-room attendant.' As a result, while her husband was paid 45s, Mrs Labrum's wage was just 10s.

---

* Catering staff were very low paid. The average pay of all GWR staff was 80s 5d for female and 123s 10d for male.

Crossing Keepers

As we have seen, women level crossing gatekeepers were habitually excluded each time wages and conditions were improved. Gatewomen and gatemen continued to be treated as two entirely different grades by the NUR as well as by the companies. In 1939 the NUR had stated: 'Male crossing keepers should not be ... in charge of any crossing for a period of in excess of 12 consecutive hours', and proposed an eight hour day for them. But women were not included in the union's demand; in fact, their very existence was not even acknowledged. Treating female crossing keepers as though they did not exist had by this time reached new heights of absurdity, because women comprised the majority of crossing keepers — 1,467 compared to 1,298 men!

A year later the NUR had a change of heart and its officials met the REC to request that female crossing keepers be given the same status as other railway employees and asked for them to be included in the National Agreements. Compared with how women crossing keepers had been treated since railways began, these demands were outrageously radical and it is not surprising that the REC rejected them.

In 1943 the REC at last agreed to standardise gatewomen, who now numbered 1,585, and to bring them into the new Conditions of Service. One effect of the re-grading was to give 75% of them a pay rise. Fortunately, women already earning more than the new rates were not going to be penalised. Despite this, women crossing keepers remained the lowest paid of all railway workers. What is more, some managers on the LMS and LNER introduced rent payments on the hitherto 'free' cottages, thus annulling the pay rise. This was clearly unsatisfactory and the women affected by this complained to the NUR. In addition, railway companies were unwilling to spend any money on the crossing cottages, which, typically, had no electricity, no bathroom, and an outside WC.

The remuneration for keepers of level crossings was based on the tradition of the work being shared between husband and wife, but men were now forbidden by their new conditions of service from operating the gates while off-duty from their main job. However, no compensatory arrangements were made to women who were obliged to perform more hours because of the new rules, or to those whose husbands were away in the forces. In both cases, the wife's workload was greatly increased, and in some cases doubled, without any enhancement in pay.

Salaried Staff

Women clerks had made little progress towards equality during the 1920s and 1930s, despite considerable effort. By 1940 their mood was described as 'acutely pessimistic'. The problem was not so much unequal pay as lack of promotional opportunities. While men were graded from 5 up to 1, then Special Class, women had only W2, W1 and Special Class. Women in W2 and W1 were paid more or less the same as men in Grade 5 and 4. Thence, men could advance three further grades, which women could not. Less than 5% of women reached Grade 1, leaving over 95% to 'stagnate' — to use their terminology — in W2. Only a tiny minority (those with professional qualifications) could enter Special Class.*

On stations, women were thought suitable for jobs as typists, telephonists and telegraphists, and as clerks in parcels, left luggage and booking offices and these were the

* For example, a secretary to a general manager — the highest position a woman could hold on the railways — would be in Special Class.

kinds of jobs that could often be retained after the war. Eileen Bridges was a telegraphist and teleprinter operator until she married a railwayman in 1952.

> There were three females, two males and a male boss. The girls and myself worked shifts: one week finishing at 6.30 p.m., another 8 p.m. No cars to take you home after work, only a bicycle to go along a very dark road in the blackout sometimes with a doodlebug overhead. My first day at work I thought, 'I shall never stay here'. The noise was horrendous: single needles clicking, a teleprinter clattering backwards and forwards and phones constantly ringing. After mastering the Morse code and the teleprinter, life became bearable. We were in a smallish environment but were not isolated from the work of the station. Our town was a military base and there were always troops on the platform – Americans, Canadians, men from all over the world. Americans squatting on the platform playing dice games, money piled around them. One of the most vivid memories is of the troop trains bringing the wounded home. A different memory is the smell of the steam trains standing outside our office in the dock waiting to be off. I can still recall that smell.[165]

In 1939 there had been just over 11,000 women engaged in clerical work, compared with over 74,000 men. Wartime substitution raised the number of women to just over 30,000 by March 1944. Some were recruited specifically to replace a man; in other cases a W2 was temporarily transferred to 'men's work' and raised in grade to a W1. This increased her pay to the equivalent of a male Grade 4, but in many cases she did the work of a Grade 3.

Being allowed to perform higher-grade work gave women the opportunity to demonstrate their suitability and competence for such positions, and to prove their labour equal to men's. This in turn helped revitalise the pre-war campaign for better promotional prospects. The practice of dismissing women on marriage was suspended for the duration of the war and many experienced clerks who would otherwise have left the service were able to continue lending their voices to the campaign.

Railway Magazine suggested in 1942: 'There seems to be no reason why [women] should not take a prominent part in railway management',[166] but companies, unions and the rank-and-file were unanimous in the belief that women were not suitable even to be station masters.

The RCA

The attitude of the RCA towards its women members was different to that of the NUR, for several reasons. There was less prejudice against women working in offices than in manual grades, and the RCA had a greater proportion of established and permanent women members. But the deciding factor was the large number of career women among the clerical staff, who were better educated and more articulate than their wages-grade sisters. They were certainly more active and vocal in their union. Furthermore the marriage bar meant that clerks, being spinsters, had more leisure time to dedicate to trade union activity. They had even managed to obtain a permanent position for a women's representative on the RCA EC, something the NUR would not entertain. The fervour of some women alarmed the RCA President, who appealed to them not to succumb to 'sex-antagonism' but to remember that, as workers, men's and women's interests were identical; however, one female member complained: 'The men do not give us the help we should have.'[167]

Women activists in the RCA quickly enrolled large numbers of war-workers in administrative and ticket offices, for which the Executive praised them. Several branches signed up every woman in their catchment area. In Yorkshire, one clerk was enrolled within 20 minutes on her first day at work. But the Women and Girl Clerks' representative on the Executive, Miss Eveline Hugill, wanted more than subscriptions: she urged union officers to persuade women to become actively involved.

By 1942 women held one in ten of the official positions within the RCA. Three of its 435 branches had a woman chair and 10 had women secretaries. By July 1945 the number of female officials had grown to 700. In 1941, 17 women attended the annual conference and two years later the number of delegates peaked at 63. This had dropped to just 25 by 1949.

Since the first RCA women's conference in 1916 they had taken place 'whenever circumstances seemed to require them'. In 1941 it was held in the same Leeds hotel as in 1916 and General Secretary Gallie remarked that they were facing 'almost precisely similar problems' as they had a quarter of a century before. The bosses sought to save money by engaging cheaper female labour and the RCA promised to 'ensure due regard for the human element and to protect its people against exploitation.' The 100 women delegates discussed equal pay and reference was made to the NUR's success in obtaining it for war-workers in wages grades. This was not wholeheartedly supported because if war-worker women clerks obtained equal pay with men then permanent, experienced women staff would earn less than 'temps'. It was also pointed out that equality with men would mean performing night work, which men thought undesirable; however, many women were already working at night — unpaid — as air raid wardens, firewatchers and ambulance drivers. Mr Gallie said that delegates were 'addressing themselves to the converted' as the RCA had submitted a claim for equal pay as early as 1919 and, more recently, in 1939. He invited delegates to provide him with evidence to support his next claim.

The long-standing demand for a woman to be appointed to deal with the problems of women clerical workers was raised and the General Secretary announced that this would be considered when a vacancy arose. Miss Eveline Hugill was appointed soon afterward and was later joined by Muriel Luntz. Women's enthusiasm was such that, in 1944, twelve candidates stood for election to one of the two vacancies.*

An equal pay claim submitted to the Railway Staff National Tribunal (RSNT) in March 1942 was rejected because there was no precedent for it in the civil service, banks, industry or in any other transport authority.† The REC claimed, enigmatically, that equal pay was 'unsound on social grounds.'[168] The issue was also raised unsuccessfully in the House of Commons in 1944 by Reg Sorenson, Labour MP for Leyton West. The REC reminded him that the railway unions had accepted lower rates for women clerks. Later, at the RCA women's conference in October 1942, General Secretary Gallie said women performing duties similar in character and value to male clerks should be paid as men.

By 1946 the RCA had 20,000 women among its 90,000 members. They were being elected in increasing numbers as organising secretaries and to women's sub-committees. Hundreds of women's meetings were held all over the country; one at Edinburgh was attended by 265 members. Thousands attended weekend schools (where one of the tutors was Anne Loughlin).‡ *The Railway Service Journal** published abundant correspondence from

* In 1947 the two women on the RCA Executive were Ethel Chipchase and Miss Leishman.

† Women civil servants and women railway clerks were paid 80% of the male rate.

‡ Dame Anne Loughlin (1894-1979) OBE 1935, DBE 1943, General Secretary, Tailor and Garment Workers Union, 1948-53, President of the TUC General Council, 1943.

women relating to inequalities in pay and promotion. Every issue carried articles for women on the subject of equality with men. The contributors were clear what they wanted: an end to undercutting; all women clerks to join the RCA; equal pay for equal work and equal opportunity of advancement.

Miss Hugill objected to the companies' claim that men were paid more because of their supposed family responsibilities. She challenged employers to be consistent by assessing every employee's personal circumstances before setting their rate of pay, knowing they would discover that many women staff had dependants while many men staff did not. A correspondent signing herself simply 'B.L.' (perhaps Betty Lamont†) reported that 30% of British men were unmarried and 60% of those married had no children, yet 50% of working women had dependants.

The war bonus, (16s for men; 12s for women) was, according to one woman activist, 'adding insult to injury, as women have to meet the same rise in the cost of living as men. It is an inequality which cannot be logically justified.'[169] Another asserted that women's economic inequality 'is still almost as bad as it was in 1914.'[170] For example, the average railway pension for a woman was so small that many were obliged to supplement it by continuing to perform paid work.

Substantial improvement was made during the 40s: in 1942, only 4% of women clerks held positions above the lowest grade (W2) but by 1949 this had risen to 11%. For those in W1, however, opportunities for advancement were still 'negligible'. A female delegate to the 1949 RCA conference explained that this increased the difficulty of recruiting women to the railway service, adding: 'If you want the best women you must be prepared to pay for them.' The delegates rocked with laughter at the double entendre.[171] Such male ridicule irritated the women, who were striving in earnest for a better deal.

The End of War Work

Many women left railway work before the war ended, for a variety of reasons. There was plenty of alternative work available offering more sociable hours, safer conditions, less heavy lifting, and a more female-orientated workplace. Juggling housewifery with full-time railway work was in many cases impossible to sustain year after year. Some women resigned in order to look after a war-wounded relative. When husbands came home on leave from the forces, or were demobbed, women were granted fourteen days' unpaid compassionate leave and, all too often, this led to the railway losing a war-worker. A typical case is that of Annie Brown (née Hughes), a former HGV driver on the GWR:

> My husband came back from the Far East on January 7th 1944. We were married on 17th, and he travelled around with me in the lorry for a week to see what my work entailed. His verdict was I was working far too hard. He said, 'I will put an end to this if it is up to me.' And so he did: I was pregnant within six weeks.[172]

The war came to an end in the summer of 1945, and by December the number of railwaywomen had dropped to 105,346, of whom 58,681 filled male grades, 15,176 worked

---

* Formerly (until 1919) *The Railway Clerk.*

† Elizabeth Lamont was an RCA activist and career railwaywoman who joined the railway as a telegraphist at Princes Street, Edinburgh, and retired in 1954 with 43 years' service.

in female grades and 31,489 were clerks. Many war-workers wished to retain their jobs but their hopes were dashed when they received a letter such as this:

> I regret it is now necessary to terminate your employment with the Railway Executive, and I have to inform you that your services will not be required from ... [date]. The Executive greatly appreciates the splendid work performed by a large number of women who have undertaken duty in the Railway service in the National interest many of them in positions which are normally occupied by men and I should like to express to you on the railway Executive's behalf, thanks for the services you have rendered.

Some did not even receive a letter, but were dismissed verbally. Former porter Gwynneth Dixon was 'very disappointed' that she did not receive any recognition or thanks, not even a letter of appreciation from the LNER: 'It was just as if we had never been,' she recalled sadly, many years later.[173] Those on the LNER who did not receive a personal letter of recognition shared a communal one published in the company magazine. It was headed 'Thank you, Ladies, and Goodbye' and concluded:

> Goodbye to you, ladies, and good luck go with you. You have done a good job of work and you leave the service of the L.N.E.R. with the knowledge that you have been of invaluable assistance to the country's war effort and your work has been appreciated by the Company. Many of you have tackled jobs which only men did before the war, and you have succeeded splendidly. You will be long remembered.[174]

While most women accepted that it was their duty to make way for returning servicemen, they resented being dismissed without notice, because this gave them no opportunity to use up any remaining free travel entitlement or to find alternative employment. However, on railways as in industry generally, demobilisation was less abrupt than had been the case in 1918-19. Although women could be summarily dismissed, they could not leave without permission, as the Essential Work Order was not rescinded until 1946.

When removed from male grades, some war-workers became housewives;† others stayed on the railway but were transferred to female grades and the rest left, either to begin new occupations or to return to their previous line of work. After leaving Collingbourne signalbox, Doreen Spackman was transferred to Savernake Low Level as a booking clerk, where she stayed until April 1949. Mary Causebrook, an engineer's chainman, returned to hairdressing. Miss Manifold, a ticket collector at King's Cross, managed to obtain a permanent position as Ladies' Retiring Room Attendant on board the Flying Scotsman. Unfortunately she was made redundant six months later.[175]

The Scottish Record Office holds documents relating to the fate of 28 female guards at Edinburgh Waverley. Only nine asked for release from railway duty at the end of the war, while 19 wanted to stay on. One secured a male wages grade position as a ticket collector; four were 'dispensed with', and the remaining 14 were sent to Craigentinny depot as

† 1947 was a record year for marriages: over 400,000 compared to a pre-war average of 325,000. Two million women gave up work after the war.

carriage cleaners.[176] Staff records cannot communicate what women felt about the sudden demotion and dramatic fall in pay and status.

Some women fought hard to retain their jobs, searching for loopholes and unearthing obscure union agreements. One, Mrs L. Greetham, had been a guard for five years when she received her dismissal notice in 1948. She discovered that a woman porter was being retained, and that this was contrary to union rules, because the porter had three months' less service than herself. After protesting through Kettering NUR branch she was reinstated, albeit as a Grade 2 porter. Her attempt to recover the six weeks' wages she lost while pursuing the case was unsupported by the NUR EC, which advised her to accept instead a £10 goodwill payment offered by the LMS. However, she continued to press for the full amount, backed by her branch.[177] The outcome of this case could not be traced.

LONDON MIDLAND AND SCOTTISH RAILWAY COMPANY. E.R.O. 21016.

Telephone:

DEPARTMENT,

STATION,

19

Dear Madam,

I regret to have to inform you that the Company will not have occasion for your services after and your engagement will therefore terminate at close of work on that date.

The Company appreciates and thanks you for the assistance given by you during the shortage of male labour brought about by war conditions.

Yours faithfully,

Mrs. ~~or Miss~~

Signalwoman Hobson's dismissal notice, dated 1946. Five years later (having remarried and become Gertrude Richardson) she was invited to return to the same signalbox (see following chapter).

The war had shown women that, in many cases, 'men's work' suited them better than that deemed appropriate for their own sex. Pat Foreman had been an engine cleaner at Kentish Town — 'a miserable place to work,' she had called it — and yet, when she left and went into 'a cosy little factory' she felt that she was 'an ex-railway worker working in a factory' and, in spite of the comfort, she was 'miserable'.[178] Similarly, former goods porter Mabel Watkinson recalled:

> I went back to my job in a grocery store and I soon found out how much I hated that. I missed being out in the open air and I felt claustrophobic, miserable and bored, and I missed the company of the railwaywomen.

Miss Watkinson discovered that men were 'getting preference not only on railways but every other job'. However in 1947 she successfully applied to be a bus conductress, in which job she remained for 28 years. Other ex-railwaywomen found themselves attracted to traditionally male jobs: Telegraphist Phyllis Wright joined the Exeter City Police and Porter Kathleen Hadfield became a postwoman, a job that was 'not as much fun as working on the railway'.

A number of former signalwomen were interviewed and, without exception, every one of them enjoyed the work, grew to love the railway and the peaceful atmosphere of a lonely signalbox and were reluctant to leave. Many recalled with great affection the old stoves, the twinkling lights, the bells, the levers and the brass instruments. Some said they were in tears when they had to leave. On their return to 'women's work', they felt they had lost something of themselves: pride in being entrusted with people's lives, self-respect from knowing they had accepted such responsibility. Above all, they missed being one of the huge family of railway workers.

A signalwoman making a pot of tea on her stove. The flowery umbrella is, presumably, hers.

COURTESY OF THE NRM

A small number of women managed to stay in male grades, but not without criticism. A year after the war ended Mr Holloway (writing in *The Railway Review*) demanded: 'Why are women kept on a number of jobs when it has always been a man's job?'[179] A later correspondent asserted that the railways ought to dispense with every married woman whose husband was working;[180] while another added that wives worked purely out of 'greed for gold' and accused them of forcing single women into prostitution by taking work at lower rates.[181] The latter comment deeply offended Miss A. Kenney,* a refreshment room waitress at Leeds, who wrote in reply that his remark was a 'horrible libel'. She upheld married women's right to work and reminded him: 'Woman is no longer the slave of man.'[182]

By the beginning of 1947, there were only 59,780 women employed by the Big Four, a decrease of nearly 50,000 in just over 12 months.† There was a national labour shortage after the war, causing the Ministry of Labour to appeal again to women to enter industry, because the workforce was too small to meet production objectives. After breaking many women's hearts (and severely reducing their financial position) by dismissing them, by 1947 the railways suffered staff shortages, partly owing to the national situation, but also because of the introduction of the 40-hour week. Mary Smethurst, dismissed in 1946 after working for six years as a numbertaker at Castleton, LMS, was invited to return in 1947. She jumped at the chance, and stayed in her post a further four years. At one point there were 900 signalbox vacancies and women — some of whom had only recently been dispensed with — were recruited to help fill them. Similarly, London Transport began to advertise for women porters (later designated 'station assistants'); not under war work arrangements but as part of the regular staff.

The Labour government, which had been elected in 1945, nationalised the Big Four to create British Railways on 1st January 1948. At this time there were still some women in male grades, happy, proficient and unwilling to leave. One of them, Mrs Macefield, who had worked at Bushbury Goods, LMS, for six years told *Carry On* magazine that she would find it 'very hard indeed' to give up her job.[183] Such women continued to be the subject of controversy. 'When are we going to see the elimination of female traffic staff on the railways?' demanded one NUR member in *The Railway Review*, but another — more realistic — railwayman explained that more, not fewer female staff were needed, if BR was to reduce men's hours and grant them more leave.[184]

In the House of Commons in 1948, Colonel Clarke MP informed the Minister of Labour that people were 'shocked' to discover that women were still working on track maintenance, which he described as 'hard and dangerous work.' However, Mr Ness Edwards assured him that the women were volunteers who were not compelled to continue, and who would be transferred to lighter work if they so requested.[185]

Four years after the war ended, the editor of *The Railway Review* published the first *Railwaywoman's Handbook*. Its front cover carried a drawing of a woman guard and inside was a list of some of the previously-male grades now open to women, including porter, guard and ticket collector. Railways, it claimed, 'offer excellent careers to the ambitious and are accessible in ever-growing measure to women of today'. The *Handbook* even acknowledged that the exclusion of women from 'male' grades had been wrong:

* Miss Kenney was an activist in Leeds 2 NUR Branch, and a delegate to the ACCUCWW.

† They were distributed thus: LMS, 19,261; LNER, 16,738; GWR, 8,649; SR, 5,432. There were in addition 9,700 women on London Transport's railways, of whom 5,650 were in male grades.

> A woman's adaptability and skill in industry are rarely admitted until she is put to the test and emerges triumphantly. In fact, her former incompetency to fill many posts was assumed, and it took a war to prove the fallacy of that belief.
>
> In the service of British Railways a wide field is open for women workers. ... The plain fact is ... that women have proved themselves capable of covering numerous jobs, necessary to the efficiency of British Railways in a way which ensures their permanent association with the industry, and that, too, explains why over 50,000 women workers are so employed today. ... Fortunately the contribution of women is recognised in Government and official quarters, and every encouragement is given to sustain their interest in the protracted obligations of railway operation. [186]

That such positive assertions should be published under the auspices of the NUR was both uplifting and promising: at last the union acknowledged women's permanent place in the uniformed traffic grades. In practice, instead of being recruited to male grades, women were ousted from the few they still held, including the ones pictorially represented in the *Handbook*. Curiously, about the same time as the *Handbook* was published, its mother paper *The Railway Review* printed the following correspondence:

> FIRE THE FEMALES. Now that we are drawing to the close of another year, will anything be done by British Railways to eliminate as many female staff as possible — and whom I consider have been allowed to remain on the job far too long. Bachelor.[187]

In reply, Mary Mosley and Miss E. Franks remarked:

> What a poor morbid creature 'Bachelor' must be; and no wonder he is a bachelor. During the war we women did our bit going to bed after the all-clear had gone at 3 a.m. and up again at 5:30 a.m. to start work at 6 a.m. Did 'Bachelor' go in the Forces? I don't think so. I suppose he stayed at home picking spots off the female staff.[188]

Later that year, some women members of Covent Garden NUR branch (war workers who had remained for four years after the war ended) put forth a reasonable request: that women who had filled a male uniformed grade for over eight years be appointed to the permanent staff. Although *The Railwaywoman's Handbook* had stated that 'a wide field is open' to women and that 'every encouragement' would be given to them, the NUR's General Secretary Jim Figgins opposed even the modest request from the women at Covent Garden and the EC upheld his decision.[189] After its first optimistic and pro-female issue, *The Railwaywoman's Handbook* was never published again.

The employer agreed with the NUR EC. When, in 1949, BR planned to shed up to 30,000 staff, the first to go were men over 65 — and all women in male grades. The wartime limit of 1cwt on parcels was abolished, prompting BR to claim that women were (once again) 'unsuitable' for jobs as porters. The only wages grades in which the number of women increased was that of carriage cleaner which, except gatekeeping, was the lowest paid, and certainly the lowest-status railway occupation.

SUMMARY

Bringing in a new group of workers, unused to the railway industry, hurrying them through their training, putting them straight into levels of responsibility not normally attained by staff until they had years of experience — and never attained by women — does seem to be asking for trouble. Yet the mishaps and problems one might have expected from such an ad-hoc workforce failed to materialise. Against all the odds, women excelled, and did so under the terrible circumstances of war.

Railway work was, however, harder for women during the Second World War than it had been for their First World War predecessors. Daily life was more affected by enemy bombings — 60,000 British civilians were killed in air raids — and railways were especially targeted. More was expected of war-workers this time: women's abilities had been established during the First World War and they were expected to live up to their predecessors.

Outside of railways, notions of feminine frailty were increasingly seen as outmoded. Women were in the army; some flew planes, others worked in shipyards; even the heir to the throne, Princess Elizabeth, was training to be an army motor mechanic. Employers followed the lead of the government, which conscripted women into the services and expected them to take part in civil defence, even operating anti-aircraft guns. Railways echoed these attitudes: women were exposed to more hazardous work, such as track maintenance and fog signalling, and were guards on heavily-bombed main lines.

While women were proud of themselves for performing such work, some men indulged in what historian Susan Briggs has described as ' "little woman" style mockery'[190] and their participation has been ignored or belittled by historians. For example, railway historian R. S. Joby had only one comment to make about war workers in his 1984 book *The Railwaymen.* It was: 'Contact with caked grime smeared their makeup.' Women are not mentioned anywhere else in the book. Even the Prime Minister overlooked railwaywomen's contribution to the industry. At the end of December 1943, the railways' busiest year, Winston Churchill expressed the gratitude of the nation to 'every railwayman who had participated in this great transport effort'.[191]

We have seen how women war-workers on the railways were subjected to criticism by railwaymen. Their attacks were often unwarranted and usually unfair, in view of the fact that the women were either conscripts who had no choice, or volunteers who had bravely agreed to work in a male-dominated industry that was one of the primary enemy bombing targets. Overall, however, war-workers received better treatment from railwaymen than did their predecessors during the First World War. There are several factors that may account for this. In 1915 women were barred from the NUR; by 1939 they had been 'sisters' for 24 years. Involvement with the trade union movement politicised many working men and raised their awareness of concepts such as socialism and egalitarianism, which led some to rethink their traditional beliefs about women's position in society. Many railwaymen, too old to be called up, had already worked alongside women during the First World War, and women themselves took comfort in the knowledge that women of their mothers' generation had successfully replaced railwaymen two decades previously. Indeed, a few older women were performing their second stint of war-work.

In wider society, women had advanced their civil and social emancipation; more than 50 had been elected to parliament, and eight were in the Cabinet. It began to seem rather old-fashioned to talk about woman's 'correct sphere' or to maintain that women had no place in public life or in traditionally male industries.

Appendices

Women employed by the Big Four *Excluding hotel and catering staff*		
	March 1939	*June 1944*
Clerical and technical	11,565	29, 512
Crossing keepers	1,467	1,693
Cleaners and charwomen	2,650	2,349
Workshop women and artisans	964	16,673
Waiting room/lavatory attendants	450	458
Carriage cleaners	739	5,014
Miscellaneous other grades	525	1,989
War-workers in male wages grades	0	41,202
TOTAL	18,360	98,890

Female wages staff at Wolverton Works 1939-47		
Date	*No. of women employed*	*% of total Wages Staff*
25.11.39	93	2.35%
30.11.40	78	2.15%
29.11.41	324	8.29%
28.11.42	724	18.91%
27.11.43	729	20.55%
25.11.44	474	13.26%
24.11.45	364	10.80%
30.11.46	267	6.64%
29.11.47	216	5.64%
Clerks and storeswomen excluded. *The figures for 1942-4 include women working on government contracts.*		

Source: <http://www.livingarchive.org.uk >

WOMEN EMPLOYED BY THE GWR, LNER, LMS, SR, LPTB AND RCH, 1939-1945					
Year	*Clerical*	*Conciliation*	*Workshop/artisan*	*Miscell.*	*Ancillary*
1939	11,226	------	635	6,126	5,566
1940	11,642	------	591	5,941	5,315
1941	14,778	9,071	1,806	5,363	5,715
1942	23,763	23,242	8,669	5,622	6,278
1943	26,624	31,109	11,943	5,768	6,406
1944	26,965	34,865	12,394	6,167	6,464
1945	27,536	34,545	10,302	6,494	6,596

Source: *Railway Gazette* 9 August 1946

WOMEN EMPLOYED IN WORKSHOPS, JUNE 1942				
	GWR	*LMS*	*LNER*	*SR*
Coppersmith	9	39	0	0
Coach bodymaker	0	6	0	0
Coach bodymaker trainee	0	0	0	33
Crane driver	37	59	84	5
Electrician	0	11	5	10
Painter	17	36	34	70
Rivet heater	28	0	36	34
Metal machinist	0	441	580	181
Fitter	37	589	24	38
Saw sharpener	0	0	0	2
Tinsmith	0	4	0	0
Miscellaneous	459	1514	1907	747
TOTAL FEMALE WORKSHOP STAFF	587	2,699	2,670	1,120

SOME FEMALE STAFF WORKING FOR THE LMS		
	31/12/44	*31/12/45*
Signalwomen	532	515
Porter signalwomen	90	80
Passenger guards	229	192
Porter guards	155	129
TOTAL	1006	916

The total number of women employed in male wages positions on the LMS at the end of December 1945 was 12,776, or 9.1% of the total wages staff.

Source: Glynn Waite, Chairman, Midland Railway Society.

Women in wages grades, June 1942				
Grade	*GWR*	*LMS*	*LNER*	*SR*
Billposter	0	0	6	0
Chauffeur	0	0	3	5
Checker	11	0	0	0
Cloakroom attendant	17	19	0	6
Crossing keeper	55	10	52	2
Guard, passenger	46	0	0	0
Parcel porter	338	438	109	63
Porter-guard	12	10	2	0
Porter-signalman	6	21	36	0
Shunter	2	0	0	0
Signalwoman	48	58	82	0
Ticket collector	202	55	13	62
Toll collector	0	0	2	2
Announcer	0	18	0	11
Train attendant	0	4	2	0
Porter grade 2	1035	2369	1549	604
Porter grade 1	112	136	27	89
Dock porter	22	0	0	0
Leading porter	16	16	7	0
Junior porter	32	33	58	19
Goods porter	2311	5155	2555	810
Vanguard	351	769	534	289
Numbertaker	14	134	55	3
Loader	32	296	67	0
PW labourer	72	88	431	58
Ganger	0	1	0	0
Engine cleaner	0	361	395	0
Loco shed labourer	44	1039	113	14
Oiler/greaser loco	20	0	0	0
Lengthwoman	0	0	1	0
Carriage cleaner	942	908	686	520
Chargewoman cleaner	0	0	1	13
Oiler/greaser carriages	0	48	74	9
Waitresses	14	212	149	16
Restaurant car attendant	17	2	20	0
Cook	8	39	38	0

Women employed on railways, June 1942				
	GWR	*LMS*	*LNER*	*SR*
Carriage & Wagon	943	963	791	550
Locomotive Dept.	141	1,666	1,580	16
Permanent Way Dept.	72	162	477	59
Goods Dept.	2,809	7,954	3,528	1,122
Traffic	2,167	3,377	2,313	894
Signals & Telegraphs	32	2	37	78
Signals & Telegraphs labourers	0	0	303	0
Dock, Quay & Marine	258*	152	55	0
Civil Engineering	153	446	598	483

**Of whom 192 were dock porters.*

There were also an unknown number of 'miscellaneous staff', these included sports ground assistants, halt attendants, storeswomen, police, lost property officers, warehousewomen, first aid attendants, laboratory workers, matrons, office cleaners, advertising clerks, messengers, and others.

RCA female membership 1939-1950		
Year	*Women*	*% of members*
1939	6,839	10.6
1940	9.068	12.9
1941	15,355	19.6
1942	20,540	24.1
1943	21,843	24.9
1944	22,497	25.3
1945	21,856	24.4
1946	17,502	20.0
1947	19,044	21.0
1948	18,289	20.5
1949	17,041	19.7
1950	16,745	19.6

Source: Wallace, M. (1997) *Single Or Return?* (TSSA).

List of Some Jobs Performed by Women on Britain's Railways During the Two World Wars

MISCELLANEOUS MAINTENANCE
Axlebox cleaner
Bogie cleaner
Carriage cleaner
Carriage lampwoman
Carriage washing machine attendant
Electric light examiner
Examiner
Globe cleaner (gas lamps)
Lampwoman
Linen porter
Messenger
Oil and gas filler
Station painter
Travelling carriage cleaner
Wheel tapper

TRAFFIC GRADES
Billposter
Brakeswoman
Bridge painter
Chauffeuse
Checker
Goods porter
Guard
Halt attendant
Lampwoman
Leading porter
Lift attendant
Lost property attendant
Luggage weigher
Numbertaker
Points woman
Porter
Senior porter
Signalbox 'girl'
Signalwoman
Station announcer
Telegraphist
Ticket collector
Ticket examiner
Timekeeper
Train attendant
Train indicator operator
Travelling ticket collector

GOODS, CARTAGE & ROAD TRANSPORT
Caller-off
Capstanwoman
Carter
Chain horse driver
Checker
Contactwoman
Crane operator
Demurrage numbertaker
Dock porter
Electric truck driver
Goods porter
Horsevan driver
Loader
Lorry repairer
Mobile crane driver
Motor bus conductor
Motor lorry driver
Officewoman
Road motor attendant
Roper
Sheeter
Stablewoman
Store leader
Vanguard
Weighbridge woman
Weigher

WORKSHOP GRADES
Blacksmith
Blacksmith's striker
Boilermaker's assistant
Concreter (making sleepers and coping posts)
Crane driver
Drop-stamp hammer driver
Electrician
Engine builder's assistant
Engine painter
Engine repairer
Engineer's labourer
Fitter
Hammer driver
Jig-borer
Machine driller

Machine shop worker
Mechanic (forges, lathes, radial drills)
Oxy-acetylene welder
Oxy-gas flame cutter
Rivet heater
Riveter
Shot blaster
Sleeper shaper
Tube welder
Wagon builder
Wood planer

LOCOMOTIVE RUNNING SHEDS
Fitter's labourer
Fitter's mate
Timekeeper

SIGNALS, TELEGRAPHS & P-WAY
Ganger
Inspector's timekeeper
Labourer
Lengthwoman
Lineman's assistant
Plan room attendant
Stores labourer
Telegraph labourer
Timekeeper
Timekeeper's assistant

LOCOMOTIVE DEPARTMENT
Ash filler
Caller-up *
Depot office assistant
Engine cleaner
Firelighter
Lampwoman
Lift machinery attendant
Messenger
Messroom attendant
Motor driver
Oiler/greaser
Pump labourer
Sand drier
Shed labourer
Stores issuer
Telephone attendant
Tool winder
Toolwoman
Tube cleaner

UNISEX OR WOMEN'S GRADES
Administration clerk
Booking clerk
Car cleaner (LTPB)
Carriage cleaner
Catering assistant
Cleaner
Cook
Crossing keeper
Draughtswoman
Engraver
First aid attendant
French polisher
Hostel assistant
Ladies' room attendant
Laundress
Matron
Messroom attendant
Needlewoman
Nurse
Office cleaner
Policewoman
Polisher
Seamstress
Secretary
Stewardess
Storekeeper
Telephone operator
Telephone supervisor
Ticket printer
Trimmer
Typist
Waiting room attendant
Waitress

*Before the universal use of telephones and alarm clocks, callers-up walked or cycled to railwaymen's houses, waking them for duty or taking messages to them.

References

[1] Bell, R. (1946) *History of the British railways during the war* (Railway Gazette) p46.
[2] Bagwell (1963) *The Railwaymen* (Allen & Unwin) p581.
[3] NUR EC Mins 1940 and 1941.
[4] Letter to the author, 1990.
[5] Letter to the author, 2005.
[6] Letter to the author, 1990.
[7] Letter to the author, 1990.
[8] *Daily Herald* 5 November 1942.
[9] Letter to the author, 1995.
[10] *Railway Magazine* February 1941. See also *Railway Gazette* 11 June 1943 and *The New York Post*, 9 July 1942.
[11] *Daily Herald* 18 July 1942.
[12] Interview with Annie Hodgeon, 1995.
[13] Daphne Hart, letter to the author, 2005.
[14] Wallace, M. (1997) *Single Or Return? The Official History of the* TSSA (TSSA).
[15] See Calder, A (1969) *A People's War* (Literary Guild) pp121 & 318.
[16] Isabella Anderson Gilder, letter to the author, 1990.
[17] Letter to the author, 2005
[18] Letter to the author, 1990.
[19] Personal interview with Louisa Jupp, 1995.
[20] Personal interview with Mrs Rowe, 1995.
[21] Personal interview with Mrs Davies, 1990.
[22] Letter to the author, 1990.
[23] *Daily Telegraph* 13 March 1942.
[24] Letter to the author, 2003.
[25] Cardiff Guard Mary Marchant, letter to the author, 1990.
[26] Mary Davies, letter to the author, 1990.
[27] Benson, T. (1941) *Sweethearts and Wives* p74.
[28] *Carry On* June 1941, p2.
[29] *Manchester Evening News* 19 December 1941.
[30] SR Magazine March/April 1943.
[31] Darwin, B. (1946) *War on the Line* (Middleton) p80.
[32] *Daily Herald* 22 June 1944.
[33] SR *Magazine* November 1945 p170.
[34] SR *Magazine* 1946, p108.
[35] Board of Trade Enquiry, 1945.
[36] Letter to the author, 2005.
[37] Letter to the author, 2005.
[38] Letter to the author, 2005.
[39] *Carry On* 27 October 1945.
[40] *The Railway Review* 10 July 1942, p3.
[41] NUR Minutes 1943.
[42] *London & North Eastern Railway Magazine* 1943 p28.
[43] Darwin, B. (1946) op. cit. p180.
[44] Darwin, B. (1946) op cit. p178.
[45] *Daily Herald* 7 April 1944. Thanks to Steve Daly.
[46] Pathé newsreels are available online at <www.itnarchive.com/britishpathe>
[47] Conversation with her son, Norman Harding, 18 July 2005.

[48] *Carry On* September/October 1940.
[49] *Railway Magazine* Feb 1941.
[50] *Great Western Railway Magazine.* June 1941, p146.
[51] Letter to the author, 1990.
[52] NER *Magazine* 1945, p28.
[53] LNER *Magazine* 1943, p144.
[54] Letter to the author, 1990.
[55] Letter to the author, 1990.
[56] Letter to the author, 1990.
[57] Nancy Walters, letter to the author, 2005.
[58] Letter to the author, 1990.
[59] Letter to the author, 1990.
[60] Letter to the author, 2005.
[61] *Daily Herald* 5 November 1942.
[62] *Daily Herald* 21 February 1941.
[63] May Westmoreland, letter to the author, 1995.
[64] Mabel Watkinson, letter to the author, 1990.
[65] Mary Davies, letter to the author, 1995.
[66] Personal correspondence with Mrs Lovsey's son, Derek, 1989.
[67] Letter to the author, 1990.
[68] Available online at <www.itnarchive.com/britishpathe>.
[69] *Railnews* June 1989.
[70] *Daily Telegraph* 27 April 1943. See also *Manchester Guardian* 10 November 1942.
[71] *Carry On* February 1943, p6.
[72] Letter to the author, 1995.
[73] Hilda Coe, letter to the author, 1990.
[74] Mrs Glasscock, letter to the author, 1990.
[75] Mrs Roberts, letter to the author, 1990.
[76] NER *Magazine* 1943, p206.
[77] NUR EC Minutes 1942 R1393.
[78] NUR EC Minutes 1944 R2186.
[79] Interview with Louisa Jupp, 1995.
[80] Edie Rowe, taped interview with the author, 1990.
[81] Letter to the author, 1995.
[82] Letter to the author, 1990.
[83] Interview with Clara Evans ,1995.
[84] Interview with Phyllis Mortimer, 1995.
[85] Interview with Edie Rowe, 1995.
[86] Ministry of Transport Accident Reports 1946.
[87] Letter to the author, 1990.
[88] Letter to the author, 1990.
[89] Steve Daly <http://www.trainweb.com/signalbox/branches/sd/signalwomen.htm>
[90] Interview with Vera Perry, 1995.
[91] Letter to the author, 1989.
[92] *The Railway Review* 31 July 1942. Letter from 'Bobby'.
[93] Letter to the author, 1990.
[94] Letter to the author, 1995.
[95] Interview with Vera Perry, 1995.
[96] *Carry On* August 1946, p2.
[97] Letter to the author 1990.

[98] Letter from Vera Williams 1990.
[99] Letter to the author 1990.
[100] Interview with Audrey Brown, 1995.
[101] Letter to the author, 1990.
[102] Judy Gascoyne letter to the author 2005.
[103] Letter to the author, 1995.
[104] National Archives AN2-532.
[105] NUR Minutes 1942, R1932.
[106] NUR EC Minutes 1944 and *The Railway Review* 18 February 1944.
[107] Nash, J. (1946) *The LMS at War* (LMS) p81.
[108] NUR Minutes 1949, R.3679.
[109] Rose Eastwood, letter to the author, 1990.
[110] Letter to the author, 1989.
[111] *The Railway Review* 14 January 1949.
[112] NUR EC Minutes 1946, R2455 and 1947, D498.
[113] Letter from Vera Williams, 1990.
[114] Letter to the author, 1990.
[115] Letter to the author, 1989.
[116] Letter to the author, 1995.
[117] Letter to the author, 1995.
[118] Letter to the author, 1990.
[119] Ibid.
[120] NUR EC Minutes March 1943.
[121] *Railway Gazette*, 27 September 1946.
[122] *Carry On* March 1943.
[123] *The Railway Review* 6 November 1942.
[124] NUR EC Minutes 1944, p18.
[125] <http://www.thisisworcester.co.uk>
[126] *The Railway Review* 19 February 1943.
[127] *The Railway Review* 11 December 1942.
[128] *The Railway Review* 1 January 1943.
[129] *The Railway Review* 15 January 1943.
[130] *The Railway Review* 29 January 1943.
[131] *The Railway Review* 12 February 1943.
[132] *The Railway Review* 8 September 1944.
[133] Letter to the author, 1995.
[134] Letter to the author, 2005.
[135] NUR EC Minutes, October & November 1943.
[136] Interview with Edie Rowe, 1995.
[137] *The Railway Review* 15 September 1944.
[138] *The Railway Review* 17 December 1943.
[139] *The Railway Review* 29 September 1944.
[140] LPTB Newsletter in *The Railway Review* 16 April 1943.
[141] Letter to the author, 1995.
[142] Letter to the author, 1990.
[143] Interview with Audrey Brown, 1995.
[144] Letter to the author, 1990.
[145] National Archives RAIL 1172 - 787 Southern Railway Staff Punishment Book.
[146] Interview with Clara Evans, 1995.
[147] Interview with Edie Rowe, 1995.

[148] Interview with Annie Hodgeon, 1995.
[149] National Archives AN2-187 Minutes of Staff Committee meeting 18 March 1943.
[150] McKenna, F. (1980) The Railway Workers (Faber & Faber) p98.
[151] Letter to the author, 1990.
[152] *The Railway Review* 5 July 1946. Conference report.
[153] NUR Minutes 1946. R.2563.
[154] *The Railway Review* 27 October 1944.
[155] *The Railway Review* 29 August 1947.
[156] *The Railway Review* 15 November 1946.
[157] *Manchester Guardian* 28 November 1942.
[158] *The Times* 4 April 1945.
[159] Letter to the author, 1990.
[160] *Daily Telegraph* 27 April 1943.
[161] *News Chronicle* 19 July 1944.
[162] *Railway Service Journal* January 1942, p24.
[163] REC Minute 3177, 24 April 1941; REC Catering Committee 5 May 1941 & 5 June 1941.
[164] GWR Census of Staff employed on 9 March 1946.
[165] Letter to the author, 2005.
[166] *Railway Magazine* July/August 1942, p207.
[167] *Railway Service Journal* November 1942, p173.
[168] *Railway Service Journal* March 1942.
[169] *Railway Service Journal* February 1943, p22.
[170] *Railway Service Journal* January 1942.
[171] *Railway Service Journal* July 1949 p297.
[172] Letter to the author, 1990.
[173] Letter to the author, 1990.
[174] LNER *Magazine* May 1946.
[175] NUR Minutes 1949 D1268.
[176] Scottish Record Office, Documents LNE/15/80.
[177] NUR Minutes 1949 D631.
[178] McKenna, F. (1980) *The Railway Workers* (Faber & Faber) p98.
[179] *The Railway Review* 4 October 1946.
[180] *The Railway Review* 8 November 1946.
[181] *The Railway Review* 22 November 1946
[182] *The Railway Review* 29 November 1946.
[183] *Carry On* February 1948, p9.
[184] *The Railway Review* 5 March 1948.
[185] *Hansard* 15 June 1948.
[186] *The Railwaywoman's Handbook* 1949.
[187] *The Railway Review* 18 March 1949 and 27 October 1950, letters page.
[188] *The Railway Review* 25 March 1949 letters page.
[189] NUR minutes 1949, R.3260.
[190] Briggs, S. (1975) *Keep Smiling Through.* Weidenfield and Nicholas. p173.
[191] *The Railway Review* 31 December 1943.

5: Postwar to 1974

> Surely, after having stood their ground through the perils of the blitz, women will not acquiesce to return to the role of inequality and inferiority to which they have been — and still are — subjected in most spheres of life.
>
> Kathrin Smith, *Railway Service Journal*, January 1942

From nationalisation in 1948 the railways were run initially by the Railway Executive, one of five transport bodies headed by the British Transport Commission (BTC), and then, from November 1953, by the BTC itself. The 37 hotels were run separately until they were returned to the railways under the title British Transport Hotels in 1962, the year that the British Railways Board (BRB) was formed. From 1964 it was known as British Rail (BR) and comprised six regions: Scottish, Eastern, Southern, North-Eastern, London Midland and Western.

From the early 50s, the railways suffered a serious decline in traffic, owing to the rise in car ownership, the increase in air travel, the growing popularity of foreign holidays and the trend to send goods by road. Even the shift away from domestic coal fires led to a loss of freight traffic. Between 1948 and 1963, 1,850 stations were closed and staff decreased by almost 27 percent. Despite this, the railways continued to make a loss, which in 1961 amounted to almost £87million. BR Chairman Dr Beeching's 1963 plan for the further curtailment of British Railways' services recommended the closure of many lines and a further 2,128 stations. These cuts made a disproportionate impact upon railwaywomen because they tended to work at stations, signalboxes and level crossings on quiet branch lines, the very lines chosen for closure.

Half a million operating staff were employed in 1960; this decreased by more than half to just 210,000 by 1977. The clerical staff, which numbered 629,000 in 1948, had shrunk to just 251,000 by 1970.* In the face of staff reductions such as these, the trades unions were very active during the 50s and 60s, and a bitter and protracted strike occurred in 1955. Between 1949 and 1980 NUR membership halved as the railway workforce declined by 70%. Women union activists were few. Their NUR membership — in both 1951 and 1971 — was only 2% of the total, although the proportion peaked briefly at 3.5% in the early 1960s.

The railways were still suffering from the effects of unusually heavy use and lack of maintenance during two world wars. Everything was out of date — most lines were celebrating their centenaries — and the industry was so massive that modernisation was going to be an extremely slow and costly process. Staff accommodation varied considerably, from spacious, modern-style offices to dilapidated, dingy goods depots that

---

* The total staff in 1962 was 475,000 and 1965 it was 365,043.

had not changed in a century. One railway clerk remarked in 1949 that only one goods station in London had a typewriter; the rest were still using pencils.[1]

That year new accommodation standards were set, with particular reference to women. Where 12 or more were employed, the following were required: a rest room in a quiet location, with 'emergency access' to lavatories; a bed or couch; bedding and hot water bottles; two easy chairs; a sink with hot water; a table; a washable screen; first aid equipment and remedies; and large and small enamel bowls. Only large administrative departments or carriage-cleaning depots employed that number of women and small depots did not attain this standard.

Overall, conditions continued to be poor. For example, in 1955 a journalist investigating carriage cleaning remarked: 'Marylebone was built in 1899 and nothing seems to have changed'. She described the women's messroom:

> The room, approached via a rubbish dump, is dark and gloomy and is used by the women for eating, washing and resting ... here is no canteen. The workers bring their own pies and soups to be hotted up, and brew their tea from an enormous black kettle on a gas ring.[2]

The Offices, Shops and Railway Premises Act 1963 was supposed to improve the provision of lighting, heating, toilets and washing facilities for everyone. In some workplaces the barest minimum facilities were installed to comply with the letter of the law; in others – particularly those used by wages grade staff on stations and in yards – there was no change and the working environment continued to be as run-down, dingy and in some cases rat-infested as it had been for decades.

Against this background railwaywomen struggled not only to retain their jobs, but also to gain equality of pay and opportunity. After the war the number of women employed by railways showed an immediate decline, almost entirely owing to the loss of war workers in uniformed grades. By 1950, of the 605,455 persons employed by the railways, about 40,000 were women; by 1956 this had fallen to about 35,000, of whom 16,000 were in wages grades and 19,000 in salaried grades.

The 1950s are usually cited as the decade in which women went 'back to the home' after their war-work; however, in reality the number of married women in employment increased until, by 1951, they comprised 38% of the female workforce. One of the reasons for this was the abolition of the marriage bar for white-collar employees. A resolution to this effect was proposed at the 1946 RCA conference, but was amended to apply only in exceptional circumstances, and the amendment was carried. This put the union out of step with the TUC, which wanted the marriage bar abolished. Between 1947 and 1950 national and local government, railways and other nationalised bodies abandoned it. Ashford 1 RCA branch was in favour of the marriage bar, and in 1950 complained about its being removed without consultation with the unions. That year the RCA dismissed one of its administrators, Margaret Cairncross, for getting married. Even though her spouse had once been a high-ranking RCA officer, her request to continue was rejected by the Executive because it contradicted the union's aforementioned 1946 conference resolution relating to women members who were employed by the railways, i.e. that they be dismissed upon marriage except 'in exceptional circumstances'. A proposal that she be allowed to continue under this proviso was ruled out of order by the RCA president.[3]

Women in Male Wages Grades

Owing to a shortage of men, many women continued to work in male wages grades long after the war had ended. Accident compensation records for 1954, for example, reveal that women were still employed as motor drivers, numbertakers, vanguards, porters, goods porters, station attendants, motor attendants, van attendants, metal machinists, shed labourers, travelling carriage cleaners and ticket collectors. Some railwaymen opposed the employment of women in peacetime. One wrote in 1950: 'The continued employment of female labour ... is detrimental to all railway workers and ... will result in chaos.'[4] However, London Transport did not agree: it employed 450 women porters and ticket collectors in the 50s and recruited many more over the next decade, effectively converting these to unisex jobs. A number of them had been recruited – along with thousands of men – from the West Indies, to help fill the many inner-city vacancies that both LT and BR had problems filling. For the same reason, some of the war-workers who had been 'dispensed with' were re-employed. One, wartime ticket collector Florrie Smart, returned in 1954 after her husband's death, in order to support her two dependent children. She became a station cleaner-cum-ticket issuer, a post she filled until she reached retirement age (then 60). She loved the job and, unwilling to leave, sought permission to continue part-time and did so for ten years, finally retiring in March 1988.

Some women who had not been war-workers were drafted in when men could not be found. A Pathé newsreel of 1951 shows a group of women working on the tracks at Stonebridge Park, London Underground, using spades to dig up weeds. The commentary stated that 400 women were so employed.[5] In 1952 a group of women who had been stood off from Leicester's hosiery factories also took up track maintenance and, in 1957, 400 women were employed to weed tracks on the LMR. Former waitress Elizabeth Hall, aged 22 and married with a child aged four, told *The Daily Telegraph:* 'I found it heavy at first, but I soon overcame the tiredness. It is cold, but when we get into the rhythm of it we are too busy to feel cold.' Their pay was £4.15s for working 7.30 a.m. till 5 p.m. Monday to Friday, and if they worked at weekends, loading up the weeds and rubbish they had cleared during the week, they took home more than £6. Their ganger remarked: 'They are good workers and with a little more experience will be as good as the men.'[6] In the early 50s Helen McGuire and Catherine MacMaster were motor car drivers for senior railway officials at Edinburgh, working from 7.40 a.m. till 3 p.m. and 2 p.m. till 10.30 p.m. alternate weeks. They wore navy uniforms, brown kid gloves and peaked chauffeurs' caps.[7]

By 1957 there were 2,000 uniformed railwaywomen. The number on stations decreased until by 1966 they comprised only 6% of ticket collectors and porters.* In 1952 there were 28,500 women in the porter grades; in 1968, only 11,000. While this constituted a sharp decline from the numbers employed during the war, it was the first time in railway history that women were recruited to these positions in peacetime. Women's permanent place in the uniformed grades was symbolised in 1957 when a dark blue beret was designed and issued to them so they could cease wearing peaked caps, which were seen as too masculine. The berets had silver piping and on the front was pinned a chromium badge with the British Railways 'lion and wheel' logo and the woman's job title.

* In 1968 the 41 wages grades were replaced with the generic 'railman' 'leading railman' and 'senior railman'. Thus, a porter became a railman; a Grade 1 porter, a leading railman; and a ticket collector, a senior railman.

MAN AND WIFE RUN STATION—AND TEND PRIZE-WINNING GARDEN

The recent announcement by the railway authorities that Raunds station had won a first prize in the station gardens competition in the Leicester Operating Superintendent's District mentioned that the garden had been tended by the stationmaster, Mr. Peter Hutchinson, and his porter-wife.

Intrigued by the description 'porter-wife' I went to Raunds a few days ago to meet young, attractive Mrs. Freda Hutchinson, who has been a part-time porter at the station for three years. She and her husband comprise the whole of the station's staff.

Although the station is tiny and two miles from the centre of the town, there is plenty of work to be done. On a single-line track from Kettering to Cambridge six passenger trains and two goods trains pass through every day and on Saturdays there are five passenger trains. The station is closed on Sundays.

Busiest day

'For its size the station has a good number of passengers. Saturday is our busiest day, for the local fishermen go to Huntingdon and Buckden', said Mr. Hutchinson. Part-time means that Mrs. Hutchinson has to do 22 hours a week, which she prefers to do over three full days. When I asked her exactly how she spends her time, she said she did everything except work the signals and assist in the shunting of goods. 'Once a week, all the signal lamps have to be cleaned and their wicks trimmed. Then I have to put them all back again on top of the signal poles.' However, when the weather is really rough and the poles sway, she persuades her husband to do the job for her.

Housework

She does her housework and shopping methodically on her free days. Meanwhile only child Brian, who is five, is collected by bus in the morning and taken to school in Raunds, where he stays until the bus brings him home at 4.30.

Born at Croxton, near St Neot's, Hunts, Mrs. Hutchinson was a chemist's assistant and worked in a shoe factory before her marriage in 1951 to Mr. Hutchinson, who was then a railway clerk at St Neot's.

'I'd no idea I would be doing this six years later,' she said. At first the couple were unable to get a house, but Mr. Hutchinson knew that one way of getting one was to become a stationmaster. He was promoted to stationmaster and took over Raunds station with the adjoining house, in 1953, when there was a full-time male porter there. 'And we had just managed to get a council house six months before his promotion!' said Mrs. Hutchinson. -- E.A.S.

THRAPSTON, RAUNDS & OUDLE JOURNAL (CIRCA 1957)

Freda and Peter Hutchinson.
NORTHAMPTON CHRONICLE & ECHO

ITEMS for the agenda of this year's Conference make it clear that signalmen are becoming aware of the vast potentialities of the new signalling systems envisaged by the modernisation plan.

There is also a demand for equal pay for women employed in signal cabins. I thought there were no women employed in signalling on our railways to-day.* Because of the lack of new entrants into the grade of signalmen, is it intended to repeat the war-time measure of employing women in our lower-class cabins? That will have to be strenuously resisted—despite the news which our old friend Harry Franklin gave us of women working cabins in Russia.

From several angles many of our cabins are not fit for women to be employed in. We will wait to hear what the delegates have to say about this when we meet at Clacton.

FEMALE CROSSING-KEEPERS

SIR,—I am pleased to find at least one N.U.R. member on the side of the residential Crossing-keepers. Oh, but how we females differ from our more fortunate males. They must have a full uniform while we the so-called weaker sex are allowed an overcoat (or Mac). The males (in most cases) have eight hours relief per week while the females are only allowed **four** hours per week shopping concession.

I asked last year for an additional hour on my concession in order to get my Christmas shopping done, and found on the next pay day our benevolent B.R. had deducted a quarter-day's pay for one hour's leave. This was adjusted after protest and the noble sum of **sixpence** for the **one** hour additional leave had been deducted. Is there any other grade on British Railways paid at the rate of 6d. per hour?

We women are supposed to be expert at cackling (gossiping) so what about it, can we cackle loud enough together to make ourselves heard?—Yours, etc.,

6d. per Hour.

Crossing Keeper Alice Foster and a colleague on the steps outside her workplace, Pool Hey Junction signalbox, Southport. A. FOSTER

Cuttings from *The Railway Review*, 1955. Above: a note from a delegate to the 1955 NUR Signalmen's Conference. Below: a crossing keeper airs her grievances.

Annie Smith, one of our few lady crossing keepers, was a challenger recently on the BBC-TV panel game *What's My Line?* Unfortunately she failed to beat the questioners and was guessed after eight "nos". Annie, along with her husband Jack, looks after the busy crossing at Rearsby on the line from Leicester to Peterborough, and they are both well-known characters in their district. So much so that one of the panel, Lady Isobel Barnett, asked to be excused, having met Annie many times before. Further proof of popularity came from Annie herself: 'The vicar of Rearsby complained to me that his congregation had dwindled considerably the night I was on TV!' Smiling Annie, who has the personality becoming of one who before her marriage was a leading chorus girl said, 'The trip to the BBC was the thrill of my life.'

Above: Magazine article about Crossing Keeper Smith.
ORIGIN UNKNOWN

Left: *Railnews*, August 1970

Below: *Manchester Guardian*, 11 September 1957

FIRST WOMAN TO BE CHIEF STEWARD

PROVIDING a spot of glamour on SR's luxury Pullman Brighton Belle is Mrs Jennifer Keogh. And 29-year-old Jennifer, here serving coffee in the first class, is a belle about as special as the Belle itself — she's BR's first-ever chief stewardess.

Jennifer got the job after four years stewarding on the Waterloo-Exeter trains, which she joined after managing an Exeter restaurant. Now, in her new capacity, she's back on the West Country run, which is ideal as she lives in Exeter.

RESCUED WOMAN FROM TUBE RAIL TRACK

In path of train

A London Transport station woman and a passenger yesterday received Carnegie Awards for "outstanding bravery" in rescuing a woman from the electrified track in the path of a Tube train.

During an evening rush hour at Liverpool Street station last November a woman passenger fell on to the east-bound track. Another passenger, Mr George Mansfield, of Brocket Way, Chigwell, jumped down to rescue her although he knew a train was due at any moment. He was unable to move her, and a station woman, Mrs Elsie Buck, of Mawney Road, Romford, also jumped down, and together they got the woman to the platform just before the train passed over the spot.

A woman working, in an unknown capacity, on the construction of a diesel shunting engine, Derby locomotive workshops, early 50s.
DERBY MUSEUMS/TALES OF THE OLD RAILWAYMEN-

Mrs Maillard, the matron at Midland lodging hostel, Sheffield, c1950.

The heading on the noticeboard reads: *Enginemen are requested to mark the time to be called & to occupy the room next to their fireman.*

MR MAILLARD, IN MCKENNA

Station Staff

Porters' duties varied enormously from one station to another. Lena Lowdell worked at Sheffield's Darnall station for 20 years:

> At 5 a.m. I opened the station and lit the coal fires in the waiting rooms and all the gas lights, then worked in the ticket office till the clerk arrived at 8.30. I had to see to all the trains, closing carriage doors and putting mail and parcels into the guard's van. I had to weigh pigeons in their baskets and send them off by train, and also received baskets of pigeons to release in the street. In between trains I had to deliver all the mail to two signalboxes and light about 19 lamps. Then there was numbertaking of the wagons being used by three local firms.[8]

Freda Hutchinson worked as a porter at Raunds, Northamptonshire, for seven years:

> In June 1953, my husband Peter became stationmaster. A few months later the porter's job became vacant, and the District Office let it be known that an application from me would receive favourable consideration. I was very apprehensive because I was not sure that I would be able to fulfil my role, particularly as I had a small son. However, I decided to give it a go. I was provided with a very smart uniform including a beret and badge.
>
> I thoroughly enjoyed my life as a porter and quickly adapted to the needs of the job. There were only six passenger trains to attend to each day, plus two freight trains. Our main customers were coal merchants and farmers and we handled regular pork pie and sausage traffic. The station boasted a working weighbridge, which I had to learn to operate, and I had to work the levers in the signalbox which allowed the twice-a-day goods train into the station yard. These levers were heavy to pull, and a certain amount of knack was required. In this respect, I was at least more successful than one relief station master who was quite small in stature. The results of his efforts were that the engine of the goods train became derailed, with all of its wheels on the ground, and the single line was blocked for three days.
>
> The ASLEF strike in 1955 had a devastating effect on the branch line. We carried on with our duties as far as we could but, with no trains, the work seemed pointless. The coal merchants at Raunds made arrangements for their coal to be carried by road, and the traffic was lost to rail forever, whilst fertilisers for the local farmers met with the same fate. Even the pork pies and sausage parcels were lost, never to return, and as a result the station began to die. I was never approached by a trade union official for me to join their ranks and, after seeing what had taken place as a result of the 1955 strike, I would have thought hard and long before taking such action.
>
> We took great pride in our little station. We won several prizes for station cleanliness and for our displays in the station gardens. It was often said by the locals that Raunds was the only station in the country were the porter gave the station master his orders!
>
> Unfortunately, all good things came to an end and Dr Beeching's axe finished both mine and my husband's career on the railway. The line, along with many others, was closed. We frequently reminisce about our days on the railway, and both agree that they were among the happiest days of our lives.[9]

Joan Percival became a Grade 1 Porter-in-Charge at a small station near Warrington:

> There were two of us to run it, one on the early shift and one on lates, changing week-about, so one person ran the station alone. This was not an unusual job for a woman; around this area they had quite a few. We had to wear many 'caps': booking clerk, ticket collector, parcels clerk, gardener, cleaner, porter and accounts clerk, doing daily, weekly and monthly accounts. The only person above us was the station master, whose office was at another station so we didn't see much of him, so we had to be station master as well. He usually came once a week to pay out the wages; sometimes he couldn't come, so I had to get on an engine to collect them, get another engine back, then pay the signalmen, the platelayers and my colleague, not forgetting to pay myself. A spare station master's hat was there to wear if we wished, and I sometimes put it on when the late trains came in full of drunks, as it seemed to steady them a bit.[10]

Railwaywomen occasionally appeared in the press for doing something noteworthy or simply for being women in men's jobs. One journalist remarked that Chester Road, LMR, had been 'transformed by a woman's touch' since Porter Edna Hulls arrived. 'Lace curtains flutter at the waiting room windows. There are carpet strips on the floor, armchairs in the porters' room and a bowl of blue hyacinths in the booking office.'[11] Veronica Glover was said to bring 'glamour' to the platform at Gretton, LMR,[12] while Edna Davis, the only woman porter at Smethick, LMS, was in the news for moving two tons of refuse and carting ten barrow-loads of bricks from the goods yard to make a border for the station garden.[13] In 1957 a woman porter saved the life of a passenger who had fallen onto the track.[14] In 1954 two working mothers, Porters Eva Richardson and Maud Harvey – dubbed 'The Two Blondies' – cultivated a platform garden 80 yards long at Streetly, LMR, won first prize in a competition. They appear to have pioneered what is now termed 'job-sharing'. The press reported that Mrs Carol Fink, the only woman axle-oiler at Redhill carriage and wagon department, frequently swapped her greasy overalls for elegant dresses to compete in ballroom dancing competitions.[15]

British Railways Magazine stated in 1953: 'There is still a Station Mistress at Deadwater'.* Violet Mace was station mistress at Berney Arms, Norfolk, a station 'in the middle of the often windswept Halvergate marshes and two miles from any road access'.[16] Pathé made a newsreel about Dolly Palmer, who by 1961 had been station mistress at Althorne, Essex, for 20 years. She walked three miles each way between her home and the station, where she and her male colleague worked nine hours each, dealing with 32 trains a day and 15 on Sundays.[17] She was filmed, at the age of 53, climbing a tall ladder to clean the signal glass and operating the signalbox and the crossing gates. In the 50s another Mrs Palmer was in charge of a busy halt on a rural line in Gloucestershire:

> They used to queue at Knightwick, where Mrs Palmer was station mistress, to load up their produce and even in the 1960s, just before closure, the station was handling 1,500 boxes a day at the height of the fruit picking season.[18]

She lost her job when the whole line fell victim to Dr Beeching's axe.

* It is interesting that BR's own magazine used the term 'station mistresses'.

ENGINEERING

After the war the number of women in railway engineering and maintenance declined sharply and few were recruited to these departments over the next 30 years. Among them was Leonie Sumpter, who worked as a carriage and wagon engineer at Toton depot, Nottingham, in the early 50s.[19] At about the same time, Gleny Walley was refused an apprenticeship in the signals and telegraphs department at Crewe because of her sex. She became a tracer and gained her qualifications at night school instead. In the early 60s she was promoted to signalling technical assistant, earning £555 a year – the same as her male colleagues. She was mainly involved in drawing track designs, plans and diagrams, and she visited trackside locations in the Coventry area. As an oddity, she drew the attention of the press:

> Whenever a report appeared about my engineering activities, it was usually linked with the fact that I played trumpet with the local band – both male dominated and so, funnily enough, I was always described as pretty or glamorous (which I don't think I was!) The report would mention that I found time for boyfriends – obviously reassuring the readers that I was still a 'normal' female.

The attitude of her male colleagues varied from friendship to 'blatant hostility'. Miss Walley remarked, 'I never asked for special privileges, yet often when meeting new groups to work with, the leader would make a point of emphatically telling me not to expect special privileges.'[20]

In 1966 seven women at Paisley carried out the electrical installation for a new line along the south bank of the Clyde. Their job was to 'locate, link and label a myriad of tiny multicoloured wires which will serve as the "brain" of the new signal box controlling the whole of the electrified route from Glasgow'. Their wages, £20 per week, were excellent.[21]

SIGNALWOMEN

Signalbox vacancies were, theoretically, open to women, but in practice local managers deemed it a 'man's job' and when women applied they were almost always rejected. The manager's decision was final and, until 1975, could not be challenged. Most signalwomen working during the 50s had been recruited as war-workers and retained in peacetime. Although between 1950 and 1978 the number of signalboxes decreased from 10,000 to 2,250 and their staff reduced from 25,000 to 8,000, there were sometimes localised shortages of signalmen. Each local manager had to balance his personal prejudices and reluctance to employ women against the necessity to keep the trains running. In most cases, women were resorted to only after every effort to obtain men failed, and then were only ever offered the lowest-graded boxes. Mr Weir of the LMS signalling school admitted that he occasionally engaged one or two female trainees because 'in some areas the positions are difficult to fill with men, owing to the counter-attractions of other industries'.[22] Women were only too glad to take the crumbs from men's table.

The station master at Newtown, LMR, was astonished when Mildred Jennings applied for a signalbox vacancy in 1952. He agreed to recruit her, but only if she first proved to him that she could operate the heavy levers. She passed this impromptu test – which no man was expected to take – and held the job for seven years. She recalled that most railwaymen treated her politely and never swore in her presence, but the signalman on the opposite shift was scornful and tried to dissuade her from taking such a 'difficult' job:

> It wasn't a difficult job at all. In fact, the easiest I have done. My lasting memory is of how lazy the majority of men were. I was paid 4s less than the man's rate for doing the same job. Women rarely complained, as men were still considered superior in those days.[23]

After leaving the army, in 1955 Mrs M. E. Smith became a porter, firstly at Heaton Mersey, then Cheadle Heath, and then Didsbury while persistently applying for signalbox vacancies. Her letters were either ignored or she was told she was 'unsuitable'. This was the code word used when rejecting a woman on the grounds of her sex, because there was no official reason why signalwomen could not be recruited. Eventually Mrs Smith succeeded and began riding her 250cc motorcycle daily to Carrington Box, between Liverpool and Manchester, where another woman worked the opposite shift. Owing to signalbox closures she was moved five times (to Withington and West Didsbury, Cheadle, Cheadle West, Cheadle North and Bredbury) before leaving the railway through ill-health in 1971.[24] She recalled that 'the men didn't like women on the railway much, thought we couldn't do it, and when we proved we could, they didn't like it'. At one box her opposite number was a man of 21 who refused to empty the toilet, which involved digging a hole in the banking and burying the contents. 'So I had to empty it after him as well, or I couldn't have used it'. At Cheadle the station master 'thought women were easy prey and had been put in the world for his own convenience'. The man lived right opposite the signalbox; 'it was a good job I'd been in the army, so I was able to put him in his place'.[25]

At the age of 48, Mary Faulkner took over her husband's signalbox at Cadishead when he became ill. He died three years later, in 1945, leaving her with seven children to support. She remained in the job for many years, managing to combine childcare with paid work. Signalwoman Joan Percival, who joined the railway in 1945 aged 19, also managed to combine her career with motherhood:

> I had no self-doubts, I loved the work and was full of self confidence. The two old signalmen who trained me made me that way. From the first minutes of my first day, they let me take charge of the box. They watched me carefully of course, because if I caused an accident, they were responsible, not me, and of course because I knew this, it made me pay attention. This is the very best way to be trained for a signal box, not in a training school. There were 12 levers in my box, they were not too bad to pull, except for the distant ones, they were a bit stiff, because one was three-quarters of a mile away and the other was a mile away. [26]

She worked until the sixth month of her first pregnancy: 'The doctor told me to leave well before then, but I stayed as long as I could because my colleagues would have to work 12 hours a day once I left', she explained. She took short periods of leave around the births of her three children. Twice she managed to get her job back, but the third time she was invited to fill a vacancy as a Grade 1 Porter-in-Charge of a station until the retirement of a signalman created the appropriate vacancy.

Hope (Penny) Wise was recruited in 1961 and after she began work at Manchester's Crumpsall signalbox her husband resigned his job and obtained a similar post nearby. Eight years later the couple was featured in a television programme called *At a Time Like*

This. Mrs Wise later moved to Queen's Road box.[27]

Signalwomen in the 50s and 60s were normally allocated the lowest-grade boxes (Grade 5), but a few made it to Grade 4 and a tiny number reached the lofty heights of Grade 3. Grade 2 and 1 boxes were closed to women, as were Special Classes A and B (the highest graded signalbox). After Joyce Wiltshire's husband became a signalman she became interested in the work and successfully applied for a job as porter-signalwoman in 1956. She said: 'I did everything from signalling to loading cattle.' Later she was promoted to a Grade 3 signalbox at Old Ford, in the East End of London.

When a local station master engaged a signalwoman the event was not widely advertised. One would occasionally come to light in a press report, from which it is known that a signalwoman at Latchford, LMR, had her grandson working at another box nearby, and that in Scotland Alice Fraser worked at Gorton Crossing Box, Bridge of Orchy, on the edge of Rannoch Moor in the Highlands. The hardy Scot had to cross some of the bleakest and wildest country in Britain to begin her shift at 3.15 a.m.[28] In the 50s four signalwomen – Lila Kent, Madge (surname unknown), Doreen Griffin and Jessie Bloggs – covered three eight-hour shifts at the 16-lever Fletton's Siding Box at Bletchley, LMR, which was in operation 24 hours a day. According to Mrs Kent (who appeared on the television show *What's My Line?*) women were considered competent to operate the box except when the Royal Train was passing; then, a senior signalman was deemed necessary.[29] She recalled:

> It was hard physical work but there were some lighter moments, in particular when a flasher appeared near the signalbox, his antics amounted to dancing about, baring his genitals and bottom, lying on the grass but craftily hiding when trains were passing.[30]

The police advised her to keep his attention until their arrival, at which point the man took to his heels and ran. He was subsequently caught, charged and fined.

Signalwoman Iris Moy worked at Custom House, east London. In 1960 *British Railways Magazine* published an article about her. Headed 'This Really is a Man-Size Job', it continued: 'A clean, bright cloth on the table, a vase of flowers and cups of tea and biscuits – it was just like being in a kitchen, except, of course, for the signal levers.'[31] The journalist explained that when Mrs Moy was 15 her railwayman father told her of a vacancy for a box 'boy' at Thames Wharf, and she'd applied. After seven years she was promoted to signalwoman at Silvertown and later transferred to Custom House after she married that station's leading porter. Her shifts involved starting at 5.30 a.m. one week and finishing at 10 p.m. the next. Even after she had a child she continued working, saying that she would not change her job for anything.

Sometimes a noteworthy incident drew the attention of the press and exposed the existence of an otherwise invisible signalwoman. In 1964, for example, one signalwoman on the LMR was found 'lying in the signalbox and singing'. She was dismissed and fined £3 by Belper magistrates for being drunk on duty.[32] This was the only negative press report that came to light during my research; all the others cited signalwomen who were a credit to their grade and even, in some cases, heroic. Mrs S. Jones of Folly Lane Box near Runcorn was told that some wagons had run away on a steep gradient and were heading for her box, as well as being on a collision course with a tanker loaded with liquid chlorine. She signalled to a driver to get his train clear, placed her signals at danger to prevent another engine from obstructing the line, and swiftly diverted the runaways into buffer stops. She was later presented with a reward for preventing a major incident.[33]

In 1955 Signalwoman Gertrude Richardson dealt with a serious fire close to her signalbox at Monk Bretton. She had gone to investigate why smoke was issuing from a paraffin store next to the box when she found a blazing inferno within. She said: 'I saw flames and shouted to a gang of platelayers. I tried to fix up a stirrup-pump but it wouldn't fit the tap.' Alarmed that her wooden signalbox might catch fire, she tried to remove a 40-gallon drum of paraffin single-handedly, but it was too much for one person. Calling to some contractors' men she organised them into a chain of buckets by providing the receptacles and directing the men to the tap in her signalbox. After making sure that they were doing what she required, she phoned Barnsley fire brigade before helping Ganger Cyril Race to remove two heavy drums, containing 25 and 40 gallons of paraffin, to a safe distance away from the fire. She then telephoned for a steam engine to be brought to the scene and asked the crew to spray water onto the fire. She then poured water down the sides of her signalbox as a precaution. A fire brigade officer remarked that Mrs Richardson was 'the heroine of the whole affair' and Mr W. Shelton, the shunter at Monk Bretton, wrote a poem about the incident, which included the lines:

> British Railways a more gallant crew never had
> They worked with skill and with speed.
> Encouraged by Gertie, the girl with the flag
> Who was proving herself fit to lead.

Mrs Richardson was summoned to Regional Headquarters at York, where she and Ganger Race each received an award for gallantry and were given framed certificates for courage and resource. Her manager said: 'She did much more than normally would be expected of a woman in such circumstances'[34] and *The Railway Review* commented:

> Mrs Richardson displayed initiative and courage in the face of considerable personal risk and but for her actions it is possible that the signal box ... might have been completely destroyed. Throughout the whole incident her coolness and organising ability was an inspiration to those she called upon to assist her.[35]

Gertrude Richardson was a signalwoman for 20 years. Although only five-foot-three she could swing on the levers 'as good as any man and better than some', recalled her husband. Originally recruited as a war worker, she had worked at Monk Bretton for five years when her employment was terminated in 1946; but in April 1951 the NE region of BR found itself short of signalling staff and invited her to return. Monk Bretton box closed in 1962 and Gertrude transferred to Crofton Junction (Grimethorpe North) signalbox as a Class 4 signalwoman. Six months into the job she sustained a nasty accident. Workmen installing central heating controls called her to the back of the box, where she fell through a trapdoor they had left open. She fell 10ft into the workings of the box. After a court case the contractors were found to be negligent and she received £100 compensation.

In 1966 Grimethorpe North was closed and Mrs Richardson was made redundant. She held various jobs outside the railways but her true love was signalling and near the end of 1969 she applied successfully for a position at Glasshouse Crossing, a box on a fairly busy road with level crossing gates operated manually by a big wheel. Seven years later she moved to Dearne Valley Colliery Sidings box, on the Leeds to Sheffield main line, as a signalwoman Class A.

Signalwoman Gertrude Richardson and Ganger Cyril Race receiving their awards, 1955.

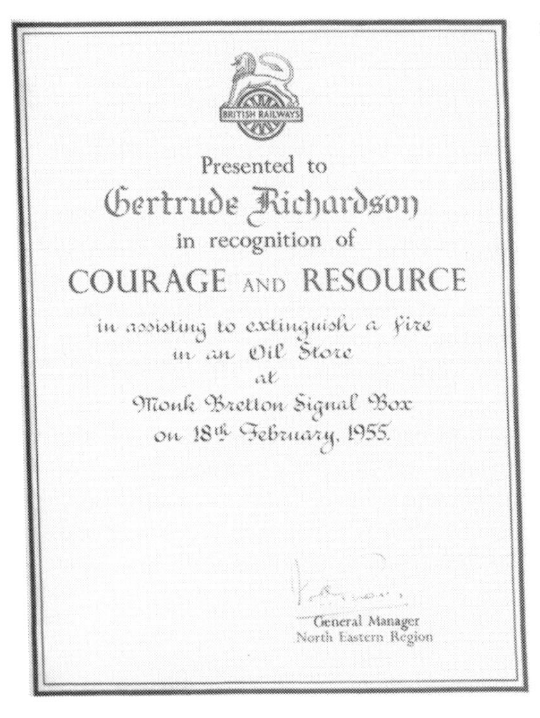

BRITISH RAILWAYS

Presented to

Gertrude Richardson

in recognition of

COURAGE AND RESOURCE

in assisting to extinguish a fire
in an Oil Store
at
Monk Bretton Signal Box
on 18th February, 1955.

General Manager
North Eastern Region

Mrs Richardson enjoying a well-earned cuppa at Monk Bretton Box, 1955.
ALL PHOTOS COURTESY OF FRED RICHARDSON

WOMEN IN A MAN'S WORLD

She took signalwoman's job to buy a washer

AFTER having a go at changing the points at a railway signal box with one of those large and heavy levers I know why this is a job mostly done by men — it's such hard work, and it needs some masculine muscle power.

In nine years attractive Mrs. Clarise Rich of Emsley Avenue, Cudworth, has developed the strength to

by

SUSAN FRANCIS

do the job of signalwoman at Monk Bretton, and Mrs. Rich, who was a nurse during the war, thoroughly enjoys being a woman in a man's world.

Mrs. Rich is not the only signalwoman in Yorkshire, but she is one of a very small band of strong women. Her husband is a signalman at Barnsley, and it was through him that Mrs. Rich first heard of a vacancy at Grimethorpe.

The normal procedure is for potential signalmen and women to work in a box as a trainee, logging down train movements and watching how the job is done. From there they go to signal schools, and then back to signal boxes. Mrs. Rich learnt her new job in five months in the box. Women started doing this work during the war.

LOCAL GOSSIP

For some time now Mrs. Rich and a signal man have run the Monk Bretton box which deals with goods traffic from the main line to the nearby colliery and glass works.

Mrs. Rich's box is linked to the main link box by telephone and by a code bell system. She hears from the shunter when trains are leaving the colliery or the glass works and then she gets in touch with the main line box to get permission for them to go.

"There is no quicker way of finding out all the local gossip than working in a signal box. News buzzes from one box to another over the phone."

Mrs. Rich at work in her signal-box.

Although Mrs. Rich is in her "box" by herself for long periods, she never feels lonely. It is not cold in the signal box either and Mrs. Rich had a cheerful fire burning when I called to see her.

EARLY START

"I only took the job originally for three months to earn enough money to buy a washing machine. I got my washing machine, but I am still working."

One week Mrs. Rich is working from 6 a.m. to 2 p.m., the next week she is working from 2 p.m. to 10 p.m. When she starts early she has to see that all the points are clear of snow. Unless they are the signal levers will not work. At this time of the year Mrs. Rich goes to work an hour earlier to clear the points with the help of the shunter.

Mrs. Rich has two sons, 13-year-old Alan, and 16-year-old Kevin. When she is off duty her main hobby is cake icing. She ices them for friends' weddings and birthdays.

Her tough strong-arm job does not seem to spoil her delicate artistic skill in decorating cakes.

PRESS CUTTING ORIGIN UNKNOWN

Mrs Richardson worked alone in her various signalboxes and it wasn't unusual for people to try the door during the lonely night shifts. She had sometimes to walk to and from work in inclement weather if transport was not available. Dearne Valley box in particular was difficult to reach by public transport. She remained in service at Dearne Valley until January 1980, when she was made to retire, having reached the age of 60. In all, Mrs Richardson had worked for 20 years and six months, spread over 39 years.

Signalling staff generally work in isolated locations and are usually out of public view. A signalman called Webster was puzzled to find an equal pay resolution on the agenda of the 1955 NUR Signalmen's Conference, as he was unaware that any women were employed in his job. When he discovered that they were, he immediately formed the opinion that they should not be, a view he aired publicly in *The Railway Review*[36] and to which Miss A. G. Beanlands replied:

> SIR. As a signal-woman of 12 years' service I would like to inform him that there are three full-time signal-women on the Birmingham-Leicester line (at Shustoke and at Arley & Fillongley) in addition to those stated by you in your postscript on the Western Region. Would he like to give us his views why the employment of women should be 'strenuously resisted'. Does he not think they could prove their worth in such jobs? Also, if many of the cabins are not fit for them to work in is this not often the fault of those already employed in them? I sincerely hope this matter will receive every consideration at the forthcoming Signalmen's Conference, with reference to the question being raised of equal pay.[37]

While the discreet employment of an individual signalwoman here and there across the country was usually tolerated by the male staff and their union, deliberately seeking female recruits caused a furore. In 1960 a lack of male applicants for signalling vacancies in the NE region forced local managers to invite women to apply. The resultant uproar was reported in *The Daily Telegraph* and official announcements made plain the prejudice against women. The managers admitted that they too had reservations about appointing 'women signalmen' and went to considerable trouble to pacify male staff and their union officials by reassuring them that the recruitment of women would be restricted to the NE region, that no man was being ousted, that they were resorting to women purely because men could not be found and that women would be restricted to the lowest-class (and thus the lowest-paid) boxes.[38] The railwaymen still grumbled, but decided not to strike.

Guards

Male guards were more militant than signalmen and would not tolerate women in their grade other than as an emergency wartime measure. It was easier for guards to exclude women from their grade because, during the war, managers had allowed women to bypass the normal promotional steps of porter, ticket collector or shunter and goods guard, and enter railway service as passenger guards. When special wartime measures were rescinded, all women had to leave the grade.

By 1948 all female guards had either resigned or been dismissed. From personal testimony it is known that a few isolated women who had been guards during the war and demoted to porter afterwards were used occasionally to work a train in exceptional circumstances but, unlike signalling, no woman could be recruited or trained to the work.

In the early 1960s the LMR was faced with a scarcity of guards so serious that it threatened the timetabled train services. Older managers remembered the sterling work performed by female guards during the war and so, naturally, they considered recruiting women, who the managers knew would be eager to take the job. The proposal caused uproar amongst men guards, who claimed that women could not manage heavy parcels or night-work and that men's promotion would be adversely affected. The issue attracted national press coverage. The NUR objected most vociferously and suggested that BR raise wages instead, to attract 'the right people' — i.e., men. LMR manager George Dow pointed out that women had performed the work without difficulty during the war, and that nothing in the law prevented them from working nights. He invited guards from several depots to meet him in a gentlemen-only bar for what he called 'a man-to-man talk'. No record appears to have been kept of the proceedings, but the men's opposition must have been solid because the LMR immediately abandoned the idea. The 1961 NUR Guards' Conference passed a resolution against the employment of women. Although the shortage of guards was declared 'a state of emergency', the bitter and prolonged rail strike in 1955 was still fresh in managers' minds and they could not risk provoking another.[39]

In 1974 BR was again faced with chronic recruitment difficulties and again considered allowing women to be guards and signallers. A letter was sent to the NUR HQ on 26th February to advise the union of the intended action. The matter was not considered by the EC but was instead listed for discussion at a sub-committee on 11th June. In the meantime, the NUR circulated Branches and District Councils for their comments.[40] Soon many letters were received opposing female guards and several branches passed resolutions against them. One branch submitted the following emergency motion to the NUR National Joint Conference of Shunters, Guards and Yard Foremen:

> This Conference ... are [sic] totally opposed to the employment of female guards. We consider that this is not the answer to the serious shortage of Staff in the grade. ... The employment of females as guards is not practicable for many reasons, i.e. Guard's duties as laid down in the Conditions of Service Book, Guard's duties as laid down in the proposed Pay Structure Review, Physical needs, etc. Also female conciliation staff are not included in the Promotion. Transfer & Redundancy. arrangements promotional tree, therefore they would be temporary. The answer to staff shortages in key grades, particularly Guards, is a much greater Rate of Pay so to attract men.[41]

The motion was carried, with a substantial majority.

At the meeting of the sub-committee on 11th June the NUR representatives said that they were not opposed to the employment of women guards (or signallers) but 'their engagement posed a number of questions which required careful consideration'. The letters received at NUR HQ, the branch resolutions and the conference motion led to their anticipating difficulty in 'securing local acceptance' of women. The NUR negotiators were prepared to progress the matter further, but only on the understanding that there would be 'no discrimination in favour of women', by which they meant that women should not be allocated the more attractive work. They were, however, reluctant to progress extending the employment of signalwomen while signalmen were being made redundant.

The BRB representatives reminded the NUR that the question of female guards was urgent, adding that they would 'greatly appreciate any assistance ... in the way of securing the co-operation of the staff at local level'.[42]

In August the EC referred the matter to Negotiating and Traffic Sub-Committees, who produced a report saying that they were unable to make any policy decision, although they thought that the employment of 'females' would 'create more problems than it solved'. The EC voted unanimously to accept the report and in December 1975 BR told the NUR that it had decided 'for a variety of reasons' to hold the matter 'in abeyance'.[43]

WOMEN AS TRAIN GUARDS

The men talk it over

By our Midlands Correspondent

Railway guards met yesterday in the "gentlemen only" bar of a Birmingham public house to discuss a London Midland region proposal to recruit women for their job. They had been invited by Mr George Dow, the divisional traffic manager, for what he described as a "man to man talk."

When the proposal was announced some weeks ago it aroused a great deal of male opposition, and protests were sent to the headquarters of the National Union of Railwaymen. Yesterday Mr Dow explained the official point of view and tried to answer the men's objections. It was, he said, "purely an information meeting." Any negotiations would take place through the normal union chapels. The guards have claimed that they would have to do more early and late shifts if the plan went through because women would not be allowed to work earlier than 6 a.m. or later than 10 p.m. Other complaints were that promotions would be affected and that women would not be able to handle the heavy parcel traffic carried by passenger trains.

Mr Dow said he told the meeting that it was proposed to settle work schedules by mutual discussion. As far as he could see there was nothing in the Employment of Women and Young Persons Act to prevent women from working the late and early shifts. There would be plenty of opportunities for the qualified man to reach the grade of passenger guard. Recently there had been so few applicants for jobs that they had been forced to advertise some vacancies five times. Some women who had been recruited during the war were still working as guards and signalmen. In one area where there were now 11 vacancies it was hoped that five women guards would be appointed.

"The staff situation is so difficult that we are once again in a state of emergency. The only difference is that now we are not at war. We shall be in serious trouble if there is a severe winter or a large sickness epidemic."

Although they were very short of goods guards, they were having to release some for passenger duties to maintain services. Women would get equal pay.

The attendance at yesterday's meeting was small. Some guards had said they would boycott it.

Women as train guards. *Daily Herald*, 24th June 1961.

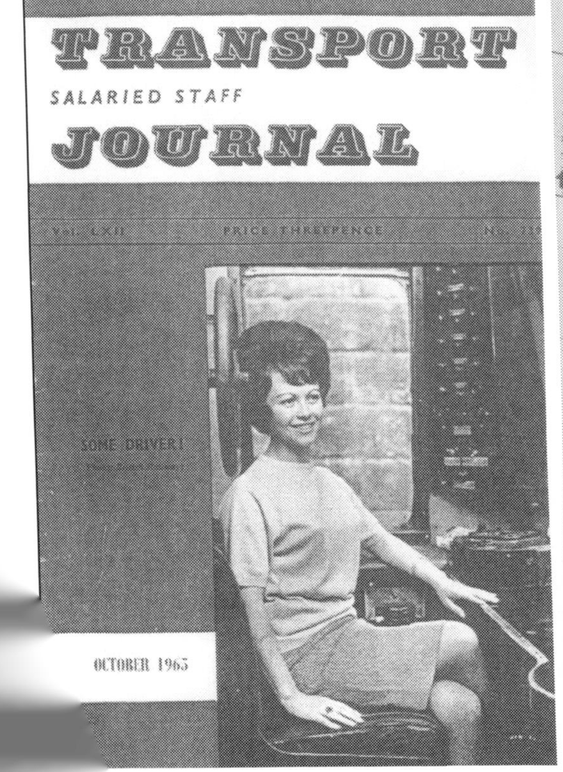

This rather ironic front cover of the TSSJ shows a railwaywoman posing as a train driver, but in reality women were barred from the job. TSSJ, October 1965

Signalling Technical Assistant Gleny Walley. G. Walley

Women in Female Wages Grades

Most 'blue-collar' women who applied to the railway for work were directed to carriage cleaning. Working in the sheds, often at night, they carried out the least-respected job in the industry. Some men objected to women's performing even this humble work. One claimed in *The Railway Review* that if his female colleagues saw 'four-legged vermin' in a coach they 'disappeared' and that, unlike the men, 'the females can do, say, and come when they like'.[44] These unsubstantiated accusations were published despite the policy of *The Railway Review* to exclude libellous material.

Thousands of women worked as carriage cleaners, out of the public eye, forgotten and unappreciated. The disparity in pay suffered by carriage cleaners in the 50s was matched by inequalities in the provision of clothing; for example, male cleaners were issued with two pairs of trousers annually while their female counterparts received just one. When women received press coverage it usually belittled and patronised them. One article headed: 'The Mrs Mopps of Farington, Preston' described a mess-room in which 'the feminine touch could be seen in the pretty curtains in the window.'[45] A more pleasing report described how carriage cleaner Mrs Ann Zabala was lauded a hero at Cardiff Canton depot for administering first aid to a goods guard badly injured during an accident involving a shunting pole. She received a Class 2 Award for Meritorious First Aid.[46] Some completed very long service; for example Annie M'Brearty worked at Larkfield, Scotland, for 40 years while her colleagues Janet Henderson and Kit Fraser completed 34 and 36 years' respectively. All three were proud of having cleaned the Royal Train.

Women continued their traditional railway work of serving other staff, carrying out menial and domestic-type tasks in the railways' 42 canteens and in their 83 staff hostels,* also known as 'lodges'.† The Midland's lodge at Sheffield, dubbed 'The Nunnery', was described by enginemen as 'a home away from home':

> The Nunnery had sixteen bedrooms, warmed by a Jumbo stove. It was decorated in 'dingy green' railway paint and it sported the inevitable railway brown linoleum. Spitoons [sic] were an interesting embellishment.‡ For many years, Mrs Maillard was the lady in charge ... and it was due to her efforts that it enjoyed such an enviable reputation among trainmen.[47]

But the job of hostel matron was doomed. Enginemen and guards disliked doing 'double-home turns', as they were called, and discontent led eventually to anti-lodging strikes between 1949 and 1955. 'Double-home' turns were gradually phased out and by the 1980s the job of matron no longer existed.

A few new jobs were added to the list of female grades; for example, from 1947 women attendants staffed the ladies' retiring room on board some prestigious trains, such as the *Flying Scotsman* and the *Elizabethan*.

---

* Taken from 1952 figures.

† Long distance train crews slept in these lodges overnight before making their return journey to their home depot the following day. Frank McKenna's *The Railway Workers* is a rich source of information on railway hostels and their matrons.

‡ Let us hope that this feature is not what made the lodge a 'home from home'.

Crossing Keepers

By 1950 women had been working as crossing keepers for a century. Typically, they worked between eight and 12 hours a day, six days a week, for 27s, while men performing identical work received 80s for a 48-hour week. Women were tired of being told that this inequality was due to agreements made between the company and the NUR. One, Mrs Duerden, observed that is was 'high time the Union got some of these obsolete agreements altered.'[48] Managers were reluctant to grant women any time off: according to the companies, a day's work for a female crossing keeper consisted of 24 hours, yet a day's leave consisted of providing a stand-in for just eight hours!

Kathleen Willingham worked from 6 a.m. till 10.30 p.m. – a 91-hour week – at a crossing near Colchester, pulling a very heavy ground frame lever 144 times a day. The LNER provided a male stand-in for only seven hours a week 'shopping leave'. Her application for a pay rise to compensate for taking over her husband's duties was declined, as was her request for a reduction in hours. LNER managers said she was classed as a part-time employee because she could 'run home between trains', adding that she knew what the job entailed when she accepted it.[49]

As we have seen, successive union agreements to improve crossing keepers' pay and working conditions had applied only to men and routinely excluded women, although they performed identical work. Incredible as it may seem, just after the war a NUR-backed campaign emerged to improve the hours, pay and conditions of *male* crossing keepers. Neither the NUR officers nor the correspondents to *The Railway Review* offered any justification for limiting the campaign to one sex. At the time there were 1,285 male and 1,591 female crossing keepers, so the usual excuse – that women were a tiny minority and therefore of no significance – was inapplicable. It is possible that the NUR thought women crossing keepers a lost cause, and one that could jeopardise the men's case. However, it continued to accept the women's subscriptions.

Despite being in the majority, gatewomen seem to have been invisible to some. One railwayman complained of 'scandalous conditions, such as inhuman hours of work, miserable wages and an utter lack of facilities for recreation' which were endured by 'heroic hard-working crossing keepers' who gave 'day and night selfless services which are safeguarding the lives of millions of passengers, not to mention the millions of tons of goods vital to the war efforts'. He concluded: 'The vested interests won't help them, but one expects the N.U.R. to start a holy crusade to assist.' But he was pleading only for men; women were not once mentioned.[50] He even described crossing keepers as 'the forgotten men of our time.' Three years later, *The Railway Review* published an article bemoaning the lot of male crossing keepers. The author said that the men were in the 'Cinderella' grades (ironic, under the circumstances, as Cinders was female). Similarly, NUR officials at a Railway Staff National Tribunal in 1947 left no doubt about the gender of the workers to whom they referred:

> Male crossing keepers ... are the only grades included in the Conciliation scheme who do not enjoy a 48-hour week ... it is contended by the N.U.R that ... Crossing Keepers are responsible for the control of traffic involving the safety of human lives and statistics indicate that comparatively few accidents occur at crossings, thus illustrating the men's devotion to duty.[51]

One railwayman suggested that 'a mild form of blackmail' was being used to force men to tolerate the poor conditions and low pay, because many were disabled and could not easily find alternative employment.[52] Although his analysis applied equally to the many female crossing keepers whose childcare responsibilities handicapped them in the job market, their existence was not even acknowledged.

The men's campaign bore fruit in 1947 when rates of pay for gatemen were raised to between 76s and 95s (inclusive of 25s 6d war wage), while the highest-graded woman earned a mere 53s (29s plus 24s war wage). Men also won 10s 6d per week compensation for being excluded from the 48 hour week, which had been conceded to all other male conciliation grades. Nothing was offered to women. Gatewoman Duerden wrote to *The Railway Review*:

> We are classified as 'Railway Workers' but when improvements are made we find another well-worn expression applies to us: 'This concession is not granted to female crossing keepers.'[53]

Marriage to a railwayman was not a very attractive proposition for a single gatewoman, for she would immediately suffer a pay cut of 8s to 10s.[54] The practice of paying a railwayman's wife lower wages was abolished after nationalisation in 1948 and, at the same time, all gatewomen were awarded a 4s rise. They were also allowed one-twelfth of their total hours off-duty but, owing to staff shortages, this was impossible to implement and they were paid 5s per week compensation instead.

Female crossing keepers continued to suffer disparity in uniform provision: men were issued a cap, jacket and vest annually, trousers every six months and a coat every three years. Women received no uniform, but BR conceded that they could have an overcoat every four years.

By 1956, crossing keepers' pay was 140s to 144s for men and 71s to 90s for women. Owing to union agreements in the 1950s, railwaymen were restricted by law to a 12-hour day, while women residential crossing keepers could work 16 hours or more. Furthermore, men were granted an eight-hour period off duty each week, while women were granted only four hours' 'shopping leave'. When one NER crossing keeper requested an extra hour off duty for Christmas shopping she found her pay docked a quarter day.[55]

Although time off duty was difficult, gatekeepers had plenty of free time in between trains to see to household duties, care for children or pursue hobbies. Even at a busy crossing like Canterbury's Whitehall, the gatewoman found enough spare time to write an 840,000-word novel between trains. Rosemary Churchill (although married to Porter Stokes she kept her own name) spent two years writing *The King's Daughter*, a fictionalised life of 'Bloody' Mary that was published in 1969.* [56]

Gatewomen occasionally appeared in the media. Mrs Smith, of Long Green Crossing, Essex, was featured in a Pathé newsreel when she retired in 1960, after 28 years' service.[57] *The Daily Telegraph* reported in 1954 that Crossing Keeper Burns, who worked at Moulinearn, on the Perth to Inverness main line, had been warmly praised in an accident report. When she was off duty her job was performed by a relief porter from Perth. One

* Miss Churchill must have abridged it considerably; a copy for sale on the Internet in 2005 had a mere 221 pages — about 100,000 words.

day he caused the death of two men by allowing their tractor onto the crossing when a train was due. The report said that Mrs Burns had previously suspected that the man did not carry out his duties properly, and had done 'all she could to bring about correct working when [he] was in charge.'* [58]

Crossing keepers' work was detailed in a magazine article featuring Anne Hollis of Barton's Lane, LMR, where there were, on average, 60-70 cars daily and 110 in the fishing season. She was on call 24 hours a day: 'Whether Mrs Hollis is eating a meal, in bed or having a bath, it is her job to hurry out as soon as she hears a car hoot.' [59]

Another gatekeeper gained her fifteen minutes of fame because she was a member of the Polish royal family. Princess Madelein von Dębinska's mother had been fighting since 1918 to prove her legal right to a huge fortune and an aristocratic title. Until this could be substantiated, her daughter had taken a humble job on the railways, operating Rodbridge Crossing at Long Melford, Suffolk, from 6 a.m. to 9 p.m., six days a week.[60]

The crossing at Melton Ross, near Barnetby was operated by three generations of women. Annie Brown (b. 1860) took over from her father and later married a railwayman. She passed on the job to her daughter, also named Annie, who married Signalman Walter Wilson. Their daughter Doris (b. 1905) married engineman George Baldock and later took over the gates:

> Doris was kept very busy. Farm carts made many journeys each day and children needed to cross to get to school and to the main road to Barnetby. The trains were very frequent and some carried coal from the Yorkshire coalfields to Immingham Docks to be exported. Other trains were carrying fish to the North from Grimsby docks.
>
> People rang a bell that hung from a post when they needed to cross. One farmer would go to the local public house every night with his pony and trap. He would return after closing time, always drunk, but the pony would take him home. When the pony got to the level crossing he — the pony — would ring the bell continually until Doris went out to open the gates for him to take his passenger home. She said there was no such thing as going to bed until Farmer Sam was home.[61]

Crossing keepers' responsibility for lives was tragically highlighted in 1950 at East Shalford, SR. Elsie Goodwin, a 19-year-old with only three months' service, opened the gates to let a car cross. A train crashed into it, killing both occupants of the car. While at first she appeared to be entirely to blame, the enquiry proved that she had been insufficiently trained, for she confused the up and down lines. Furthermore, the instructions for operating the crossing were ambiguous and were 'interpreted differently by the Area Inspectors and the two assistant Stationmasters, all responsible officials'.[62] Miss Goodwin had taken over the crossing because her sister, the previous keeper, had died. She had moved in with her brother-in-law to look after her late sister's child, and took over her gate duties, too.

The closure of branch lines put hundreds of crossing keepers out of work. In 1952 there were 1,432 and by 1968 only 849. Women bore the brunt of the cuts because they

---

* The crossing no longer has a keeper; it now has barriers controlled by road users. A collision between a car and a train in May 2001 resulted in the death of a car passenger.

manned the lower-graded crossings, which were most commonly found on branch lines. Some of them had been in railway service for many years; in some cases, decades. Alice Tubbs had taken over Durley Halt Crossing, SR, from her father in 1906. Forty-eight years later, in 1954, she was forced to retire because of a decline in traffic: the line that once carried seventeen trains a day now saw only two. Mrs Tubbs had to move out of the cottage in which she was born and had inhabited for all of her 65 years. Unable to break her lifelong attachment to the railway, she rented a smallholding just 150 yards away.[63]

Mrs J. Smith was crossing keeper at Wainhill, near Chinnor, WR for over 24 years:

> My husband was working at Chinnor station, he was only earning 50 shillings and had to collect and deliver parcels to earn a few extra bob.* My father-in-law noticed the job going and suggested it would suit me.
>
> I must have been crackers to move there with a baby. It was an old cottage: two up and three down, no electric, water in the well, the loo round the back. I was paid eight shillings a week, and no rent to pay. I had red and green lights on the gates, a light on the platform. The first engine was 4.20 a.m. and there was no 'letting the gates go swinging', as some did. In the late 1950s the line was closed for people, then later for cement, and so no job for a crossing keeper.[64]

Fred and Freda Box operated Bruton Road crossing near Evercreech, Somerset & Dorset Railway, from 1938 till 1966.

> It was not an easy existence, especially with three children to bring up; no running water, no electricity, no gas, our lights were paraffin lamps and warmth was a coal fire. Our water was delivered in five-gallon cans by train. If the crew were a friendly bunch, as most were, they would supplement our coal ration with some extra coal off the tender. In the garden we had a large wooden butt for rainwater which we used for washing. We had an allotment in the garden which kept the family in fresh vegetables.
>
> Fred and I worked 24 hours a day between us, seven days a week. What amazed us was that when we had a short holiday, the powers-that-be sent three men to work the gates over the 24-hour period. We had a small hut next to the cottage where the wheel was kept. I used to count how many winds it took to manoeuvre the signal; it was in fact 20 and over 25 years it must have run into thousands. It couldn't have done me any harm as I'm now in my 80s and I could still do it today (once).
>
> Summer Saturdays were very busy. It was lovely to see the *Pines Express* roaring through with its happy holidaymakers going to Bournemouth. We always thought we were doing our bit for this famous express; when we travelled on it we thought we were royalty. I remember in late 1962, when the snow was nearly as high as the crossing gates, the children and ourselves moved heaps of snow off the track to make sure we kept the crossing open. The engine with its snow plough would come up and down the track to keep the trains moving; we made sure that the crew had steaming hot cups of tea.
>
> One busy Saturday Fred was going to Bruton to get some shopping and we had locked the gates as an express was due. One of my sons, seeing his dad on the other side of the gate, wanted to join him. He somehow opened the wicket

---

* 'Bob' was a slang term for a shilling.

gate and was about to run across the track. I just managed to grab him and pull him away as the train hurtled through – what a fright. It was always a worry bringing up a young family with trains going by a matter of yards from our front door. You always had to be vigilant.

In 25 years at the crossing we only had one accident. One morning a passenger train went through and we knew that a light engine would be following. Unfortunately we only opened two of the four gates because of a crisis in the cottage. All of a sudden we heard a bang that was the class 2P engine knocking the gates down. We rushed outside and apologised to the crew. We thought we would lose our jobs but we only got a slight ticking off.

Fred and I thought the railway would never close. Bruton Road crossing was our home and life, and we opened those gates in all types of weather – wind, rain and snow. Now Dr Beeching was kicking us out. When we closed those gates in 1966 for the last time, tears were in our eyes, it was goodbye to our Somerset & Dorset friends. The only way of life we had known was at an end.

After four years as a booking and parcel clerk at Wisbech, Marjorie Cook married Porter Arthur Phillips and they moved to Ferry station, where he became the leading porter and she the crossing keeper:

It was a lovely house but there was no electricity or water. Drinking water came by train. We had some lovely fires as the train drivers would throw off lumps of coal. There was an outside lavatory with a bucket that had to be emptied. There was no specification of hours and my husband was allowed to cover if I had to go out. The only times that the gates were opened to traffic was when produce was being loaded into trucks in the yard, this was from the nearby farms and was mostly by horse and cart, and there was nothing at weekends after Saturday lunch time. I do not think that I belonged to a union but I was quite satisfied with it all. Mr Beeching decided that the line had to be closed. We were so sorry, as we were very happy at Ferry.

We then took on what we thought was a similar job at Bleasby. My husband was one of three porters on the station. They worked the gate as well as issuing tickets and other jobs between 6 a.m. and 11 p.m. I was to be responsible for the crossing between 11 p.m. and 6 a.m. We really got a shock when we got there. This crossing was completely different in that it was open to the road for most of the time and the gates were closed when a train was due. There were a lot of latecomers from the pub down at the river and so one of us had to sit outside in the hut until about 1 a.m. Fishermen would start to move at about 4.30 a.m. We didn't get much sleep. There was a loud bell on the house for people to ring when they needed to cross and some impatient clients gave this the works! We really had not expected that amount of traffic.

There were no trains between 1 p.m. Sunday and 4 a.m. Monday and, although we knew we shouldn't, we would leave the gates open to the road after 11 and set our alarm for about 2.00 a.m. to get up and close them.

There was a big crash once when the mail train went through the gates! It shouldn't have happened because there were fixed signals, but the driver came past them. I had to go to Lincoln to a disciplinary hearing. It was decided soon after this to have someone employed on the crossing 24 hours a day.[65]

In 1951, at the age of 34, Ivy Sisson became keeper of Crossing No. 9 on the Louth to Willoughby single line at Farlesthorpe, LNER:

My husband had been a plate layer and wished to change his work to a porter-signalman. To take the job at Mumby Road his wife had to take the crossing keeper's job. This was a good chance for us to earn more money and still be together. I worked from 7 a.m. train to 8.30 p.m. train with seven trains in between. I always kept my gates locked across the road, but one Saturday I left my husband in charge (which was allowed). On return at the top of the lane, I saw to my horror a large engine puffing outside my home. My husband had been on early shift. He'd let the butcher over the crossing, left the gates open for him to return when he was ready, and fallen asleep in front of the fire. Luckily the train driver had a good look out. I got a No. 1 [a Form 1, a formal disciplinary charge]. for this as the gates were my responsibility. That was my only mishap in five years.

My husband got promotion to Sutton-on-Sea and I took over Crossing No. 10 at Huttoft village. I had an indicator on a post to inform me if I had a train in section up line and down line. I didn't have any telephone. All went well for us until the floods of 1953. My crossing gates were put across the road after the last train on the down. At 10 p.m. we went to bed. In the adjoining field something shone like a mirror. Didn't take any notice, but at midnight our neighbours knocked us up as our house was completely surrounded with water. We were evacuated to Lincoln; my husband was left behind as he had to man Sutton-on-Sea to receive trains carrying ballast for the sea wall.

In 1956 we moved again. I no longer did the gates as they were operated from Roxton Sidings signal box where my husband worked. If he was called out to another crossing, I would be called upon to cover any road traffic in the night – for which I was paid handsome money. We lived there until 1981 and then retired. [66]

Crossing Keeper Kathleen Willingham pulling a ground frame lever.

Railway Romance

PRESENTATION TO PORTER AND CLERK

THERE WAS A happy little ceremony at the Wisbech East Stationmaster's Office yesterday (Thursday) afternoon, when two employees, who were married at March on Tuesday week, were presented with an eight-day clock and candlesticks to match, subscribed for by the Station staff.

The happy couple, to whom hearty congratulations and best wishes for their future happiness were extended, were Mr. and Mrs. Arthur Phillips, of Gatehouse, Redmoor-lane, South-brink, Wisbech, the bride being formerly Miss Marjorie Cook, of 27, Maple-grove, March.

Mr. Phillips has been a porter at the Wisbech East Station for 12 years and his wife has been a clerk there foi three-and-a-half years.

On Monday Mr. and Mrs Phillips will take up a new joint position at Ferry Station, where they will live in the Station House.

In congratulating the couple, Mr. J. Rose (Stationmaster) thanked them for the work they had put in, adding that he was sorry to lose them.

FIRST TIME

Mr. B. Bays (Chief Clerk) thought it was the first time at the Station that the operating and commercial departments had merged into wedlock.

Station Inspector F. Anker, Mr. H. C. Gladwin (Accounts Clerk), Miss M. Oglethorpe (District Relief Clerk) and Mr. H. Covill (signalman) also spoke.

Mr. and Mrs. Phillips suitably replied.

Clerk Marjorie Cook married Porter Arthur Phillips and together they moved to Ferry, LNER, where Marjorie operated the crossing while her husband worked at the station. One of their small daughters is seen playing happily in the back yard, alongside a train berthed in the siding.

CUTTING: *WISBECH STANDARD*, 15 JUNE 1951

PHOTOS: M. PHILLIPS

SHIPPING

Women continued to be employed in the railways' shipping division, both ashore and at sea. Three – Stewardess Roseann Baxter and Bureau Assistant Mary Close, from Larne, and Stewardess Catherine Clark from Gourock – lost their lives in the worst maritime disaster in British railway history: the loss of the *Princess Victoria*, a pioneer roll-on-roll-off ferry operating between Stranraer and Larne. On 31st January 1953 she hit a storm, and the stern gates to her car deck were forced open. She foundered off Belfast Lough and 136 people on board were drowned, including three MPs. Only 44 persons survived, all of them men. According to marine historian Stephen Cameron, testimony from survivors related that the two stewardesses were seen helping all the women and children into one lifeboat, and it seems that they joined them. The boat was caught by waves and smashed against the hull of the ship, throwing all the occupants into the icy sea. No women or children survived.[67]

Senior Stewardess Kit Holt was interviewed in 1961, when she was working for the Eastern Region of BR aboard the SS *Arnhem* between Harwich and Hoek van Holland. She was in charge of 19 cabins containing 37 passengers. Her shift began at 8 p.m., checking cabins and passengers' tickets, after which she was on call all night. In the morning she issued landing cards and helped passengers disembark before finishing at 11.30 a.m. – a 15½ hour shift.[68] Nellie Horne was for 32 years a stewardess on the Harwich-Hoek van Holland route, retiring in 1959. Margaret M'Geehen, who had held a wartime post as Chief Purser on the Wemyss Bay to Rothesay steamer from 1916 to 1920, remained in service ashore until 1957. Stewardess Rose was based at Harwich Parkstone Quay for 37 years until her retirement in 1957, having spent 14 years at sea.

WORKSHOPS

In 1951 there were 468 workshopwomen, of whom more than half worked for the LMR. Their pay began at 26s and rose to a maximum of 78s. Typical women's tasks included polishing carriage brass-work, lacquering, trimming, re-covering and re-carding horsehair seats, electroplating, French polishing and sack and sheet repairing. They also sewed diaphragms – the black, concertina-like curtains that were fitted between connected carriages. Engraver Marjorie Gunson, a war-worker, stayed on at Leyton signal and telegraphs workshops into the 60s. Classed as a Fitter, 3rd Grade, her task was to engrave labels, dials, seat numberplates, signal lever plates and signal tablets. In the late 1950s, Mrs M. Clarke was among the few women employed at Wimbledon signal engineer's depot to engrave cable test cases, relays and signalling instruments. Her husband, three sons and a daughter were also in the service of the SR.

Although many women spent their whole working lives in railway workshops there was little scope for advancement for any of their sex, and most stayed in the lowest grades performing repetitive, routine work. Elsie Cook worked as a seamstress for 42 years at Doncaster trimming shops before she was promoted to chargehand in 1962 (supervising six women) by which time she was 64 and just months from retirement.

CATERING

Railway buffets, bars and restaurant cars were extremely busy in the post-war period. Most catering staff were female and their working conditions very poor. Many lived in, sharing four to a room. The NUR exploited this to the full with an impassioned article, massively headlined 'Slave girls of the refreshment rooms', which on closer inspection was actually a thinly disguised union recruitment advertisement.[69]

Mella Shannon spent 44 years in railway catering, for which she was awarded the BEM. At the age of 14 she took a job at Omagh station as a washer-up. After three months she was sent to work on a train from Londonderry to Belfast making tea and sandwiches, and aged 16 she began as a cook on a 30-seater dining car, full meals and afternoon tea. In 1966 the 'Derry' line was closed and she transferred to Belfast to work on the prestigious *Enterprise*, which ran non- stop between Belfast and Dublin.

> My life was very happy on the train; most enjoyable, I met many VIPs, pop stars etc. Life got hard when the civil unrest started. Terrorists blew up the line, one bridge on the border between Northern Ireland and the Republic was blown up 25 times. When that happened myself and the head waiter put our supplies in boxes as far as Newry station, then off the train on to a bus to Dundalk station where we opened up our own train which was stuck there all night. Got the cooker going: sausages, bacon and eggs. Some of our regulars set up the tables, helped us so much. This sometimes lasted for weeks, but we kept the service going which made us feel good. The icing on my cake was being presented with the British Empire Medal by the Lord Lieutenant, at Hillsborough Castle. [70]

From 1973 railway catering was renamed Travellers Fare and was privatised in 1987, from which time its staff were no longer railway employees.

POLICE

After the war many policewomen were dismissed, but a meeting of the railway chiefs of police at Euston in February 1946 acknowledged the contribution of women and concluded that a quota of female officers in each force was desirable, particularly for dealing with incidents involving women and children. Colonel Jesper of the LNER recommended that when not engaged on police duties, policewomen could be deployed as clerks and typists at divisional offices. Not unexpectedly, this suggestion was rejected to avoid conflict with the railway unions, particularly the RCA.

With nationalisation the four main line railway police forces merged into the British Transport Police (BTP), and this was followed by a series of 'firsts' for women officers. The first female sergeants were appointed in 1950 when WPCs Snell (Paddington) and Barrett (Liverpool Street) were promoted. In 1957, there were so many female trainees that the first all-woman course was held at Tadworth training centre in Surrey. By 1959 there were 127 women and 2776 men in the BTP. The first female inspector was appointed in March 1961. Vera Lee, originally from the North Riding Constabulary, was made head of the Women's Unit. She was subsequently promoted to the rank of chief inspector in 1963, a groundbreaking event in the police service.

The Whitbread Shield was awarded to Woman Sergeant Staniforth in 1967. Following a train crash near Stetchford Station, Birmingham, she set up and managed a temporary mortuary, where the nine victims were taken for identification. A curious incident occurred in March, 1965. *The Daily Mirror* reported that, following a new issue of fine poplin blouses, BTP's 150 policewomen had been warned against wearing black bras under their uniforms because, said a spokesman, 'the girls would attract more attention than they do already.' Anyone ignoring the order would be 'quickly pulled into line by her sergeant'. In 1969 a new style of uniform was introduced with a shorter skirt and a jacket tailored to fit the female form. At the same time, out went the old-style peaked cap and a design known as the 'patroller' was introduced across the service. [71]

WAGES GRADES' PAY, PERKS AND PENSIONS

After the war the Labour government cited its wage freeze as a reason to continue to withhold equal pay from women. The issue was, nevertheless, kept alive: the 1950 TUC Women's Conference passed three resolutions for equal pay, and the following year 3,000 people protested at a meeting in London, and hundreds marched to Parliament to demand equality for women. In 1956 the government granted equal pay to some of its white-collar female employees. The principle had at last been conceded, albeit to a very small number of the seven million women employed in the UK. Further hope was given by Article 141 (ex 119) of the 1957 Treaty of Rome, which required legislation on equal pay to have been passed before Britain could enter the European Economic Community.* This had no immediate impact, however, since it was many years before Britain would have to comply.

In 1963 a six-point charter for women was passed by the TUC, including a demand for equality of pay and opportunity. However, when Labour returned to power in 1964 it broke its pre-election promise to pass equal pay legislation.

On railways the practice of paying women lower rates than men created many absurdities and stark injustices. For example, during the mid-1950s male announcers were paid the ticket collector's rate, while females were designated as 'women train announcers' and paid far less. Similarly, women ticket printers earned 127s, while men working alongside them on identical tasks and hours enjoyed 163s. Male hostel attendants earned 124s but their female colleagues received 94s; again, for exactly the same work. Perhaps the most breathtaking injustice was the case of female chargehand cooks. They were paid 118s, and for that they had to train and supervise male assistants earning 135s.

BTC finally agreed in 1957 that equal pay ought to be awarded but did not implement it for more than a year. London Transport granted pay equality to all women in wages grades on 28th October 1958. Shortly afterwards, BTC informed the NUR (on 22nd January 1959) that equal pay would be implemented for women in wages grades (except crossing keepers) and the award would be backdated to January 1st 1958. London Transport then backdated its own scheme to that date. At that time there were 32,145 women out of a total railway staff of 550,123.

Further union negotiations resulted in a few 'paper' victories for women. Gatewomen at the higher-graded level crossings finally obtained equal pay with men. However, lower-graded crossings were excluded and — predictably — most gatewomen operated those very crossings. In February 1968 workshopwomen were granted equal pay if they filled a male grade. Those grades were — of course — almost without exception closed to women.

In the late 50s, just as railwaywomen approached victory on the issue of equal pay, the unions were giving consent to new arrangements which treated them less favourably than men in the provision of free travel, sick pay and pensions. A 1955 agreement ruled that a railwayman could obtain free travel passes for his wife and dependent children, but his female colleague could obtain them for her children only if her husband was incapable of any employment, and if his or the children's income did not exceed a certain limit. A railwaywoman could claim free passes for her dependent children only if she was married. Employees' female housekeepers were also entitled to free passes. A single man could obtain them for his sister or mother if they acted as his housekeeper; a single woman

* After the First World War Britain had been a signatory to Part 13 of the 1920 Treaty of Versailles, which required equal pay for women. It was not implemented.

could claim only for her mother, but not for her brother, because male housekeepers were not recognised. When a married man was being transferred, he and his wife were given a free ticket to visit the new location to look for a home, but if the worker seeking a transfer was a married woman her husband was not entitled to a free ticket.

The 1956 British Railways wages grade sick pay scheme discriminated against women. To qualify for a flat rate of 30s a week sick pay, men had to be 21 and have a year's service; women had to be 25 and have five years' service. Only after ten years' service were women treated equally with men. This adversely affected many hundreds of young women who worked for a few years and left to start a family. If they later returned to work, they had to re-start their qualification period.

While negotiating a pension scheme in 1953, BTC excluded all women. The NUR General Secretary felt this was a 'serious weakness' but asked only for 'certain female grades' to be included. Even this was refused by BTC, which declared:

> Female employment on the railways was of a transitional character. Young females ... do not look upon the railways as a career. They are more concerned about marriage. Some women employees are already married and consider their responsibilities to be more important.[72]

This was a kick in the teeth to the many hundreds of women who gave several decades of service. The NUR leadership had to accept the exclusion of women from the pension scheme, which became operative from July 1954. By 1962 the delegates to the NUR AGM voted for 'urgent action' to include railwaywomen in the scheme and, at the 1964 AGM, women were dubbed the 'Legion of the Lost' for being the only employees without pension rights.[73]

British Rail eventually allowed women into the scheme in 1967, but this was too late for women like Porter Cleaver, known as 'The Grand Old Lady' of Camp Hill Goods depot, Birmingham, retired in 1956 with 28 years' service, during which she married and raised 16 children.[74] Other women who left without a pension include Mrs Palmer, ladies' waiting room attendant at Liverpool for 34 years; Mrs Allen, waiting room attendant at Henley-on-Thames for 30 years; Mrs Stemp, ladies' room attendant for 42 years; and Margaret Scott, a storekeeper with 49 years' service. Miss M. Brinnand, who came from a family of six boys and five girls who between them had a total of 250 years' service, worked in the refreshment rooms at Euston, Carlisle, Whitehaven, Accrington, Blackburn, Preston, Blackpool North and Birmingham New Street in a career that spanned 33 years from 1919 to 1952. Miss Owen was refreshment room manageress at Huddersfield for 37 years and Miss Stephenson fulfilled the same role at Middlesbrough for 48 years. Margaret Johnston worked from 1915 to 1957. Working successively as a guard, carriage cleaner and mess-room supervisor, she completed 42 years on the railway. Carriage Cleaner Lena Spence retired in July 1955 after more than 40 years' service. None received a pension, because 'female employment on the railways was of a transitional character',

Miss Spence had been a member of the NUR longer than any other woman, having joined on 16th October 1915, just three months after it admitted women. In 1955 she was the first woman to be awarded the NUR Gold Medallion, Gold Bar and Ribbon for 39 years' service as a staff representative, recruitment officer and subscription collector for Darlington 1 Branch.[75]

SALARIED STAFF

After the war there was a massive transfer of routine clerical work to women and by the 60s such work was almost entirely in female hands. They dominated numerically in typing pools, paybills offices, traffic statistics offices, accounts, switchboards and administrative work of all types, with the notable exceptions of train crew rostering and ticket offices. Smaller numbers worked as tracers.

While most women were employed in large groups and in female dominated offices, a small number found themselves working alone and in close contact with male wages grades. For example, shed-master's clerk Miss L. Dowell was the only woman employee at Laira Diesel Depot. When interviewed after working there for 14 years she declared herself to be 'very happy'.[76] Maisie Bell joined the railway at South Shields in 1963 at the age of 40 and worked until retirement 20 years later, working in the parcels office and later the ticket office, and was promoted to chief clerk of both before moving to the travel office at Newcastle. Joyce Pluckrose joined Southwark goods depot in 1958 as the lowest grade clerical officer and became the rolling stock clerk, working under the goods agent:

> We worked six days a week and I started at 7 a.m., earlier than most, as I had to have the whole movements of wagons summarised for the previous 24 hours by 10.30 a.m. I started my day by collecting all the numbertakers' sheets from the chief foreman's office at Blackfriars Goods, walked to Southwark depot, again collected the numbertakers' sheets and then took the whole lot to my desk in the chief goods' clerk's office. I had to keep an accurate record of all types of wagons passing through the two depots. The type of wagons received, unloaded and then held on hand or despatched, either empty or loaded, to other parts of the British Isles or returned empty to their stations of origin, mainly Dover or Folkestone for the continent.
>
> We were moved to Hither Green, where there were eight ladies and 24 men clerks, and about 100 uniformed men and eight supervisors. The ladies were all treated with respect but were expected to work hard and pull our weight equally with the men. I became a customs clearing clerk, a job that entailed travelling to London Bridge daily to pay the duty on behalf of BR's clients.
>
> Later I became the staff clerk, dealing with the pay and welfare of the whole staff and as the depot was closing I moved to the staff office at Beckenham divisional manager's office, where I stayed until retirement.[77]

Marjorie Phillips started work at Wisbech East Station as a clerk in the booking and parcels office in 1947, when she was 16. She recalled:

> I lived at March, about 11 miles away. Occasionally I had to cycle but most of the time travelled by train. In the fruit season, I used to go out on the train to other villages to make out consignment notes, so that the fruit (mainly strawberries) could be transferred to the other trains without delay. I loved the old steam trains and once rode home from Wisbech to March on the engine at the invitation of the fireman.[78]

Josephine Ball of Pickering joined BR in 1950s as a junior clerk at Manchester Victoria:

> I left there in 1963 and became an auditor for all the little goods stations in the Stockport area. I also unofficially worked in a signal box, went on the footplate of a shunt engine and learned to drive it.[79]

G. Margaret Penning was the booking office clerk on the LNER from 1945-47:

> Penistone was nationally known as the coldest station in England. I thought it would be rather boring at such a comparatively small station, but not at all. All trains stopped here, and in fact it was important enough, connection wise, to be listed on the boardings above the carriage windows of the London trains. Charlie was my opposite number and we worked the two shifts alternately – 5.45 a.m. to 1.45 p.m., or 4 p.m. to midnight (or after the mail train had gone). I loved cycling to work on a summer morning, seeing the sun rise through the viaducts, to get there in time for the first workman's train from Huddersfield. On the other hand, I was tentative riding past the churchyard as the clock struck midnight.
>
> I worked — alone — in a sort of cabin about 3 x 4 yards in area, set in the luggage entrance hall. This was probably a wartime arrangement as, some years later, it was removed and the clerks returned to the original Victorian booking office. Various staff would pop in for a chat, even the station master. The train register lad from the nearby signal box called in one day and began swinging his legs, with both arms on the desks either side. He somehow brought down a full rack of tickets — hundreds of them.
>
> There were individual tickets to almost everywhere. Monthly returns, daily returns, singles, workman, privilege, and blanks for those we had to write out if they weren't in stock. We had a reference book for every fare. We also had four timetables, blue for LNER, red for LMS, green for Southern, brown for GWR. There was a special rack for LMS tickets, mainly workmen's.
>
> Tickets were booked at one window and collected at the opposite window, tickets being about two inches of green card, returns printed in two parts for tearing off at the end of the outgoing journey. The card was date stamped by punching it into a noisy gadget.
>
> My husband was a signalman for 48 years. Over the years the family travelled a lot with the free passes and quarter fare privilege tickets.
>
> We worked every third Sunday. There were fewer trains of course, but I had to do more travelling with my having to cycle the two miles each way three times —for the early trains, the midday trains and the evening trains. The LNER must have saved a lot of money that way. Sunday evening was the busiest time of the week — three or four deep on the platform. A lot of them were military; they all had warrants, of course. The second busy time was when Sheffield Wednesday were at home, the station inspector often having to hold the train several minutes or more, whilst everyone got their tickets and scrambled aboard.
>
> I dealt with incoming and outgoing parcels including weighing foundry patterns from various works in the area. Also wrote out a delivery list every day for the drayman. I also dealt with all enquiries, train times, train routes, answered phone enquiries — our phone number was Penistone 198. Also dealt with messages and the internal phone. Many a time we got the message 'VANCO' and time of a train. This meant a coffin, a van attached to the end of a passenger train. It would be detached from the train and shunted to the cattle dock until the coffin was collected by the local undertaker.

> One day the porters deposited a coffin just inside the entrance hall. There was a body in it. Travellers tripped over themselves trying to avoid it as they came off the platform, such surprised faces. It was there two hours.
>
> When it was quiet and the weather was decent, I liked to go on to the platform and take it all in, with the gas lighting, the big two faced clock, the tiny newspaper kiosk, which only opened in the mornings, the letter box on the wall, the red penny chocolate machine and the barrow, ready for action at the end of the platform. Looking back, it was like a film set. There was even a roaring fire in the third class waiting room with a bucket of coal at the side for passengers to use. The long horsehair benches and large framed paintings. I remember it all with affection.[80]

Cynthia Coleman (now Phillips), a railway clerk's daughter, joined Birmingham's Lawley Street Goods as a parcels' clerk in 1952 when she was 16. She recalled unofficially riding on the conveyor belt down to the canteen to eat her lunch, usually the only girl among a hall full of railwaymen eating, talking, drinking tea and smoking cigarettes, and larking about in the office. One day she, another woman and ten lads from the office went outside and had a snowball fight while the managers watched through their windows. Another time she found her boots full of the pea-sized balls of glue. The office was filled with old documentation and was extremely dusty as well as being generally dirty. When after two years' service she and another girl contracted tuberculosis it was widely believed that constantly breathing the dust had caused their illness, but nothing was proved. She was off sick for 14 months and then began to work at Birmingham New Street as a reservations and sleeper clerk. Mrs Phillips described the atmosphere on the railways of the 1950s as one in which people just accepted the conditions they worked in: 'There was no thought for health and safety in those days; we didn't think to complain. The same attitude was held towards a man who, at every opportunity, groped the young girl clerks: 'We just avoided him, and warned the other girls. It didn't occur to any of us to complain to anyone in authority. In those days you learned to look after yourself'. She left the railway in 1956 to attend secretarial college and, many years later, was pleased when her daughter Heather became a ticket office clerk at Bristol Temple Meads.[81]

Clerical opportunities for women were expanding, albeit slowly. In 1950 the Eastern Region introduced 'Holiday Runabout Salesgirls', in other words, mobile ticket sellers. These unfortunate women were engaged at Norwich and other towns to walk the streets outside the stations with a weighty mobile ticket office hanging around their necks.[82]

In 1957 the LMR reintroduced a secretarial service for 'business men' between Euston and Manchester. The first was Ann Lowe, who revealed that she 'felt like a lamb for the slaughter'. On her first trip she dealt with only one client – ironically, a woman. She remarked, rather acerbically, that she would have managed to serve two more had she not been surrounded by journalists and photographers.[83]

Some railwaywomen on the clerical and technical side distinguished themselves by winning prizes and competitions. Tracer Joyce Young, a member of the locomotive drawing staff at Brighton, SR, won a prize in 1962 from the Draughtsmen's and Allied Technician's Association for her technical drawing of a motor-tug. She had previously worked for the War Office, tracing boilers. Miss E. Davies, senior shorthand typist in the divisional signalling office at Chester for 41 years, was the only railwaywoman to pass the higher signalling examinations with merit, on two occasions. She didn't intend to become a signalwoman; she simply felt that a thorough understanding of the system would help with her work.[84]

Both the WR and LMR employed female travel advisors or hostesses. Their task was to stand on the concourses of the main stations, inviting travel enquiries and assisting passengers. They were issued with a uniform that included twelve pairs of nylons per annum (presumably, each pair had to last a month) and a pair of high-heeled shoes, totally unsuitable for a job that involved standing all day. One journalist called them 'the new feminine phenomenon of the Railways Executive' and they were described as 'adding incidental touches of glamour to drab stations'. Thelma Whitehouse, who was employed at Birmingham Snow Hill, remarked unsurprisingly: 'my feet are suffering most.' Despite this, she admitted that she preferred the job to being 'behind bars' in the inquiry office.[85] Her colleague at Cardiff, Vera Bray, was once ambushed by a male passenger who proceeded to embarrass her by loudly and publicly airing his views on 'the error of careers for women' and propounding instead 'prolific motherhood'.[86]

When male railway managers needed temporary staff for special promotions they hired only female applicants, and selected them purely on the basis of physical attractiveness, as William Becket explained:

> We used to hire a couple of pretty faces for a few days, dress them up in some sort of garb and get them to hand out leaflets. The qualifications for the job were purely aesthetic but I remember on one occasion I had a disappointed applicant who demanded to know why she had not been appointed. Quite apart from being the wrong side of 40, she resembled Kruschev with tits.[87]

Winifred de Bierre recalled that although in theory by the early 1960s women were able to apply for any post, in practice there was discrimination:

> At interviews women were asked if they were contemplating getting married. Posts that involved being over male staff were ruled out — especially male wages grade staff, such as office van drivers. As promotion required 'suitability', the female applicants could be deemed as 'unsuitable' for those sorts of reasons.
>
> In the 60s one or two avenues were opening where sex discrimination was applied less and women were able to get into the lower senior grades (e.g the first grade of management). These were the 'boffin' areas. I was lucky enough to get into two — research and computing. In each of them I was the only female.
>
> If I went to a meeting or a training course, I was generally the only female and it was impossible to relax. Such a fuss was made by the men — I was treated like a piece of china, everyone was very courteous. But if I made a business comment, perhaps slightly controversial, the men just looked uncomfortable that such a thing could happen. We were meant to be 'ornamental'. The men, being totally unused to a female at these meetings and courses, used to get a bit frisky — quite a strain!
>
> I found that the top bosses had breadth of vision and saw us as equal to the men; it was our own male colleagues who didn't. There was also animosity from their wives, that we were with their husbands all day, but in particular if we got promotion before a married man. Both the men and their wives seemed to think this. We were accepted in lower management but there was awful resentment if we got promoted higher.[88]

During the 50s and 60s more women began to enter technical and professional areas of BR as computer experts, engineers, chemists and architects. Angela Levy recalled:

> On graduating from architectural college in 1957 I started work in the architect's office of British Rail, Eastern Region at Kings Cross. My father was Chief Mechanical Engineer to BR. When being interviewed for my job at Kings Cross I was very concerned that no one knew of my father's position as I wanted to obtain the job on my own merits — which I did!
>
> The offices of the Eastern Region Civil Engineers and Architects were alongside platform one at Kings Cross — steam trains on one side and a very busy road on other side — a very noisy, dirty environment. There were about 50 male architects and one female technician in the office when I joined; I fitted in easily as I had been one of seven girls and 70 men in my year at college so was quite used to being in a considerable minority. Some of the civil engineers with whom I had to liaise found me a bit of a problem but generally I won them round quite easily. One trade rep who was trying to sell me some building products told me that he couldn't (as he would with a man), take me out to lunch as his wife wouldn't like it; he gave me an advertising scale rule instead!
>
> One of the first projects I worked on was designing a lady carriage cleaners' amenity building (washrooms, canteen etc.) All the fittings had to be locked on or chained, otherwise they were removed and taken away by the said ladies.
>
> I was employed there for four years, and worked on a wide variety of schemes and enjoyed most of it immensely. We would have several trips a year as an office outing to visit railway and other buildings on the continent — Amsterdam, Brussels, Zurich — and of course we had free first class travel.
>
> When I first joined the office I did not have equal pay with my frequently less-qualified male colleagues. We started work at 8.30 in the morning but, as I had a full social life outside the office, I sometimes got in a bit late. I said that when I got equal pay I would be meticulously in on time — which I was.[89]

After the war more care was taken of staff welfare. Women's welfare officers — a wartime innovation — were renamed welfare officers and attempted to advise on all difficulties, whether 'legal, moral, financial, matrimonial or domestic' to staff of both sexes.[90] Kate Henderson, Women's Welfare Supervisor at York, was awarded the MBE in 1957 for her sterling work in this difficult and stressful area, which required considerable tact and diplomacy as well as common sense.

Railway staff organised an enormous number of sports and social clubs, hobby groups and personal improvement associations, mainly run by clerks. These included fire-fighting teams, ambulance teams, bell-ringing groups, building-a-house-from-scratch teams and also a wide range of competitive sports including motorcycle scrambling, hockey and racquet sports. Participants' achievements were published, complete with photographs, in the various regional editions of the *British Railways Magazine*.

Ethel Panting, secretary to the Swindon Works manager, who had 38 years' railway service, was awarded the MBE in 1969 for her 30 years' voluntary service in railway ambulance work and 25 years' work promoting the National Savings movement.

Salaried Staff's Struggle for Equality

Before dealing with the stance taken by the NUR and RCA towards equality for women on the railway, it is edifying to take a brief look at how they treated their own clerks. As employers, they unashamedly advertised separately for 'male clerks' and 'female clerks', offering lower rates of pay to the latter. They also restricted women clerks to lower grade and 'female' office work until February 1951, after which they (supposedly) had equal opportunities with men.[91] However, it took until 1985 for the TSSA to appoint a woman as a senior official; she was Caroline Hodges, editor of the *Transport Salaried Staff Journal.* The first ex-railwaywoman to be appointed to a senior position in the TSSA was Marion Campbell, who became Finance and Education Officer in 1991.

During the 1940s clerical grade railwaywomen made fair progress, in that they enjoyed more opportunities for advancement than ever before. Just before the war, 94% of women railway clerks had been in the lowest grade (W2); by 1952 this had dropped to 88% and by 1956 it stood at 85%.

Behind the massive headlines of the industrial trades union struggles of the 50s, including the railway strikes of 1955, female clerks both within and outside the railway industry continued their little-reported but nonetheless determined campaign for equal pay and equal opportunity. It had become predominantly a middle-class movement, especially since the 1944 Royal Commission decreed that only professional or higher-grade women clerks performing equal work with men ought to receive equal pay. From 1946 women in the higher grades of some local authorities and nationalised industries won pay parity with men, but from 1948 the Labour government's pay freeze halted the spread of equal pay before it reached the railways. In 1950 female trade unionists stepped up the campaign, but by the time the Labour government was voted out of office in 1951 it still had not bowed to the pressure.

In December 1953 the BTC expressed a willingness to revise pay structures. The TSSA* (but not the NUR) requested common scales of pay for men and women clerks. After a year's negotiation men were given new scales of pay while women were merely promised that their employers would 'consider improving' their promotional structure. The Conservative Party's election victory in 1951 coincided with a shortage of clerical staff and this proved to be in women's favour: one by one the local authorities, public utilities and services and the civil service conceded equal pay. The Railways Executive had always refused to give women equal pay on the grounds that the government did not pay it, and so railwaywomen assumed that their struggle was, at long last, over. The women were exasperated when the employer still refused to concede equal pay, promising only 'further consideration'.

In 1955 the starting salary for clerks aged 16 was £165 a year for males and £145 for females. After twelve years' service, a woman of 28 would find herself in receipt of an average of £365 a year while her male counterpart enjoyed £450. At this time there were over 67,000 salaried staff on the railway, of whom 18,000 were women, including 5,800 shorthand and copy typists, 3,800 machine, telephone and teleprinter operators and 9,000 in miscellaneous clerical work.[92]

The TSSA had over 20,000 female members in the mid 50s, among them many determined and energetic activists working on the 'shop-floor'. One, Gladys Jones, a goods clerk at Port Talbot and an RCA/TSSA member since 1928, was awarded the TUC Women's Gold Badge in 1962 for services to the trades union movement, during which time she had been a delegate not only to RCA conferences but to those of the Labour Party and the TUC.

* The Railway Clerks' Association became the Transport Salaried Staffs' Association in 1951, after being opened to clerks in all transport industries. Its peak membership, 91,514, was reached in 1952.

Also in that year, TSSA activist Ethel Chipchase became Secretary of the TUC National Women's Advisory Committee.* It was owing to the efforts of such women that resolutions for female equality were debated — and sometimes even carried — at TSSA conferences. These conferences gave a platform for many intelligent and determined railwaywomen to express their views on the unequal treatment of their sex.

Popular history claims that during the post-war era women retreated into domesticity and feminism was dormant, but female railway clerks made their grievances abundantly clear. In 1949 one TSSA delegate was perturbed because 'the chances of a progressive career are negligible.' while another complained that women had a 'raw deal.'[93] At the 1955 conference Miss Hayward asserted: 'It is often said that women cannot accept responsibility. Nonsense. You can't accept something that hasn't been offered you',[94] while Sylvia Morris described how women with 20 years' service were forced to suffer the indignity of seeing young men being newly recruited and then promoted above them.

Women clerks had been complaining for decades about the lack of promotional opportunities, but nothing had changed. There were still only one or two senior positions available to them, as supervisor of a typing pool or telephone exchange and, once they were filled, the incumbents had nowhere further to go, and so never vacated the position until they retired.

Another discriminatory practice was revealed at the 1956 conference: some clerks' jobs required the appointees to be geographically mobile and take lodgings wherever they were sent. Because it was *assumed* that the parents of *some* young female clerks *might* not allow them to leave home, these posts were closed to *all* women indiscriminately. At the same conference the TSSA itself received criticism in relation to women. One railwayman criticised the union's leadership for finding the problem of women's rights 'as difficult as the ascent of Everest', while a Miss Brewer declared: 'We are one-fifth of the membership of this Association, we pay the same subscriptions and we demand the same treatment.' Thinking that an equal pay resolution would fail, the women instead proposed a more modest one calling for more higher-grade posts for women and a general increase in their salaries. The resolution was carried, but the general secretary voted against it.

TSSA women seem to have converted many of their brother activists to their cause, and must have been delighted when two attempts to pass conference resolutions unfavourable to women were unsuccessful. In 1954 delegates rejected a motion from Motherwell branch to treat all married women clerks as temporary and in 1955 a resolution was proposed to the effect that, in cases of redundancy, wives should be dismissed before spinsters. The TSSA Women's Officer, Betty Kent,† disagreed: older women had less chance of finding alternative employment, she argued, and often had dependants. The motion was defeated. In 1964, an attempt was again made to treat all married women clerks as temporary, but this also failed.[95]

* Ethel Chipchase MBE. RCA Executive 1945-1948; TUC Women's Conference 1948-1950. First female member of the RCA to stand for Parliament, in 1950. Later joined the RCA staff. TUC Women's Officer 1962-1980; member of the Equal Opportunities Commission.

† Elizabeth Kent, Glasgow Central RCA branch. Joined the RCA 1933; Executive Committee 1953-1960. Chairman, Scottish (Western) Divisional Council; represented the TSSA at Scottish TUC Women's Advisory Committee, which she chaired in 1958 and 1968. Wrote *A Page For Women* in the *TSSJ*. Awarded the TUC Gold medal, 1969.

In October 1955, almost two years after equal pay was conceded to women in the civil service, public utilities and local authorities, the BTC unexpectedly announced that it would be granted to women in clerical and technical grades: rates would increase gradually from December 1956 until parity was reached in 1961.

As this news emerged Betty Kent was on her way to address a meeting of women clerks. She announced jubilantly that their 25-year struggle had finally borne fruit: they had won equality of pay with men.

> The effect was almost embarrassing. For what seemed like five minutes, but, of course, was only a few seconds, there was dead silence. It appeared as though my audience weren't at all impressed, but as my words sank in and they got their breath back, their facial expressions and applause showed their very great pleasure. Quite obviously, this was something none of them had expected.[96]

Miss Kent described the agreement as 'the most important milestone to date', representing 'a lifetime's work and ambition.'

When the settlement was scrutinised, however, it transpired that the BTC had excluded from the settlement the following workers: office-machine operators (such as telephone, tele-printer, adding-machine, punch card and calculator operators);* clerks who worked in docks, shipping, hotels, catering and workshops; and all employees of London Transport. In addition, to qualify for equal pay, a woman had to perform work that was 'predominantly performed by men'. One of these jobs was tracing; however, all 270 female tracers were refused equality with their 121 male colleagues, on the grounds that only men were dubbed 'trainee draughtsman' while women were called 'tracers', even though many female tracers became draughtswomen.

The TSSA's official, understated response was that it was 'quite frankly surprised'; but its female membership was nothing short of devastated to find that they had been duped once again. The only women eligible for equal pay were clerks in booking-, parcels-, and goods-offices; telegraphists, senior clerks in accounts, costing and paybills and station masters' clerks. Of the 18,607 female clerical and technical staff who believed that they had been awarded equal pay, a mere 4,500 — just 24% — qualified for it.[97]

The TSSA tried to re-negotiate the settlement. According to NUR leader Jim Campbell, the TSSA 'dropped a bombshell' in February 1956 by asking the BTC to abolish women's scales altogether and introduce one scale for clerical staff and another for machine operators, irrespective of sex. The NUR publicly criticised the TSSA for changing its mind, while the TSSA openly condemned the NUR for failing to support equal pay for women.

After nine months of negotiations the dispute was passed to a Railway Staff National Tribunal, chaired by Sir John Forster QC. The BTC's request that the hearing be held in private was declined and women TSSA members from all over Britain eagerly filled the public seats. They were not disappointed: the Tribunal upheld the TSSA's demand for equal pay for clerks without the necessity to prove that their work was exactly equal to that of men. Female grades were abolished, giving women the opportunity for progress to the former male Grade 1. Equal pay was to be brought in by stages from December 1956 until parity was reached in December 1961.

* Civil servants in these jobs had won equal pay in 1956.

Although the TSSA had failed to get office machine operators included in the equal pay scheme, an increase in their pay was obtained. New scales were inaugurated: Class A consisted of typists and machine operators; Class B, higher-skilled machine operators and shorthand typists who had attained a certain competency; Class C contained tracers and some other skilled grades. The employers argued that they should not have to pay the male rate for 'routine office work'. The TSSA pointed out the absurdity: they paid it to *male* clerks engaged in the same routine tasks. The union's HQ was inundated with correspondence from women in grades still excluded from equal pay. Eventually a Working Party was appointed and after negotiation the excluded grades were integrated into the clerical structure, and in 1968 equal pay was finally achieved for all women within the BRB.

But it had been a long and hard struggle, and women's patience had run out, as a member of the TSSA remarked:

> Unfortunately, negotiations have been protracted and difficult and, as a consequence, there has been considerable unrest, disappointment and dissatisfaction among the women concerned. ... These negotiations conclude a quarter of a century's efforts to secure reasonable rates for women salaried staff in all grades and end, we hope for ever, the wide disparities purely on grounds of what was previously described as social distinction, but was, in fact, sex discrimination. Those at present in the service who will derive full benefit from the settlements will, we know, acknowledge the debt they owe to their predecessors, who persistently fought for this ideal when times were not propitious and the possibility of success remote.[98]

The writer criticised the NUR by adding: 'The T.S.S.A. is entitled to the credit for this very real improvement, for on it alone fell the burden of argument.' Indeed, the NUR had taken almost no part in the campaign for equal pay for female clerks (although it happily recruited them as members).

The TSSA next turned its attention to BTC's other undertakings and, by June 1957, it managed to obtain equal pay for women clerks in headquarters, regional and district administrative offices of hotel and catering departments. But clerks in the actual hotel and catering establishments were still excluded, on the grounds that equal pay was not operative in the hotel trade generally. Once again the senior railway management insisted on waiting for other industries to make the first move in giving equality to women.

Once female clerical grades were abolished in 1956 the path should have been open to complete equality of opportunity with men, something many women thought even more exciting than equal pay. There would no longer be men workers and women workers, just railway workers and women could apply for any salaried staff vacancy. It is what women had wanted for decades, and Betty Kent was overjoyed. She remarked:

> The most important thing is that women will now be allowed to apply for posts from which they have hitherto been barred and, what is even more important, have the right to expect equal consideration with male applicants.[99]

Delegates from BR, the NUR and the TSSA met in 1956 to discuss what kind of higher-grade work women might do. Predictably, 19 of the 20 persons present were male. Poor Betty Kent, the token woman, was crestfallen when she discovered that the promised equality was – yet again – merely a hoax. Although separate men's and women's grades

THEY SAY 'NO' TO A STATION MISTRESS

By Harold Webb

BRIDLINGTON, Tuesday.

IT'S becoming a woman's world in many places—but not on the railways. Top jobs there are still for men only.

For instance, why not have women stationmasters? Certainly not, says British Railways.

And women controllers? No again.

Result of this attitude is that three-quarters of the 18,500 women employed on the railways are barred from reaching the goal of the modern woman in industry—*equality*.

Because of this, the Transport Commission was strongly criticised by women and men at the conference of the 90,000-strong Transport Salaried Staffs' Association here today.

For the MEN, Mr. W. J. P. Webber, general secretary, declared: "I see no reason why women should be excluded from the job of station master. *From the men delegates came cries of "Hear, hear!"*

Mr. Webber continued: "Women should have the opportunity to become station masters, shed masters or controllers if they have the ability."

But he warned that equality for women would not mean "equality plus." They would then have to do the inconvenient turns just the same as the men.

He then revealed that the union Executive was not satisfied with the Transport Commission's attitude towards equal pay. The matter might have to go to the Railway Staff National Tribunal for a decision.

Women fed up

Then came the WOMEN. Clerk Joan Aberdeen of Glasgow, declared: "Our patience is wearing out. We are fed up with words. What we want is action."

And Miss M. Brewer, of Bristol, protested: "The longer this procrastination continues then promotion for women will be held up and they will be passed over by junior men."

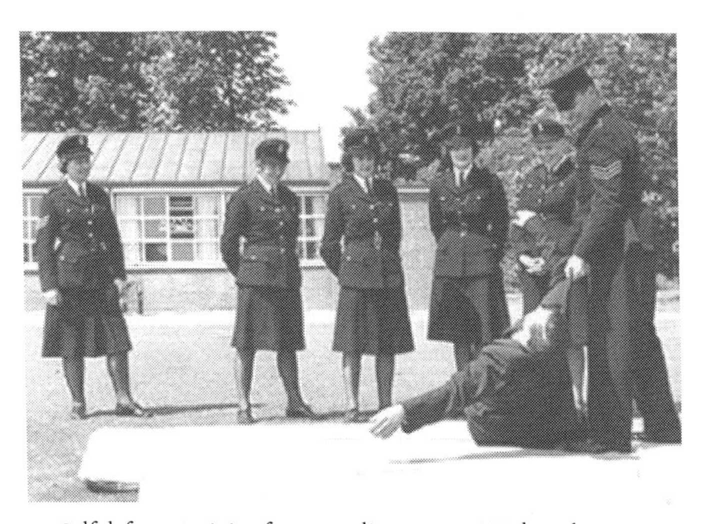

Self defence training for BTP policewomen at Tadworth. BTP

Report from the TSSA conference.
DAILY HERALD, 30 MAY 1956

were abolished, the male delegates believed that it was 'unlikely that women would be suitable' for most supervisory jobs in docks, workshops and railway operations, because of the 'nature of the duties'. Yet again, men and men alone assumed the right to decide which jobs women were 'suitable' for, using their clichéd stereotypes, entrenched prejudices and — not least — their self-interest in keeping all the best jobs for themselves. Men were adamant that a woman must never be placed in charge of men, just in case she was called upon to perform the work herself, which she clearly could not, since it was 'men's work'.[100] For example, if a female booking clerk were promoted to station mistress she would be in charge of porters, trackmen, signalmen and shunters, whose duties, it was assumed, she was incapable of performing.

Some TSSA men supported women's quest for equality. At the union's 1956 conference men cried 'Hear, hear' when the general secretary said he approved of station mistresses, but Clerical Officer Joan Aberdeen declared: 'We are fed up with words. What we want is action.'[101] She got it: the delegates passed a resolution that female clerks should be allowed to apply for all vacancies, and that women should be considered for any salaried post including those of 'station master or yard master'.

The women may have convinced many of their union brothers, but huge obstacles still existed in the shape of the Executives of the RCA and the NUR, and senior railway managers. The latter announced that certain posts were — and would always be — reserved for men. These included station master, yard master, locomotive shed master; assistant station master; goods, passenger and parcels agent, workshop, railway and dock supervisor; electrical, technical and supervisory staff; and electrical control room and rectifier staff. A spokesman for the BTC appealed to railwaymen's paternalism:

> One need only to emphasise the duties of a yardmaster in a large marshalling yard to recognise that to have a lady appointed to that post would not be in her best interests and certainly not in the best interests of the staff whom she would need to control, quite apart from the danger attaching to the job.[102]

Of course, had he cited the duties of a goods agent instead, his objection would not have sounded so reasonable, and the judicious use of the word 'lady' instead of 'woman' emphasised the unsuitability of such people for the job. The BTC had further reservations:

> There are offices at stations and depots where it would be wrong to employ a woman on her own during the hours of darkness. ... There are offices in busy marshalling yards where running lines have to be crossed; again, it is often undesirable that a woman should be employed in such circumstances.[103]

The fact that many railwaywomen already worked nights and crossed yards and tracks was, apparently, irrelevant. Clearly, it was perfectly safe for them to do so as carriage cleaners and crossing keepers, but not as supervisors or station mistresses.

The deep-seated prejudice against women united railway managers and NUR leaders. In 1956 the union's general secretary echoed BR's attitude when he asked, rhetorically, on the front page of *The Railway Review*:

> Can any practical railwayman imagine a woman Yard Master at, say King's Cross, supervising Yard Inspectors, Yard Foreman, Clerical Staff, Checkers and Motor Drivers — all men with a wealth of practical experience in their grade?

This provoked journalist Margaret Stewart to write a scathing piece in the *News Chronicle* condemning the NUR leadership. In their fight with the Railways Executive, women had won the principle of equality; but, she asserted, 'Our railwaywomen have another battle on their hands – against railwayMEN.'[104] Six years later, in 1962, BRB chairman Dr Beeching told the Women's Press Club that 'really bright, well-educated people' should be encouraged to join the railways. He then added that prospects for women were 'not good' and turned down a suggestion that he should give station mistresses a trial to prove themselves.[105]

It was in theory possible for a woman to take advantage of the opportunities open to them in railway office work, although they were often subtly discouraged from doing so. By the late 50s, Mrs K. Odell had completed 20 years' service and was working as a secretary in the Staff Office at Derby:

> When equal pay for women was introduced, I and the other secretaries decided we would apply for an advertised job on the clerical side in the office where I was working. This would mean a rise in salary. The all-male interview panel persuaded all the others that they didn't want the job. It didn't work with me, I was bored with my job so had nothing to lose. To the surprise of all concerned, I got the job.
>
> I didn't come across any hostility as a woman in what had previously been a man's job. At first I only had to supervise a couple of the male sex, but I tried to do this in a sensitive manner. It was in my existing office and, of course, I knew the men. There had been women working there, but they had always been paid a lower salary than the men and were confined mainly to routine work. I stayed in the section, rising a little, until I took early retirement in 1977.[106]

Farewell to the Victorians

One of the characteristics of railway offices during the late 50s and very early 60s was the retirement of the many railwaywomen who had joined the industry between 1910 and 1920. This was the end of an era: by 1961 almost every Victorian-born railwaywoman had either left or been obliged to retire at the age of 60. Here is a list of some of those with over 40 years' service (those with 30 to 40 years' service were too numerous to include):

46 YEARS' SERVICE

Irene Dening (1914) P.A. to stores manager, Swindon, GWR.

45 YEARS' SERVICE

Eva Lawson (1912), women's supervisor, electrical engineer's department, London Bridge.
Miss L. Tichner (1914), shorthand typist, Marylebone.
Miss V. Willey (1912), typing supervisor, LMR.

44 YEARS' SERVICE

Alice Etherington (1918), supervisor, Waterloo Exchange.
Jenny Blackwood (1914), audit office clerk, Scottish Region.
Miss W. Bliss (1915), clerk, district goods manager, Gloucester.
Miss E. B. Cape (1915), clerk, Scotland.
Miss H. Coombs (1915), assistant supervisor, telephone exchange, Paddington.
Miss Hardman (1917), shorthand typist, accounts department. Crewe.

Mabel Hayes (1913), goods clerks' supervisor, Bradford.
Miss M.D. Smith (1915), typist, stores (Scotland).
Miss G. Walters (1914), clerk in charge, Swindon.

43 YEARS' SERVICE
Miss E. Bevan (1916), supervisor of Punch Card Centre.
Miss E. Dexter (1913), secretary, Peterborough.
Miss A. Hardie (1913), senior typist, Chester, GWR.
Elizabeth (Betty) Lamont (1911), telegraphist, Edinburgh.
Ivy Payne (1912), typing supervisor, Euston.
Miss J. B. Taylor, (1916) clerk, DR & MO.
Isabella Valance (1916), typing bureau supervisor, Glasgow.
Miss M. Watkin (1916), personal Clerk to District Officer, Newport.

42 YEARS' SERVICE
Miss J Gardner (1914), personal clerk to the docks manager, NER.
Ethel Clarke (1914), telephone supervisor, Euston.
Helen Cockburn (1917), clerk, Dundee.
Mrs E James (1913), clerk, Euston dining car office.
Miss F. M. Glidle (1915), typing supervisor, Leeds.
Miss E. Gutridge (1913), supervisor, Swindon works telephone exchange.
Miss D. Robbins (1917), clerk, Regional Accounts, WR.
Miss H Wallace (1915), clerk, Supplies & Contracts Office, King's Cross.

41 YEARS' SERVICE
Miss Olive Appleton (1915), accounts clerk, Nine Elms, SR.
Margaret Archer (1916), clerk, Motive Power Depot, Parkhead.
Miss A. N. Clark (1915), personal Secretary to Asst General Manager, Waterloo SR.
Miss Gladys Cooper (1914), telephonist, later supervisor, Southampton.
Miss E. Davies (1918), senior Shorthand typist, Chester.
Miss K. D. Fuller (1913), clerk in charge, South Lambeth Goods, SR.
Miss R. Ireland (1918), area welfare supervisor, ER.
Elizabeth Johnston (1914), typing supervisor, Glasgow.
Hilda Kendall (1916), personal secretary to chief parliamentary officer, BTC HQ.
Miss M. Kittow (1915), typist, Southampton marine department, SR.
Madge M'Culloch (1915), goods clerk, Greenock.
Miss B. Noble (1916), clerk, Bradford.
Miss F. Simpson (1917), clerk, regional accounts, Newport.
Annie Slack (1914), clerk, London.
Medora Swann (1915), paybill supervisor, York.
Olive Taylor (1918), clerk, goods office, Paddington.

40 YEARS' SERVICE
Mary Atkinson (1917), typing pool supervisor, York.
Miss D. Bentley (1915), telegraphist, Ruabon, WR.
Margaret Burness (1920) clerk, staff section, Dundee.
Miss R. Cheetham (1914), clerk.
Miss F. Codner (1920), secretary, public relations & publicity, ER.
Miss E.B. Ellis (1918), typist, Scottish Region.
Gladys Foster (1917), senior typist, Edinburgh.
Miss F. Glide (1915), typing bureau supervisor, Leeds.

Gladys Limb (1915), clerk, Middlewich.
Miss Jenny Panter (1915), telegraphist, GCR/LMS.
Miss F. Ryan (1917), clerk, Newport.
Kathleen Saull (1915), supervisor of typing bureau.
Miss W.E. Solman, (1916), clerk, Winchester.
Daisy Stewart (1916), telegraphist, Glasgow St Enoch.
Miss C. Surridge (1916), typist, Knebworth.
Miss K. Ward (1917), telegraph supervisor, Shrewsbury.

The above roll of honour makes no claim to be complete. It includes only those women who, for one reason or another, were featured in the staff magazines that the author read, up to 1961. There are likely to have been many others with forty years' service and more. Here are some details of a few.

Miss M. Enderson — known affectionately as 'Endy' — began her long and distinguished career at the bottom of the ladder, as goods clerk at Stewarts Lane, SECR, in 1917. Always adding to her skills and ever looking for ways to improve her career prospects, she transferred to Waterloo where she eventually rose to personal secretary, firstly to the general manager of the SR, then to the general manager of the BTC. Her final appointment was as assistant (female staff) in the manpower department of BTC headquarters. She retired in 1962 with 45 years' service.

Elsie Hamlyn became a telephonist on the GWR in 1915, supervisor in 1937 and chief supervisor in 1945. In 1952 she received the BEM for services to railway communications. She retired from Paddington telephone exchange in 1959, after 44 years' service.

Miss C. Blackwell joined the rolling stock superintendent's office at Crewe in 1916, transferred to HQ at Euston and studied for secretarial qualifications. Her job involved dealing with railway works, equipment regulations, works orders and progress reports. She became a Fellow of the Royal Society of Arts in 1920 and an Associate of the Chartered Institute of Secretaries in 1922. Miss Blackwell won the Prince of Wales Gold Medal of the London Chamber of Commerce in 1936 and, during her long career, won a sheaf of First-Aid certificates. As a first-class personal secretary, she served eight consecutive general managers before retiring in 1960 with 44 years' service.

Station master's daughter Miss R. Ireland began working life in 1918 in the ticket office at Brough, Yorkshire, moving firstly to York traffic statistics office and then to divisional accounts in London. After spending the Second World War as a clerk in the city manager's office, she was appointed welfare officer in 1946, then area welfare supervisor for the eastern counties, from which post she retired in 1959 with 41 years' service.

Gladys Limb, who joined in 1915 as a clerk at Middlewich, was leader of the LMS Ladies' First Aid team for 16 years. She was, in 1943, the first railwaywoman to receive the Order of St John. She retired in 1955 with 40 years' service.

Pearl Edith Wadham was born in 1892 and joined the LNER during the First World War with a qualification in Pitman's shorthand and typing and worked her way up to personal secretary to the general manager at Liverpool Street. During the Second World War she dealt with secret documents at Hitchin, for which she was awarded the MBE. On retirement Miss Wadham was presented with a montaged cartoon depicting her as cox in a racing boat containing the eight general managers for whom she had worked. She died in 1983.*

* The cartoon is held at the National Railway Museum.

Summary

During the immediate post-war years, a few lucky women managed to retain their jobs in male operating grades. In most cases, the management took a laissez-faire attitude to an individual woman who was obviously competent at her job, but NUR officials and – most especially – railwaymen sometimes complained until the woman was dismissed and replaced by a man. Between 1945 and 1975 there was, in theory, nothing to stop a woman from joining the railways as a porter, engineer or technician although this was not common knowledge. As far as Labour Exchanges and recruitment posters were concerned, these were male-only occupations. Progression from carriage cleaner to porter, ticket collector or signalwoman was also, in theory, possible, but it rarely happened. No woman could become a shunter, guard or motorman, and no woman had ever been employed as an engine driver or fireman when steam was abolished in 1968.

Women who aspired to railway work continued to be directed to one of the 'three Cs' – cleaning, catering or clerical. The employment of women in other areas was not merely discouraged but was concealed in printed recruitment material. Government careers booklets always referred to railway staff as male; for example, in one typical publication, reference was made to 'boys who want to be signalmen'.[107] The NUR played its part in the stereotyping. When *The Railway Review* ran a series of photographs depicting a wide range of railway workers, it had a golden opportunity to seek out women in non-traditional roles, in order to illustrate the wide range of possibilities for women. But the only woman in the series was Mrs Hutchinson, who served tea in the station buffet at York.[108] Within the railways, the word 'staff' was synonymous with 'man'. For example, one booklet explained that the Staff Association was open to 'all grades of the staff, and their wives',[109] while another, for salaried staff, stated that 'a married householder means a married male member of staff'.

Anyone reading such material would assume that women were not admitted to railway operating jobs. Misleading people into making such assumptions has in practice the same effect as barring women from the work, for the vast majority of women at that time, being accustomed to occupations being designated as men's or women's, and knowing that most jobs in industry and transport were for men only, are unlikely to have pursued the matter further. It was, in effect, a well-kept secret that women were eligible to apply for all kinds of wages grades jobs.

Railway staff, 1959	*Female*	*Male*
Administrative, clerical and technical	19,569	56,025
Carriage/wagon cleaners & examiners	3,731	12,789
Civil engineering	83	20,516
Goods and cartage	1,550	48,514
Locomotive workshops	108	36,137
Police	127	2,776
Signals and telecommunications	8	11,897
Station, goods and yard masters	0	7,254
Traffic controllers	4	2,320
Wages grades	2,437	105,693

Despite their absence from recruitment material there were so many isolated instances of women in male wages grades that, nationally, they amounted to several hundreds; but, such was the enormous size and wide geographical spread of the industry that it was possible for a railwayman to work for years without ever meeting or hearing of a woman working as anything other than a carriage cleaner, crossing keeper or clerk.

Whereas a man simply had to apply for a job for which he was eligible in order to get it, a woman had to be single-minded and prepared to suffer setbacks and disappointments while maintaining an unwavering belief in her ability to carry out a job designated as suitable only for men; and she would need determination to carry on trying, in the face of hostility and even obstruction. Few women would have wanted, say, a porter's job that desperately or had a level of self-belief sufficient to make them persevere. And yet some women fell into railway work easily, hearing of a porter's vacancy and applying, or being invited by local managers to take a uniformed job; while a few wartime signalwomen were sought out and invited to return. It all depended on the location, the availability of male labour and, most of all, the attitude of local managers towards women.

In the years between 1945 and 1975 women were habitually omitted from rules' books and other publications and were routinely treated less favourably than men in the provision of sick pay, pensions, uniforms and free travel passes. Lack of equal pay legislation, coupled with the NUR's compliance in paying lower wages to women, led BR to financially exploit the situation by gradually increasing the number of female staff in the areas of carriage-cleaning, gatekeeping, and routine clerical work, until (most) railwaywomen were granted equal pay between 1958 and 1961.

In 1962 the TUC launched its Women's Charter. This called for equal pay and equal opportunities, and for training facilities for women returning to work after having children. The struggle for equal pay gained impetus in 1968 when 850 women workers making car seat covers at the Ford motor car factory (members of the Transport and General Workers' Union), went on strike, bringing Ford's entire British operation to a standstill. They won almost equal pay with their male colleagues (who did exactly the same work): they settled for 92%. The case became a *cause célèbre* and a delegation of strikers was invited to tea in Whitehall. They inspired many other women and their case prompted an Equal Pay Bill to be introduced in 1970 by Barbara Castle, Minister of Employment in the Labour government. It passed and, although it was of great benefit to all working women, it had its limitations. After all, women in 'women's work' had no man to be equal with.

The Act gave employers five years' notice before it had to be implemented. Some grades of railwaywomen had been excluded when equal pay was granted to their female colleagues in 1958 and 1961. In 1973 and 1974 their wages were raised incrementally until parity was reached in 1975. The final stage was implemented when workshopwomen were granted equal pay on 29th December 1975 — just two days before the legal deadline.*

* An equal pay act was, in any case, inevitable, because Britain needed to comply with EEC entry requirements. After the First World War Britain was signatory to Part 13 of the 1920 Treaty of Versailles, which required equal pay for women but, as stated earlier, it was not implemented. The 1957 Treaty of Rome required legislation on equal pay to be passed before Britain could enter the European Economic Community.

After the passage of the Equal Pay Act in 1970, it became clear that if women and men continued to be segregated into different work the Act would be meaningless. And so (after several abortive attempts by individual MPs between 1967 and 1972 to bring in private members' bills) the Sex Discrimination Act (SDA) was proposed by the Labour government in 1974 and became law the following year.

The fact that both Acts passed into law under a male dominated parliament suggests that the timeworn beliefs about women had changed significantly over the preceding decades. Public opinion had been influenced by various campaigns and issues including the suffrage movement, women's work during two world wars, years of campaigning by women's groups (such as the Six Point Group and the Fawcett Society), by women in trades unions promoting the TUC's 1962 charter, by the 1960s women's liberation movement (with its marches, conferences and publications), by the increased percentage of women in the workforce and by the high number of women MPs, all of which contributed to a sea change in the status of women. There was also a growing awareness in society of human rights and of the unfairness of discrimination against anyone who was not white, heterosexual and male. The campaign for women's equality was assisted by the election of a Labour government in 1964, which was more susceptible than its Conservative predecessor to pressure from women in trades unions. Last but not least, after women 'proved' themselves in a thousand ways during the Second World War, it became increasingly untenable to regard them as inferior.

The part played by women war workers on the railways and elsewhere in gaining equal pay and opportunities for women is impossible to gauge. Equally difficult to judge is whether female members of the railway trade unions had any influence in getting the Sex Discrimination Act passed. There were no women in ASLEF, and the number of female activists in the NUR was very small. In contrast, women in the RCA/TSSA had the numerical strength to get themselves heard and were able to send women to TUC conferences and to its women's committee, giving some railwaywomen a voice within the trades union movement.

The SDA made it unlawful for employers to 'discriminate against a woman: (a) In the arrangements he makes for the purpose of determining who should be offered that employment, or (b) In the terms on which he offers her that employment, or (c) By refusing or deliberately omitting to offer her that employment'. It further decreed:

> It is unlawful for a person, in the case of a woman employed by him at an establishment in Great Britain, to discriminate against her (a) in the way he affords her access to opportunities for promotion, transfer or training, or to any other benefits, facilities or services, or by refusing or deliberately omitting to afford her access to them.

And with that law in place women could enter any railway occupation on the same terms as men.

References

[1] *Daily Herald* 25 May 1949.
[2] *The Railway Review* 23 December 1955.
[3] Wallace, M., (1997) *Single or Return? The Official History of the* TSSA (TSSA).
[4] *The Railway Review* 28 April 1950.
[5] Pathé News, 1951. Available online at <www.itnarchive.com/britishpathe>.
[6] *Daily Telegraph* 28 December 1957.
[7] *British Railways Magazine* Scottish Edition, 1954, p108.
[8] Letter to the author, 1995.
[9] Letter to the author, 2005.
[10] Letter to the author, 1990.
[11] *British Railways Magazine* LM Edition, 1955, p131.
[12] *British Railways Magazine* LM Edition, 1956, p56.
[13] *British Railways Magazine* LM Edition, 1952, p195.
[14] *British Railways Magazine* Southern edition, 1960, front cover feature.
[15] *British Railways Magazine* LM edition 1954, p11.
[16] Hutchinson. S. (n.d) *Berney Arms Past & Present.*
[17] Pathé News (1961) *One Woman Show*. Available online at <www.itnarchive.com/britishpathe>
[18] www.thisisworcester.com 27 May 2005.
[19] *Daily Herald* 20 February 1953.
[20] Letter to the author, 1990.
[21] *The Scotsman* 4 November 1966.
[22] *British Railways Magazine* LMS Edition, July 1958 p260.
[23] Letter to the author, 1989.
[24] Letter to the author, 1990.
[25] Letter to the author, 1990.
[26] Letter to the author, 1989.
[27] *Railnews* May 1969.
[28] *British Railways Magazine* Scottish Region edition1954, p146.
[29] Interview with Elsie Scriven (n.d.)
[30] <www.livingarchive.org.uk>
[31] *British Railways Magazine* Eastern Region Edition, 1960, p294.
[32] *Manchester Guardian* 9 October 1964; *The Times* 13 October 1964.
[33] *British Railways Magazine* LMS edition 1954, p66
[34] *British Railways Magazine* Scottish Region edition1954, p146.
[35] *The Railway Review* 19 August 1955.
[36] *The Railway Review* 11 March 1955.
[37] *The Railway Review* 18 March 1955.
[38] *Daily Telegraph* 29 October 1960.
[39] *Daily Herald* 24 June 1961; *Manchester Guardian* 21 November 1961; *The Times* 21 November 1961 NUR EC minutes, 1961.
[40] Head Office Circular to all Branches MC2/34/1 No. M9422/18928.
[41] Appendix A.73, E.C. Minutes, August 1974.
[42] Appendix A104, EC Minutes, August 1974.
[43] Noted in NUR EC minutes, Decision 2350, December 1975.
[44] *The Railway Review* 10 November 1950.
[45] *British Railways Magazine* Western Region 1957, p17.
[46] *British Railways Magazine* London Midland Edition, 1959, p282.

[47] McKenna, F. (1980) *The Railway Workers* (Faber & Faber) p204.
[48] *The Railway Review* 29 March 1946.
[49] *The Railway Review* 7 November 1947 and caption on a photo at www.corbis.com.
[50] *The Railway Review* 10 November 1944.
[51] NUR EC Minutes 1947.
[52] *The Railway Review* 11 November 1949.
[53] *The Railway Review* 14 November 1947.
[54] *The Railway Review* 24 October and 31 October 1947.
[55] *The Railway Review* 9 September 1955.
[56] *Railnews* December 1969.
[57] Pathé News 1960. Available online at <www.itnarchive.com/britishpathe>
[58] *Daily Telegraph* 8 September 1954.
[59] *British Railways Magazine*, London Midland Edition, 1959, p282.
[60] *British Railways Magazine*, November 1960. Pathé News has a short newsreel of Miss Dębinska available online at <www.itnarchive.com/britishpathe>
[61] Letter from Mary Baldock of Oxshott.
[62] *The Railway Review* 1 September 1950.
[63] *Daily Herald* 19 April 1954.
[64] Letter to the author, 2005.
[65] Letter to the author, 2005.
[66] Letter to the author, 2005.
[67] Email to the author, June 2005.
[68] *British Railways Magazine* Eastern Region edition, 1962, p14.
[69] *Railway Review* 24 February 1950.
[70] Letter to the author, 2005.
[71] Thanks to Steve Daly and Kevin Gordon.
[72] Bagwell, PS. (1982) *The Railwaymen* Volume two (Allen & Unwin) p342.
[73] Bagwell, PS. (1982) *The Railwaymen* Volume two (Allen & Unwin) p344.
[74] *British Railways Magazine* LMR edition, 1956.
[75] *The Railway Review* 5 August 1955.
[76] *British Railways Magazine*, Western Region, 1959, p45.
[77] Letter to the author, 1990.
[78] Letter to the author, 2005.
[79] Letter to the author, 2005.
[80] Letter to the author, 2005.
[81] Telephone conversation with the author, 15 July 2005.
[82] *British Railways Magazine* Eastern Region 1950, p84.
[83] *Daily Telegraph* 17 September 1957.
[84] *British Railways Magazine* 1959, p337.
[85] *Daily Telegraph* 28 March 1957; 10 June 1957; 19 November 1957; *Manchester Guardian* 11 June 1960.
[86] *British Railways Magazine* Western Region 1958, p47.
[87] Posted to the GWR e-group, Yahoo online groups, 13 July 2005.
[88] Letter to the author, 1990.
[89] Letter to the author, 2005.
[90] *British Railways Magazine* Western Edition 1962, p261.
[91] Wallace, M., (1997) *Single or Return? The Official History of the* TSSA (TSSA).
[92] *Transport Salaried Staff Journal* July 1954.
[93] *Daily Herald* 25 May 1949.
[94] *Daily Herald* 17 May 1955.
[95] Wallace, M., (1997) *Single or Return? The Official History of the* TSSA (TSSA).

96 *Transport Salaried Staff Journal* November 1955, p438.
97 *Transport Salaried Staff Journal* November 1956, p429.
98 *Transport Salaried Staff Journal* April 1957 p130.
99 *Transport Salaried Staff Journal* November 1955, p438.
100 NUR Minutes 1956 RSC Meeting 24 January 1956.
101 *Daily Herald* 30 May 1956.
102 *Transport Salaried Staff Journal* November 1956, p436.
103 Ibid p442.
104 *News Chronicle* 27 November 1956.
105 *Manchester Guardian* 7 December 1962.
106 Letter to the author, 2005.
107 *Choice of Careers* No 88 HMSO, 1960.
108 *The Railway Review* 24 February 1950.
109 *Facts & Figures about British Railways* 1957, p44.

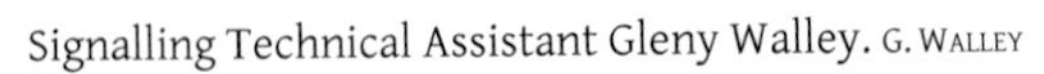
Signalling Technical Assistant Gleny Walley. G. WALLEY

6: Railnews

Railway companies both before and after nationalisation published staff magazines, in which were reported all manner of events including weddings, retirements, promotions and awards. Women, being such a small percentage of the staff, were featured only infrequently, but were initially depicted and treated in exactly the same way as men. However, around the time that equal pay was conceded to (most) railwaywomen, staff magazines began to develop a new attitude towards them, in which women were trivialised and treated primarily as decorative or sexual objects. Railwaywomen's physical attractiveness was emphasised as though nothing else was important — their work paled into insignificance.

One of the earliest examples of this occurred in 1958 when Dawn Timpson (whose work as a tracer involved her in an exciting and important project: the new colour-light signalling for the line to the Kent coast) was featured in *Railways Executive Magazine.* The article included photos of her in a swimsuit and at home, cooking.[1] This heralded the beginning of a 'swimsuit and housewifery' angle on most stories featuring railwaywomen, an attitude that had full rein in BR's newspaper, *Railnews.** From its inception in 1969 until the middle of the 1980s, *Railnews* portrayed railwaywomen in a manner that undermined their struggle for equality and respect and encouraged their male colleagues to regard them in ways that were detrimental to women's career prospects.

All adult female staff were called 'girls', even those with 30 years' service or more. For example, under the title 'Girl in the Box' readers were invited to 'Meet one of the prettiest outdoor-job railgirls on BR', a crossing keeper who was married with two children. No man of that age would have been called a 'railboy'. Worse that this was the seemingly never-ending array of gratuitous 'glamour' photographs included in every issue. Women (often semi-naked) were photographed alongside fully-dressed railwaymen as though such juxtaposition required no explanation. In some cases the women were railway workers. One front page carried a photograph of a Rail-Air Hostess meeting some primary-school children from a train. *Railnews* did not explain why the children were wearing cardigans and sweaters while the hostess wore a bikini. Even in winter, articles ostensibly about fashion always featured bikinis, swimsuits, skimpy underwear or baby-doll nighties. In 1980, for example, swim-suited women appeared 13 times over 12 issues; in addition a woman was pictured in a bikini bottom, another in a leotard, another wearing only a towel and another in what *Railnews* described as a 'provocative' nightdress. This pattern was repeated year after year while, simultaneously, railwaywomen were making their first attempts at equality with men.

Throughout the 1970s female staff were posed atop bars, walls and tables and photographed from below so that their bare legs dominated the photograph. Headings applauded their looks, never their labour. *Railnews* featured female staff for no other reason than as decorative or sexual objects. It even set them up in competition with each

---

* Called *Rail News* until March 1979.

other to be voted the prettiest, in a 'Dolly of the Month' contest. There was even one for the 'Dolliest Dolly'. Despite the abundance of voyeuristic imagery, when one railwayman was asked in 1972 for his opinion of *Railnews*, he replied that he wanted 'more girlie pictures'. The paper did not dispute his terminology, and subsequent editions show that his wish was granted.

Railnews trivialised many of the pioneers who entered traditionally-male railway occupations. The first woman chief steward was described as 'providing a spot of glamour'; a photograph of the only woman studying for the Higher National Diploma in Building was captioned: 'We like the construction of 20-year-old ...' Chemist Mary Drew, a highly qualified specialist in fuel research, was described as a 'pretty girl', as was the first woman to drive an articulated lorry for BR. In March 1978 *Railnews* showed similar disrespect for the first female shunter in railway history to be employed on the same terms as men. The headline 'She's the prettiest shunter we've ever seen!' described her as 'an attractive wife and mother'. In an article titled 'Woman in a man's world', *Railnews* interviewed a member of a Sealink gang whose duties were unusual and interesting; they included berthing ships, shackling vehicles onto vessels and driving a luggage tractor. Of all possible questions, the reporter chose to ask how she coped with her housework. Even women in senior positions did not escape this treatment. One with 35 years' service was called a 'girl'. The first woman appointed to a BR Regional Board, Catherine Hall CBE, was described as 'adding a touch of femininity'. The first woman physician to be appointed chief of a Railway Medical Centre was described as 'incredibly attractive, with the sort of figure that would add glamour to a pair of baggy dungarees'. The angle of the accompanying photograph leads the reader to peer up her skirt.

BR's got a 'fair' share

YES, Anne Jackson on the November letters page is pretty. In fact, BR has lots of pretty girls the public never see.

Rail News always finds them. More power to your elbow! — R. A. WAGSTAFF, 78 Inglethorpe Street, Fulham.

Railnews, January 1970

One headline — 'Shall we see the day when women drive the locos?' — suggested an intelligent article about equal opportunities but the content was disappointing. It included an interview with a female member of the testing team on board the trial runs of the Advanced Passenger Train. The reporter admitted that he had 'automatically assumed' that she would do the cooking on board. She replied that her male colleague was the one renowned for his culinary skill, prompting the *Railnews* reporter to describe her as being 'mildly in a bra-burning mood'. In fact, he was so preoccupied with his sexist assumptions and baseless accusations that he forgot to say what her job was.*

Railnews offered its female readers a shorthand-translating quiz and Joan Bisson's page, which dealt mainly with domestic, not occupational, matters; but Mrs Bisson did comment on the social and political issues that concerned women. Her views were inconsistent: she ridiculed 'Woman Lib' [sic] and openly scorned women for wanting equality; yet she frequently displayed intense irritation at her own inferior status as a woman and complained bitterly that men did not do their share of the housework. And yet, at other

* I suspect she was a computer technician.

times, she said she was 'bored' by 'woman liberationists demanding their rights'. In 1974 she attacked the acceptance by 'the authorities' of the option of Ms as well as Mrs and Miss, ran a quiz to discover 'How much of a feminist are you?', told all women over 40 to keep their flesh covered and described women over 60 as 'revolting' when undressed. This incited the (male) editor to invite readers over 40 to send in glamorous photographs of themselves for publication, thus further encouraging railwaymen to drool over and be judges of their female colleagues' bodies.

It seems bizarre that a woman writing for female employees in a workplace magazine should oppose equal employment legislation, but Mrs Bisson did so unashamedly, asserting that it was 'morally right' to give a job to a man with a mortgage and a family rather than a single female. (Predictably, she did not comment on whether a widow with dependent children should be favoured over a bachelor.) Her analysis of the lack of women in top jobs was: 'They didn't apply for them.' Guard Ian Macmillan of Kirkdale Depot felt the need to defend women:

> How much longer do we have to endure the invidious pronouncements and constant trivialisation of women presented in the Joan Bisson column [in which they] are portrayed as insignificant, mindless creatures. ...
>
> What kind of make-believe world is Joan Bisson living in? If she comes by Liverpool, I shall be glad to introduce her to a selection of ... thinking women, concerned with the values of life, education, politics, peace, the quality of the environment, building a caring community. Such women ... demand the right not to be stereotyped, but considered as whole people, fully and rightly concerned with all the wider issues of life.[2]

While *Railnews* habitually treated female staff as eye-candy, it forgot that they existed when referring to railway workers in general. In 1969 it replaced its short-lived 'Miss *Railnews*' contest with a competition to find 'Mr and Mrs B.R.' The text made it seem that only male employees and their wives were eligible to apply: 'We are looking for the man ... whose enthusiasm for his job is shared by a tolerant and understanding wife.' The fact that either spouse could be the employee was hidden in the small print. Similarly entrants in the Railway Queen competition had to be a staff member or 'daughter of a railwayman'. What about daughters of railwaywomen? Were they excluded? *Railnews* also ran a Sportsman of the Year competition. Janet Dickens, a tracer at Euston, won it in 1968, but the title was not changed even for that year.

The front page of the February 1979 issue featured the first four female station managers, prompting *Railnews* to admit that hitherto there had been a 'gentleman's agreement' with the unions that no woman would be appointed to that post. This contradicted an article published just three years earlier, in which *Railnews* had claimed: 'Equal pay and equal opportunity have been standard conditions on BR for many years.' A later issue included a letter from a railwayman deploring the appointment of women station managers, describing them as 'good-looking dolly birds'. One of them, Pennie Bellas – who held a BA in Economics and Industrial Relations – responded by attacking the 'dumb blonde stereotype' image and *Railnews* printed her photograph again, no doubt to remind readers how pretty she was. *Railnews* seemed to enjoy the controversy: in May 1980 it used the provocative headline 'No to women' above a letter that was not, in fact, against women. (The correspondent deplored the appointment of graduates as managers, preferring those who had worked their way up through the grades they were to manage.)

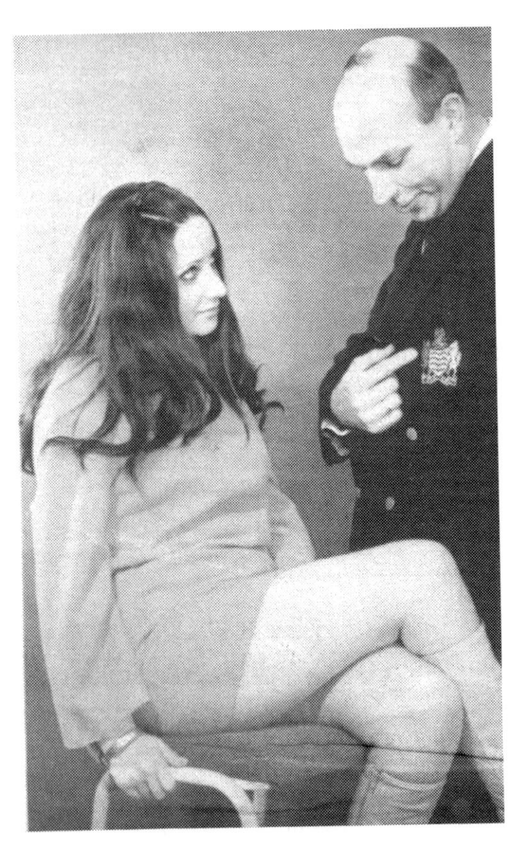

Above: Senior Technical Assistant Geraldine Shaw of Derby Technical Centre's electrical research division was involved with building a computer for on-board train control. *Railnews* called her a 'computer girl'.

RAILNEWS JULY 1970

New badge designed

PRETTY girl looking at the new SR Staff Association badge is 15-year-old Corinne Anderson, who works in the welfare department at Charing Cross.

And showing her the badge is Waterloo branch chairman Arthur Woodhouse, who is with NCL.

The new badge—shown below—is designed to conform with present-day SR boundaries. It is available to members from branch secretaries or the general secretary at 39 Craven Street, Charing Cross.

This news feature is ostensibly about a new badge. Instead, it invited railwaymen to ogle the thighs of a 15-year-old girl.

RAILNEWS FEBRUARY 1970

Mary Drew, a top specialist in BR's fuel research, examining the possible effects of bacteria contamination in a fuel tank at Old Oak Common Depot. *Railnews* called her a 'pretty girl'.

RAILNEWS DECEMBER 1970

From the 1980s a more respectful attitude to women began to emerge in *Railnews* but by 1988 it was still demeaning women sufficiently to provoke Dave Hillam, a controller at Swindon, to complain about women employed on track maintenance being described as 'a bunch of lassies', 'petite', 'willowy' and 'the fairer sex'. Mr Hillam declared: 'It would appear that BR's equal opportunities objectives have not yet penetrated the *Railnews* offices'. He continued:

> If there is to be a serious attempt to change attitudes in this area, then more thought must be given to your reporting in the future. Or is this (totally unnecessary) use of adjectives to be extended to male members of staff, and can we expect for example to see the BRB managing director of personnel routinely described in your pages as flyweight or petite? Of course not. Nor should women attempting to break down the barriers which undoubtedly exist have to find themselves labelled in this way.
>
> Is it any wonder, with coverage like this, that women are reluctant to apply for posts in male-dominated areas of BR?

Beneath the letter, the author of the offending article, Eddie Toal, responded:

> Adjectives like willowy and petite are perfectly valid when used to describe people doing tasks from which they've hitherto been excluded because of these very qualities. ... Apart from being a trifle pompous, the notion that banning words will change attitudes to women doesn't come backed with evidence ... Do you really think that the advancement of women in the workplace can be brought forward any quicker by a rigid, thought police type imposition of the sort you advocate?[3]

Despite Mr Toals's impassioned defence, *Railnews* did change its ways and its terminology. In November 1988 the magazine passed a milestone by reporting on a woman cricketer without using a single patronising or demeaning comment. Fortunately, the newspaper today bears no relation to its former self; indeed the current editor helped the author by supplying and allowing her to use many images from past issues.

References

The above was based on a study of over 250 editions of *Railnews* from 1969 to 1989.

1 *British Railways Magazine* Southern edition, July 1958. Front cover.
2 *Railnews* February 1983.
3 *Railnews* August 1988.

It's only man's work because women rarely apply

TRACKWORK

If you're a woman who has lots of stamina, likes the outdoors, enjoys teamwork and gets a real sense of satisfaction from skilled physical work, this could be the job for you.

At British Rail, we have thousands of miles of track to maintain and improve. We want to recruit more women, because our female trackworkers have shown they can do the job, enjoy it and do it to high standards.

In a typical working week, you'd work from 7.15am to 3.45pm, Monday - Friday and there are also frequent opportunities for weekend overtime.

You'll need to be physically fit with good hearing and eyesight, and able to take anything the British climate can throw at you (although we will provide protective clothing!).

So why not make tracks to one of our Open Days on Monday 17th, or Tuesday 18th June at The Reading Job Centre, Broad Street Mall from 10am - 3pm. We look forward to seeing you there.

Alternatively, write to the Recruitment Office, Personnel Section, British Rail, ACEO CP51, Western Tower, 18 Station Hill, Reading RG1 1NQ.

Because women are under-represented in this area of work, this advertisement is run under section 48 of the Sex Discrimination Act, 1975. All applications from women and men are considered on the basis of their abilities for the job.

British Rail - working towards equal opportunities.

7: 1975 AND BEYOND

> Women entering some parts of the business still need a little pioneering spirit, although they need have no doubts about the welcome they will get.
>
> *WORKING WITH BRITISH RAIL, 1984*

By 1975 women's participation in railway operating had barely altered in a quarter of a century. Because comprehensive statistics are not available, it is possible only to make broad generalisations about the numbers and distribution of railwaywomen at that time. There were no female shunters, travelling ticket inspectors, guards, train drivers, rolling stock technicians or track-workers, nor were there any female supervisors or managers of men in uniformed grades, nor any female station- or yard-managers. There were fewer than 30 signalwomen and only a very small percentage of station and workshop staff were female. A tiny number were professional or technical officers, tracers, and supervisors of female staff in telephone exchanges and typing bureaux. About half of all crossing keepers were female and women constituted the majority of carriage cleaners. Women greatly outnumbered men in catering and cleaning.

When the Sex Discrimination Act (SDA) came into force on 1st January 1975 it became illegal to refuse to consider women for vacancies in jobs previously open only to men. Within BR the Act came into effect inconspicuously and made no immediate impact on the staffing arrangements. No effort was made to recruit women into former male grades or to let existing staff know that transfers to 'men's jobs' were now available to them and BR did not implement an equal opportunities policy until 1986. Unsurprisingly, there was no flood of female applicants; the appearance of women in train maintenance and civil engineering, as train crew and as station supervisors and managers happened gradually and began with isolated pioneers across the country.

Unlike laws, attitudes cannot change overnight and when a woman considered applying to work on the railway in a formerly-male grade, she frequently met with discouragement and disapproval from her parents, husband and friends, as well as being put off by comments made by Jobcentre clerks, railway personnel officers and station managers, who would, with varying degrees of subtlety, hint that these posts were not *really* suitable for women, and would — slyly or forthrightly — steer them towards carriage cleaning or office work. Simply being informed that there were no toilet facilities in their intended workplace was enough to dissuade women from continuing their application. Others were deterred by heavily exaggerated tales of the hazards of railways and of the dangers of working alone with men, especially at night.

Typically, women were quizzed about their domestic responsibilities and intentions to have children, were sternly warned to expect 'no special treatment' and were told that, if they wanted a man's job, they would be treated 'as men', an expression that was often said in slightly menacing tones but always left undefined. Complaining about this treatment was simply not possible. Potential new entrants to an industry would hardly wish to jeopardise their chances of a job by complaining and being branded a 'troublemaker'.

WAGES GRADES

CROSSINGS AND SIGNALBOXES

During the 1970s and 1980s many manually operated level crossings were either replaced by overbridges or de-staffed, a new type of automatic half-barrier crossing (AHB), taking their places. Of the remaining crossings, about 50% were staffed by women. Despite this, they were still referred to as being unusual and novel on the rare occasions they were mentioned by the media.

Railwoman Pat Hanson worked at three crossings between 1965 and 1984, while raising three children. At her final posting, at Swatlands, SR, the family moved into a gatekeeper's cottage at a nominal rent. She worked eight hours and a railman, working from a track-side hut, worked another eight. BR wanted to abolish residential crossings, and when Mrs Hanson was retired on medical grounds in 1984 a permanent separation was made between the house tenancy and the crossing job. The gates were operated only from the hut and, after Mrs Hanson's death, her husband (a guard) and later her daughter, Debbie rented the cottage. When one of the gate jobs became vacant in 1992, Miss Hanson applied. As a child she had helped her mother with the gates, and: 'It was right on my doorstep, just fall out of bed and I was at work.' A year later BR replaced the manual gates with automatic ones. 'The day that they ripped those barriers out to put in the half-barrier, all the hairs on my body stood up on end, because it had been such a part of my life', Miss Hanson recalled.[1]

The recommendations of the Hidden Report* were implemented by 1992. This meant that railway workers could not work more than 72 hours a week and must have a day off after 13 consecutive days worked, but residential crossing keepers were excluded from this directive. In 1996 *Railnews* published a full-page article about 32-year-old Debbie Williams of Tunstead Crossing in rural Norfolk. She revealed that she was available for work for nearly 94 hours a week: 'You get about 20 minutes between trains, if you are lucky', and explained that her usual time off between shifts was less than six hours. However, as a mother of two small sons, she liked the job because she did not have to arrange childcare.[2] In 1999, when Jean Richards retired from her job as gatewoman at Minety, WR, after 23 years' service, she was still working 24 hours a day:

> My hours of duty were 'continuous'. I only had a 12 hour 'rest' day once a month! Most weeks I had two periods off duty, sometimes three. They consisted of one or two 4 p.m. to 6 p.m. and one of 2 p.m. to 10 p.m. The pay was around £30 a week with £5 being deducted at source for rent. I belonged to the union – it was a closed shop so I really had no option.
>
> In the beginning I had signal levers outside the cabin and the indicators and phones were housed in a box (on legs) also outside. One of my duties was to clean, refill, trim the wicks of the paraffin lamps on the gates and to make sure they were alight 24/7.
>
> Because of the isolation I had no real friends in the village only acquaintances. I rarely had any contact with other railway folk, except my relief men who were generally the porters from Kemble station.

---

* Named after Sir Anthony Hidden, whose report was produced as a result of his enquiry into a major train crash at Clapham Junction in 1988.

> Lots of folk who passed by used to say how they would love to do the job until I pointed out the many snags — weather and sleep for example. In fact we rarely were bothered late at night. Apart from the dreadful tie it was marvellous for someone with children. I was 40 when I started and the option of another post was never a viable proposition, as for instance I would have lost my home. So I hung in there until I was 63.
>
> We had some great times there. If I'm honest, yes, I think I would do it all again, but would insist on more time off.[3]

After she retired BR had to pay two men to cover her job, each working a 12 hour shift.

Judy Finch started work at New Barnetby, Lincolnshire, in 1978. It was a Class 1 crossing and Mrs Finch was restricted to working 12 hours a day. In 1983 she moved to a Class 2 crossing at Sloley, near Norwich, where her hours increased to 17 a day over seven days, with one-and-a-half days off a week. There were no restrictions on how many hours she worked. If a special train came through during the night she had to attend to the gates without any compensatory time off being granted, and was also expected to do her full shift starting at 5.30 a.m. the next day. Her first eight hours were paid at full rate, but after that she received only a quarter-hour's pay for each hour worked. After performing the job for 18 years she was made redundant when the gates became automatic.[4]

Despite the job of signaller being open in theory to women since the First World War, by 1984 there were only 37 signalwomen on BR, compared with 6,671 signalmen. Because they worked out of the view of the public, the employment of signalwomen came to light only if one did something newsworthy. In 1975 *Railnews* reported that Janet Girvan had prevented a train robbery, and that her intervention had involved her in a physical struggle with the raiders. The article mentioned that she had operated Glen Douglas box since 1971, and that she was a mother of six children whose husband worked in the same box on the opposite shift.[5] Signalwomen Vera Cunningham and Marjorie Smith were mentioned in *Railnews* on the occasion of their retirement, with 25½ and 28 years' service respectively, in 1985. They had both worked in various heavy-levered, manual boxes on the Liverpool-Manchester line and Miss Cunningham declared that she had 'loved every minute of it'.[6] During the 1980s, until its closure in 1989, the signalbox at Battersby Junction was manned by two signalwomen, giving rise to the Esk Valley Railway becoming known locally as 'The Petticoat Line'.[7]

Former Residential Crossing Keeper Kate Lee managed to make the move, via working at Norwich station, into signalling. She started at Spooner Row signal box in 1985, where she found 'mixed reactions' to her appointment:

> I would often get comments from drivers along the lines of 'Women are starting to get everywhere these days', to which my stock reply was: 'Well, we have a woman head of state and a woman prime minister, so what do you expect?'
>
> One day I had a barrier failure at an automatic crossing between my box and the next (Attleborough). I stopped a train at the box to caution the driver and he started laughing and asked 'Where's Tony, then?' I told him I was the signaller on duty. Again the driver laughed and, looking up to the signal box to see if Tony (my colleague on the opposite shift) was there, said: 'He sent you down as a joke, didn't he?' I had to get quite cross with him to get him to take my caution seriously, and at last he departed. A short while later I got a phone call from the signaller at Attleborough, saying that the driver had stopped at his box to ask if I really was the signaller or if someone was having a joke.

> Being the only signalwoman in the area at the time meant that a lot of people who I didn't know knew who I was. My partner was with his young son on a train and, as it passed a signalbox, the boy asked: 'Daddy, is that Katie's signalbox?' The guard, who was nearby examining tickets, turned round and said: 'No; Kate works at Spooner Row'. God knows who he was, but he certainly knew of me, although I did not even work on that line.
>
> I have had to develop a thick skin over the years though. Respect can be gained by 'giving as good as you get' and being able 'to take it as well as dish it out'. I try not to resort to bad language if I can help it, however.[8]

Twenty-two years later, Kate works in an automated signalling centre where she holds a Grade 9 position, the highest grade.

Kate Lee at her signalling desk at York IECC. K. LEE

RAILWOMEN/RAIL OPERATORS

In the 70s the lowest wages grades were railman/woman, leading railman/woman and senior railman/woman, and officeman/woman. These terms were later changed to rail operator etc. Most women in wages grades were in the lowest grade of railwoman and were employed as carriage servicewomen, but were always known simply as 'cleaners'. Very few were promoted above the lowest grade.

Cleaning trains could be unpleasant, especially as it involved dealing with all manner of disgusting items discarded by the travelling public, including half-eaten fast food, vomit, excrement, and disposable nappies thrown behind seats or discarded in toilets. But to counter these disagreeable tasks there was a great deal of camaraderie amongst the women, and some became union activists and health and safety representatives. The shiftwork suited many of them and a number preferred to work nights, either to fit in with childcare or because of the higher pay. The SDA had little impact on carriage cleaners because, although they could transfer to a former male grade, very few did so. Apart from female companionship and supervision by members of their own sex they had proper toilets and changing facilities. The isolation and awkwardness of being the sole female in a male environment was not appealing and they would have to work more extreme, or (in the case of train crew) irregular shifts, which made childcare difficult.

The remainder of women in the lowest conciliation grades were station staff or office-women. It was rare to see women working on provincial stations and even rarer to find them in a grade above railwoman. None became a station supervisor until 1981. In the 50s and 60s thousands of new workers came from the Caribbean and for the first time black women worked as ticket collectors at London termini, graded as senior railwoman.

Judith Swain (now Hobson), whose father, uncle and grandfather had worked on the railway at Pickering, York and Malton, went to work at Scunthorpe, a station where eight railwomen on various shifts covering 4 a.m. till 11 p.m. worked under a male foreman:

> We saw to all the trains; early morning paper, mail train and all passenger trains. All the cleaning: brass, windows, waiting rooms, ticket office, polishing floors on our hands and knees. No electric polisher then, and yet the floors gleamed. We whitened the platform edge and had to maintain the flower boxes. We even went to unstaffed stations along the line to shovel snow off the platforms. If we were on at 4 a.m. we had all the barrows to unload with parcels from the mail train, up to 50 some days, then sort them into areas ready for 9 a.m. when the van men came, and then we went out on delivery with them. The last shift finished about 11 p.m. It was hard, heavy work but we always had a good laugh. We were told the passenger came first and to be helpful and polite. I worked at the station for about six years then left to have a family. No people working there apart from the ticket office.[9]

Such places were the exception rather than the rule: a woman station worker was often the only female at her workplace and her happiness depended largely upon how open-minded her male colleagues were in regard to women's role. A leading railwoman employed to cover for men's absence and leave at various stations on the Hinchley Wood to Guildford branch line, SR, in the early 1980s said:

> I was taught to couple and uncouple trains and used to do the work on odd days when the shunter was absent. I'd be paid as a senior railwoman only for those days. Had I been a man, due to union agreements I would have been permanently re-graded to senior railman and always paid that rate, even on the days I did only station work, on account of having learned the extra skills. But they could not — or would not — officially grade a woman as a shunter.[10]

Women working on stations were sometimes treated as the butt of many a joke, as a bit of a liability and as inferior to men as workers:

> The men think that *they* are the ones who can do the job, and they think that women are not *really* quite up to it, to the point that sometimes — and this probably sounds a bit weak — you start to question yourself a little bit. It's very subtle. It's the way they talk over you, or answer a question addressed to you. You're not really as good as the men, not *really*. And if you were to talk to honest men, they'll say that it's not really a job for a woman.
>
> But, in all honesty, when I worked on the platform I hated it. I didn't think it was a woman's job, either. But that goes against women doesn't it? I think mainly it's that I didn't like the image that I gave. I didn't like holding up that

> stupid baton. When they wanted me to split and attach the trains, I refused, and yet another woman who started work there, she couldn't wait to do it.[11]

If she was lucky (or perhaps unlucky) an opportunity would eventually arise for a woman to show that she really was as good as her male colleagues. Leading Railwoman Dawn Jennings (aged 27) was approached by a woman at Bath Spa station who claimed she had placed a bomb in the toilets and began running away. Mrs Jennings set off in pursuit and, after bringing the woman to the ground in a flying tackle, frogmarched her to a toilet, locked her in and called the police. No suspicious object was found and the woman was successfully prosecuted. Mrs Jennings remarked: 'It was all just part of a day's work.' Rail Operator Janet Ellis was on duty at Margate in late 1993 when her supervisor, Peter Evans, was being beaten up. Mrs Ellis, who was 54 years old, did not hesitate to rush to his assistance: she waded into the affray while raining down numerous blows with her train despatch baton and chased the attackers out of the station.

Police

Until the mid-1970s policewomen were considered capable of dealing only with women and children. Indeed, J. R. Whitbread wrote in his 1961 book *The Railway Policeman*: 'Women are not, needless to say, expected to deal un-aided with holiday crowds, drunks, or violent males.'[12] It was not until the SDA came into effect that women were put on an equal footing with, and had to perform the same duties as their male colleagues. One or two resigned but the majority welcomed the opportunity to prove themselves. During the 80s the term 'woman' was dropped from use as a prefix before the title 'Constable', 'Sergeant' etc. Women began to take on roles not previously filled by them such as Tutor Constable, Scenes of Crime Officer and Detective. In 991 Chief Inspector Betty Glover was appointed the first woman Commandant of the Training School at Tadworth and was later the first woman to be placed in charge of policing at London's largest railway terminus, Waterloo.

Throughout their history, railway policewomen have displayed the same skill and courage as their male counterparts and some have earned awards and commendations. In 1985, PC Jean Rose of Euston was awarded the Royal Humane Society Testimonial on Parchment for preventing a woman who had taken a drug overdose from jumping from scaffolding on a building. In 1996 Probationer PC Jill Spencer of Birmingham disarmed and arrested a man who, in a frenzied attack, had stabbed his estranged wife to death at Birmingham New Street station (having already murdered his four children elsewhere). PC Spencer also tried in vain to stem the flow of blood from the dying woman. She was awarded the Whitbread Shield.

The statistics for 2003-2004 show that there were 316 women BTP officers, which represented just over 7% of the force. This figure has increased since, but there has still never been a woman promoted above the rank of chief inspector. Female special constables and community support officers have also lately been recruited.[13]

Two women BTP employees were awarded MBEs in June 2005. Constable Margaret Lyall, described as 'a tough no-nonsense Scot', received hers for 28 years' dedicated service. After joining in 1977 aged 19 and 'looking for a bit of action', in 1982 she became the first female dog handler and later patrolled Glasgow Central station. Norma King received hers after 36 years' service, ten of them as area safety adviser in the North East. Ms King was also a health and safety representative in the TSSA for 25 years. She said of her award: 'I thought the whole thing was a hoax. I didn't think people like me got this kind of thing. It was a major surprise, a great honour'.[14]

Former Male Grades: Some Pioneers

It is impossible to establish which women were the pioneers in various railway jobs as such records do not exist. The following information comes from press reports and, therefore, may not be accurate.

In 1975 Joyce Wellings was reported to be driving a 32-ton articulated lorry for BR.[15] In 1977 BR engaged its first woman craft apprentice, an electrical technician.[16] In August 1980 Catherine Potter was reported to be the first woman to work in a Sealink berthing gang. Her duties at Harwich Parkstone Quay included berthing and releasing ships, shackling and unshackling vehicles on vessels and driving luggage tractors.[17] In October of that year Barbara Ralph, BR's first woman radio officer, began work on a Sealink ship. Patricia Woolven was a shunter at Redhill, Horsham and London Victoria. She said: 'I never thought of myself as a woman; I just did a job I like doing. All my working life I have done what most people think is men's work'.[18] After working as a telegraphist in the RAF for four years Ginnie Day became an apprentice welder for a bet, and worked in that grade for four years before joining the railways, where she became the first woman welder at Gloucester Train Maintenance Depot in 1980, working on heavy rolling stock frames.[19] In 1986 carriage cleaner Linda Morgan moved to Glasgow's Yoker depot and was promoted to general purpose relief. This meant that shunting was now a part of her duties. She said:

> I enjoy shunting work, although it can get a bit lonely at times when you're away down the bottom of the yard. I've had quite a few soakings, too, because the work has to go on no matter what the weather is like.[20]

ASLEF's first female member was Beryl Weedon of East Ham branch, a trainee driver on LUL who joined the union on 2nd April 1977. But it was Hannah Dadds who, after nine years as a stationwoman at Barbican, became LUL's first woman driver when she passed her exams in October 1978 and joined Barking depot on the District Line. These pioneers hardly opened the floodgates; by 1992 LUL employed only 21 female drivers (compared with 2,023 men).

On BR, 19-year-old Karen Harrison, based at Old Oak Common, WR, was featured in *Railnews* in July 1980 as the first woman drivers' assistant, but Anne Winter, of Waterloo, SR, became BR's first female train driver on 17th February 1983. Fiona Johns became the first woman to drive Eurostar services to France and Belgium, having previously been the sole woman at both Old Oak Common and Hastings depots. Sue Ricketts, who had been an HGV driver before joining BR in 1986, was the first woman to drive trains on the Isle of Wight's Island Line. She qualified in 1994 when she was 49.[21]

Female train drivers were not universally welcomed. In the late 1980s BR stated that it wanted to recruit more, but its Chief of Personnel, Trevor Toolan, announced that all future drivers must be at least five feet four and no taller than six feet four. The Equal Opportunities Commission said: 'This amounts to discrimination because 48 percent of women in Britain are under 5ft 4. BR say they want to hire women and then exclude half the potential candidates. It is ridiculous.'[22] But Mr Toolan was not anti-female; he once said: 'I cannot think of any job within BR that couldn't be done by a woman.'[23]

In 1991 journalist Mary Kenny wrote an article titled 'Do women really want to drive BR's trains?' She doubted it:

Crossing Keeper Debbie Williams, Tunstead. COURTESY OF RAILNEWS

The author, September 1995. AUTHOR'S COLLECTION

> I wonder if substantial numbers of women have the sustained concentration powers that train-driving requires ... There is a male ability to concentrate that few women have ... concentration is the essential ability required in guiding a train to its destination safely — not falling into a reverie over hundreds of miles of railroad track. ... Spending millions of rail travellers' money in seeking to recruit and train women drivers could be a disappointing and wasteful exercise in gender engineering. Left to their own devices, few little girls are even going to dream of climbing into the train drivers' cab.[24]

Since that article, the number of female train drivers has increased considerably. For example, in 2001 there were 100 female Tube drivers; a year later, 176. In 1992 ASLEF had 144 women members, of whom 106 worked for BR, 36 for LUL, and two for the Tyne & Wear Metro. In 1999 ASLEF had 313 female members of whom 201 worked for the (former BR) private railway companies, 42 for LUL, two for the Tyne & Wear Metro, 64 for Eurostar and four for Eurotunnel.* In 1994 BR employed 55 women as train drivers (or 0.4% of the total of 14,780) and 3% of its drivers in training were women.

Passengers who noticed that their train's driver was a woman often reacted with astonishment and some were worried. Anne Winter said:

> I am amused by male passengers who make a point of telling me that they considering travelling on another service because they'd rather not be driven by a woman. They really think I care whether they board my train or not.[25]

Driver Carrie Simpson revealed that some passengers would step further back behind the yellow line when they saw her at the controls of a train entering a platform: 'They seemed to think they might be in danger because a woman was driving'.[26]

As far as can be established, the author of this book was the first female guard employed by BR on the same terms as men. Based at Wimbledon Park, SR, my training began in December 1977 and I took charge of my first train on 23rd March 1978. About four months later *The Evening Standard* ran a prominent feature on the 'First woman guard on BR', a colleague at Cannon Street who had worked her first train that morning. (This illustrates the unreliability of press reports.) On 22nd June 1980 *The Sunday Times* also featured 'Britain's first woman railway guard': Brenda Joyce, a volunteer on the 'Poppy Line', a preserved railway in Norfolk, drawing protests from several other preserved lines, including the Nene Valley Railway, where Beryl Dore and Doreen Foster had been volunteer guards since 1968.

British Rail Youth Training Schemes brought more young women into traditionally male jobs. In 1984, seventeen-year-old Karen Clark of Hanwell spent a year maintaining track, shifting ballast, changing sleepers and maintaining points for the WR. One press report claimed that a 'government lifting restriction' prohibited women from track maintenance, and so, at the suggestion of her instructor, she applied to be a train driver instead.[27] In 1989 Tracy Kerwick, aged 16, joined the scheme as the only girl on Scotrail's civil engineering course, and much of her 12-month training took place on the track.[28]

In 1988 the North East Equal Opportunity Group carried out an experiment in which female paybills' clerks did a day's work as platelayers. The trial was a resounding success

* Figures are ASLEF members only; some drivers (especially within LUL) are in the NUR, others are non-unionists.

and proved that 'ordinary' women were capable of the work.[29] Later, 13 clerks successfully laid 240 yards of new track, without any plant or mechanical tools, on the Aviemore to Boat of Garden tourist line.[30] Shortly afterwards, 28-year-old Mrs Lesley Fraser was engaged as BR's first female trackworker. 'I saw the job in the paper but I never thought I'd get it', she told *Railnews* in 1990, adding: 'The first day they had me gravel packing and I thought I was going to die.' However, her fitness and strength improved and after six months in her otherwise all-male gang she was able to assert with confidence: 'I can do anything anyone else can'.[31]

A number of women responded to a carefully-worded job advertisement that invited applications for the post of 'trackperson'. Western Region managers remarked that the applicants had remained undeterred when warned of the practical problems such as the lack of trackside toilets. A gang of six was recruited and, wearing hob-nailed boots, they handled concrete sleepers weighing 6cwt, heaved steel rails and swung pickaxes. Louise Bird, a former nurse, preferred being taught in an all-female group because there was 'no harassment from males while trying to learn'. Their supervisors were, of course, male. One of them said: 'I was not convinced women could do the job: it is hard, dirty, heavy work in all weathers.' Trackwoman Nicky Smale explained: 'It was painful at first, getting fit and strong enough, but now it is no problem — I have plenty of muscles and we can do every job a man can do.'[32] Andrea Draper revealed that they had put up with a lot of ribbing from men, but were now accepted as equals, and Louise Bird said:

> Many men — most even — thought we would not be able to do the work, and would not stay anyway. Many couldn't believe we could like it. After three years it is obvious that we can do everything that the job involves, although obviously a small person cannot lift the same weights as a large person — this does not put us at a disadvantage because the railway employs some small men!

The gang remained as a distinct unit for about a year before being disbanded and assimilated individually into various male gangs. Trackwoman Bird pointed out that this was inevitable, because 'equality was the true aim, not being set apart'.[33]

Above: Driver Terrie Hogarth in 2003; right, Driver's Assistant Karen Harrison in 1979. RAILNEWS

Railwaymen's attitudes

A woman filling a former male grade would usually find herself the sole female in that grade at her depot or station. Many were made to feel that the railway was male territory into which women were unwelcome interlopers, and it was common for a woman to face incessant remarks regarding the work being 'unsuitable' for women and 'unladylike'. Some men observed that all mess-rooms would have to be fitted with mirrors (based on the assumption that women are obsessed with their appearance); others complained that they could no longer relax in the mess-room because they would have to 'mind their language' if there were 'ladies present'. Some men opined loudly that women would not 'stick the job' because of the shifts, the bad weather or the night-work and would 'go to pieces' in emergencies others assumed that women would be off sick 'one week in every four' and, moreover, that management would turn a blind eye to such absence, thus giving women special treatment. Others thought women downgraded the status of railway work: 'When people see girls driving trains they'll think there's nothing to it!' One man was cross that females had been brought in without negotiation with the unions: 'It's a bloody cheek, if you ask me; nobody asked us if we wanted to work with women!'[34]

The attitude of railwaymen to their female colleagues depended largely upon the woman's age and appearance. Those who were young and pretty often found that their male workmates could not see past their physical attributes and treated them in ways that would now be described as sexual harassment. Older women, tomboys and the less attractive fared a little better, although they too suffered unkind remarks.

When Crossing Keeper Debbie Hanson was made redundant in 1992 she went to work on the platform at Tonbridge, where 'you're out in all weathers and — oh — the winters out there are terrible!' She was received well by the men, but said 'there is this feeling you get, as a woman, because there are so few of you.' When an attractive female passenger was spotted, the men would radio from platform to platform, until every man on the station was ogling her. They treated their female colleagues with much the same attitude, as Miss Hanson explained:

> When a woman first starts, all the men ask is 'What does she look like?' All they want to know is, 'is she shaggable?' That's all they really think about you, not 'Can she do this job?' And if you are 'shaggable', then they think that you are probably not much good at the job.
>
> A new woman started lately, and we've had, 'What does she look like?' And another woman who is going to be starting here already has been labelled as kinky and rumours are going about relating to her sex life. [35]

If a woman was warm and friendly, she was a 'tart'; if not, she was a 'stuck-up cow'. If she wore sturdy boots and trousers, she was rebuked as unladylike; if she wore dainty shoes and a skirt she was criticised for being dressed inappropriately for the job. If bare-faced, she was 'dowdy'; if made up, she was 'tarty'. Some women were insulted with comments such as: 'Why work outdoors in all weathers when you could earn double indoors on your back?', endured salacious gossip and were the subject of lewd graffiti. Some received anonymous letters with pornographic images via the internal post.

When Celina Roccia, a former hairdresser, was the only female driver at London Victoria, some of the men were so anti-woman they refused to speak to her. She moved to Marylebone, a smaller and friendlier depot with a handful of female train crew and a woman ASLEF branch secretary, Karen Harrison, who remarked:

> There are a lot of nice people in the railways but it's the nasty ones, the big-mouths, who make themselves known. I get a lot of abuse and there's gynaecological pornography all over the walls, and yet, if I swear, the whole messroom descends into silence. But ... I'm damned if I'm going to be driven out of my job by a load of ignorant people.[36]

Female train crew heard it suggested that physical intimacy would inevitably take place on trains when the sexes worked together. One driver said he feared working alone with women because: 'All she has to do is cry "rape" and that's it: my job, my marriage, my pension, all down the pan – and me banged up in prison!' While no evidence was found of such false accusations there were many cases of women suffering unwanted and indecent touching when alone with a man in a driving cab, signalbox or station, especially on night shifts. One female driver suffered three such incidents:

> While I made my anger known to these individuals I was far too ashamed to report them. The incidents all played on my mind for many months after they occurred. The only way I could reconcile myself to what had happened was to make myself see them as the sad characters they were.[37]

If a woman managed to pluck up the courage to complain to her manager, all too often she was told: 'If you can't stand the heat, get out of the kitchen!' Driver Karen Harrison declared that 'the standard rejoinder to any legitimate grievance was: "You forced us to employ you, so stop complaining and get on with it".'[38]

The older woman, married and with a motherly demeanour, was usually exempt from gossip, graffiti and other sex-related harassment, and was sometimes well-respected. If her personality appeared gentle, men assumed she was not sufficiently tough to do her job effectively; if assertive, she was labelled a 'battleaxe'. Men got on well with the tomboy type who could chat about cars and football; however, some men would criticise her lack of femininity or even spread rumours that she was a lesbian.

Often an individual woman's behaviour was used to generalise about all women. The resignation of dozens of men would pass unnoticed, but when a woman resigned it 'proved' that women couldn't 'stick the job'. If a woman was involved in an incident her male colleagues would afterwards discuss and scrutinise her every action in tiny detail, eagerly searching for any shortcomings that would confirm women's inherent unsuitability for railway work. A trainee rolling stock technician found that any error she made was cited as conclusive proof that all women were unsuited to technical work. As a result she had to be twice as good to be (grudgingly) considered (almost) their equal. She said, with a sigh, that she hated 'having to keep proving something about women'.[39]

Women also made some stalwart friends among railwaymen. Some behaved like old fashioned gentlemen – opening doors, offering to carry heavy bags, curbing their language; others acted like fathers or brothers and defended women from unfair criticism. A few – often the left-wing union activists – were very vocal in their support of women's liberation and were ridiculed by their colleagues. With friendly men, women found great comradeship: they were taught to play cards and darts and to roll cigarettes. There was much flirtation, many affairs and some marriages. One couple, guards at Dorking, married and raised a child jointly by working opposite shifts.

Accommodating a female workforce

A number of practical changes need to be made to a previously-all male workplace to accommodate female staff. Toilet facilities were a problem in many locations, and it was often left to individual women to force the issue with BR and the unions. Women did not press for their own messrooms, however; although where large groups of both sexes worked together, such as in carriage servicing departments, messrooms had traditionally been separate and continued to be so.

Where women had not previously filled a grade, various ad-hoc arrangements were made until a uniform arrived. Some of the more androgynous-shaped women got by wearing clothes cut for the male figure from the uniform stores; others had an outfit designed for them. The first female station manager was issued with what appeared to be an air hostess's suit, while the author, a guard, was affronted when issued with a carriage cleaner's uniform. Across BR, women in all grades complained about uniform issue: they were treated unfairly and the clothing issued was often unsuitable for the job; for example tight, straight-cut skirts allowed no freedom of movement to women who had to clamber in and out of trains, up ladders and across the tracks. As late as 1991 no uniform had been designed for signalwomen. One, Iris Jackson of Chetisham, complained that she was allocated only 70 points compared with her male colleagues' 90 points, to spend on items in the uniform brochure. Men received cotton shirts while women's were polyester which, she pointed out, caused the wearer to 'sweat profusely'. Mike Carter, Uniform Clothing Project Manager, denied any intention to discriminate against female staff.[40]

BR's Equal Opportunities Policy, operative from 1986, was specifically targeted at women in salaried grades. Among the benefits offered were flexible working, including part-time, job share, and term-time only; gender recruitment targets, women's seminars, pilot well-woman health care schemes and career break schemes. While these looked very impressive on paper, and were no doubt praised in boardrooms across the country, they were rarely applicable to women in wages grades. For example, managers insisted it was impossible to employ train crews part time, and the unions resisted the introduction of part-time working. Marylebone guard and NUR activist Tessa van Gelderen called the Policy 'so much hot air' and 'a desperate measure taken to stop the Equal Opportunities Commission from taking British Rail to task'.[41]

Driver Celina Roccia, who had a child in 1990, found the state maternity allowance so meagre that she returned to work quickly and, although BR helped by allowing her to work a regular daytime shift, this meant losing her unsocial-hours payments, just when she needed extra money. She thought BR ought to provide crèches or at least help towards childminding costs.[42]

Susan Edwards joined LUL in 1983 and qualified as a train driver in 1987. That year she had a baby but successfully continued to work by swapping duties with other drivers to create a shift pattern that fitted in with childcare. She was forced to resign in 1992 because LUL, after rejecting a scheme that would have helped her continue working, introduced a new rostering system that made it impossible for her to swap shifts. With the support of the EOC Driver Edwards won her case at an Industrial and Employment Appeal Tribunal. LUL appealed against this but, in May 1998, the Court of Appeal upheld the Tribunal's decision.

Signalwoman Veronique Melvin.

Courtesy of V. Melvin

Trackwomen Jan Sutherland, Louise Bird, Nicky Smale and Andrea Draper. COURTESY OF RAILNEWS

Driver Jean Cochrane, London Victoria, 2004. AUTHOR'S COLLECTION

Crossing No. 9, Sloley, Norwich, the crossing keeper's cottage and the ground frame levers, early 1990s.

Crossing Keeper Finch, seen from the crossing, operating the levers. BOTH PHOTOGRAPHS J. FINCH

On Sunday 20th October 1991, Conductor-guard Dorothy Rees of Pontypool became the first female guard on British Rail to work a steam-hauled train since the war. She is pictured at Cardiff Central on the footplate of a BR standard tank locomotive No. 80080. Conductor Rees has just given Driver Faulkner (seen peeping out of the cab) details of the train (how many coaches etc) before setting off to Treherbert. The train was run to commemorate the 150th anniversary of the inauguration of the Taff Vale Railway. David Rees

An End to Harassment

In 1990 the NUR National Women's Advisory committee formulated the wording of a document explaining what sexual harassment is and how to deal with it. BR used this as the basis for its own policy, which took effect in 1991. The literature made it clear that open denigration of females or harassment of individual women could eventually lead, after warnings, to dismissal. There were a few die-hards amongst the men, who resented being dictated to, but sexist comments gradually became less frequent.

BR introduced training sessions for its managers and provided volunteer harassment counsellors for victims to talk to and by 1992 there were 143 counsellors nation-wide. Women Against Sexual Harassment reported that the number of cases reported to them by railwaywomen had declined from 106 in 1990 to 39 in 1991, and to 10 in the first half of 1992.

The instigators of BR's sexual harassment policy probably never envisaged that a woman would be dismissed on that charge. However, Mrs Jan Hustwitt, a 37-year-old guard at Harrogate, had already been disciplined for repeatedly pressing unwanted sexual attentions onto a male train driver and, when she committed the same offence against another, she was dismissed in 1994.[43]

In 1998 LUL had to pay £25,000 in damages to two women — a manager and a driver — who were hounded from their jobs on the Bakerloo Line by offensive innuendo in an unofficial magazine produced by male staff. This case seems to have prompted LUL to take drastic action, for in 1999 it introduced a sexual harassment policy and hired consultant Terry Day to review equal opportunities. She said: 'People were accepting things that any decent person would say were unacceptable.' These included crude sexual remarks, threats of gang rape and real sexual assault. The perpetrators were colleagues, managers and subordinates. Interviews with eight women — four white and four black — who had been persistently harassed, showed that the black women were experiencing a 'horrible cocktail of racism and sexism'. Ms Day was subsequently engaged as LUL's Equality Officer.

LUL's mishandling of complaints caused women even more distress. No one knew how to deal with harassment. Despite several Industrial Tribunal cases, no records were kept of incidents among the 12,370 staff, 85 per cent of whom were male. About 50 volunteers, including train drivers, station assistants, secretaries and managers were trained as advisers. To bring the problem into the open a 'zero tolerance' message was broadcast to all staff using videos, noticeboards, newsletters, briefings and training courses. In the first two years of the five-year programme, 86 victims came forward, compared with a mere handful in the previous two years. Disciplinary action was taken against 21 workers, and six were dismissed. In 2002 Cherie Booth QC presented LUL with an award from Opportunity Now, a business-led campaign to advance women in the workplace, for the excellence of its harassment policy.

The Equal Treatment Directive, brought in under European law, has lately been amended to split the two forms of sexual harassment, because of the confusion that has often arisen from using one term to mean two different things. The definition of sexual harassment is still 'unwanted verbal, non-verbal or physical conduct of a sexual nature'; but a new term — 'sex-related harassment' — is now used to describe ill treatment which is due to the sex of the victim, not because the conduct complained of is sexual. Sex-related harassment encompasses graffiti, disparaging comments about one's gender etc, and 'is a display of power over the victim rather than a sexual advance'.[44] It means bullying, intimidation or verbal abuse of a woman at work *because* she is a woman.*

The Equal Treatment Directive became operative in October 2005, 30 years too late for the female pioneers in previously all-male workplaces. Perhaps it should have been inaugurated simultaneously with the Sex Discrimination Act in 1975, but maybe the authorities never envisaged that men in traditionally male jobs would be so nasty to women entering their ranks.

Salaried Staff

By the 1970s women comprised about 40% of railway administrative clerical officers and over 90% of telephone exchange and typing bureau staff. Few worked in jobs closely related to railway operating: the majority of booking office clerks were male and women rarely performed work such as train crew rostering.

In January 1976 Evelyn Duffy became the first woman senior technical officer. She worked at the CCE in Glasgow, designing track layouts, and was required to work on the track, not just in the office.[45] The same month, Bounds Green carriage cleaning supervisor Margaret Welch became the first woman to attend the Eastern Region's Supervisory Management Centre at Leeds.[46] In October 1980, the first woman joined the British Transport advertising sales force. Janice Williams joined Eastern Region as a traffic apprentice in 1980 and was the first woman supervisor at Dagenham Dock. She encountered a lot of prejudice: the area manager addressed her as 'boy' and she had to be tutored by another apprentice because the staff refused to train her.[47]

Helen Smith became the first female station supervisor when she was appointed at Oxford in June 1981, at the age of 23.[48] Christine Taylor was the first female traffic manager in Wales. At the age of 22 she took the post at Machynlleth after graduating in philosophy and maths at the University of Kent.[49] Lorna Lawson, a typist at Elgin for 25 years, was chosen for Scotrail's experimental accelerated promotion scheme in 1990 and, after six weeks in signalling school and three months on-the-job training, she was appointed Traffic Supervisor responsible for all commercial and operating matters affecting the signalboxes and stations on a 60 mile section.[50]

Humanities graduate Gillian Fisher was appointed Assistant Station Manager at Redhill in 1979, when she was 25. She was 'overwhelmed' by the reaction and the congratulatory letters, which included one from an 85-year-old former suffragette. She later became one of the first female station managers when appointed at West Croydon. Pennie Bellas held the same position at Burgess Hill and Hassocks. Having been told at interview that women were 'not up to' being station managers, she felt it important to take her full share in emergencies, dealing with points problems and getting her hands oily, to gain the respect of the staff. In 1981 Susan Hughes became station manager of Elmers End and its 93 staff, while Susan Carey was appointed at Tolworth, where she managed four stations and a freight yard.[51] By the 1990s the appointment of female station managers was so commonplace that it ceased to arouse comment among the staff.[52] Karen Smith said in 1995 that she had received no sexist comments, but passengers at Radlett were still surprised when, asking for 'the man in charge', they were directed to her.[53]

Janet Wall held managerial posts on the Chiltern Lines, at Wolverhampton Freight Terminal, in the Projects Department and in Railfreight Distribution before landing the

* Of course the new law applies equally to bullying or intimidation of a man, owing to his being a man.

post of station general manager at Manchester Piccadilly in 1994. Caroline Starmer, formerly a ticket office clerk and later station manager at Faversham, filled the same role at Ashford where, in 1995, she was placed in charge of ten stations and 80 staff.

Women had worked in railway engineering departments for many years, but only in certain jobs such as tracer and draughtswoman. Betty Saunders, a technical officer in the Civil Engineer's Office at Peterborough, had joined the LNER around 1946, a time when, she recalled: 'It was very difficult for women to be accepted into the male domain'; but by 1986 she felt that 'after much perseverance, women have now become an accepted cog in the wheel.' * In 1990 Anne Harrison spent a year investigating the training and recruitment procedures of Doncaster's signalling department and found that only eleven of the 700 signal and telegraph technicians were women.[54]

Senior Technical Officer Lindsey Locke joined BR in 1981 and qualified as a civil engineer in 1986. By 1988, when she was 29, she had responsibility for the day-to-day technical management of the renovation of the vast 'umbrella' roof at Bristol Temple Meads. This involved climbing up the scaffolding and working 125 feet above the ground.[55] Civil engineering graduate Niamh Partridge spent four years designing bridges, stations and depots, and in 1998 was appointed assistant project manager. [56]

Carolyn Griffiths graduated from Birmingham University in 1979 with first class honours in mechanical engineering and found herself 'seduced by the practical content of the British Rail Engineering Graduate Training scheme.' Her first boss recalled:

> Carolyn came to me for her first job ... There was fire in her belly and she fixed me with a gimlet eye of Thatcherian intensity. She wanted to go to Old Oak Common [Paddington] as a Shift Foreman but I said no, not yet. If looks could kill she gave it to me Force 9 but to Paddington she had to go.[57]

Miss Griffiths recalled: 'By the end of my training I had become fascinated by the 24 hour world of depot operations.' After a short time at the loco section at Paddington she was placed at Cardiff Canton Traction Maintenance Depot.

> It was here, working alongside the supervisors, electricians and fitters, that I learned the ropes of diesel loco maintenance, dealing with real time pressures and a lot about the rough and tumble of depot life. ... I signed up to work shifts and also became a member of the 'breakdown gang' — the accident recovery and crane gang.

She was trained on Class 47 locomotive maintenance and overhaul and soon qualified to change cylinder heads, big end bearings and to carry out major repairs — 'hard graft and great fun'. In 1983 she became senior shift supervisor at Stratford Maintenance Depot, in charge of 130 locomotives, a shift of two supervisors, 25-30 fitters, electricians, fitters' mates and the activities of three maintenance sheds:

> I spent as much of my shift as I could out on the shop floor, working with and supporting the shift staff; by now, I had some practical capability for trouble shooting on diesel locomotives and I was still learning.

---

* In 1965 women were admitted to the Permanent Way Institution, and Miss Saunders was one of its first 12 female members. In 1985 she was elected its vice-president, the first woman to hold that position.

In 1984 Miss Griffiths moved to Selhurst Traction Maintenance Depot, where she learned about electric traction. She was promoted to Maintenance Assistant, in charge of 70 staff and the maintenance of 100 trains and in November 1985 became Depot Manager at Brighton, in charge of 140 staff involved in cleaning and maintaining 170 electric units. She was the first woman to fill such a post.

> One of the most rewarding aspects of my work whilst at Brighton was managing accident recovery work in the Chichester/Horsham/Redhill/Hastings area. For this I was on call one week in two. On average my team had one call out each week to derailments and other accidents, usually requiring use of the depot's 50 ton rail crane or road-rail vehicle. Some were minor, others not and unfortunately some involved fatalities.

In 1987 Miss Griffiths left BR to work for the new Mass Rapid Transit system in Singapore. Eventually, she was to land the very top job in railway inspection (see page 369).

When Kate Burt graduated from Imperial College in 2005 with a BSc in Mechanical Engineering she too was determined to find a hands-on job rather than one that involved sitting in front of a computer. She joined Network Rail and was placed in the Rail Vehicle Engineering Section, where she began four years' training in looking after the company's 2,000 track maintenance vehicles. Of her first placement (at Selhurst) she said, 'It did seem strange at first, being one of the few women, but everyone gets used to you pretty quickly'.[58]

In 1984, TSSA staff representative Julia Hammond set up two Women at Work enquiry meetings at Rail House, Euston. The secretaries, clerks and middle managers who attended wanted to implement a positive plan of action for reform. This included clearer career structures, more accurate job specifications and more opportunities. The women said they would welcome flexitime and job-sharing. It emerged from these meetings that many women were irritated by chauvinistic attitudes. They spoke of being patronised, of feeling 'kept out and kept down'; they were actively discouraged from undertaking training and denied the opportunities to do so. They complained that at job interviews they were frequently asked about marriage and family commitments. One mentioned the attitude of personnel officers, who assumed they would leave in a year or two to start a family; another felt: 'they are just looking for reasons to reject you'. Personal assistants complained of having to perform inappropriate chores for male bosses, for example sewing on a button.

The women were also unhappy that single men were seen as dashing bachelors while career women — especially those with long service — were labelled neurotic and frustrated. Some men even told their female colleagues that they were not wanted on the railways in any capacity. One said, bluntly: 'I don't approve of women in offices.'

As well as chauvinistic behaviour some women experienced varying degrees of discrimination and even lewd comments from male colleagues. Sometimes even the managers acted objectionably. At King's Cross Travel Centre, for example, female staff complained that their manager insisted they wear skirts. They submitted a petition asking to be allowed to wear trousers and a few months later this was granted.

Mary Dickson, Managing Director of Scotrail. COURTESY OF *RAILNEWS*

Kate Burt, Rail Vehicle Engineer at Selhurst. COURTESY OF *RAILNEWS*

When East Anglian rail operator One* chose a virtual person (a 'Lingubot') to guide people around its website and answer questions, a representation of a woman was chosen. Called 'Valerie' (Virtual Assistant London Eastern Railway Interactive Expert), it was modelled on Senior Stewardess Dionne Mobbs, who remarked: 'my boyfriend says it's a really good impression of me, especially the angry look.' The company, anticipating that Valerie might suffer sexual harassment, have programmed appropriate responses. If asked: 'Do you fancy me?' she replies: 'I have a high opinion of all my visitors.' A spokesman for One said 'there have been quite a few questions that are censored'.[59]

Higher Management

The 1981 *British Rail Directory* names all officers of the rank of Area Manager or higher. Among the many hundreds of male names are just 16 women, of whom 12 were secretaries. The highest ranked was Miss Prudence (Prue) Leith, a restaurateur and cookery writer who had in 1977 become the first woman appointed to the British Transport Hotels, a subsidiary of the BRB, as a non-executive member, specifically to advise on catering. (Miss Leith revealed that dinner invitations from the BRB asked her to wear a black tie and bring her wife.[60]) Other women in the *Directory* included an Economic Survey Officer, a member of the Design Panel, an officer in the Finance, Planning and Computers section, and an Industrial Relations Planning Officer. The 1982 edition of *Who's Who in Britain's Railway Industry* reads like a list of members of a men's club (which, in a way, it was), as not one female name appears.

Since then, the change has been revolutionary. More women have been appointed to the BRB, including one in an executive capacity: Alison Lesley, who was head of the British Rail Property Board.[61] Although they got off to a fairly slow start – the number of female senior managers increased from two in 1980 to 36 in 1990[62] – hundreds of women have since held higher-management positions and, in the last decade, three have been appointed to the highest positions anyone can hold on Britain's railways. Chartered accountant Janette Anderson was Director of Network Rail in Scotland for six years (she resigned in June 2003 to work for a rail maintenance company). In August 2004 Mary Dickson was appointed Managing Director of First Scotrail at the remarkably young age of 34. *The Sunday Times* described her as: 'A marketing course's dream graduate, a vision in pastel shades, from the pristine hair to the cream suit.'[63] In February 2004 Alison Forster became the first woman Managing Director of a train operating company, the First Great Western. A graduate of the London School of Economics, she joined BR's graduate training scheme in 1980 and held a number of station manager posts on the SR before moving to Swansea to become area passenger operations manager, responsible for South West Wales. She was later station manager at Bristol Temple Meads, then operations manager on the newly privatised Great Western Railway. In 1998 she was appointed First Great Western's operations and safety Director, a post she filled for nearly six years before her promotion to managing director. According to reporter Paul Clifton, 'Ms Forster doesn't conform to the stereotype of a railway MD. She wears her lapel name badge, just as any platform staff would do. Orange and yellow hi-vis jackets hang on the coat rack. Visitors are given the impression of someone who can get her hands dirty'.[64]

---

* 'One' is the irritating and confusing name of a railway company covering the services previously provided by Anglia Railways, First Great Eastern, the West Anglia part of the WAGN operation and the Stansted Express.

UNIONS

In 1978 there were 9,145 women in the NUR, most of them carriage servicewomen and catering workers. Women comprised 5% of the total membership, a figure that was bolstered by the closed shop agreement of 1975. There were few women activists. In 1979 there were, for example, no female secretaries of railway branches.* By 1980 the total railway workforce had declined 70% since 1949 and NUR membership had halved. In 1983 women still comprised less than 1% of branch secretaries (four out of 543), and there were only nine women on the union's Sectional Councils, of which seven represented retail and catering grades.

The first woman delegate to the NUR AGM† was Mrs J. Brightman, a gatewoman at Middle Road Crossing, March, who attended in 1978. Only two women have been on the NUR Executive; the first was Ann Laverick, elected in 1982. NUR historian Dr Philip Bagwell asserted that the reasons so few women attended the AGM or were elected to the EC ranged from 'the prevalence of male chauvinism in some branches to the difficulty married women have in reconciling ... [union] activities with their domestic responsibilities'.[65] Caroline Stephens experienced the former when she attended the 1982 AGM:

> My branch moved a resolution to examine the position of women in the NUR and ways of implementing the TUC Charter for Equality for Women. There were 19 votes for and rest of conference against. A motion to change the name of the union from 'Railwaymen' to 'Railwayworkers' was also lost, with 20 voting in favour. The Mayor of Middlesbrough said there were only two places for women and one of them was at the kitchen sink and Sid Weighell, the General Secretary, said 'If you think we're changing the name of this union for a load of women you're very much mistaken'.[66]

In 1984 women's share of NUR membership was only 3.5%, a reduction of 1.7% in six years. This was caused by the loss of shipping, hotel and catering staff as BR curtailed or sold off those departments. By 1992 the proportion had returned to 5% (c6,000 women). The union created a National Women's Advisory Committee in September 1988 and two years later amalgamated with the National Union of Seamen, which forced a change of name to the National Union of Rail, Maritime and Transport Workers (RMT). In 1994 the union held the first of its women's conferences. RMT membership at December 2004 was 71,544, of which 7,534 (9.48%) were women, a proportion not seen since the last war. There are no women on the EC, but eight branches (of 230) have female secretaries. The union is currently holding a telephone canvass campaign to try to get more women actively involved. Efforts are also being made to establish regional and branch level Women's Advisory Committees.

A 1984 booklet called *Introducing ASLEF* contained the words: 'Brothers in Unity for Mutual Help — a motto to be proud of' and in 1997 Philip Bagwell described ASLEF as 'a craft union looking after the fraternity of locomotivemen'.[67] In 1984 ASLEF had eight women members (and 21,164 men) and by 1992 there were 144.‡ Karen Harrison made

* There were two in branches for bus employees.

† The AGM is the union's highest body; it outranks even the EC.

‡ This list includes only ASLEF members. Some drivers were in the RMT, others were non-unionists.

history in 1995 when she was elected Chair of the union's Annual Assembly of Delegates. The union had an extant Women's Consultative Committee at the beginning of 2003; however, at the time of writing the most recent set of minutes posted on ASLEF's website was dated February 2003, and numerous emails sent to the secretary of the Women's Committee over a period of nine months received no response. ASLEF's head office declined to give any current information about its female members.

The TSSA Executive Committee of 29 persons included two women in 1978, the year the executive seat reserved for a woman was abolished because there was no longer any need for it. In 1983 the union had about 60,000 members, of whom 21% were railwaywomen. Currently about one-third of TSSA members are women but not all work for the railways as the union also recruits from other transport industries.

Wanted: Railman

Wanted: Railman was an Equal Opportunities Commission report, published in 1986, that stands as a damning indictment of sex discrimination within BR. Researcher Diana Robbins noted that, of a total staff of 170,000,* there were 11,000 women on BR (6.5%). Of these, 61% were in clerical work and 25% were in the lowest uniformed grades and, of those, 77% were carriage servicewomen. Of the 61% who were clerks, 95% were in the lowest grades, a figure almost identical to the 1939 statistics. Ms Robbins remarked: 'Some employers might have felt that the statistical evidence of gross imbalance and occupational segregation by sex justified internal scrutiny of procedures, leading to a program of reform'. Not BR, which required 'proof' that the organisation was directly to blame. She said that the attitude amounted to: 'If women do not come forward, if women have no ambition, if our jobs do not appeal, why should we do anything about it?'[68]

Ms Robbins tried to determine whether women's aversion to railway work, lack of ambition, or some other factor was responsible for their lowly position. But when (male) managers spoke frankly to her about which work was suitable for women she discovered an exact coincidence with the jobs women already performed, suggesting that managers' prejudices had a direct bearing on which sex was hired for which job. She remarked that where male managers could see women being of use was for 'their domesticity, their sexuality and their capacity for routine work'. One manager thought 'lady guards' would be 'quite nice'; 'I would be looking for the air-hostess type, I would capitalise on their femininity'. Another said that most men like to see a woman around, 'even if it's nothing more than to goggle at'.[69]

The report included dozens of quotes that reveal an entrenched hostility to women who stepped outside the narrow range of 'women's jobs'. A number of men cited their female relatives as a benchmark for all women and then labelled certain jobs unsuitable because they would not like their wives to perform them. Others opined:

> A woman is good at certain things; a man is good at certain other things. That's the difference in their physical make up. Now OK there's some jobs a woman does much better than a man – take carriage cleaning. You can't beat a woman on carriage cleaning. I suppose it's their domestic nature.[70]

In fact, carriage servicing bears little resemblance to domestic cleaning. Ms Robbins described it as 'heavy, dirty and can be dangerous, yet apparently despised by the very

---

* Railway workers only, not including ferry, hotel or engineering staff.

kind of men who believe women incapable of heavy work'. Cleaning carriages was habitually used as a punishment for insubordinate railwaymen: 'The point of the punishment of course is to put the men in a degrading and unpleasant situation — the daily work situation of women cleaning carriages' Ms Robbins remarked. The carriage servicewomen said they were treated as 'the lowest of the low, like rubbish' by management and union alike.[71]

Ms Robbins asserted that small details can create an environment from which women feel excluded. Job titles such as signalman, booking-boy, secondman, foreman; the lack of toilet facilities; the difficulties and inequalities with uniform, all served to make women feel like square pegs in round holes. Recruitment leaflets assumed all applicants were male and depicted only men in photographs. Indeed, Diana Robbins named her report *Wanted: Railman* after seeing those very words on an advertisement outside a station. She was not surprised that, in 1983, 85% of new recruits were men.

The report found men sneered at women's lack of ambition, but remarked 'when women are ambitious they risk being labelled as "pushy".'[72] It also discovered that the 1% of railwaywomen who were signallers, guards and drivers suffered more than other railwaywomen from harassment, including obscene graffiti, insults, unwanted sexual advances and touching. One signalwoman resigned after a series of incidents, including having the fire brigade sent to her signalbox as a joke.[73]

The report listed the outcome of all the sex discrimination and equal pay cases against BR between 1975 and 1984. There were seven, of which three were brought by men, and in all but one the plaintiff lost, although a second case was won on appeal to the European Court. This was a case brought by TSSA member Eileen Garland, an accounts clerk with BR Engineering Limited at Wolverton. Even after the Equal Pay Act of 1970, BR continued to deny women equality in regard to the traditional railway workers' perk of free train tickets. Retired railwaymen received free travel not only for themselves but also for their wives and dependent children; retired railwaywomen received it only for themselves. The NUR endorsed this discrimination: in 1975, its AGM voted against part-time and retired railwaywomen's having equal travel facilities with men. Eileen Garland had the full support of her union when, in November 1976, she complained to the Equal Opportunities Commission, which backed her case at an Industrial Tribunal. She lost, but an Employment Appeal Tribunal overturned the decision. BR took the matter to the Court of Appeal and won, and Mrs Garland applied to House of Lords, which referred it to the European Court of Justice in Luxembourg. On 22nd April 1982 the Court found in her favour and on 1st April 1983 BR implemented the new arrangements. The case took six and a half years and cost the TSSA £40,000.

In personnel departments Ms Robbins found 'goodwill toward women', but the general consensus among lower managers was that women were incompetent, weak (emotionally and physically) and unsuitable for many jobs, even those being performed by women at the time. She concluded:

> This report shows unequivocally that women as a group are at a disadvantage compared with their male colleagues. Indications of prejudice, of harassment, of unfair treatment, of conscious and unconscious acts of injustice, of potentially unlawful sex discrimination (both direct and indirect) appear throughout the report.[74]

After the report was published, an Equal Opportunities Manager was appointed to the BRB; the first was Lesley Holland.

SUMMARY

Although this chapter has been mainly dedicated to describing the experiences of pioneers in formerly all-male grades, it must not be forgotten that they comprised a tiny proportion of the total female staff. In the 70s and early 80s two-thirds of all railwaywomen were clerks, of whom 95% performed routine administrative work in the lowest grades, and three quarters of women in wages grades were carriage cleaners.

In 1982 women comprised only 7% of BR employees; a decade later this had risen to 10% of a total staff of 136,000. The same number of women were employed in 1992 as had been in 1914, and they were still disproportionately concentrated in clerical and cleaning grades. Only one in 20 railwaywomen was in a wages grade, and only one in 100 was a signaller, driver or guard. By 1994 the proportion of women had risen by only 0.6%. There were twice as many women in railway management as there were in wages grades: 9.5% compared with 4.7%, and women comprised 22% 'other salaried staff'.

Since the railways were privatised and split up into many different companies, statistics for 2005 are impossible to obtain; however, it is clear that women can now hold any manual or managerial post on the railways. Sex discrimination is at an all-time low and in some circumstances had been eradicated completely. This is not due directly to their predecessors, or to those who performed men's work during the two world wars, or as a result of any endeavours by the railway unions. It is because of the Sex Discrimination Act.

Despite the Act, in some ways women recruited in the 1970s and early 80s were treated less favourably than war-workers. During both wars the decision to recruit women was a momentous one and the sheer numbers suddenly appearing on the staff meant that railway managers had to make special arrangements. The problem of female WCs, mess-rooms, uniforms and maternity had to be addressed and resolved quickly. But the post-1975 recruits found that none of these issues had been tackled and, in the vast majority of cases, it was left to individual women to fight identical battles in separate locations with varying degrees of support or opposition from their colleagues and union officials. War-workers certainly suffered less sexual harassment and insult than did railwaywomen who joined after 1975. This was because during the 1940s considerably more men exhibited 'gentlemanly' behaviour towards women than was the case by the 1970s, by which time there was increased antagonism between the sexes, that was still present when women began to storm the male bastions on the railways.

The Railways Act 1993 privatised the industry and the BRB was disintegrated into one hundred separate parts, each one sold or franchised separately. Train operation was franchised and ownership of the infrastructure (i.e. track, signalling and stations) passed to Railtrack, which was privatised in 1996. Railtrack's job was taken over by the non-profit body Network Rail in October 2002.

Some people believe that women do better within profit-making businesses, while others think that there will be even more sex discrimination, because considerations such as seniority and turn-taking for promotion will be replaced by 'suitability' and the Old Boys' Network. There is also the danger that the unions will lose even more power, leading to worsening conditions for non-managerial staff of both sexes. The negative effects of privatisation have already started to show. Most carriage cleaning, for example, is now contracted out to cleaning companies, whose employees are not railway workers and so do not receive the many benefits that their predecessors enjoyed, such as free rail travel, entry to the railway's excellent pension scheme and an active trade union.

Appendices

Distribution of some railwaywomen, 1984		
Position	*Female*	*Male*
Senior officer	0	8
Senior executive	2	589
Management	169	7,868
Supervisors	26	9,304
Professional/technical officers incl. trainees	237	3,755
Clerical staff	5,651	11,955
Train drivers	0	18777
Drivers' assistants	5	1720
Guards	64	11,011
Signal(wo)men	37	6,671
Trackmen / Overhead line technicians	0	20,746
Rolling stock technicians	2	1,374
Railmen, Leading Railmen, Senior Railmen (including carriage cleaners)	2,279	20,479
Road motor drivers	2	521
Hostel staff	74	3
Office cleaners	223	0
Canteen staff	28	2
Adapted from Wanted: Railman, Diana Robbins, 1986.		

A written enquiry on the number of female staff was sent by the author to every train operating company in September 1999. Virgin, Northern Spirit, and Railtrack replied promptly, the GNER replied in August 2002 with apologies for the delay, and Thameslink refused to give any information. Despite being sent a reminder in April 2002, no other train operating company even acknowledged my letter.

Virgin Trains, female staff, September 1999			
	Female	*Male*	*% females*
Casual	7	9	43.75
Catering	401	367	52.21
Clerical	285	475	37.50
Drivers	7	726	0.95
Managerial	142	308	31.56
Railway supervisors	3	33	8.33
Senior conductors	43	381	10.14
Traffic	4	69	5.48
TOTAL	892	2,368	27.36

The following grades on Virgin Trains contained no women: Chargeman Shunter, Train Controller and Train Controller Instructor, Train Driving Instructor, Management Staff grades 1, 2 and 5 at headquarters. In 1999 an advert for train drivers was worded specifically to attract women applicants, but 94% of respondents were men.

RAILTRACK, FEMALE STAFF, OCTOBER 1999		
	Females	*% of total*
Management	704	19
Clerical	779	60
Technical	8	4
Signalling & Supervisors	222	4
TOTAL	1713	16

Note: Railtrack offered maternity arrangements over and above the statutory requirements.

NORTHERN SPIRIT, FEMALE STAFF, OCTOBER 1999		
	Females	*% of total*
Booking office clerks	42	19
Administrative	59	60
Technical	33	4
Station staff	39	16.9
Carriage cleaners	11	23.9
Drivers	13	1.9
Conductors	73	12.4
Traincrew support	5	7.8
Revenue Protection	5	14.7
TOTAL	280	12.1

NB: Northern Spirit offered slightly higher maternity pay than the statutory minimum.

References

[1] Personal interview with the author, 2003.
[2] *Railnews* March 1996 p17.
[3] Letter to the author, 2005.
[4] Letter to the author, June 2005.
[5] *Railnews* January 1975.
[6] *Railnews* January 1975.
[7] <http://web.onyxnet.co.uk/Auffret-onyxnet.co.uk/railways/battersby/batt15.htm>
[8] Email from Kate Lee, 30 June 2005.
[9] Letter to the author, 2005.
[10] Personal interview with the author, 1989.
[11] Personal interview with the author, 2003.
[12] Whitbread, J. R. (1961) *The Railway Policeman,* Harrap & Co.
[13] Thanks to Kevin Gordon and Steve Daly.
[14] *Railnews* July 2005.
[15] *Railnews* August 1975.
[16] *Railnews* November 1977.
[17] *Railnews* August 1980.
[18] Email to the author, 2005.
[19] *Railnews,* February 1980.
[20] *Railnews* June 1991.
[21] *Isle of Wight County Press* 25 November 1994.
[22] *Today* 17 January 1989.
[23] *Railnews* February 1989.
[24] *Daily Mail* 9 May 1991. Ms Kenny refers to Karen Harrison as BR's first woman driver.
[25] Taped reminiscences of Anne Winter, 1995.
[26] *Metro* 3 July 2001.
[27] *The Times* 7 September 1985; *The Times Educational Supplement* 20 September 1985.
[28] *Railnews* July 1989.
[29] *Railnews* May 1988.
[30] *Railnews* July 1988.
[31] *Railnews* August 1990.
[32] *Railnews* June 1991. They were Jan Sutherland, Louise Bird, Nicky Smale and Andrea Draper.
[33] *Daily Telegraph* 6 June 1991.
[34] Conversation with the author, 1979.
[35] Personal interview with the author, 2003.
[36] *Guardian* 10 December 1986.
[37] Letter to the author, 1999. Victim wishes to remain anonymous.
[38] *Morning Star* 12 April 1990.
[39] Personal interview with the author, 1986.
[40] *Railnews* November 1991.
[41] *Railnews* August 1988.
[42] *Guardian* 5 April 1991.
[43] *TV Quick* 17 October 1994.
[44] Article 2 of the Equal Treatment Directive.
[45] *Railnews* January 1976.

[46] Ibid.
[47] Letter to the author, 1996.
[48] *Railnews* June 1981.
[49] Frater, A (1983) *Stopping Train Britain* (Hodder & Stoughton) p 88-90.
[50] *Railnews* July 1990.
[51] Equal Opportunities Commission (1982) *Breakthrough* (booklet).
[52] *Railnews* October 1981.
[53] Letter to the author, 1995.
[54] Railnews, *February* 1990.
[55] *Railnews* December 1988.
[56] *Track Record* November 1998, p17.
[57] Hardy, R. (n.d.) *Railways in my Blood.*
[58] *Railnews* March 2005. Special supplement.
[59] *BBC news online* 27 May 2005
[60] *Railnews* June 1984.
[61] Gourvish, T.R. (2002) *British Rail 1974-97* (OUP) p559.
[62] Gourvish, T.R. (2002) *British Rail 1974-97* (OUP) p584.
[63] *The Sunday Times* 17 October 2004.
[64] *Rail Professional* April 2004.
[65] Bagwell, P.S. (1982) *The Railwaymen Volume Two*, (Allen & Unwin) p111. Dr Bagwell devotes only two paragraphs to railwaywomen in this book of 418 pages.
[66] Reminiscences of Caroline Stephens, 2005.
[67] In Simmons, J & Biddle, G. (Eds) (1997) *The Oxford Companion to British Railway History* (OUP) p24
[68] Robbins (1986) *Wanted: Railman.* HMSO, London. p22.
[69] Ibid, p33-4.
[70] Ibid. p22.
[71] Ibid. p71.
[72] Ibid. p39.
[73] Robbins, D. (1986) *Wanted: Railman.* HMSO, London. p37.
[74] Ibid. p.86.

Ann Henderson driving a Class 37 locomotive on the West Highland Line, 1992. A. HENDERSON

The author changing a headcode stencil, 1995. AUTHOR'S COLLECTION

8: Ten Personal Histories

Caroline Stephens – Railwoman, Numbertaker & Manager

I joined British Rail in 1976 aged 21. I had finished university and been to India, but somehow, my education had failed to point me towards a particular career. It was not long after the Sex Discrimination Act and I was aware that women could now do men's jobs. Despite this, it didn't occur to me that I could have a man's job on the railway.

I went to a builders' yard and asked for work. The man looked at me as if to say: 'You won't be able to do the job, love', but he didn't say this; instead he took me into the yard and threw a hundredweight bag of plaster into my arms and told me to toss it up above my head into the lorry. I failed miserably. Looking back at my railway career, I can see now that this man was indeed enlightened: he kept his mouth shut and gave me a test which was relevant to the job.

As I was living in a squat next to Clapham Junction station, I thought I might get a cleaning job there, but to my surprise the station master offered me a job on the platform. I accepted and eventually worked there for nine years. He warned me that I would have to climb a ladder and clean the lampshades, which were about 13 ft off the ground. I told him that I had done rock-climbing and mountaineering for a number of years and he took me on. Later I found that none of the men would climb the ladders to clean the lampshades anyway, and this quickly became my job.

I was told that I was the first woman to work on the platform since the war and was treated as a complete novelty. I wore a man's uniform because I didn't like the skirt: it was straight, grey and itchy. I quite liked the waistcoats. I had one with lots of buttons and black and red striped sleeves. I was indoctrinated quickly into the workings and the culture. My supervisors were from the old railway days; they looked after me and showed me the ropes. I stayed in the job for nine years.

The whole station smelled of dirt and brake dust and, as the platform was covered, it was never cleaned by the rain. Old men and youths in anoraks stood on the end of the platform taking down the numbers of trains. They couldn't believe their luck — a woman on the platform. They hung around with their tongues hanging out. Yuk.

Most of the workforce were immigrants — West Indian, African, Indian and Irish — and I enjoyed their company. Male passengers and employees would ask me if I was married before making any other conversation. They would also tweak me in the ribs because I was female. I found that invasion of my body space bizarre and it really annoyed me. The tweaking stopped when I punched one bloke and then warned others what happened to the last man who did that to me. Of course, these days I'd be sacked for that.

The railway was like an alien world, totally hierarchical, with its own set of rules, names and abbreviations. It was as if the clerical and managerial workers were people and the blue collar workers weren't. For the first 10 years of my railway career there was no sick pay for us, although clerical workers got it. Clerical workers got more holidays and didn't have to do the terrible shifts that we did. Of all the things on the railway, the thing I found hardest was the shift work. I remember turning up 10 minutes late for a 5.30 a.m. shift once and being sent home without pay — a real shock to my system.

It was totally a man's world: the culture was dominated by men's jokes, men's concerns, men's interests. There were pictures of naked, sexually provocative women in all the mess-rooms. Many of the men were not lean and fine of character, but were beer-swilling misfits who couldn't have got a job elsewhere. The culture consisted of doing as little as possible. It was not uncommon for platform workers to go to the pub in their break and some were very heavy drinkers. I remember one enormous West Indian who, when drunk, would boom announcements in a sing-song chant and who used to cock his head on one side when he saw me, smile and say, 'Do you like me?' One day, I was seeing out his train home and he leaned out of the window and said 'Give me a kiss, darling', before being sick down the outside of the train.

Women were in the minority and somehow you couldn't be yourself. The men just seemed to be themselves in their male culture, playing with their trains and their bits of metal, with myriad personalities, some of them downright weird or nasty. But just being a woman in this culture made you stick out and could be seen as difficult. To survive as a woman, somehow you had to be particularly careful not to upset anyone.

Being sent to the station master was like being sent to the headmaster. He looked rather like a vampire and wore a pin-striped suit. One of his clerks frightened the life out of me when he shouted at me for changing Miss to Ms on my Privilege Railway Ticket and made me cry. He told me that railway workers had fought for a long time to get these privileges and I shouldn't deface my card. I said I wasn't defacing it and women shouldn't have to say whether they were married or not, because men didn't have to, and you could use Ms on your passport. Nowadays, I would have just explained it nicely to him and I grew to really understand his point of view in time as I represented the men, who also did not have a voice, but I was really only a young girl then and I felt very hurt at the time.

The working conditions and environment weren't very nice and I soon found that not many people would take up their rights. Someone gave me an NUR Conditions of Service book and after my probationary period, I put in for six of us platform staff to be upgraded from the bottom grade to the next grade up because we announced trains. I won the claim and it had ramifications for all the platform staff on BR. The claim was discussed at the Regional Management/Union Committee and we won. Afterwards, the management representative said to the union side, 'Oh, by the way, Miss Stephens does have a degree in mathematics and she is a Marxist.' What are they talking about? I wondered (both my parents were Tories) and I went back to my flatmates to ask what a Marxist was. From that day, the platform staff around me protected me from the onslaught of sexist comments and whenever a man came up to me making improper suggestions they would warn him: 'Lay off her, she's our union representative.' Soon I was the NUR shop steward and health and safety representative. Not because I was political but because the people needed a voice. I helped people write letters, got them extra overtime and dealt with hundreds of basic workplace problems.

I found the carriage cleaning women more frightening than the men. When I used to go over to the yard and ask whether they wanted the union to do anything for them, they would shout at me, saying, 'Nobody's interested in us, nobody does anything for us' and they were really intimidating. You should try addressing a room full of enormous, angry West Indian and African women and thin, wiry Scottish women. I felt really scared of them, but persisted in trying to listen to their concerns, and some of them are still my friends to this day. They had a really horrible job and very low pay. Later on in my career, I set up the first ever meeting between senior management and some of these women, where they could report some of their concerns face to face to those bosses. I was very proud then. Another group of women closeted away in Clapham Yard were those who looked after the oil lamps. 'Hello', I said, 'I'm your new union rep. Is there anything I can do for you?' 'Ha', they laughed, 'the union won't do anything for us.' I said, 'Well, would you like a crèche?' — at which they exploded in laughter. Maybe their children were all grown up or maybe it was the absurdity of the railway providing a crèche. It was difficult to imagine young children in such a dirty and dangerous environment. There was a sharp divide between home and work life. Women, with their periods and pregnancies, were a nuisance to the system, but drunken, incompetent men were OK.

After I had got us all upgraded one supervisor, Dick, took me into the shunting yard to teach me to couple and uncouple trains. We had to be able to do this, even though in reality there were always shunters available. Lifting the 90lb buckeye coupling was often cited as one of the things that women would never be able to do. Little Dick was very short and had a hernia down to his knees (perhaps swinging buckeyes isn't very good for women or for a lot of men). But I had to pass this test to be upgraded.

Late one night, he said: 'Come on Caroline, I'm going to show you something' and we left our platform unmanned in between the trains which I was supposed to attend. He took me clambering over running lines and juice rails out into Clapham Junction's enormous shunting yard and we wove in between stationary trains in the dark with our little lamps until he found a suitable train. He taught me how to couple and uncouple carriages with the knack of swinging the buckeye coupling. This meant that when I went on my course, I would be able to show them I could do it and wouldn't get picked on.

The tracks at Clapham Junction are very numerous and the density of trains is frightening. Later, Dick taught me how to cross all of the tracks in one go, dodging moving trains as we went. This includes all the trains out of Waterloo and Victoria Central and is unbelievably dangerous. We walked up the tracks as far as Battersea Park, where we were responsible for the wooden bridge that often caught fire from people throwing cigarettes out of train windows. At this point, the electric rail was knee-high for me and nearly up to Dick's groin. You have to step over the running rail and the electric rail together, so you can imagine the contortions that you have to go through, balancing on one foot with 800 volts between your legs, whilst looking out for a machine that could make mincemeat out of you. The sound of the train wheels against the iron rail is really frightening. In one second, you can be dead. To this day, I still have the greatest respect for the men who work on the tracks on a daily basis. Indeed, when I became a branch secretary, I had to deal with numerous accidents involving track workers, including a number of fatalities.

When I started to go to union branch meetings, I felt quite scared to speak. I was always the only woman. When I went to my first, I shook with fear when I spoke in front of the group of men. After a year, they elected me to attend the National Grades Conference and, again, I shook with fear as I moved our resolution on something really banal in front of a hall full of railwayworkers from all over the country. Here, I got a feeling for the whole railway network, regional accents, and the concerns of manual workers in poorer parts of the country. I met some other women there, carriage cleaners, who were really nice, but no other 'women in men's jobs'. It was here that I first met Tony Donaghey, who is now President of the RMT and one of the finest and most dedicated men working for working class justice. He was totally encouraging of women. At this conference I had numerous offers to be taken to bed, which I just laughed off. But one bloke was so ugly and fat and disgusting that I found his offer quite upsetting, particularly when he persisted and followed me back to my digs. It seemed as if because I was a woman and he was a man that somehow he felt he had some claim over me. And indeed, I suppose that's part of how sexism works — women submitting to men's wishes. But he was so revolting it was unbelievable. Nowadays I'd just tell him to eff off, but I was young and more polite then, and it left me feeling quite shaken.

I was a union and safety rep for 11 years, during which I learnt an enormous amount about the concerns of my fellow workers, about the system and the inequalities of working class life. My Divisional Officer was Jimmy Knapp, who became the General Secretary of the NUR. He was always really helpful and encouraging. We won quite a few victories. On one health and safety walk, I asked the station manager to check what the white stuff was around all the pipes in the carriage cleaning shed. This stuff was everywhere and was often knocked by the trolleys the carriage cleaners used. He thought it was nothing dangerous. It turned out to be brown asbestos, and the whole carriage cleaning shed had to be closed down and sealed, while it was specially removed by men in white suits at a cost of £30,000.

I moved to Battersea No. 1 NUR branch in about 1977 and was proud to be part of a very active branch with a strong history. The branch had a lot of trackworkers and signal technicians, platform and yard staff and carriage cleaners and I learned the harsh realities of railway life, how the union really worked, including how incredibly bureaucratic and controlling its head office was. When the assistant branch secretary died (how many men did I see working all their lives on the railway and dying before their retirement?), I was voted in. At that time it was assumed there had never been any women branch secretaries but being his assistant meant that in due course I would become the secretary. I really felt I belonged and was very proud.

My life changed big time in 1982 when I became pregnant. I attended the NUR AGM five months pregnant and took over being branch secretary with a one-month old baby. I attended my predecessor's retirement party, a presentation by Jimmy Knapp, holding my new baby and very tired. I think I only missed one branch meeting and carried on with all my union work throughout my maternity leave.

By now, I had been elected onto Sectional Council 'C', the NUR's regional negotiating body. Again it was thought that I was the first woman. I represented all the railmen and leading railmen on the Southwest Division. I learned what could and could not be done at regional level. The meetings with management were always full of smoke and, worse, the management chairman smoked cigars. I always felt like I couldn't breathe. One day, while I was on maternity leave, I took my new baby to see them all and sat at the back. My baby got hungry, so I breastfed him. This caused raised eyebrows, embarrassed comments and jokes. I told the chairman: 'Of course you know that cigars are nipple substitutes.' He laughed and months later asked me if I was still giving my son cigar substitutes. It was funny, but it wasn't the welcome a new mother deserves. You never saw anyone with a baby at any railway meeting or event and, now that I am older, I am still jealous when I see women with babies taking them to work where there are groups of women who coo over them and take them into the society of mothers. No time for pre-natal groups, with full-time shift work, five union jobs and trying to make women's history. I had a home birth, which was ground-breaking at the time. No women to talk about this with. The biggest event of a woman's life — irrelevant. The railway kept on running and I had made myself one of the brothers and lost something of my womanhood in that.

I wrote to the station manager asking if I could come back part time or job share, but the answer was that there was no provision for it. So, with a seven month old baby, I returned to shiftwork. Breasts aching and overflowing, I found some international directive which allowed women breastfeeding breaks at work, but how could I feed my baby if he was not there and where were the facilities? The concerns of women were not on the agenda.

I thought that I was totally accepted by now, by management and union alike, but one day, after I had done nine years on the platform, I received a phone call from the secretary of the NUR Sectional Council who sounded very worried. He had had a phone call from the area manager, who told him: 'I've got that Caroline Stephens!' I was accused of having falsified my timesheet and claimed pay when I had not been there. When I checked the details, it turned out that I had been at a union meeting on that day and the management had not noted this. It was a salutary reminder of the fact that some people didn't want me to the extent that they would sack me, despite all the efforts I had made to get on with everyone and fit in. This was to haunt me for the rest of my railway career.

The union's divisional officer negotiated a day job for me as a numbertaker in Clapham Yard as recompense. It was a relief not to be on shift work, but the job was deadly boring. I had to walk around the yard and write down the numbers of the carriages and wagons and enter them into a tracking system so that someone, somewhere would know where things were. Despite my having four A levels and a degree in mathematics, the system made no sense to me at all.

The shunters' cabin was above the pointsman's cabin in the middle of the tracks and, when there was no work to do, the shunters would lie down on the hard wooden benches at the side of this cabin and snooze or engage in banter or insulting each other. The walls were covered with pictures of naked women with their legs spread open, but there was no point my making an issue of it because I didn't want to alienate the men. There was a particularly nasty, aggressive shunter who said something really offensive to me one day, as I also lay in the manner of the men, with my back propped up against the wall and my feet up on the wooden bench. He showed me some pornographic magazines and said he liked big tits and that he could f*** me up and down like this (with actions) for hours. I told him to eff off, and he grabbed my legs and forced them apart and said he'd pull me apart like an effing wishbone. There was another man there who didn't do anything, but he saw it; perhaps if he had not have been there, my attacker would have done more. He got off me and I burst into tears, ran down the stairs to the pointsman's cabin and told the supervisor what had happened. He couldn't look me in the eye. He said: 'That's terrible, swearing at a woman.' He'd missed the point that I'd been sexually assaulted, and had no way of dealing with it. I went to see the personnel manager at Waterloo and told him all about it. He asked me to give him the man's name, but I decided not to, because I was the man's union representative and I didn't want to alienate the people I represented or get the man sacked. Later on, I was to work on BR's policy on sexual harassment and would find that this sort of incident was not uncommon. Looking back now, I am amazed at what I was prepared to accept so as not to rock the boat.

In 1986, after two years in the shunting yard, I noticed a job advertised for a tutor with the Youth Training Scheme (YTS). I talked with my husband, without whom I couldn't have sustained my extremely low paid railway 'career', and we agreed that it was time for me to get a 'proper job'. The job was teaching life and social skills. The grading system at that time was Railman (sic), Leading Railman, Senior Railman, Chargeman, Supervisor A, B, C, D, E, so when I got the job, I jumped six grades to Supervisor D. I was well qualified for the job but, being a woman, the word went round that I had slept with somebody to get it. Although I remained secretary of Battersea No. 1 branch, the rumour made me feel awkward about having a leaving party so, after 11 years of working there and helping hundreds of people, my leaving was not marked in any way, and this made me very sad.

The new job was very exciting. I was part of a team of 14 other trainers, all men except three women. I attended a Day Release Certificate in Training course, where I met trainers from other industries. Most of them were women and I found it really strange and enjoyable to be in an all-women group. I didn't realise how starved I had been intellectually until I got involved in this further education. It seemed as if I spent one day a week in the real world. I had got so used to being a railwayman, that the rest of the world seemed a little strange. I had to travel round to the different schemes and teach the trainees about sex, drugs and rock and roll. This turned out to be harder than I expected. The spotty youths in question, mainly boys with the odd girl thrown in, didn't like the classroom. It reminded them of school, from which they had just escaped and they didn't like talking about the personal stuff I was supposed to engage them in. I didn't have to wear a uniform and I suddenly found it excruciating wearing dresses and skirts and attempting to look smart in 'normal' clothes. Somebody gave me a knee-length black-belted long-sleeved dress with a sort of scarf attached to it which you tied in a bow at the neck. I felt uneasy in it, maybe the trainees picked up on this and a couple of them said I looked like a prostitute in it. It was another salutary reminder of my femaleness and their maleness, even though they were only 16.

Equal Opportunities (EO) was an integral part of the YTS. I read training resources to do with gender at work with interest. With the support of my boss, I investigated male/female turnover and organised meetings of female trainees to provide support and training in EO. I learnt a lot from these meetings. The young women were very shy and their expectations were often lower than those of the young men.

When the scheme was devolved, I continued in the department as a divisional supervisory trainer. Now I was in an open-plan office and could see how the management side of things operated. Compared with the common culture I had been brought up in on the stations, I found the culture here rather weird. On the platform, it was all plain speaking; in the office, there was this veneer of teamwork and politeness, but underneath you didn't really know what was going on. In between teaching interviewing skills and so on, I continued on my mission of gathering women together and getting their voices heard as much as I could. This was accepted because now there was a BR EO manager and EO policy and various initiatives had been set up including a Return to Work Scheme. I was surprised to learn that there had been a Southern Region EO Steering Group, made up of all grades and functions, from 1986 to 1988, which had ceased for no apparent reason.

By 1990 EO initiatives for women on Southern Region had largely ground to a halt, with the exception of plans for a pilot women's development course. The number of women had not significantly increased, although there was no way of investigating this, because no monitoring systems were in place. There was no evidence that any initiatives had lasted or that any strategy was in place. There was no evidence that managers or supervisors understood EO for women or their responsibility under the law. No national EO policy was available at regional level. Few women knew that BR had an EO policy or manager and virtually none had heard of the Return to Work Scheme.

I asked if I could hold meetings with women to let them know about EO and find out if they had any concerns. This was a really exciting time for me, as I managed to get clerical women and women who were in men's jobs together. The women faced numerous problems. Lack of toilets was a major one. One woman was raped by a customer and was so upset by the manager's handling of this that she left the industry. Several had been humiliated in training school. One had been physically assaulted by male employees on three occasions and not reported it in case the men got the sack. One had had her body compared to a blow up doll. A woman was taunted that she could not lift heavy weights until she worked out a system to lift the item with a rope, at which point her foreman 'went crazy'. Several had been 'cornered' and had their breasts felt. Numerous women had left after having babies because they could not be accommodated. Some were subjected to constant verbal 'jokes', requests to 'go out' and male embarrassment at having to work with a woman. Even women who had been involved in initiatives for their own sex said that inconsistency in the progress of equal opportunities left them feeling distrustful and let down. Ethnic minority women were at a particular disadvantage on BR. They constituted 1% of the workforce and were concentrated in one of the dirtiest and lowest-paid jobs in the industry: carriage cleaning. Interviews with these women indicated total demoralisation, especially amongst the older West Indian population, many of whom had been employed by BR for many years. The highest graded black woman was a recently appointed chargewoman who had taken 30 years to get there. I proposed setting up women's support and discussion groups throughout the Southern and pilot groups were set up. Three male supervisors from the engineers department carried out research into sexual harassment on Southern Region in 1990. The project concluded that one in five women and one in twenty men had been sexually harassed. The most common form of harassment was verbal — 69%. Physical harassment was also high at 47%. One in five women felt that the harassment had affected their performance at work. A further one in five had taken time off as a direct result. All the cases of harassment took place at work and some continued outside work. Many women felt that the procedure for reporting incidents was inadequate, because in many cases the harassers were in positions of authority. Most women took the problem very seriously and felt that something needed to be done, whilst most men did not. Porn calendars tended to make the work environment intimidating and degrading for women and led to derogatory remarks and suggestions.

The BRB issued a draft policy on sexual harassment. I asked if I could get involved and was upgraded to MS2. After a year's work it was launched in April 1991. It was highly progressive and included training for all managers, a counselling system to support victims, women's support and discussion groups, and help for vulnerable and isolated women. This made it potentially difficult to introduce because it was so far ahead of current understanding and practice. An initiative called Quality through People was being launched, which encouraged staff who wanted to address a problem to get together and make recommendations. I managed to get women's and ethnic minority groups under this scheme. At last, this was official consultation on these issues. They found that women faced problems associated with being in a very small minority in a male-dominated industry. These problems were complex and divided into: sexual discrimination (including sexual harassment); racial discrimination; lack of training; lack of promotion; lack of support and counselling; problems related to child-bearing and child-care; sexist attitudes; physical danger and lack of adequate facilities. The key problem was outdated attitudes towards women and the key area for improvement was 'to change behaviour towards women and increase communication between workers and management'. Twenty-two of us presented this to the senior managers. It was agreed that an overall strategy was needed. This was one of the proudest moments of my life. It represented the first time that a group of senior managers, all white men with the exception of one white woman, had been addressed by a group of lower-graded staff, all of whom were women and 40% were ethnic minority. I felt that the voice of those carriage cleaners at Clapham Junction had finally been heard. The faces of the women were positively glowing.

We sent out a questionnaire on sexual harassment to the workforce, which supported previous findings. I set up training for managers and a counselling system for victims of sexual harassment and we introduced the sexual harassment policy on Southern Region.

This was a very exciting time and I felt that I was really making a difference for women.

Like all good things, it had to come to an end and I was dumped back into my Supervisory D training job. My new manager was a 24-year-old woman who had started as a YTS trainee. I had been brought up with the old BR culture, which said that time-serving was important. I had come up through the grades from Railman on the platform and found myself feeling like one of the old men would have felt: why should I be told what to do by a 24-year-old girl who had seen nothing of the industry? I set about my work grudgingly whilst putting in for as many promotions as I could. I had a Diploma in Training Management (NVQ Level 5) and was ready to be a training manager. Despite putting in for a lot of positions and the rapid promotion of many younger people, I didn't get any of the jobs. One training manager refused to employ me on the basis that I was 'difficult to manage' and had 'poor interpersonal skills'.

I became more disillusioned as I saw the sexual harassment policy and the women's initiatives falling apart. It had been flavour of the month and now they were on to new things. I made a complaint about my lack of promotion, but this didn't get anywhere, so I applied to an Industrial Tribunal, claiming discrimination under the Sex Discrimination Act and as a trade union representative. Suddenly I was appointed as a training manager in the Total Quality Management Initiative (TQM). I interviewed well for the job and would like to think that I got it on merit. Our job was to improve quality on the line from Waterloo to Exeter. Passengers became customers and we were to improve communications between different departments. I was again in a job which I found interesting and challenging. I believed in what we were doing — I had seen so much miscommunication at ground level — and wanted to make a better railway. I would like to think that TQM would have been set up anyway but, as it was, its job was to move the company towards privatisation, which I did not believe in.

After ten years as a union branch secretary, I resigned in 1992, so now I had firmly moved from change through union activity to change through management activity, but what is important is that I still felt that I was helping people on the ground. The TQM manager above me was lovely and we were going to do great things. I was to manage five trainers. We set up the training programme, but the goal posts kept changing and I didn't find managing a team easy. I went on a managing skills course and was doing fine until my lovely manager came to talk with me as part of the course. He said: 'You do know they don't want you'. I asked: 'Who?' and he replied: 'the management, they just don't want you.' I was mortified. I had tried so hard to adapt, to improve my skills. Earlier, I had been leaning over the photocopier when the personnel manager (nipple-substitute cigar smoker) for whom I had introduced the Sexual Harassment Policy, pinched my bottom and said: 'Let me sexually harass you.' He always used to comment on my clothes and do things like tap me on the head with his pen. I had become used to this sort of thing, but felt it was demeaning. I was used to sexual harassment of course and, when I had been on the YTS, one of the trainers had touched my breast, I just told him off. But what do you do when the Executive Officer for whom you have introduced a policy on sexual harassment for 21,000 staff, pinches your bottom? I did what the policy told us to do: I went to see his manager, who happened to be the Divisional Director. 'What do you want me to do?' he asked. I said 'Nothing, but I want you to know.' The policy provided for confidentiality of complaints and agreed action with the complainant, but he must have told the man concerned because he said: 'You badmouthed me', and didn't talk to me for a year.

The following year I took three weeks leave and, when I returned, my job had gone and I had been seconded to the safety department to help with the safety validation in preparation for privatisation. TQM was nearly over and who knows whether I should have been honoured or insulted at my move? Maybe that's the way all managers are treated. Once again, my job was to be sent out amongst the staff on the ground, to interview them and make a report on safety. I suppose I should be proud that I as a woman could slip into any messroom and converse easily and be trusted by those people, but I felt disappointed that I had been taken off the other job. The new organisation was set up and my job was gone. I was offered a lower grade retail trainer's job. I asked the Divisional Director 'Is there a place for me in this organisation?' He replied: 'Sometimes there's square pegs in round holes in organisations.'

I decided to take redundancy. I thought there would be a few more weeks for me to come to terms with leaving the workplace I had had this love-hate relationship with for 18 years, but no sooner had I made the decision than I received a letter saying: 'Thank you for your service; we will require you no more from Monday.' I felt devastated. No one seemed to care that I was leaving; in fact some people must have been pleased to get rid of me. I had no retirement party and that was the end of my railway career.

Looking back, I wonder whether we achieved anything. But at least, if a woman works as a driver, manager or guard, she is going to earn much more than being a carriage cleaner. I think there were more changes to the railway during this period than in any other time and that young women expect more than they used to and will put up with less. I hope it was all worth it. I still feel part of the railway family and have lifelong friends there.

Eleven years later, Caroline works as a Yoga and Pilates teacher. Her son is 22 and her daughter, eight.

Pennie Bellas – First Female Station Manager

I didn't set out to be a railway manager, I hardly thought of railways at all. Then came the graduate 'milkround' and the need to get a job. My degree was Economics and Industrial Relations but I didn't see myself as an economist and was drawn to general management.

The interview for British Rail fell on my 21st birthday, which made me consider quite seriously whether to go or not. The gentleman who interviewed me was charming and 'old school' and addressed me as 'my dear' throughout. At one point in the interview he asked me what job I would see myself doing at the end of the 18 month training scheme. Having read the brochure, I said that being a station manager had appeal. He laughed and said 'Well my dear, I'm told we must take ladies now as Traffic Management Trainees, but we certainly don't have them as Station Managers.' That was it, a red rag to a bull, having been told I couldn't do something, it became a challenge I had to accept.

Six months later I was through the two-day assessment at Westfield College and at The Grove, Watford, being inducted as one of 24 management trainees, the class of 1978 having three other women. Interestingly none of us had any previous links to the railway and we were all to marry railwaymen.

The training scheme was a mixed bag. It involved a tour round all the railway departments with spells at The Grove and occasionally the operations training centre at Crewe. Time spent in the Divisional Manager's Office tended to be the most frustrating. With hindsight, the almost annual imposition of a trainee who knew nothing, but in a few years would be senior to many of the people there, must have caused some resentment. Certainly some people who were supposedly 'training' me were inclined to have me just sit in a corner and read files/manuals etc. Others went out of their way to introduce me to interesting people and situations which stood me in good stead later. In general, training out on the areas was the best part, it was practical and many people I came into contact with were passionate about what they did.

Reactions to my being a woman were mixed. Some were patronising, some didn't make an issue of it at all and others clearly enjoyed it. The chief reservation was whether a woman would have the strength to 'lift the buckeye', a coupling link weighing some 110 lbs. A kind shunter at New Cross Gate showed me the technique and after that I demonstrated it successfully on a number of occasions. I probably hold the record for being the person who has most often lifted a buckeye. Did I ever actually need to do it operationally? Of course not!

Other concerns expressed were about going into dark tunnels or dealing with suicides. I pointed out that police women or nurses had to deal with similar issues and that I was no more squeamish or afraid of the dark than any male colleague. The only area where I conceded being female would be an issue was if one was heavily pregnant and on-call. Call outs could involve long track walks, sliding down burning embankments or chasing vandals. This might be impractical when pregnant, but I wasn't planning on motherhood at that point, so it was a non-issue.

Being a female operations trainee often caught people by surprise. I was almost physically removed from the drivers' cab of a train after a signalman had seen me and phoned the next station to report 'a woman in the cab'. It was assumed I was the driver's girlfriend. Another driver who got a rude surprise was one who picked me up from a signal in a cutting which I'd be flagging following a failure. The weather was dreadful so I had my hair tucked up into my hat and my collar turned up. As I climbed into the cab the driver saw the opportunity of company to vent his frustration at the state of the railway, the weather, management etc. Having let him vent his spleen I removed my hat and shook my hair out — his face was a picture, his comment unprintable.

Towards the end of the training scheme I was seconded to do a project for the chief executive on Gatwick Express. I really enjoyed that because it was a real problem to get my teeth into rather than the old chestnut which always got given to trainees and in which no-one had any real interest. It also brought me into regular contact with the station manager at Gatwick Airport, whom I married in December 1981. Despite all the jokes about 'marrying above one's station' and how long my 'train' would be we are still together 24 years later, and our son is just off to university to read Transport Planning so we are possibly founding a railway dynasty.

It was my appointment as station manager in Burgess Hill — 'The first woman Station Manager' — which brought my 15 minutes of fame. *Railnews* had run a couple of pieces about female trainees, though the emphasis seemed to be on our decorative qualities rather than competence. Despite this preoccupation with appearance the system had been totally unable to provide me with a uniform.

Male station managers wore made-to-measure black suits with a fine white pinstripe. The plan for women was a fetching pale blue which looked more like an air hostess outfit and would be totally impractical. Eventually it was conceded that I should have a suit similar to the men's, but it wasn't ready in time for the my appointment so I wore a grey suit and purloined a rail air hostess hat and sewed my three gold 'Station Manager' rings onto it. I was later to inherit my predecessor's 'carnival hat' which was the most practical for wearing on the track and later still a bowler for meeting royal trains etc.

The day of my appointment was obviously a 'slow news' day. I ended up on the front page of most of the UK dailies and even have cuttings from papers from far flung places such as the *Sydney Sun Herald* and the *Johannesburg Star*. Best of all, several cartoons appeared in the press and the divisional manager tried unsuccessfully to buy the original Giles one for me. This coverage was later to bring interviews whenever people were writing about 'first women', a lot of requests for after dinner speaking, and invitations to events such as the Women of the Year lunch. This latter I attended with Gill Fisher who was a 1977 trainee and had become the first woman assistant Station Manager at Redhill while I was still in training.

Pennie Bellas. *RAILNEWS*

What expectations did people have of a woman station manager? Mixed I think. A lot expected stereotypically female preoccupations and suggested I would hang gingham curtains in the waiting rooms. Others thought a woman might be more 'person' focussed rather than 'train' focussed and that this would be good for customer service. My staff, 20 men, were chuffed to find themselves in the papers and interviewed by TV and radio.

The passengers were very welcoming and dealing with angry passengers turned out to be where being female was an advantage, almost alone of my colleagues I was never hit or physically intimidated and most muted their verbal abuse.

Interestingly it was some of my fellow station managers who were probably the most resentful of my appointment. One pointed out that it lowered their perceived status that a 'slip of a girl' was doing a job they had worked up to over twenty, thirty or even forty years. A few were deliberately unhelpful, refusing to speak to me or even setting traps for me to fall into. I was also the recipient of volumes of pornography, presumably as a reminder of what my role as a woman should be.

I wanted to show that I was serious about being a railway operator and so embarked on the London University Certificate and then Diploma in Transport as well as attending the Railway Study Association lectures. Through these I met people who helped and mentored me and was delighted to emerge from the diploma with the highest mark of my year group despite being seven months pregnant when I took the final exam. I came to enjoy attending talks that started 'Pennie and Gentlemen'.

My subsequent jobs on BR included a move to Liverpool Street as Travel Manager, Station Manager and acting as Area Passenger Manager, during which time I discovered that my real love was training people. At this point an opportunity arose to be Director of Studies at The Grove and so I found myself back at my first entry point helping to train the graduates of 1984. I spent four years there, during which I had my son and started my MBA at Henley. That showed me that the skills I had developed as a manager, trainer and internal consultant were transferable and I resigned from BR on my 31st birthday – ten years to the day after that first interview.

Anne Winter – First Female Train Driver

I should have realised it wouldn't be easy when I rang BR's Wimbledon office in the summer of 1979 to ask if it was possible for a woman to be a train driver, and was answered by hysterical laughter. My interview was not a comfortable experience. I sat at a desk opposite the Area Depot Manager and one other and answered questions and listened as they seemingly tried to put me off the job. Luckily, I'd been to my local library and read up about my prospective duties, so I was able to answer their questions. Much was made of the danger and loneliness of the job and the lack of toilet facilities for women was discussed as well as very personal questions about my periods and how I thought I'd manage without toilet facilities all shift. At the end I was asked if I still wanted the job and when I said 'Yes' I was offhandedly told: 'Well, go for your medical then.'

At 9 a.m. on 6th August 1979 I began my first day. As I left the Assistant Depot Manager's office at Victoria, the clerical officer said: 'I wouldn't be you for all the tea in China'. On arrival at Norwood Junction depot I found that certain individuals took delight in increasing their swearing in front of me or being crude. I was very offended by this. I went to the training school and was in a class with another female who was on her second attempt. I was treated fairly well, but during meal breaks it was implied to me by a number of trainees that no woman would ever be allowed to pass out as a driver. I found that very upsetting and threatening.

In December 1979 I passed out as a Driver's Assistant, or 'Secondman'. I spent two and a half very happy years at Norwood. I hated taking annual leave and could not wait to return to work. I was treated very well although all the time I was aware that I was different from the others. It was as if I'd suddenly obtained lots of dads and big brothers. No doubt was ever voiced to me about my eventually making the grade of driver; it was an automatic assumption that I would one day be working with them as an equal.

Being new, and as a woman in the industry, it took many years for me to feel I could request my rights and so I was rather a downtrodden member of the grade. The general attitude was that, as a female, I would not be around long enough to warrant the expense of toilets or regular uniform issue. Having no uniform, I was once accused of being the driver's girlfriend, along for the ride. Whereas my colleagues' uniforms arrived automatically, for about ten years mine did not. When I questioned the uniform stores I was told that, as a woman, there was some doubt as to how long I would be staying in the job and so it would be necessary for me to submit a uniform request annually.

I transferred to Waterloo in the summer of 1982. Then began six months of extreme stress and excitement as we headed towards those three days of exams which would decide whether we were to be drivers or not. For myself and the other female there was the added pressure that all eyes were on us waiting to see if one of us would be the first woman to qualify as a train driver on BR. A number of juvenile characters tried to whip up competition between us, even comparing our looks and lying about what one of us had said about the other. We got on very well and agreed to ignore their lies. The other woman took her exams three months before me but she failed. Even so, she helped me with my studying. After I passed out on 17th February 1983, she presented me with a congratulatory card and a Paddington Bear, which she had dressed up in a train driver's uniform. When she passed out I gave her a Class 33 loco model. We were both very much aware of what we had achieved. All of us who were in competition to be the first woman driver were being carefully monitored by the various Press Officers across the country, and there is no doubt that I was the first to qualify.

I had another medical and started my road learning, and waited to work my first train. It seemed an eternity before my first solo drive. The longer I waited the more nervous I got. Eventually on Sunday May 1st 1983 I told the supervisor that if he did not give me a train to work soon I didn't think I would be able to do it! At 22.31 I found myself setting off for Kingston on my own. I'll never forget it. I kept looking over to the secondman's seat because I couldn't believe I was really on my own. I was on a high: totally elated when I returned to Waterloo. To this day I am still thrilled to be paid to do a job I love.

Once I got my driving job my colleagues definitely started to take me more seriously, but management were a different story. I have been patronised when raising a genuine safety concern. I have experienced problems with management, which have been due to their perceptions of male psychology, which don't apply to women. Male pride dictates that men don't usually ask for help until they are just about at breaking point. Women, in the main, looking ahead and seeing a problem arising would start making plans to alleviate it, which probably involves approaching someone in authority. Being used to dealing with men, authority tends to go into 'headless chicken' mode when approached by a woman requesting help with something which has yet to become a problem. The person responsible for welfare was the same person responsible for discipline, and if approached with a welfare problem they often remove the person from the track. It is a ludicrous situation. Female drivers tend to seek help on our own or elsewhere.

For a few years women were invited to attend women drivers' workshops. These were intended to gain women's input on how BR could attract more women to the grade and how more flexibility and support for all drivers could be included in the proposed drivers' restructuring. The woman who ran these workshops spent a year putting together a full report for the BRB with the help of external consultants and equal opportunities experts. When it was submitted, it was ignored and none of her proposals or findings was implemented. The two main points were the lack of flexible arrangements for people with dependants, and lack of flexibility regarding depot transfers for welfare reasons.

The latter became an issue for me in 1990-91. I was married to an MOD police dog-handler who was moved to Salisbury and required to live there. I applied for a transfer to Salisbury depot on compassionate grounds. This was declined. My doctor, seeing the early signs of trouble with my health, wrote to BR, but to no avail. Travelling 101 miles each way every working day around my shifts took its toll, and I was getting about 4 hours sleep in each 24 hour period. After a year I suffered a nervous breakdown and my doctor, who was furious at what had happened, told me I would not be returning to work until I could work locally. My illness had been totally avoidable. Had BR heeded my doctor's warnings I would not have suffered that dreadful condition and they would not have been paying me to be unproductive for three months. During those three months I did not receive a single letter or phone call from my manager enquiring how I was. The strong loyalty I had felt for BR since 1979 was gone. It never returned. Luckily my transfer to Salisbury, under the normal transfer procedures, came about in October 1991 and the next month I returned to work. I was warned that it would take two or three years to recover fully, which was true. It was a sad chapter in my life and I am still angry because it was totally avoidable.

At the current time morale is low in both sexes and most grades due to uncertainty about privatisation.* Private companies will not promote people by seniority, which is traditional on the railways, and I think women will be treated unfairly as a result. Companies in the business of making money, when faced with two candidates – a woman of childbearing age or with family responsibilities, and a man – will choose the man. In the run up to privatisation people are increasingly willing to turn a blind eye to potential dangers or unfair practices. We are all very aware that nobody wants to be labelled a troublemaker: people who take the risk and raise their heads above the parapet are likely to get them shot off.

Despite everything, I'm doing a job I love and am proud of, and nowhere outside will you find such a feeling of community as you do on the railway. You can be lost in any town in Great Britain, but if you make your way to the nearest railway station and say you're staff, you will be given the customary cup of tea and help will be heaped on you.

Sandie Arscott – Station, Crossing and Office Worker

> Sandie Arscott is a real traffic stopper. All she has to do is come out of her office and she can halt a line of cars. And they don't move again until the pretty, 26-year-old redhead gives the go-ahead.
>
> *Ipswich Mercury*, 3 December 1987.

I spent almost nine years on the railway, beginning as platform staff at Southend Central in 1986, when I was in my mid 20s. I and another lady were about the only railwaywomen in the area. She didn't stay very long, as we used to get 'stick' from some of the male staff, and others would 'pull our legs' a lot. I really enjoyed the work and was determined to stay despite the 'ups and downs' with the males. I ended up getting on with most of them in that area as I used to go to other stations for overtime.

In 1987 I became a crossing keeper on the Felixstowe branch. I absolutely loved it. In fact I would say it is the best job I have ever had in my life, I would go back to it like a shot if they still had manned crossings in this area. It wouldn't be everyone's cup of tea; you need to be able to stand your own company for quite long periods of time; but there were times when the public would stop and chat and then during a quiet period the signalman would invite me up for a coffee and a natter.

The first time I was on nights was at a very small crossing on a country road. All you had there was a very small hut to sit in right at the side of line. I had shut the gates, gone back into the hut and was waiting for the train to pass through. It was pitch black and all I could hear was this rumble. At first I couldn't see anything out of the window. The noise got louder and louder and then I could see a light in the distance getting bigger.

The ground was then starting to shake and within seconds the hut was rocking from

* Britain's railways were privatised in 1994.

side to side. The light outside was on top of me now, clear through the window, just one single light. I thought my days were numbered; the train was so close I thought it was coming straight through the little hut. That was my first experience of a class 37 diesel engine with about 25 wagons behind it. I soon came to love these magnificent engines — I even got to have a ride in one. Even now if I hear the sound of one it makes the hairs go up the back of my neck.

Sadly I stayed on the crossings only for a year: I was made redundant as all the gates were automated along that line. I went to Ipswich as the Train Crew Supervisors' Assistant. I was the only lady there amongst 150 men, and all bar two or three of them treated me like a queen. I had almost five years of fun and made many friends, some I still have to this day. Unfortunately for me I had attracted a stalker. I wasn't aware of it until I went to the train crew depot where he worked. This however wasn't going to spoil things for me and I carried on as normal enjoying my job and social events that the NUR used to lay on for us.

My job came to an end when they decided to cut down on most of the staff at the depot. I went to the stores at Liverpool St. It wasn't too bad if you were busy, but the afternoons would drag and my colleague and I ended up each day clearing all the shelves and completely sorting out the stores. This caused me to get a chest infection that turned so bad I was left with asthma. It was due to working in the basement with recycled air, the dust we had created through clearing all the filthy shelves and also the dust that comes off the brakes as the trains pulled into Liverpool St. On top of all this my stalker had followed me, found where I was working and was sending letters to me.

I was moved to an office over at Ilford, working for Freight Infrastructure. I hated working in an office, full of 'office type' people, I was getting extremely run down and ill with having to get up at 5 a.m. and not getting home until 7.30 p.m. — if the trains were running on time. I took redundancy. I had had enough and the railway wasn't what it used to be with all the privatisation going on. I had also had enough of looking over my shoulder every day I travelled to work with my stalker still at large, but the railway did one last big favour to me, that was make this man who had been pestering me for seven years sign an agreement never to come near me, or try to contact me again.

I had good times and bad times, but if I could do it all again I would, only not now: the railway has been totally ruined, gone are the old days and they'll never come back.

Susie Bosworth Brown – Conductor-Guard at Bletchley

When asked what I wanted to do when I left school, I replied 'a railway guard'. This was unheard of and met with disapproval. My grandfather worked in Signals & Telegraphs and because my father was a guard at Rugby I already knew about the job and I'd been to work with him a couple of times.

In August 1989, aged 17, I became a booking office clerk with Network Southeast. Working at Northampton I got to know a lot of guards and drivers as they picked up their pay packets or paid in fares collected. When I finished late shift I often sat talking to the guard while travelling home to Rugby. From my booking office window I could see trains arrive and depart and felt closed-in behind the toughened glass, so I decided to make the change and get out.

Aged 19 I applied to be a guard and was invited to Watford for some tests and an interview. I was accepted and told I would be based at Bletchley and would work trains from London Euston to Birmingham New Street, Bletchley to Bedford and Bletchley to Aylesbury. I then found out that my father had asked my manager to turn me down. When everyone knew I had been accepted I was told stories of the terrible things that went on and advised to be a driver as it was a lot safer than being a guard. I stood my ground and in April 1991 was transferred to Bletchley.

I spent a couple of days assisting the train crew supervisor and was then sent out with various drivers on various jobs. Imagine my excitement when one of them asked if I wanted to have a go at driving! I was so nervous but at the same time proud that I was driving a big Class 31 loco with four carriages all the way from Wolverton works to Willesden. But I had to keep it quiet, as it wasn't allowed. I also spent a few days with a guard on a job with local trips. He found me a smock and gloves and showed me how to couple up and do brake tests. Then he allowed me to do it all myself. Now I felt I was proving a point as many people said I wouldn't be able to couple a train together.

I was introduced to the only other female guard at Bletchley, who advised me to keep my life to myself and not get involved with anyone. (Oh, how I wish I'd listened.) I was sent to Waterloo to pick up a new uniform and it made me stand out from the men. Their shirts were white with blue stripes and mine blue with white stripes.

On the guards' course in June 1991 I was the only female. The course involved weeks of learning the Rule Book, so we would know what to do in the event of any emergency, and practical training in coupling up locos, lifting a buckeye and assessing freight trains to make up a TOPS list (Total Operations Processing system.). I had to train for both passenger and freight and it was hard work. I was treated by the males as 'one of the lads' but various female staff asked: 'What do you want to do a job like that for?'

Unfortunately when it came for us to take our rules and regulations examination the whole group failed and we were retrained by guards' instructors. Second time around, we all passed. We learned the routes, gaining knowledge of stations, sidings, crossings and announcement landmarks. One instructor said to use a field with chickens in, but the following day the field was empty! We walked around all the sidings, pulling points, climbing in and out of different rolling stock and performing numerous brake tests. Our last bit of training was to have knowledge of the 321 electric multiple units. At weekends we would go out on engineering trains and the overhead wiring train to learn about possessions. The most frequent question asked was: 'what are you going to do when you need the loo?' to which I replied: 'have a strong bladder, drink little tea and hope there is a station nearby; if all that fails find a discreet bush.'

It needed a lot of confidence to walk into the mess-room on my own with all those men who would look round at anyone who walked in. It was male territory and I was intruding. It was dirty with teabags stuck on the ceiling and stained with nicotine but it was normal to them. When I gained more confidence I began joining in conversations and numerous people attempted to teach me various card games but I just couldn't get the hang of them. I enjoyed talking to the older drivers (some were ex-steam men); they could sit and talk all day about the 'good old days'. The language in the mess-room improved so much when I was around as many men were embarrassed to swear in front of a 'young girl'.

There was a male staff toilet, but women had to cross the overbridge to the other side of the station and use the public toilets. Eventually this was addressed and the staff toilets were totally rebuilt to include two for females. The RMT representatives at the grand opening jokingly said they would get some fluffy seat covers and how lucky us girls were to have our own toilet when all the men had to share. Our locker room was shared and many men used to cycle into work and change into uniform there. I used to feel uncomfortable when catching someone with no trousers on.

I was well known and knew staff from all over the network. Station staff would come out and meet me if they knew which train I was on. One Asian railman would wait for me on the platform with fruit and Indian sweets. At Euston the railmen and supervisors would make me tea and coffee, wash up my mug and carry my bag out to the train and even open the cab door for me.

The good times were spoiled by the fact that I was seen as 'fair game' by some men. Many were quite forward, saying that they would like to have a 'good time' with me. Although quite flattered at first I soon became fed up with it. Worse, I was groped and had advances made whilst in the back cab or alone with a driver in the middle of nowhere. Sometimes they would lean across me to make announcements on the P.A. and would try to kiss me. One driver was very persistent and would not accept no for an answer. After a while I tried my best not to be alone with him anywhere. One late night, we were taking an empty train from Rugby to Bletchley and I was sitting with the driver – as everyone did – and we were caught up in a points failure. As we sat there in the dark, the driver got out of his seat and came over and tried to 'get friendly'. I pushed him away and he never spoke to me again. Years later, reading that other female guards had similar experiences reassured me that it hadn't been me attracting unwanted attention but it was the men. I'd been blaming myself for perhaps leading men on.

I was gossiped about and had supposedly been doing all sorts of things with many people. By the time I left I was supposed to have been with at least one man from every traincrew depot from London to Birmingham and countless managers. Graffiti started appearing on cab walls. I began swapping my day shifts for nights, partly in the hope that the gossip about me would die down.

I was battling with pain from a prolapsed disc but felt I had to carry on with freight work just to prove that I was up to the job. After I had an operation the railway doctor restricted me to passenger work only, and many colleagues saw this as me getting out of the heavy, dirty work associated with freight and engineering trains. (Unfortunately I am disabled now because of recurring prolapsed discs in my lower back.)

Some men were genuine friends (I think). I went on a depot trip to Newbury horse racing, and I was the only female on the bus. Everyone looked after me. The one thing that made it a special day was no one tried it on.

Once I found a guy sitting in an empty first class compartment on an otherwise full train openly playing with himself. My driver radioed for the police to meet us. The passengers began complaining about the delay, and my driver asked one of them: 'What would you do if he'd done that in front of your wife?' I was quite surprised that he had defended me. It was a different reaction when we got back to Bletchley. I had to make out a report and then the jokes and crude remarks came out and it went on for days.

The management announced that they were phasing out guards and increasing the number of conductors. I applied but was turned down with no reason being given. Some months later, without notice, I was sent on a conductors' course, where I met a woman from St Pancras whom our train crew leader took under his wing. A year later a female guard accused him of sexual harassment during her training. He lost his job and no one would speak openly to her.

I was the first female conductor in our area. The passengers accepted it well and the male ones would try and use their charm to avoid paying if caught without a ticket. So I'd flirt back until they paid.

Certain drivers I worked with called me a jinx, as something would always happen. I was involved in an accident at Euston: my driver had a heart attack approaching the platforms and the train ran in to the stops and pushed them back a fair way. We were lucky as it was at low speed. The joke was we were trying to make a cross-London link.

I tried to learn everything about the 321 units just so I didn't have to ask a man how to reset the doors or the heating etc. I had a good knowledge of most things, as I was not going to give anyone the satisfaction of saying I couldn't do my job. A lot of men offered to couple-up trains for me but I always refused and did it myself. Most drivers let me drive if we had an empty train.

I met my husband, Paul, whilst working. He was a conductor at Birmingham and one of my supervisors tried his best to get me on duties that would give me a bit of time there. When I worked the 'Nightmare' train Paul would sometimes spend the shift with me. A few colleagues warned him that he'd better look after me and treat me right. When in 1995 we announced we were getting married, some men thought they would give it a final try and volunteered to be my 'last fling'.

Looking back, I miss the job. I enjoyed the freedom of being given a list of trains to work and being left alone and trusted with such responsibility. I loved seeing the countryside change day by day. My favourite time of the year was when it was frosty and misty in the early morning. I can still see the green flashes from the pantograph as it runs under the overhead wires. When it was foggy all you could see was red mist glowing from the tail lights. When I left, in 1996, I knew of at least ten female drivers and conductors. I wonder how they are treated now.

Sarah Friday – Guard and Driver

I left school in 1984 with a couple of 'A' levels and, after working in several government departments, I was bored with office work, fed up with the nine-to-five routine and the inanity of office politics. My brother's job a secondman at Hither Green sounded much more exciting than mine so I applied for a guard's vacancy at Waterloo. This was the beginning of my 12 year career in train crew.

I did not tell my family I had applied. I was apprehensive about it myself and thought they might try to put me off. In fact I very nearly ended up with another office job; initially I was mistakenly interviewed for a job in the offices. It crossed my mind that perhaps I should not say anything and let the interview run its course, but I summoned up courage and the interviewer (to her credit) encouraged me to go for the guard's vacancy.

After I started my guards training course I told my family. They were surprised, and concerned about how I would cope with the shift work and travelling up and down to London at all hours of the day and night (I lived 25 miles from London).

I found the course a struggle because it was all new to me. The biggest challenge was lifting the buckeye coupling. If we could not do this we would not pass, so drastic steps were necessary: underneath my overall I wore a brand new padded jacket. I thought that the padding would help; it did, but the jacket was ruined by grease from the buckeye. Thus was I plunged into the wonderful world of the railway.

It was invigorating to have rejected the monotony of the nine-to-five routine;

however, much of the work was not, and I got to the stage where I could not get on a train without a book or a newspaper to keep me from boredom. A perk of the job was the amount of free time within a duty to look round the shops. I began to appreciate the history of the railway and loved hearing stories about the times when rail workers were 'really militant', and about the characters they had known over the years.

One highlight was working the early morning paper train. I loved riding in the drivers cab and watching the sun rise over the New Forest and I could not believe I was getting paid for this. I was finished by about 11 a. m. (if not earlier) and had the rest of the day to myself.

But all was not wonderful, I did encounter problems; these were fuelled by a guard whose amorous advances I rejected. As a result he made my life hell and encouraged his workmates to do likewise. There was graffiti about me on the brakevan walls. I started to go out with a guard who was a popular mess room character. As a result many of my tormentors backed off.

Some of the managers were very creepy, one particularly serious and austere guards' training manager came to life when he saw me in my guard's uniform for the first time and even asked me to 'do a twirl'. A supervisor made me recoil by putting his arm around me when trying to persuade me to work a train not on my roster. When I did not succumb to his persuasive charms he made sure that he 'stitched me up' whenever he could. Later I heard he had bothered a woman his previous depot, and rather than dealing with this management had simply moved him to Waterloo. A few years later he harassed a new woman guard, and told her to keep quiet if she wanted any overtime.

In 1990 I applied for a driver's job. It was purely a practical decision, not because I wanted to be a woman pioneer. It meant more money and it was rumoured that guards would be made redundant owing to driver only operation (DOOP). I was the third woman driver at Waterloo (there were about 150 drivers at the depot, and only about 26 women drivers in the whole country) and consequently there was still animosity towards women coming into the grade. The animosity was compounded because of the Train Crew Concept of 1988. This gave guards the opportunity to apply for drivers' vacancies.

ASLEF opposed it because it reduced the driver training period from about five years to a year and abolished the old 'secondman' system of training drivers. Opening the grade to guards meant opening it to black and women workers. The hold of white working class men on the grade was broken. The first guards to be promoted were resented because of the reduction in the time spent training and known as 'boil-in-the-bags' or 'muppets'. When I qualified this resentment led to drivers' refusing to let us learn roads with them. Unlike some of the men I passed out with I decided I was not going to be intimidated and decided to take my breaks in the drivers' room. Initially it was not pleasant because of antagonism towards 'boil in the bags' and to women. Apparently a couple of female train drivers had (for unknown reasons) worked during a strike ('scabbed') and so the drivers were suspicious that we would be 'scabs', too. Most drivers came round in the end, probably because much of the control rail workers have over the horrible shifts is achieved through changing duties with others. So in the long run it was in their best interests to be on good terms with the 'muppets', the 'boil-in-the-bags' and the women.

Some men acted peculiarly when I was in the mess-room; one in particular always made a great play of not having done his trousers up properly after coming out of the toilet, pretending that he had not noticed me and then making a big show of doing up his flies.

The flip side of the problems I encountered in the mess room was the privileged position I found myself in, of being a woman in a male environment. Away from the bravura of the mess room some of the men would open up to me, and I had some fascinating discussions with them, particularly in relation to their view of women's lives. I am not sure that I could have had this sort of relationship and known men in this way through any other circumstances. This was in part the extreme nature of the shifts we worked, working with people through the night or in the early morning means you get to know them in a different way than you would in the normal nine-to-five routine and also, because I was a woman in their environment, they dropped their guard and talked in a way they would not have done in any other situation.

I was driving for a couple of years before I learnt the route to Weymouth, this became my favourite route and it bought home the perks of working on the railway. I was getting paid to drive through glorious countryside on beautiful summer days, and even had some time to spend on the beach when I got there. Weymouth was also special because I had a toilet built especially for me in the depot as I was the first woman to work trains there; I was very keen to christen it! My local union reps had maintained that I could not sign for the route until the toilet was built. My reps were good: they fought hard for us women. They were also concerned that women drivers would not be able to carry the emergency evacuation ladder on the new trains on the Waterloo and City line and put it in place from the front door of the train to the track, because it was too heavy. One rep suggested that there should be a separate ladder for women, this caused much amusement in the mess room, along the lines of perhaps the ladder should be painted pink or have ribbons on it. But no concessions were made, and women had to lift and put the ladder in place in order to pass the training. In a scene reminiscent to me of lifting the buckeye coupling the instructor and the other trainees stood and watched as I struggled. I managed to get the ladder out of the train, but had problems in controlling it while I held it above my head and trying to put it in place. The others were instructed not to help; as it was, they had to jump out of the way to avoid being whacked on the head with the ladder. Finally, I managed to get it into position.

The display of pornographic pictures, magazines and movies was something I felt uncomfortable with. In the guards' room it was not too bad: if a porn picture went up on the wall, one of the men would usually take it down (on the grounds that as women used the mess room they should not put such pictures on the wall). In the drivers' room it was more of a problem, particularly in relation to porn movies. What I disliked was their embarrassment when I walked into the mess room: they would scramble to switch off the movie before I saw it. I stopped going into the room and did not return until they stopped watching the movies. About seven years later it started up again. I did not see why I should have to keep away from the mess-room. I phoned my union rep to ask if he could sort it out without mentioning my name. The next day I went into work and the whole depot knew I had complained! After getting over the ribbing, the reaction was supportive. The men stopped watching porn, but I found out that this was because a man had complained and management had the system fixed so they could no longer do so.

My life became very wrapped up in the railway culture, principally because the shift work restricted us to socialising with other railway staff. I spent quite a lot of time in Waterloo railway club, an insalubrious place which, like much of the railway, was hide-bound by hierarchical structures. There was a section of the bar where the drivers stood, another just for guards and a padded table reserved for the old West Indian guys to play dominoes. Because I was a driver going out with a guard I was usually in the guards' section of the bar.

Another part of the railway culture was trade unionism. I became involved in the NUR and switched to ASLEF when I became a driver and became assistant secretary of Waterloo Nine Elms branch. ASLEF negotiated a deal that increased our working week to 66 hours and our working day to up to 11 hours. We could now work a maximum of seven hours before a break and that break might be as short as 30 minutes, even in an 11-hour duty. The deal also meant other railway workers would lose their jobs. I realised that ASLEF were giving up terms and conditions that drivers had spent over hundred years fighting for as well as selling other rail workers' jobs.

Because of this I left ASLEF and rejoined the RMT, becoming Health and Safety Representative and branch chair. ASLEF negotiated with South West Trains for driver only operation (DOOP) on passenger trains. I was concerned that guards would lose their jobs, and that drivers would have to do two jobs. My branch opposed DOOP very successfully and, after winning a region-wide ballot for industrial action, South West Trains withdrew their proposals. But I was to pay the price for humiliating the company.

In my view, South West Trains were keen to recruit women drivers because they thought we would be more compliant than men, less union orientated and more likely to break strikes, but we did the opposite. I launched a campaign to highlight the detrimental impact the extension of our working hours had on railway safety. I doubt whether many managers had met a female trade union rep before. They did not know how to deal with me. I took grave offence when the Train Crew Manager called me a girl (I was 35) and submitted a claim to an Industrial Tribunal of sexual discrimination against him. While this claim was still outstanding he suspended me. The suspension arose after I had spoken with him in relation to a trade union safety inspection. He drew me into an argument, I asked if I could speak to my union officer and he refused. I said I had to go to the toilet before working my next train and took the opportunity to phone my union officer. For this I was suspended and, after two hearings, I was dismissed.

My fellow trade unionists and I fought hard to get my job back but were not successful even after three days of strike action. South West Trains had taken revenge for the part I played in the DOOP victory, for the part I played in raising the health and safety issues around long working hours and, I believe, for being an outspoken woman. This is not what they had employed me for.

I miss my colleagues and feel that my railway experience moulded my life in a way that no other job could have done. I miss earning a 'man's wage'; however, when I stopped working on the railway my health improved considerably, away from the shift work and long hours, and I felt much better in myself.

I always had difficulties in picturing myself as an older woman working on the railway, now that is a problem I will not have to face!

Ann Henderson – Railwoman, Guard and Driver

I joined the industry in December 1982, aged 26. Whilst looking for work in Glasgow, at a time of high unemployment, I had decided to sign letters enquiring about job vacancies using only my first initial, in case being known as a female applicant led to rejection. British Rail held my name on a waiting list, and I was called as Mr Henderson for interview on the 23rd November 1982. I was the only woman to attend for an interview, and it seemed to come as a surprise both to the Area Manager and to the other applicants. There were a number of questions about how I would get home at night. Was I aware that the shifts meant working late into the night? I had answered confidently, this having not really occurred to me as an issue. Getting up early was a bit harder to get used to.

Ten new staff started together, and I was allocated a post as a Leading Railman at Hyndland Station in the North Clyde area of Glasgow. In 1982 all local stations were staffed, and the trains (electric multiple units) were staffed by a guard and a driver. This was the biggest suburban rail network outside London. At Hyndland station, staff were responsible for selling and collecting tickets, for setting up the trains and for manually operating the points at the junction should this be required during a points failure. I therefore quite quickly had to learn some basics about railway operation. Knowing the difference between the up line and the down line was crucial, as it would make all the difference in describing a signal fault or in dealing with a derailment or other emergency.

Hyndland was a busy station, with 26 trains an hour. I spent eight hours a day in a draughty little ticket hut at the end of the island platform. I collected tickets and made sure train doors were closed, checked signals, and helped passengers with pushchairs and information. There was no disabled access to that station and we all got to know which regular passengers would require assistance. I was outside in all weathers. I wrapped myself up in a donkey jacket, thermal underwear and Doc Marten boots. I got to know the passengers and the staff, and whilst the initial response may have been surprise to see a woman in the job, I don't remember any hostility or problems. In fact, most of the members of the public probably thought I was a boy anyway, as I had short dark hair and was permanently wrapped up from head to toe. I certainly often had to answer to the call of 'son'.

There were not many women employed within BR at that time. In the immediate area there was Maureen working at Garscadden station and Ann Maley at Partick station, Christine from Motherwell was a guard on the trains, the only one in the region at that time, and we got to know each other as her train passed through Hyndland. The fact that everyone knew the women's names is an indication of how few worked in the area. There was a traincrew and maintenance depot at Hyndland too, and the station was busy as traincrews changed over, and took their rostered breaks. I knew other women elsewhere in the country who were working as guards, and being aware of the better wages and differences in industrial strength, I applied for a guard's job.

In the early 80s appointments were on seniority so, after a couple of years, it reached the point where I was the senior applicant for the guard's job, and yet I did not get allocated the first post that was rightfully mine. I took this up with the manager with the support of the trade union, the NUR. One of the barriers turned out to be a manager's view that the traincrew depot would have to be adapted to provide toilets and changing facilities for female staff. I think there was also a basic assumption that women should not do these jobs. This was resolved eventually, and it was agreed that when the next vacancy came up for which I was eligible I would be given a try, and could use the supervisors' toilet facilities.

In 1985 I started work as a passenger guard at Hyndland depot. At that time most of the units we worked had a separate guard's compartment, and it was not possible to walk through the train. The guard's primary role was operational, working with the driver as a team, with familiarity of the routes covered, including line speeds, and station and signal locations, and emergency safety procedures. We worked with station staff and signalbox staff.

A number of changes had come about by 1987, with unstaffed stations and the introduction of some Driver Only Operation services in North Clyde. Local traincrew and maintenance depots closed, as did local signalboxes, and train crews and signalbox staff were centralised at the Yoker Operations Centre. The purpose-built depot there did reflect the changing times, in that there was locker and changing room provision for women, but with a reduced overall staff complement, as Driver Only Operation services increased.

In September 1988 I moved to Glasgow Queen Street Station. I was the first female freight guard, and I later went on to be the first female passenger guard there. On 19th September 1988 I started at the freight guards' training school at Haymarket depot. For those of us who had come from working on the electric multiple units the freight guard's job came as a bit of a shock. It required more operational knowledge, and I rapidly had to learn far more about railway working. We realised that we needed to know how to stop a train that did not have a through-braking system, to have a detailed knowledge of the risks of all forms of freight traffic, and to learn about ballast and track maintenance trains. When out training on the job, we were working alongside older and far more experienced railwaymen. Whilst I was questioned about my interest in a 'man's job', I was not deemed unsuitable, and I received as much support and training as was necessary. There was an assumption that I would not be able to deal with the heaviest part of the job, to lift the buckeye coupling for joining the wagons together, but it was in fact one or two male members on the course who found it hard.

Mastering the rulebook and all the operating instructions was more of a challenge, and before being judged competent to take a freight train out myself, I had to resit the test twice. There was a view that the local guards' inspector had been unnecessarily hard on me, and maybe being a woman in a man's world means being that bit better than some of those around you, but for myself I wanted to be absolutely sure that I understood all that I needed to know and to have the confidence to be a guard in that environment meant being sure that I was right. The help of older and wiser guards was forthcoming and invaluable.

When I started work in Glasgow Queen Street Station I reported for duty, signed on, and was shown to the women's locker room. This was occupied by female carriage cleaning staff, and I was told in no uncertain terms by one of them that I had no business to be in there as I was traincrew and I should go next door to the men's locker room. This did not happen, and we settled into an understanding that it would become an all-grade women's locker room, even if initially I was regarded as a bit odd, and not welcomed by some members of staff. Subsequently some female ticket staff and other guards joined the depot. The bothy [mess-room] at Queen Street was shared by cleaners and traincrew alike. Some of the bothies where we took rostered breaks had their share of pornographic calendars and posters, but gradually this became much less common. When learning the routes and stations, walking into a new place for the first time as a female was sometimes quite hard. I did feel as if everyone was looking at me, and quite probably they were.

I enjoyed the freight job, although own up to being nervous at first. The drivers and other guards were in the main helpful and, once I became more confident, I really liked the job. The solitude in the back of an engine out on the line with a freight train, and the responsibility when getting a train prepared, are memorable. Watching the sunrise was lovely, and working ballast trains on Sundays paid well. The shifts often involved very early starts, but also early finishes. It was good to have the rest of the day to yourself. Even the experience of working out in all weathers had something going for it.

The issue of toilet and sanitary provision however took on a whole different dimension. I had been critical of other railwaywomen, who appeared to have become obsessed with the issue of toilet facilities, but being stuck up the West Highland line in the snow with a failed diesel locomotive and with no facilities whatsoever, put things into a different light.

At Glasgow Queen Street the local arrangements were such that the line of promotion meant that freight guards were given first offer on passenger guard vacancies as they came up. My option for a passenger guard's job came up fairly soon, and I transferred into the passenger link. I worked as passenger guard at Queen Street for about three years, on routes that included Glasgow to Aberdeen, Oban, Edinburgh and Cumbernauld. By this time the guard's duties, whilst still primarily operational, included revenue protection, selling and checking tickets on the train. There would be some surprise from members of the public to see a woman guard, but seldom hostility. Difficult situations could sometimes be diffused more readily by a female guard. In 1989 I became the local NUR Branch Secretary and a shop steward. With the final stages of privatisation approaching, Eastfield traction depot was closed and freight traffic and crews all transferred to Motherwell, to come under a different company. Queen Street became a ScotRail passenger depot.

Following a national, and highly controversial, productivity agreement known as the Traincrew Agreement, guards were given the opportunity to apply for drivers' jobs. I was appointed to such a post at Queen Street in January 1992. Moving into the world of the 'gold button men', as train drivers were known, was another story. I did not think I would ever understand how a diesel engine worked, but then came to realise that not many of the men who were training with me understood either, and that knowledge on a need-to-know basis would be adequate! The traction instructor did have an inability to teach a session without mentioning sex, which got a bit tiresome – and all the rhymes and allusions that had been devised for remembering particular switches and lights on the engines, involved sexual innuendos. He said this was the way it had always been, so it was staying that way.

I was the first female driver at Queen Street, driving Class 37 locomotives and then sprinter diesel multiple units. I did take a certain pleasure from driving trains in and out of Edinburgh Waverley Station, through the Princes Street Gardens, under the footbridge on which we had stood as children, watching steam trains with my father. Train driving was the job in which I got the most public response. At that time there were so few women drivers in Scotland, and none on the routes out of Glasgow Queen Street or Edinburgh, and so it was a topic of conversation and comment. It was nearly always favourable, with women stopping to talk and parents pointing me out to their young children. The local newspaper carried an article when I qualified, and I did feel a sense of achievement. By example it is possible to change options and choices for others, and it was good to be part of that process. ScotRail sent me one day to do a careers talk in a secondary school in Glasgow, alongside a woman firefighter and other women in 'non-traditional' jobs, and the discussion that ensued amongst the children was really positive.

I joined the NUR the day I started with the railway, and remained a member until I left the industry. I soon started going along to meetings and getting involved. There was a lot to learn about the union structures, machinery and process, and about the BR Conditions of Service. There were usually no other women at the meetings and I remember attending a joint branch meeting in Partick Burgh Halls where I was asked whom was I with and whom was I waiting for, on the basis that I could not possibly be a railway worker.

Having held official positions in the NUR makes it hard to separate out experiences as a woman working in the rail industry from my experience as a trade union activist. It was unusual for those positions to be held by a woman, and I did learn that the traincrew at Stirling knew me as 'Ann the man', so I guess that was their way of managing something different!

For me, much of the attraction of coming in to the industry was the opportunity to learn about the union and to be involved. Being a woman labour movement activist gave me other networks and supports, reducing some of the isolation that I think it might have been possible to feel as a woman in such a male environment. In 1988 the NUR AGM decided, by a vote of 33 to 32, to set up a Women's Advisory Committee, and I was the only member from a Scottish branch for a number of years. It was an important source of ideas and sharing experiences, allowing for issues of concern to women members to be placed on the agenda of both the EC and of the AGM. We had the support of a number of male members and won others over, too. The union began to send women representatives to the women's conferences at the Scottish TUC, and to the Scottish Labour women's conference, and there we were able to talk to other women working in traditionally male environments.

My experience as a woman in the industry is completely mixed in with trade union activity. As the industry made further savings and cutbacks, part time revenue collection staff were brought into a number of stations and onto key shifts for on-train ticket collection. Many of them were women with childcare or other family responsibilities. At the 1988 NUR AGM there was an extremely heated debate over unionisation of the part-timers. I was amazed to hear how strong the opposition was, as delegates explained their jobs were being taken away and that therefore those workers should be excluded from the union. The decision was to recruit and represent all workers, whether part time or full time. I think this was an issue on which women had a different reaction, and we did not see it as an offence to work part-time.

Campaigning against sexual harassment, and the goal of creating a safe working environment for all staff irrespective of gender, sexuality or race, was very much on the trade union movement agenda in the 1980s. New policies were adopted, leaflets produced, guidance issued to branches and agreements over procedures negotiated with managers. For the NUR it was a new discussion, although certainly not a new experience for some of the members. At a local level I think women members felt more comfortable coming to me with concerns. Male members would refer women to come to talk to me from quite a wide geographical area. Even after leaving the industry, phone calls would come from members seeking advice and help.

The idea that sexual harassment should not be tolerated in the workplace was one thing; it was another step to work out that it also should not be tolerated within the union. I had been working on the railway for less than a year when I was sexually assaulted following a union meeting. This introduced me very quickly to the difficulties posed within the application of the union rulebook over 'conflict of interest', there being no avenue through which a complaint could be raised against the male union member. With widespread trade union membership, sexual harassment at work would also often involve two trade union members, and the union needed to find a way of dealing with it. Eventually I represented myself at a Criminal Injuries Compensation Board hearing, which found in my favour. Despite there being no union procedures, there is no doubt that with the support of my local branch officials (all male), my ability to participate in union activity without fear for my safety was defended. Support also came from friends and family and from women within and outwith the industry.

Sexual harassment has not gone away as an issue for women in the rail industry, but the trade unions are all certainly much clearer about what is right and wrong, and what is required of the union in terms of protecting all its members. 'Conflict of interest' cannot be used to protect those who create a threatening and insecure environment, on either racial or sexual harassment grounds.

Ann Henderson driving a Class 37 locomotive on the West Highland line in 1992.
A. Henderson

As a shop steward in Queen Street I was approached by a young woman guard who, on returning from maternity leave, had been denied any annual leave that would have accumulated. I sought advice from the Equal Opportunities Commission, and then the union agreed to take on the case. Top legal counsel was provided, and a tribunal hearing took place in October 1993. The union was successful, the young woman guard got the annual leave to which she was entitled, and a precedent was established for the whole of BR, thereby improving conditions for all women in the industry. On a personal level it was very satisfying to know that an instinctive reaction to an injustice had resulted in a national improvement to our Conditions of Service. Would that have been dealt with differently had the member approached a male rep? There was certainly not a culture of taking up 'women's issues' across the industry.

In 1994 I was 38 and expecting my first child. I wanted to work on for as long as possible, as the maternity pay arrangements with BR were only the statutory minimum. This again was an area where the NUR had not had to face up to pressure from members to improve conditions. With women forming less than 10% of the workforce, and not many of them seeing the union as relevant, it had not been an issue. Improvements in leave entitlement and in maternity payments have since come through the enforcement of European directives and latterly through some union negotiation. However, for me the first basic question was what to wear. As a driver I always wore sturdy boots and uniform trousers, as there was a requirement to climb in and out of the driving cab onto the track from time to time. A large navy maternity smock that was offered was clearly not suitable. (This was the only available BR issue maternity wear; it came from the clerical grade uniforms.) So some large men's BR trousers were procured, and later an arrangement was reached whereby I could be reimbursed for buying some plain trousers from Mothercare.

I was fit and healthy throughout my pregnancy, and had followed the health advice I had been given that it was fine to continue in my usual job for as long as I felt able. It was probably others who worried more. I remember being called in by the Depot Manager at one point, when I was about seven and a half months pregnant, and being asked how long I intended to go on driving trains. He said that passengers had raised concerns with him, after watching this heavily pregnant train driver walk down the platform. This may or may not have been true, but what did transpire was that some of the male train guards were not comfortable about it. I could not quite understand this, as we were working in an area never far from good medical care and, in any event, it seemed unlikely that I, for myself, would continue driving if I felt in any way at risk. However, I came off my driving duties at about eight months and spent a couple of weeks on other duties, giving out Weekly Operating Notices in the depot and other work. The best part of that was not having to worry about the frequent toilet visits that were now required! That had been a bit awkward on the longer train runs.

There is no doubt that I was more tired, but in hindsight it was nothing to how tired I felt once the baby arrived, but then there was always the option of swapping shifts with other drivers to find later starts. The flexibility of shift work was better managed in those days, with an understanding at local level that swaps could be approved which still ensured all the trains were covered, and ensured a happier workforce. In fact I realised that a number of my male workmates shared childcare and school arrangements, as in many families both parents worked, and the nature of the railway industry required juggling childcare around with the shifts.

Having been off work on three months maternity leave, after which the minimal wages ran out, it was necessary to return to work. Having been away from driving for a few months, some revision of the routes to be worked was necessary. This was better than returning straight onto the roster, and created what was essentially a phased return to work, at a time when I wished to continue breastfeeding my son, Iain. It was difficult to be back at work full time when our son was small. My partner worked on the railways too and we worked opposite shifts and swapped our son over at home or in the station. But the shift work gave me time to be with my son during the day, and with a bit of support it was possible to continue feeding him myself for that first year, albeit moving onto mixed feeding. Later in the year I was faced with a warning in the first stage of the absence monitoring procedure after being off work sick with mastitis, but this was challenged and later withdrawn. Certainly I did not find the railway environment conducive to starting a discussion about provisions for breastfeeding mothers' expressing and storing milk, but not every fight had to be fought at once.

One of my treasured memories from 1995 is of the opening night of the *Oh Mrs Porter* exhibition about women on the railways, at the National Railway Museum in York. On Thursday 20th July I went down from Edinburgh with my son, then eight months old. There were women there whom I knew from union activity from other parts of the country, and women I had not met before, all having contributed in their own way to changing the male face of the railways in Britain. My photograph was there, as a train driver. We admired Stephenson's Rocket, listened to music and to women from a local group singing, and my son crawled around the floor in the Great Hall, near the turntable for the engines, having a lovely time. It was a snapshot of women making a difference, and I loved it. Elected politicians often talk of it being a privilege to have the opportunity to represent people and to pursue a political career; that evening I felt proud to have worked alongside so many railway women and men, protecting each others' conditions and rights, and changing the perceptions of what was and was not possible for women and girls.

I had started out in the railway in 1982 with a strong commitment to the benefits of collective action, and to the need for trade unions. Politics took me in to the railway industry, not some burning desire to be a train driver. The experience reinforced my political beliefs and commitments. Interestingly, though, it was not possible to be a relatively anonymous part of a collective process. The very fact that less than 10% of the rail union membership was female, and that a whole number of us had ventured into traditionally male jobs within that, meant that our names were known and our pictures were on display.

I left the railway in 1996 and went to work in a women's community project in Glasgow, where the atmosphere was quite different. My past work experience often comes as less of a surprise to those in the industry than to those outside. Maybe that says something about the acceptability there is now in the railway industry that women can do the whole range of jobs there, from traincrew to engineering and across management. That is in part a tribute to all of the women who broke barriers and challenged perceptions in the industry in the past, and I know that I feel proud to have been part of that collective experience, as well as the individual sense of achievement I feel from working on the trains.

The railway for me was about the union, it was about progressive change, it was about essential public transport networks, it was about engines and train tracks; but it was also about families and friendships and even, occasionally, feminism.

Ann Henderson lives in Edinburgh, working part time as a parliamentary assistant in the Scottish Parliament, and part time for the RMT.

Vanda Braid – Railwoman and Conductor

In 1989, aged 46, I took a job on the platform of Penrith Station. I was the only female, but the chaps didn't seem to mind. I was the general purpose relief for two years and as such did a variety of jobs. I had the pleasure of working at Oxenholme and Windermere, and also at Appleby and Settle on the well known Settle-Carlisle line. The work was varied and so were the shifts. I did platform and booking office work. The late shift could be a bit lonely and I confess that at night I always carried my 'Bardic lamp' [a chunky and rugged handlamp made of steel] with me. It gave me a bit of confidence and security.

One of the interesting aspects was 'lamping': replacing the oil lamps at the top of the signal posts, at Appleby, Long Meg and Garsdale. It was good to get out on one's own and enjoy the lovely countryside. On a good day all was fine but on windy days, one's patience was tried to the limits. Just as you'd got to the top of the post with a fresh oil lamp to pop into the container at the top, the wind would blow the lamp out. After this happened three or four times the air could get a bit blue. In the winter it was icy going up the ladders and one's fingers frozen, but I always enjoyed the 'lamping' trips. Another pleasant occasion was being at Kirkby Stephen when the Queen visited. It was an unstaffed station and I'd been sent out there to clean it up. As a reward I was allowed to be there for Her Majesty's visit.

After a couple of years, I got a conductor's job at Carlisle, the only female among 100 male train crew. There I did get a bit of harassment but I'm sure it was all done without any maliciousness, so it didn't really bother me. In those days the mess room was always full, and it did take some getting used to all those men, passing wind from both ends — loudly at that! I don't think I ever got quite used to that. There were one or two chaps who seemed to think I was 'doing a man out of a job', but I needed to support myself, so I didn't take a lot of notice. I really enjoyed the job. I worked over the Settle-Carlisle line down to Leeds, across the Tyne Valley to Newcastle, up to Glasgow via Dumfries and Kilmarnoch and down the Cumbrian coast to Barrow and the Windermere branch.

I worked shifts, the earliest starting about 5 a.m. and the latest finishing about 12.30 a.m. Every day was different. On a summer's morning it was lovely, and I nearly always saw wildlife such as deer or foxes. I didn't get a lot of trouble; I didn't go looking for it and I wasn't argumentative, but in the evening drunks could be a problem. One evening going to Glasgow, a group of about eight young men got on the train at Carlisle. All spoke pleasantly to me as they got on, but one learned to judge people, and I suspected trouble. There was. North of Dumfries a passenger came to tell me there was a naked man in the front carriage. Sure enough there was. After a while and a request, he did don his clothes. Thankfully most people (it was a busy train) thought it was funny, but there were two ladies who were rather offended, and I had to pacify them. Another evening we stopped at Haltwhistle and I noticed a strange movement through the carriage window. It was a couple 'having it away'. I couldn't believe it.

I was the only female train crew at Carlisle until my last 18 months, when another female conductor started. I was on the railway for 14 years, finishing under privatisation. Sadly, with privatisation, a lot of the camaraderie went: we weren't all one big happy family but all different franchises. Going back to work at 46 was a bit daunting but I never doubted my capabilities of doing the job. One certainly needed a sense of humour to cope with the travelling public and with the chaps I worked with, and all the cheek I got, not to mention the farting, belching and swearing; but if a female enters a male dominated work environment, she must accept these things.

Amanda Speake – On-Track Machine Operator

I started in 1996 on the civil engineering side, typing, filing, faxing. I'd type up reports for the tunnel examiners after their weekend inspections. I asked my boss if I could tag along one weekend and see what was involved in the examination itself. He agreed. I was kitted out with a high-visibility vest and sexy little steel toecap boots and dispatched into a van with five big burly men. I was given a ten foot pole and told to walk down the side of the tunnel and bang hell out of it. If the tunnel was still standing then it was safe. Eight hours and five tunnels later, I was hooked. I ached all over and due to all the falling soot from the tunnel roof, looked like an extra from the Black and White Minstrel Show!

Our company lost the contract and I found work in various other departments over the next two years, typing, filing etc. By this time I wanted to get out onto the track. One day I saw an advert for 'On-Track Machine Operators'. It explained briefly what it was about, so I sent off a CV. I wasn't 100% sure what it was I was applying for; all I knew was that I'd be outdoors, working on the track and I wouldn't have to get dressed up and do my hair every day — fantastic! When told that the interview included a short test on mechanical engineering I went to pieces (I'm as mechanically minded as my dog) so I phoned personnel and a guy explained that it was very basic and begged me to have a go — I think the 'novelty woman' factor intrigued him — so I did. There were about 50 applicants that day and 50 the day before. The test wasn't that difficult, really; a lot of it was common sense, probably the reason why most of the men failed. I was offered the job on completion of a psychometric test, which I sat a few weeks later (I'd rather have a coil fitted than go through that again!) and started the job 3 months later.

I suppose it's nice being the first woman to do anything, especially in this job. I had no idea I was until they told me once I'd started. I can't say I was surprised. I will be the first to admit that this is not a job for all women, for example, I couldn't see my mother bobbing round the back of an old, rusty wagon for a pee, wearing orange made-for-men overalls and working with people who all appear to suffer from Tourette's Syndrome. There's a lot of banter about people giving people 'one', boob jokes and penis descriptions; this would probably offend some women. The secret is to give it back tenfold. Women are far more quick-witted and it's great fun to see a man blush with embarrassment in front of his colleagues after his attempts at a 'put down' have backfired. I would like to think that I'm asexual now in their eyes; at work anyway, I'm treated as one of the lads, although some of the older guys still insist on carrying heavy things for me and not swearing in front of me. I can see in their eyes the fear that this should ever happen to their daughters and I think they feel I've been made to do the job, as no woman in her right mind would do this by choice. They've probably got something there! On-track machine operators have always claimed their job is the worlds best kept secret. I agree.

People still regard women workers on the railway as such a bizarre notion and what a novelty we must be, and of course we must be feminists or dungaree-clad lesbians. I recently went on a seminar with our Operations Manager. We had never met and upon greeting me he announced: 'Bloody hell, I was expecting someone different.' 'A raving dyke?' I asked. 'Well, yeah' he replied. I must admit I had rather overdone it with the make-up and hairspray, but it's not often I get the chance to in this job (though I keep my toenails painted constantly to remind myself I'm female!)

It's taken three years to make it as just a normal Machine Operator and not a 'woman-operator', and I've won round some of the hardest chauvinists in the job — just. Now it's all about to start again with a new challenge: I'm five months pregnant, and they only found out last week.

Helena Wojtczak – First Female Guard

At age 19 I was working for BR as a switchboard operator at Waterloo with half a dozen women, all much older. The work was relentless. There were thousands of incoming calls and a buzzer sounded whenever a call was waiting. It buzzed incessantly. A colleague told us her husband had a new job — he was a guard. She said he travelled about in a private compartment, unsupervised, watching the scenery go by, reading newspapers, meeting new people every day and — most enviable of all — his pay was double that of ours! Everyone grumbled that men got all the best jobs, and although someone remarked that a new law meant women could get them, too, my cynical colleagues said that such laws were just theory: no way was BR going to let women guard trains. Everyone agreed, but someone suggested that one of us should apply anyway, and either obtain fame as the 'first lady guard' or a fortune from suing BR under the new law for refusing to let a woman have a man's job. Suddenly, all eyes were on me, as the youngest, to be that person.

At 5.05 p.m. I stood on platform two at the frantically busy Waterloo station and watched as guards blew their whistles to hasten passengers aboard, waved their flags and jumped onto the train as it moved way. Gripping the handrail with one hand, they rode on the running board as the train accelerated, and bellowed 'Stand away!' at commuters who attempted to board. If a foolhardy passenger opened the door of the moving train and attempted to leap inside, the guard had to make an instant decision whether or not to stop the train. It seemed to me that the commuter's life was in the guard's hands and butterflies went wild in my stomach as I tried to imagine myself in the role.

Before long I was in the divisional manager's office at Wimbledon, being glared at across a huge desk by three intimidating men in pin-striped suits. One addressed me sternly as 'Young lady', before informing me that the railway did not employ 'females' as guards; 'but', he continued, 'it appears that, owing to the new law, we cannot prevent you from applying.' The others made similar comments. I was too timid to object to their attitude, but inside I boiled with rage. I'd never been called a 'female' before and I didn't like their assumption that women could not do the guard's job. The managers had transformed my hitherto mild interest in the job into a zealous determination to get it.

After passing the physical examination at BR's medical centre I attended a week's Induction Course at Eastleigh, As the sole female I was under constant scrutiny and the subject of much interest, but my fellow trainees were friendly and flirtatious. To my delight, my payslip showed £60 instead of the usual £36. It was the most I'd ever earned.

I was at a great disadvantage during training because even the rawest recruit was familiar with electrical and mechanical terminology from childhood hobbies and boys' education. Many were railwaymen's sons and all had railway experience. It was strange and daunting, especially as I had never before worked with men (I'd even attended an all-girl school). We learnt the basics: railway law, rules, safety, first aid and a little about railway operating. We each had to extinguish a fire, which was created outdoors by igniting a large square tray filled with paraffin, and give artificial respiration to a dummy. I passed at 91% and progressed to a two-week shunting course (classroom and goods yard), an exam, a two-week guard's course (classroom), another exam, six weeks 'learning the roads' and a final, oral exam face to face with the guard's inspector who had never before worked with a woman. It was December 1977, and the next shunting course did not begin until January so, for a month, I worked at Wimbledon, a very busy, ten-platform station, where the only other women were a lavatory attendant and two buffet staff.

The atmosphere and the banter were completely different from when I worked with women and the work was unlike anything I had done before. I carried out all the usual platform duties, but was excused from cleaning the gents'. Nor did I clean the ladies', because a woman attendant was employed. No longer an anonymous, faceless voice, I was the centre of attention. I'd swapped a clean, warm, safe, office environment, for a dirty, draughty station. My pretty skirts and girls' shoes were gone and I wore a man's uniform jacket, jeans, a sweater and Doc Marten's boots.

I'd been a shy teenager who had worked only on a switchboard since leaving school and so working on a busy station made an amazing difference to my personality. The 'bush telegraph' had spread the news far and wide about the first female 'learner-guard'. I found it highly embarrassing at first but after a while grew accustomed to the constant barrage of remarks and questions. One day the actor Michael Robbins chatted to me. I'd seen him in the film *On the Buses*, in which men objected to working with women. I hoped it wasn't a bad omen! Guards would leave their brakevans and subject me to a hurried (but friendly) interrogation; then they waved their flags and, as the train moved away, stepped backwards into the brakevan, pulling the door shut as they did so. As I watched them the doubts crept in. Could I *really* do that?

I soon learned that 'men' and 'management' were warring factions: neither side would give an inch unless forced to. No man would do anything that was not in his job description or stay one minute past his day. Being as awkward as possible was a stance many railwaymen took pride in. I never heard of anyone being praised; a manager would call an individual into his office only to reprimand him, and it was standard practice to refuse an interview with any manager without having a staff representative present.

At the shunting course I encountered hostility from railwaymen for the first time: my training was 'a waste of time and money' because 'women could not stick the job'; I was 'poaching men's work'; women had 'no business with trains, except to clean them'. When we filled in our uniform applications I was told not to bother: I'd never pass my training; it would be a waste of material. I was only 19 and completely unprepared for such venomous, undeserved and relentless attacks. I couldn't complain: my mission was to prove myself, not to become a nuisance to management by whingeing, nor could I show any weakness that might be attributed to my gender. I worried constantly that any day they would think of a reason why I should not be a guard. I didn't want to 'put my head above the parapet' or give them any excuse to get rid of me.

In a snow-covered freight yard I learned how to test brakes, pull points, carry out emergency isolation of the electric traction current, and attach and detach vehicles. Heavy-duty mechanical machinery was unfamiliar to me and the novelty was exciting. Each of us had to physically grapple with points handles, brake levers on the sides of freight wagons, air- and vacuum-brake pipes and steel couplings. Everything was huge and black and greasy and much of it was frozen. We each had to demonstrate that we could couple units together. I was a bag of nerves as I gripped the frosty handrails of an electric train and hauled myself up the steel ladder that led to the driving cab door. Scared of heights, I dared not look down as I edged my way tentatively along the running board. My fingers gripped the horizontal rail but, when I reached the gap between the two units, both hands were needed to connect the pipes, so I wedged myself between the vehicles, terrified of slipping on the icy steel. Somehow, my frozen fingers managed to bend the stiff rubber air-brake pipes to connect them, and to engage the heavy 27-pin jumper into the correct position. I then carefully retraced my steps and felt a great relief when the soles of my shoes once again made contact with terra firma — or, in this case, icy ballast.

Next, each of us had to lift the notoriously heavy buckeye coupling. Many people had told me that this would be my downfall: it was far too heavy for any woman to lift. When my turn came a semicircle of tormentors gathered around. So, this was how my brief sojourn on the railway was to end: I would exit, utterly humiliated, to a chorus of jeers from my harassers. The thought of this, and knowing that all women would be judged on my success or failure, gave me the strength to lift it. But there was no applause, and not one man had the graciousness to apologise.

After passing my shunting exams I progressed to the two-week guards' course. Here we learned the bylaws relating to passengers and the regulations governing trains in transit. We were taught how the various signalling systems worked, and procedures for dealing with every type of emergency, such as collisions, derailments, fires and breakdowns. I passed the guard's exam and began six weeks of route learning. This involved accompanying a senior guard from my depot throughout his shift, days and evenings. Most of the senior guards at my depot were West Indians recruited during the post-war staff shortage. None was hostile to female guards and many called me 'darter' (daughter), a great compliment. They had a wonderfully laid-back attitude, in some cases too casual. On arrival at a deserted terminus late one night, the middle-aged Jamaican who I was training with shocked me by nonchalantly urinating onto the track in my presence!

After six weeks' route learning I took my final examination, which lasted half a day. Our depot required particularly extensive route knowledge and it was a mammoth task to memorise it.* For the first part, I had to recite all of the 'roads' aloud to our guards' inspector who, clearly unnerved at being alone with a teenage girl in his tiny office, avoided making eye contact. In reciting the route I had to include all stations, signalboxes, tunnels, viaducts, level crossings (and what type), catch points and junctions, and say which signalling system was in operation at different places. The second part consisted of an extremely detailed exam on emergency procedures, in which the inspector drew plans of lines, complete with tunnels and viaducts etc, and then told me my hypothetical train had broken down, divided or derailed at various locations and asked me to explain the correct protective and other procedures for each type of emergency. When he passed me fit for duty I felt a glow of pride that, in spite of everything, I'd qualified.

We'd been thoroughly drilled to take heed of the stripes on uniform clothing, because they indicated everyone's place in the pecking order. Guards displayed two silver braid stripes on their sleeves and on their peaked caps to indicate that they were two steps up from a railman and one down from a station supervisor. I was exceedingly proud to be the only woman with the right to exhibit those two stripes and could hardly wait to get my uniform so that I could wear it to Wimbledon station and show my ex-colleagues that their protégée was now sporting a 'lady guard's' uniform, something none of them had ever seen before. But when my uniform arrived it had no stripes. It was, in fact, a female carriage cleaners' uniform but with gold buttons (as worn by drivers). No peaked, badged and braided cap for me but a blue cloth beret devoid of adornment, which fell off if I moved my head. I felt insulted and humiliated, as though BR was informing me that my achievement counted for nothing, that I was not a real guard but some species of carriage cleaner. When subsequently wearing the uniform out and about, nobody recognised me as a guard because, given the size of the south-western and the huge number of staff, railway

* We had to know the routes from Waterloo to the following destinations: Portsmouth, Reading, Windsor, Eastleigh, Salisbury, Shepperton, Chessington and Hampton Court, plus the 'roundabout' routes from Waterloo to Waterloo via Hounslow and via Richmond and to the maintenance depot at Stewart's Lane. We also had to know the layout and working methods at the sidings and depots at Fratton, Strawberry Hill, Guildford, Woking, Clapham Junction, Wimbledon Park, Effingham Junction and Staines.

workers could not know everyone personally and so they had to rely on the stripes, braid and hat. For a long time, station staff would approach me with a message, parcel, letter or leather cash-bag to be signed for, glance quickly over my uniform looking for stripes, then peer over my shoulder into the brakevan and, seeing it empty, asked me where was the guard and who the hell was I? Then I'd have to convince him that he was addressing the guard. This met with disbelief, laughter and a demand that I be serious and tell him where the real guard was. These debates would take place within the earshot of my passengers and sometimes delayed the train. I am quite certain that none of these embarrassing situations would have happened if I had been supplied with a female version of a male guard's uniform, but that didn't happen for several years.

Helena in a 4-sub unit in 1981 wearing her carriage cleaner's jacket with golden buttons. AUTHOR'S COLLECTION

Guards' uniforms were designed to accommodate the myriad of small items they were required to carry. As well as two reinforced outer pockets the jacket had three inside pockets and the waistcoat supplied a further four. But my jacket had no inside pockets, nor did I receive a waistcoat. Fortunately, BR was lax about uniform and we wore what we pleased, provided we wore the correct jacket for our grade. A colleague donated a guard's peaked cap, which kept rain, snow and sun out of my eyes and gave me, at last, my two silver braid stripes. Then another man gave me a male guard's jacket. It was rather too large across the shoulders and chest, and a bit tight on the hips, but I wore it for years.

Each time uniforms were redesigned a female version was created, with a choice of trousers or skirts. There was also a female-style hat, but I discovered that people took me less seriously when I wore it, whereas a man's cap brought instant recognition that I was a figure of authority. Everything was winter-weight and on hot days we sweltered in nylon-lined, wool garments.

On 23rd March 1978 I worked my first train alone: the 1246 Waterloo (Main) to Waterloo (Windsor). I was anxious from the moment I waved my flag and we moved off, because whatever emergency happened, 'the buck stopped here'. But I soon ceased being nervous and enjoyed the job enormously. All my working life I'd had a colleague sitting either side of me and a superior constantly watching over us, in a windowless room in which we were not allowed to eat, drink, read or smoke. I was thrilled at being able to have everything exactly the way I wanted it: windows open or closed, heating on or off, a fag, a can of Coke, a sandwich; plus, of course, we got all the daily newspapers free of charge. It was wonderful being out and about all summer, shopping in Guildford; eating fish and chips at Portsmouth Harbour while watching the ferries cross the Solent; speeding through the countryside with my inward-opening door clipped open or my window pulled right down; seeing sunsets and sunrises across fields, sighting rabbits, badgers, pheasants and foxes that, as a city girl, I had never seen before. I was content, comfortable and earning more than double my previous wage.

As I opened my brakevan door on arrival at stations en route, the station staff would nudge each other, point and stare at the *lady guard*. Within a few weeks I grew irritated at being subjected to remarks on my gender dozens of times a day, but it was something I was to endure for many years. In the autumn a commuter alighting at Strawberry Hill handed me his *Evening Standard*. Inside I found an article headlined: 'Granny guard makes her rush-hour debut.' The 'first woman guard', based at Cannon Street, had worked her first train that morning. Seeing her proud, smiling face beaming up from the page, I felt hurt and annoyed that someone else was getting recognition for what was *my* achievement; however, I did not think to complain to anyone.

Most trains I worked had no toilets. The law states that toilets must be provided at places where we were rostered to take meal breaks, and must be separate from those used by the public or the opposite sex. BR ignored this. I was rostered to take breaks at 21 places;† in addition, we had turn-arounds at four stations.* At most I used public conveniences, which were dirty, vandalised and frequently out of order. At my home depot there were toilets within the carriage cleaners' accommodation, but it was only open during the day. Fratton Yard's accommodation had been built in the 1970s without female toilets and I had to use the gents' while male staff fidgeted outside waiting for me to emerge. At some locations I was led by an amused railman into a cobweb-infested cupboard under the stairs, containing an ancient lavatory pan unused for decades. Of course there was never any paper or a washbasin. Sometimes there wasn't even a seat and, in one case, no door! At Woking a special toilet put aside for me within the public facilities and I had to ask for a key from the staff, who took the opportunity to make vulgar remarks. These makeshift solutions were illegal and I submitted many complaints, but little was done.

The question of toilets was, of course, a pressing one, and being made to wait while a succession of union subcommittees and working parties creaked and cranked their way through the machinery of negotiation was frustrating. After three years nothing had changed so I started proceedings via the Equal Opportunities Commission. BR forced me to withdraw by threatening dismissal and my NUR branch secretary condemned me for bringing in 'outsiders' to interfere with a union matter. When reminded that three years of complaint to the NUR had resulted in nothing, he retorted: 'It took a century for us to get *men's* toilets — you cannot expect things to happen overnight!'

All of our stock was electric, but we had a wide range of different units including the 1940s-built SUBs (suburbans). At termini the SUB's paraffin tail lamp had to be swapped from one end to another. If the lamp was not on the platform side, I had to open the offside cab door and, dangling from the train with one hand, grope around the outside, unhook the lamp, and swing myself back inside, then carry it to the other end and reattach it. The trains had no intercom between guard and driver; our sole method of communication consisted of a red and a green flag by day and a steel Bardic lamp with three colours by night. If a reckless passenger pulled a door open after the train had started I would dash across the brakevan and slam down the red brake handle, which brought the train to a shuddering halt. On a sharply curved platform, I walked yards from the train in order to obtain visual contact with my driver, waved the green flag or lamp at him, and dashed frantically back to my brakevan, leaping in as the train moved off.

† Eastleigh, Fratton, Portsmouth, Reading, Basingstoke, Windsor, Strawberry Hill, Stewart's Lane, Clapham Junction, Effingham Junction, Woking, Guildford, Farnham, Epsom, Dorking, Horsham, Alton, Staines, Wimbledon, Wimbledon Park and Waterloo.

* Chessington, Shepperton, Hampton Court and Weybridge.

The cosy, feminine world of the telephonist drifted off into my past. Now, being outside, in all weathers, day or night, and dealing with heavy, dirty equipment and potentially dangerous situations was my usual day's work. Every duty was different and I had a huge range of situations to deal with. Sometimes I'd find my brakevan packed with dozens of heavy mailbags and I often had to unload them unaided. Sometimes I acted as 'secondman' on a diesel engine; more often I guarded diesel-hauled trains from the dingy train yard at Clapham Junction. Walking between the trains by the light of my hand-lamp, I'd kick the brake pads where they touched the wheels to establish if any handbrakes were screwed on, causing the depot's rats to scurry about on the path. If a handbrake was on, I had to climb into the train and unscrew a huge, red-painted, horizontal steel wheel, which often required considerable exertion to release. A battered, grease-ridden paraffin lamp would be collected from the shunters' lobby and I'd struggle to hang it onto the hook on the rear of the train. Standing on a rail, on tiptoe, balancing the lamp on the tips of my fingers, I held my breath and stretched my body to its utmost length in order to hook the lamp over the bracket. Leaning across the buffer I invariably smeared my jacket with gelatinous black gunge. After a hand signal to the driver I performed a brake test, which involved unleashing an unruly and filthy vacuum pipe. This sprung wildly from its bracket and sucked air into the system. Having replaced it, I'd take my place in the secondman's seat in the huge, throbbing diesel engine and enjoy a driver's-eye-view of the magnificent, multi-track approach to the great terminus of Waterloo.

Being a guard wasn't boring because in between stations we had things to do: logging our train's timekeeping, making announcements (when we had the equipment to do so), reading books or papers, or chatting with colleagues who were travelling 'on the cushions'. Sometimes a passenger would approach just for a natter. In the summer of 1984 I chatted to a passenger who said his father-in-law had been a railwayman at Swindon. Later the ticket collector at Windsor told me that the man was Alan Lake, the husband of Diana Dors, who had died some weeks before. Shortly afterwards, I was shocked to read in a newspaper that Mr Lake had committed suicide.

I had my share of problems. My first happened one night near Clapham Junction: two drunken Englishmen were beating up two American tourists. I got between them and raised my arms, pushing the aggressors away while shrieking at them to 'break it up'. Their astonishment at a teenage girl intervening ended the violence and the victims escaped. Then I realised that all the other passengers were staring at me and so I sloped off, red-faced, back to my guard's van. Over the years there were so many different incidents to deal with: people taking drugs; epileptics having fits; cushions deliberately set alight; a man exposing himself; someone having a heart attack; a commuter being locked in a toilet; a vagrant travelling about all day with no ticket, just to keep warm. We had to think on our feet in each circumstance and do the right thing, quickly and authoritatively.

The railway culture was, of course, very masculine, and I always felt like an outsider who did not belong anywhere. I didn't fit in with women because I was in a male grade; I didn't fit in with men as, clearly, I was female. The groups of women cleaners whom I passed on the walkways of my depot occasionally whispered comments of the 'who does she think she is?' variety. Drivers invited me to the cab of empty trains for long and intimate conversations, but most would 'disown' me when we arrived back in the mess-room. Some men were very good friends at work but if they had a girlfriend or wife it was not possible to continue this off duty and if single they expected more than friendship. My closest friend was a gay man. At the age of 21 I left my partner after five years' cohabitation and for the next 18 years all my boyfriends were railwaymen.

Among groups of railwaymen crude and sexist banter abounded, and many laughs were had at my expense. Always the only girl among a group of men, and still a teenager, I squirmed at their comments. Being the subject of ribald teasing was profoundly embarrassing but rarely could I escape, so I armed myself with a selection of put-downs and wisecracks and soon developed an array of retorts so impressive that I was able to emerge from such situations as victor, not victim. It was customary for train crew to bitch about one another by writing insulting graffiti on brakevan walls. The introduction of female staff brought in a new dimension: sex. Soon, every brakevan was filled with obscene drawings and writings, firstly about me and then about each new female recruit. One brakevan went about for years with a different comment about me on each wall: on one I was a nymphomaniac, on the second, frigid and on the third, a lesbian.

I received several lecherous propositions and when I was 20 one driver (who was about forty years my senior) approached me and touched my breasts. My hand flew up in defence, colliding with his face. A week later the relief station manager summoned me to his office and produced a letter from the driver, complaining that I had assaulted him. The manager snapped at me: he'd always known that employing 'females' was 'a big mistake'; any more trouble and I'd be 'out the door'. After drying my tears I related the incident to my union representative, who rebuked me for going into the 'lion's den' without him.

While there was little overt hostility from guards or drivers, many cited the nightwork, the environment and the physical hardships as reasons why women should not be guards (or drivers). But carriage cleaners also worked nights and performed heavy labour. In fact, it was so unpleasant that it was routinely used as the standard punishment for train crew guilty of a serious misdemeanour and was only slightly preferable to being sacked.

I was very pro-union and wore my NUR badge with pride. I found the very left-wing union activists very forward-thinking when it came to women and they took us seriously as workers and equals. When I was 23 I was elected as a staff representative and health and safety representative for guards. I was probably the first female to fill these positions, which I held for two years. My branch twice delegated me to the annual NUR Guards' and Shunters' Conference. At the first, in Brighton, as I reached the front of the queue to register my arrival the union organiser glanced up at me and snapped: 'No wives here, please, just delegates!' Not the welcome I had hoped for. Eventually I found the endless disputes with management so stressful that I not only went no further in the union but also ceased to be a representative or a conference delegate.

In 1987 my boyfriend (also a guard) and I moved to the south coast, where I returned to being the first and only woman in the whole depot, apart from the carriage cleaners. I hadn't realised how progressive my London colleagues were until I worked at Ramsgate, where I met with hidebound prejudice and provincial narrow-mindedness. Despite my nine years' service, I had once again to go through the tedious process of 'proving' that a woman could do a guard's job. My partner was younger than myself and had two years' less service. Our inspector told him that while route-learning he could come and go as he pleased, but I was rostered with specific guards and made to complete the whole duty, often working till midnight, which meant the unnecessary expense of a taxi home. Naturally, I complained of being treated unequally to a man, contrary to law. The inspector insisted that I 'had to get used to working at night', despite my protest that I had worked nights for nine years, and so I complained to the depot manager, who told me to do as instructed. When I mentioned sex discrimination and said I'd go to the union he threatened to sack me. I tried to complain to the welfare officer but he refused to take my calls. Although burning with resentment at the injustice of it all, I had no choice but to accept being treated differently to my boyfriend for six infuriating weeks.

Several colleagues subjected me to offensive remarks and accusations of being 'unladylike' as well as some Victorian comments on 'women's place' and their unfitness for railway operating. One night I extracted a tiny bit of revenge. A driver informed me that women were not fit to be train crew. 'Well it's your monthlies isn't it?' he explained. We set off and twenty minutes later screeched to a halt: he'd overshot a semaphore signal protecting Chartham level crossing. The signal lamp had gone out and he hadn't seen it. Almost incandescent with triumph, I marched up to the cab and asked him sarcastically: 'Time of the month is it, driver?' His humiliation was complete when the signalwoman (thank you, Fate, for rostering a woman that evening!) leaned out of her window and roundly scolded him for not knowing the rules.*

Despite seemingly hundreds of attempts to change the railway culture, by the 90s managers still knew only how to use the stick, not the carrot. There was no encouragement or praise; guards who did a hard day's work containing a wealth of good deeds and service beyond the call of duty were ignored — until they did something wrong; then the whole force of the stringent disciplinary procedures was brought crashing down on them. I myself was thanked only once in twenty years. A man opened a door and threatened to leap out of my train onto the multiple tracks approaching London's Cannon Street in the rush hour. At great personal risk I managed to grab his sweater and, clinging on desperately until my knuckles bled, somehow managed to haul him back to safety and shut the door before it was hit by another train. The police took the man away. My written report met with stony silence. Only after writing a letter pointing out that I had not only saved a life but averted a foul-up of the entire rush hour service did I receive recognition in the form of a customer care certificate and a cheque for £25, in a hasty 'ceremony' held in the locker room at Ramsgate as I was hurrying to get out to my train.

About 1988 I was delegated by my NUR District Council to attend meetings of the union's Women's Advisory Committee, a body that was purely advisory to the all-male EC. In 1988 I declined the opportunity to become a driver (under the Train Crew Concept) and in 1989 turned down the offer of a university place. I decided to remain as a guard and study part-time. I also began to research for this book. Having parted from my boyfriend I became involved with a colleague from Hastings, who persuaded me that I would be much happier there, as the depot had several female guards and drivers, all of whom 'took no nonsense from the men'. I moved in 1992 and although I found less hostility and fewer sexist comments, the men abused me with anonymous graffiti and insulting nicknames.

The Hastings line was more lively and interesting than the Kent coast. Among my passengers were Princess Margaret, Baroness Fookes and Glenda Jackson. I frequently sold tickets to Lord Longford and Lord Thomson of Montifieth; it amused me to see their names written on their Senior Railcards.

The guard's job had changed dramatically over the previous two decades: we had lost a lot of operational duties, the emphasis was on selling tickets and the rules were more strongly enforced and were getting pettier: one printed directive ruled that women train crews' tights had to be no thicker than 40 denier. Twelve pairs a year were issued, but we needed about 300 pairs because such thin, sheer tights would catch, snag and run very easily whenever one's leg brushed past a heating grid, bicycle, step-board, rucksack or suitcase and rarely survived to the end of a duty.

By 1994 my historical research entered its fifth year and I was invited to be consultant

* The rule book explains that drivers must know where the signal posts are, even in the dark, and a signal showing no aspect at night must be treated as red.

historian to the National Railway Museum for a forthcoming major exhibition on railwaywomen, *Oh Mrs Porter*. This ran for nine months and attracted the attention of the media, and I appeared in newspapers, magazines and on BBC television and radio. Professor Jack Simmons invited me to be a contributor to *The Oxford Companion to British Railway History*. I graduated as a Bachelor of Science after just four years of part-time study instead of the usual six. This drew further media attention, the *Daily Mirror* ran a feature about me and my university cited me in its literature. It was rare for anyone in train crew to get a degree: in 20 years I only knew one other guard and one driver who did so. Many people assumed that I would now apply for promotion, but I've never been a money-chaser and nothing on the railway appealed to me as much as being a guard. Nor would I ever leave the industry: I had worked on the railway for 90% of my adult life, and could not envisage doing anything else. I continued studying for a further three years and was awarded Honours in 1997. My next ambition was to get a master's degree and to research, write and publish a complete history of railwaywomen, while still working as a guard.

Helena in 1995, writing an early draft of *Railwaywomen* on a word-processor.
RAILNEWS

One effect of the publicity and of mixing with people in a professional and academic capacity outside of the railway was to draw attention to the sharp contrast between the contemptuous way I was treated by some railway managers and some male colleagues, and the respect I received elsewhere. To an extent, the railway culture had demoralised me somewhat but, through my extra-curricular activities and since being awarded a degree, I had developed a greater sense of self-worth. When I became embroiled in a long-running dispute with my depot manager, I was more inclined to stand up for myself and to challenge him when I felt that he was mishandling my case. I noticed that, while my conductor-manager was proud and supportive of my achievements, the depot manager (who was his superior) was more than a little scornful.

In late 1996 I slipped on diesel fuel leaking from a unit on the Brighton to Ashford line and damaged two vertebrae in my spine. My GP banned me from climbing into trains from track level, meaning I could no longer be a guard. This devastated me: I could not imagine myself doing any other job. Friends said that at least my high level of literacy and numeracy, my Honours degree and my computer skills made it easy to progress via the salaried grades into supervision and management. What happened astonished me: my manager had nothing for me to do and stood me off indefinitely on full pay.

Connex employed thousands of staff in hundreds of locations, but it was seven months before I was finally placed. It was a temporary position at the Telephone Enquiry Bureau at Tonbridge, which was scheduled to close down ten weeks later. During my training the supervisors sent me home early almost every day, knowing I was studying at home and for two hours a day while I commuted. At the end of three weeks of study and on-the-job training on the two computer systems, I qualified as a travel advisor in half the usual time. I felt I had proved to management that I could change from being a manual worker to an office worker and learn anything faster than anyone. I saw a bright future with Connex. What a way to celebrate the 20th anniversary of my joining the railway!

On the morning of my second day of proper work I was called to the conductor-manager's office. I expected him to congratulate me, but he suspended me, pending dismissal, for 'falsification of my time sheets'; in other words, for leaving early during my training. I waited at home for ten days, frantic with worry. He concluded that I had indeed left early, but only with permission, so all charges were dropped. Despite this, and despite now being a qualified travel advisor, I was not allowed to return to the Bureau, with no reason being given.

I was again stood off indefinitely on full pay, awaiting a 'suitable' vacancy. After seven months it was brought to my attention that a male colleague with less service than me had also been removed from guard's duties for medical reasons and was immediately engaged as a clerk at Hastings' ticket office. Shortly afterwards I was informed that they had found a job for me, too. I travelled to the depot manager's office at Tonbridge to find out what it was. There, I was coldly informed that I was to clean trains — the stereotypical punishment for delinquent train crew. If I refused, I would be sacked. None of this made sense, for on reporting to the cleaning shed I could not climb into the trains from the track (that is why I could not be a guard!) It was very mysterious. My GP removed me from the shed, specifying that I was fit for clerical work (the certificate stated 'no cleaning!') and expressed bewilderment that Connex could make no better use of a graduate with 20 years' service.

I waited anxiously at home for weeks, biting my nails, wondering what was going to happen next. Suddenly I was accused of 'inventing' my medical condition and summonsed to London to be sacked. My GP swiftly called in the Mayor of Hastings in whose presence (as a JP) he swore an affidavit confirming the results of my MRI scan and faxed it to London in the nick of time.

The stress upon me had reached intolerable levels, particularly as I had no idea what next was in store for me. The trauma of the accident; concern about my spinal injury; the roller-coaster of starting the new job, being suspended and almost dismissed; the humiliation of being ordered to clean trains; the shock of almost being sacked; combined with the stress of having just taken on a mortgage alone and also of having recently split from my long-term partner, all took their toll and some days I felt I was on the brink of a complete breakdown. I burned with resentment at the injustice of it all: why did my male colleague get a ticket office job while I, with 20 years' service and a degree, was deemed fit only to clean trains? I pursued the only logical course: I sued for sex discrimination. Owing to a legal agreement with Connex I am unable to reveal the outcome of the case.

Given all that had happened, the only possible way forward was for Connex and myself to part company. I resigned in December 1998, twenty-one years after working on the platform at Wimbledon station. One month later I sued Connex for personal injury. Owing to a legal agreement with Connex I am, again, unable to reveal the outcome of the case.

Seven years later, all I miss is the free travel.

Helena is now a full-time author, publisher and web-mistress. A more detailed version of the above story is available at www.railwaywomen.co.uk/gd1/html

Engine driver Heidi Mowforth on the footplate of the B12 8572. Mick Blackburn

Engine Driver Margaret Radway, Dean Forest Railway. M. Radway

9: Preserved Railways

The preserved railways are living museums of railway history. There are currently over 80 preserved and miniature railways in Britain and hundreds of women work on them, some as volunteers and others as employees. They are important in the history of railwaywomen because they have provided the first opportunities for them to fire and drive steam locomotives.

The first opened in the 1950s and over a hundred more have emerged since steam was abolished on BR in 1968. They operate as tourist attractions and most staff are volunteers who attend when they can; for many this means weekends only. The restoration work, cleaning, catering and operating are carried out by unpaid volunteers, while some administrative and managerial staff are employees.

From the outset, women — the majority of them wives, girlfriends and daughters of steam enthusiasts — were invited to help with retail sales, cleaning and catering, although some became involved with the restoration of old carriages, locomotives, signalboxes and a host of other artefacts needed to recreate the 'golden age of steam'.

By the 1960s a small handful of women became volunteer porters, ticket collectors, guards and signalwomen, and by the 70s a few expressed an interest in learning to fire and drive locomotives. There was a little hostility from some men, who saw steam trains as their territory. While a man needed only to show a mild interest to be entreated to join and help share the workload, a woman had to prove herself more serious, knowledgeable and dedicated than the average male volunteer.

Anthea Hanscomb has had a lifelong passion for steam engines. Through her son she visited the proposed railway centre at Quainton Road in 1969 and later helped him to set up a signalling system. On the line's first open day the signalling was operated by the Hanscomb family, including a daughter. Mrs Hanscomb later helped to rub down and repaint signal cabinets and restore a steam engine, and worked as a roster clerk. From August 1971 she began to learn everything about the engines and eventually qualified, first as an engine cleaner and then as a fireman. (Women who stoke fireboxes like to be called 'firemen'.) This involved performing a wide range of dirty, heavy and gruelling tasks connected with engine maintenance and repair. She fired her first engine in October 1972 and began learning to drive at Easter 1973; however, she did not qualify.

At 53 she found the couplings too heavy to manage and did not want to continue knowing that she could not perform all the duties. She much preferred firing because, as she said in her book *The Steaming Granny*: 'Every driver was different, every delivery of coal was different, every engine was different. No two firing turns were ever alike.' Mrs Hanscomb gave up firing engines in 1977, and worked instead in the refreshment room as a washer-up, and as an attendant in the society's small museum. For her 80th birthday, in July 2000, she drove a steam engine on the Severn Valley Railway, an experience she described as 'Absolute magic.'

Janice Uphill joined Quainton as a volunteer with her husband in 1969, when she was 36, and qualified as a fireman and later as a driver. Margaret Radway's love of steam engines began in 1961. When they were withdrawn in 1968 she joined first the Severn Valley Railway and later the Dean Forest Railway, where she helped in sales for several years before being given the opportunity to learn to fire and drive a steam engine in 1978. She did not even stop to consider whether the work was suitable for women, and found that the men accepted her. After retiring from the footplate in 1989, Mrs Radway travelled around the world by train.

Since 1984 the Kent & East Sussex Railway (KESR) has held several Ladies' Days, with all jobs being performed by women. Having no women except catering and retailing staff, it had to borrow them from other societies for the first event. Janice Uphill was one of five female drivers 'imported' for the occasion. She was not impressed with some of the hastily trained women she met: 'The signalwoman at Tenterden was wearing a skirt and three inch heels, so it was obvious she was not serious about the job', she said. When taking part in the 1986 two-day event, Mrs Uphill felt it was 'patently obvious that KESR male crew members wanted their own girls on the footplate, whether they were trained or not'. In 1994 and 1995 Quainton held its own Ladies' Days. 'Because it was on home ground I was able to sense the ambivalence among some of the men, but the women also,' said Janice. The mechanical engineer had to stay on site, for no woman could do his job, but he kept a low profile. Mrs Uphill argued in the members' magazine that a Ladies' Day should be just that, or abandoned, and they have not had another one since.

By the beginning of 1999, Quainton had several women in its operating grades, and the male/female distribution was as follows: steam locomotive drivers: 15 men, one woman; DMU drivers: 10 men, one woman; diesel drivers: 11 men, no women; passed firemen: seven men, no women; firemen: 13 men, two women; engine cleaners: four men, one woman; guards: 13 men, three women; station masters: 17 men, three women. (Some people hold more than one position.)

Today, all over Britain women are working in many different roles on the preserved railways, from press officers to engine cleaners, from cafeteria staff to paint-scrapers. It isn't as difficult for a woman to get accepted by the male volunteers as a fireman or driver, thanks to the determined spirit of the pioneers in breaking down the barriers of prejudice. Most of them seem to want to play down their gender; most of my appeals to various railways produced no response from their female volunteers, but the ones who replied were all train crew, and are very aware of their achievements as the first women in British railway history to fire and drive steam locomotives. They are all women of great spirit and determination, and it was a pleasure to make their acquaintance.

Tragically, the first woman driver on the Romney, Hythe and Dymchurch Railway,* Suzanne Martin, aged 43, was killed on 10th July 2005 when the train she was driving collided with a car at an unmanned level crossing. She had worked on railway since her teenage years, as a volunteer and a paid employee. She met her husband Danny while working there and, at the time of the crash, he was the railway's General Manager. Mrs Martin was the first woman train driver in Britain to die in a train crash.

* The RHDR is one-third scale steam hauled tourist line.

Janice Uphill – Volunteer at Quainton Road

In 1969 there were a few women members at Quainton, and these did refreshments, collecting money on the gate etc. Working in the NHS, where women often held higher positions, it came as quite a surprise to me that at Quainton women were subtly pushed into catering, particularly tea making. It took a long time for the other members to realise I seriously wanted to become steam locomotive crew and go through the training. Funnily enough the main opposition came from women; one in particular was very much against my joining the training scheme; she wished to get to the top by what I can only call 'foul means', i.e. getting on the footplate by doing the bits of the job she liked and letting the men do the rest. I, however, insisted on going through the scheme the same as the men.

My duties were identical to a man's. I was never an athletic person, but I did pound the manual typewriter for thirty years so had very strong arms for a woman. Of course one has not got the strength of a man, so I found ways round the job, for example where a man would put six shovelfuls of coal round the firebox I would put twelve half shovelfuls. One of the trainers said his best fireman was a woman (me), which was very nice.

On the whole the men were supportive, but there were some jealousies. When I breached a Rule it was reported to the Executive Committee and I was suspended from the footplate for three months, yet other 'crimes' went on which were not reported when done by men.

The hours on a footplate are all day, which means lighting up at about 6.30 a.m. and finishing after dropping the fire at about 7.30 p.m. Shovelling coal is hard work, but lighting up can be worse, particularly when the weather is bad and the wood and paper are damp. On the plus side it is so rewarding to see the train going through one's own efforts. At first the men tried to do some of the nasty jobs, for chivalrous reasons, but I made it clear I wished to do it all myself and learn properly. 'If you do a man's job you must act like a man.' I wore the same as the men: overalls, grease top hat and boots. Because of this and having short hair, in the early days I think the public assumed I was a man, and I have been called 'Sir', 'Governor' etc. Every now and again one would hear astonished remarks: 'I think that one in the middle is a lady.' A Belgian said in disgust to my husband: 'A woman on the footplate, whatever next!'

I still do not understand why in all the preservation railway societies there are so few women. I can only think that the average woman does not want to get dirty, and yet to me that is half the fun; after all you are dressed for the part. Some women thought I was letting the side down, doing such a dirty job. A woman must be prepared to work hard and get dirty, and perhaps try and be better than the average man as it is still such a man's world. You have to be able to get on with men as colleagues.

In the 1990s two newish members took over the rostering. One seemed determined not to admit I was a driver and did not want me rostered at all; I had to be quite fierce and point out I had been trained and qualified the same as the men. The other was incapable of understanding I knew anything about footplates and started showing me where the oiling points were in the cab. I shut him up by telling him I had served my fireman apprenticeship exclusively on that engine. I don't think he liked me much after that. There were a few people who did not want to be on the footplate with me when I was driving, but whether it was just because they did not like me or because I was a woman I shall never know.

From 1977 to 1991 I was co-opted onto the Executive Committee, the only woman among eleven men.

Heidi Mowforth – Bluebell Railway

I have been on the footplate since 1982 and driving since 1994. I started on the Bluebell Railway and became their first female fireman in 1988, later going on to become the railway's first 'Senior Fireman' (a sort of yard pilot). With my husband and two children, I spent my family holidays on the North Norfolk Railway (NNR), and it was there that I passed out to drive in 1994. Later, following an appeal for crews from the KESR, I joined there as a driver in 1997. My husband is also a driver and our son is a fireman.

When I joined the Bluebell as an engine cleaner in 1982, there had never been any women qualified for the footplate. Despite considerable opposition from 'above', the loco inspector stuck to his convictions and passed me out for firing, thereby changing Bluebell history. One of the things that I had to do on the day was drive and fire the engine (Schools Class 928) with a seven coach train single handed for a distance of five miles. This is something that no other woman has ever done, and I was proud to have achieved that. So was the inspector, as he had carried his point! The Bluebell now has three other female firemen, and I like to think that it was partly due to my initial efforts in storming the citadel that they were able to achieve this with greater ease than I had.

Engine driving is still primarily a man's job and probably always will be — the majority of women just don't see its appeal. Sometimes I get totally absorbed in the job and temporarily forget that I am the 'wrong sex', so that when someone points out the 'woman driver' I don't immediately twig that it's me to whom they are referring.

The vast majority of disparaging and derogatory comments come not from colleagues but from passengers. Some can be hurtful, particularly when they doubt one's ability. Most comments, however, are actually pretty amusing. I am often asked whether they 'let me' drive or shovel coal. The obvious answer, of course, is that they have to let me drive as I am the only person on the engine qualified to do so. Once, when I was supervising the fireman driving, the guard told me that an elderly gent had made a comment about woman drivers, to which his friend had replied: 'Yes, but at least they've got a man on the brake.' This was particularly amusing, as it was a 'man on the brake' who had dumped that same engine in the dirt and broken her axle boxes just a few weeks previously. Some ribbing is done in a jovial manner and provides harmless amusement all round. To men who laughingly object to having a woman driver I always suggest that they set off walking immediately if they want to be home before dark, and it's always worth pointing out that, over the last 150 years or so, 100% of railway accidents involving steam engines have been caused by men. Sitting on the footplate at Tenterden one evening, I heard a vociferous gentleman commenting about women on the engine. As Tom, the fireman, and I leaned over the side of the cab, the man ignored me and addressed his question to Tom. 'Good evening, Driver', he said, 'and who's that lovely creature you've got on the footplate with you?' 'That's Tom', I answered swiftly. 'He's my fireman.'

It can work the other way, of course — after a few memorable non-stop runs I have had the honour of passengers coming up to me to shake my hand and congratulate me on a good run, just as they would if I were a 'proper' driver!

Adverse comments from colleagues are rare. One or two make faintly jovial sexist remarks, but they are usually from the lower ranks anyway and fairly easily slapped down. However, I did hear one railway inspector say that he wouldn't consider having a woman drive because they wouldn't be able to cope with the reversers on some of the engines. I've driven 85 different engines (probably more than the inspector concerned), and encountered many difficulties and problems, but never a serious one with a reverser.

I've had plenty of incidents to deal with, most of which would have happened to anyone. However, I do sometimes have to cope with 'gentlemen firemen' who feel uncomfortable about allowing me to couple up or throw out the fire. Sometimes they seem to restrain themselves with difficulty from opening the cab door for me and helping me on with my overall jack, bless 'em. Lovely chaps without exception, and great company.

On one occasion my son Henry, then aged sixteen and newly passed out, was firing to me, and making up the fire at Tenterden station whilst I went to the toilet. A passenger asked him something and, without thinking he replied: 'I'm sure it'll be all right, I just need to ask my mum.' Of course, it never occurred to the person concerned that 'mum' was the driver, and he obviously had Henry marked down as a Private Pike!

I have always received the same respect as other drivers of my experience. My opinions are sought as much as anyone else's would be, my advice to firemen is ignored just the same as any other driver's, and my mistakes and omissions are admonished just as anyone else's are. In mess room conversation and technical discussions my opinions and experiences are listened to and argued with the same as any other driver's.

It has to be said, unfortunately, that this is not the case on all railways. Some still pride themselves on being bastions of misogyny, with pornography scattered on mess room tables and women's worth in the department judged on how much drink they can put away on a night out. The majority of men, to be fair, appreciate what it has taken to achieve what I have and respect me for that.

The job of an engine driver is difficult for anyone. It's dirty and uncomfortable, and everything on the engine is hot, stiff and heavy. The hours are long and exposure to the elements excruciating in extremes of hot or cold weather; burns, scalds, cuts and bruises are an everyday occurrence. A certain amount of physical training is required to build up the necessary stamina and endurance, which is probably harder work for women to do than for men, but not impossible. Female athletes manage it, after all.

Driving a GWR prairie tank engine on the NNR.

MICK BLACKBURN

Both the NNR and the KESR are proud of their women in operating grades, and station staff will often say: 'Today we've got a woman driver' with a certain amount of pride. Recently, the KESR, hard pushed for volunteers of either sex, managed to rustle up a woman signalman, guard, driver and trainee fireman, quite by chance, all on the same day, which was viewed by other volunteers as a positive thing and worthy of note. I also appeared on North Norfolk Radio as the NNR's token female driver, to promote the railway and appeal to would-be volunteers of either sex.

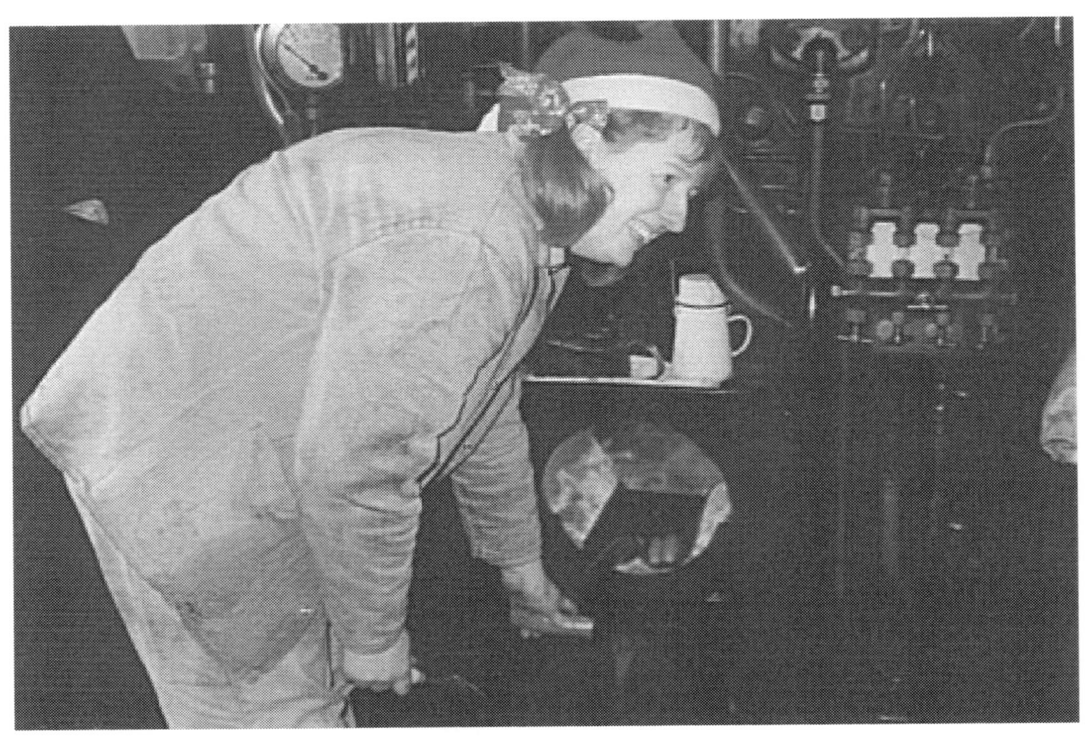

Fireman Wendy Turner, West Somerset Railway.
W, Turner

Guard Ann Tayler, Quainton Rd.
Adrian Hancock

Anthea Hanscomb "The Steaming Granny".
A. Hanscomb

WENDY TURNER - WEST SOMERSET RAILWAY

In the summer of 1994 my younger brother (with whom I had visited many preserved railways) joined the WSR and I went along for moral support. While there I was talked into filling in the forms as well. The co-ordinator raised his eyebrows when I said that I would only 'join up' if I didn't have to do traditional female tasks. I wanted to get my hands dirty! I have never been particularly 'ladylike' and as a child I was always the one to come home grubby. Ironically, my brother has never done a day's work for the railway whereas I became an engine driver.

My first hurdle was to join the steam locomotive restoration group of which the majority are footplate crew and trainees who meet regularly to work on the latest project. I was made to feel very welcome, shown around the site and workshop and assigned my tasks for the evening. There was one other female present who was very shy and who came along with her boyfriend but was obviously accepted and liked by the team. Most of the men were curious to find a redheaded, 26-year-old nurse among them and many asked why I wanted to work in the shed and on the footplate. At no time can I remember it being suggested that I — as a female — might find other roles on the railway more acceptable. I went along knowing that it was their domain and did and still do respect that. Many apologise if they swear or mention anything which they deem to be unsavoury but as a nurse there is not much that bothers me and many have now given up apologising. I am also keen to learn and not afraid to ask for help or advice. I have never been belittled or sneered at but my questions have been answered and guidance given.

Over the first two years I went through the 'firing school' and went on to pass my firing exams. This training consisted of learning how to fire a steam engine and how it works, the rules and regulations of the railway, how a railway runs, shunting and coupling railway rolling stock together etc. My biggest challenge was the buckeye coupling that is used between coaches. This is probably the heaviest duty a fireman has to perform. I did struggle as did some of the men but I achieved this skill through determination and brute force. I have never expected any preferential treatment but I am aware of my capabilities and those concomitant with being female. I accept that I am not as strong as the average man but that does not prevent me from carrying out my role as a fireman. If in doubt I will always ask for help especially when lifting very heavy objects but that is out of respect for my back not necessarily because I am incapable.

The time scale over which I passed my exams was no different to that of most of the men. Being a fireman is a job very much in the public eye and people often peer into the footplate. It is from them that I have faced prejudice and disapproval. One man suggested that the only reason I was there was that I must be married to the driver. When I explained that I was single and not dating anyone from the railway but was a volunteer of my own free will, he changed tack and said that it was not authentic to have women on the footplate. I agreed with him but carefully pointed out that times had changed. He left unconvinced. Many men have approached the footplate in disbelief questioning my motives and capability of the job and then often made a condescending remark about having a 'female driver'. I always reply politely but firmly and they appear satisfied with my response. Most women visitors are very complimentary and supportive using remarks such as 'Good for you!' or 'Nice to see a woman on the footplate.'

Why do I do it? Well the railway runs along 21 miles of beautiful Somerset countryside from the Quantock Hills to the seaside. To smell and hear the engine working hard as it makes its way through the hills taking people along the line is an experience I never tire of. To 'light up' an engine and prepare it for the day ahead is wonderful. There is no one else around except the driver and all is peaceful except for the engine slowly crackling and hissing into life. At the end of the day, pleasantly tired from the fresh air, I dig out the fire, smokebox and ashpan to leave them ready for the following day.

I have made many friends through the railway and have earned their respect and friendship, which I value greatly. One of my colleagues paid me the ultimate compliment: 'Wendy, you are more one of the lads than a lot of the lads' and I think this sums up how railway life is for me. I am still part of the Association restoration team and take my allocated jobs as seriously as the others.

JUDITH EMMERSON – QUAINTON ROAD

I joined Quainton as a joint member with my husband about 1984. At first I thought steam trains were dirty and smelly things; they still are but it gets in the blood, festers and then you are hooked. It never occurred to me that I could ever get interested enough to work there but the thought of becoming the railway equivalent of a golfing widow every weekend was not very appealing. We began by going on odd weekends and helping with the restoration of an engine, just the odd bit of metal bashing and painting. Then Alan joined the Quainton crew training scheme, so that by the time the loco was ready there would be people to drive it. I rashly suggested that they could learn the steam side and I would have a go at learning to drive the diesels so that when the loco was restored to a rolling chassis I could have the easy job of towing it up and down the line to run it in. Little did I realise the hours of blood, sweat and tears that would ensue in the following years.

Owing to the operating rules, in order to become a diesel driver I would have to start at the bottom of the steam training course so I would know where all the various levers etc. in the cab of the steam loco would have to be set, so as not to damage engines during shunting. And so I started as a cleaner. Getting dirty never bothered me but I had not bargained on the early starts; dawn was a time that I had rarely ever seen and even now I question my sanity on a freezing cold December morning when the rest of the world is still under a warm duvet.

For those people who suffer from insomnia I recommend *The Engineman's Handbook*, a book that I was to become very familiar with over the next few years. It took me years to read through to the end as I only managed a couple of pages each night before I fell asleep. Having not the faintest idea of how a steam loco worked when I started meant long hours of studying before I took the first of my exams and became a passed cleaner, which meant I could begin learning to fire the loco. A couple of years later I was informed by my husband: 'I've put your name down for your fireman's exam.' 'Aaagh!' was my first thought, but take the exam I did and passed under the very watchful eye of Dick Hardy.

Several more years passed as a fireman before the next exam to become a passed fireman and therefore able to drive. That was at the end of 1999 and I have been driving ever since.

The reactions I get from the other members can be a bit mixed but I have only had trouble with one male crew member who felt there was no place for women in railway preservation, but as I am now a driver and he is still only a fireman I can only assume he is jealous. The reaction from people ranges from: 'Why do something you don't get paid for?' right through to 'That's a woman driving the train!' I don't care what people say, the fact that I've made it to driver is good enough for me.

The fact that I'm a woman has never been an issue with the crews I've been rostered with (except the one I mentioned earlier) and some even say I'm better than most of the men. I admit to having thrown the shovel in the firebox once, it sailed clean through the fire hole door and then stood up in the fire against the side of the box taunting me. I got quite a lot of ribbing about it, but I've got broad shoulders and gave back as good as I got.

I did get to drive the diesels and also qualified to drive our DMU, and the last exam I took was to be a guard – much more civilised, no getting up at the crack of dawn, and no getting dirty. I once had the honour of driving Thomas the Tank Engine with Tony Blair, Cherie and their little son, Leo, on the train behind me, and for one fleeting moment I thought of the supposed 15 minutes of fame that everyone is supposed to get once in a lifetime but then thought that if I was the one to injure the Prime Minister it might just get me more than my allotted 15 minutes so I was extra careful on that trip.

Why do I do it? The power that comes from one little match!

Porter Jocelynne Herriott on pointsman's duty giving an engine crew the green flag as permission to set back into Smallbrook Junction, Isle of Wight Steam Railway, 2005.

10: Final comments

> The history of men's opposition to women's emancipation is more interesting perhaps than the story of that emancipation itself.
>
> Virginia Woolf

The railways are imbued with maleness to their very core. Everyone connected with the creation and operation of railways was male: businessmen and financiers, architects and engineers, navvies and bricklayers, managers and operating staff. The masculinity of railways was reinforced by military uniforms, a strict hierarchy of rank and severe disciplinary procedures, all of which were modelled on those of the armed forces.

Before 1915 the exclusion of women from almost all employment on the railways did not need to be justified, or even explained. It went without saying that railway work was 'man's work'. Women were hired by railway companies only in two circumstances: either to perform work that only women could (or would) do, or to replace men in jobs where they could be paid less.* Gatekeeping had both elements; often only a railwayman's wife could obtain a position because it was intertwined with his job. If widowed, she was retained because she was cheap and needed no training. For reasons of propriety only women could work as ladies' room attendants and as ships' stewardesses to attend to lady passengers, while laundering and sewing were regarded as women's work. To save money women were utilised wherever possible as cleaners, clerks, French polishers, hostel attendants and canteen staff on less pay than the lowest-paid men.

In 1915 a third reason arose: the staff shortage caused by the First World War. The companies' proposed introduction of women to uniformed grades provoked men to vocalise what they believed women's limitations were, although they rarely provided a rationale. It was deemed self-evident that women could not, for example, climb ladders, shift heavy luggage or guard trains. Specific reasons were offered, however, to explain why men opposed women signallers: it was because women were 'constitutionally unfitted', 'apt to lose their heads' and therefore 'a danger to the travelling public'.[1] According to John Holford, male opposition to women in uniformed roles was due to the railways' 'highly mechanistic organisation':

> The grade and classification structure was the foundation of an intricate system of status differences, and in peacetime an individual's progress through them was slow. During the war it accelerated: thus the social meanings attached to the various jobs, or work-roles, were severely dislocated. Very often the short-term response was a vigorous defence of existing standards.[2]

---

* Provided, of course, that women were considered suitable for the work.

During the Second World War the strongest objections were against female guards, who — it was assumed — would not be able to cope in emergencies. Despite the fact that during each war women climbed ladders and worked as porters, guards and signalwomen, when peace came they had to go: railwaymen protested at women being retained and the companies feared industrial action.

Having proved themselves during the First World War, there was no practical reason why women should not have been recruited in peacetime to any uniformed or salaried position from 1918 onwards. That they were not is attributable to male chauvinism within railway management and objections from railwaymen. During the 20s and 30s, and again during the 50s and 60s, owing to the enormous size of the railway industry, most railwaymen had no knowledge of the women station porters, signallers and halt attendants scattered across Britain, often in isolated locations, and those who knew of them turned a blind eye; but attempts in the 60s and early 70s to employ women as guards and signallers provoked fierce opposition from railwaymen. Meanwhile, women in salaried grades were blocked in various ways by their male colleagues, the TSSA and managers, who condemned the employment of wives, objected to women working at night and publicly ridiculed the notion of 'female station masters'. Again no specific reasons seem to have been given.

The Sex Discrimination Act changed everything by opening all railway work to women. As we have seen in chapters 7 and 8, many female pioneers in male wages grades were treated as nuisances by managers and subjected to sexist abuse and harassment from their male colleagues. The Act allowed women to enter all traditionally male industries and services, such as road, sea and air transport and to take increasingly dangerous, front-line roles within the armed forces, the police and the fire brigades. An independent enquiry found that most policewomen had experienced sexual harassment at work; an RAF internal survey published in 2005 revealed that almost half of the women serving in its ranks had suffered it and NUMAST, the British naval officers' union, reported that 76 per cent of its women members on board ships had encountered it. A Home Office report found that fire-fighters were strongly opposed to women in their ranks and considered they were not 'up to' doing 'a man's job',[3] while inspectors discovered evidence of sexual harassment in all ten brigades visited. Women bus crew and lorry drivers were also harassed by male colleagues, who wrote graffiti about them and accused them of taking jobs away from men. These attitudes and incidents were strikingly similar to those experienced by the pioneer women in formerly male railway work.

Uniforms, transport, discipline, danger, machismo and having been traditionally an all male workplace link the industries and services in which women have been reviled by their male colleagues, and the railway encompasses all of these characteristics. Some men were drawn to these types of workplaces precisely because of their masculine character, and because they did not want (for whatever reason) to work alongside women. No wonder they were angry when women joined their ranks — angry enough, apparently, to try to harass them out of the workplace.

EXPLAINING MALE HOSTILITY

In 1990 Train Driver Karen Harrison* wrote an article in the left-wing newspaper *The Morning Star* in which she put forth her analysis of why women were excluded from train crew for most of railway history and why the post-1975 pioneers were treated with such hostility. She asserted that 'sex equality almost exclusively seems to be a privilege of the middle class', and continued:

> Look closely at the inroads women have made in jobs which are traditionally male and where do you find most of them? In the middle-class 'professions.' Women doctors, solicitors and managers positively abound compared to female plumbers and bricklayers. There are more women flying planes than driving trains.[4]

It is regrettable that Ms Harrison did not specify who, exactly, prevented women from becoming plumbers but, by pointing out the lack of obstruction from middle class men towards women of their own class, she came perilously close to suggesting that working class men might be to blame. Ms Harrison continued to walk a political tightrope by protesting against the sexual harassment of railwaywomen while simultaneously trying not to alienate her readership by blaming the culprits:

> The problem of sexual harassment is an issue which BR is incapable of dealing with. BR has so far never taken on the responsibility of ensuring that the workplace is not hostile ... Freshly recruited women are usually plonked into all-male workplaces and may face antagonism and resentment — with the bosses turning a blind eye to the harassment.[5]

Although this statement is true for the most part,† by laying the blame entirely on the shoulders of middle-class managers Ms Harrison implied that working class men were incapable of taking responsibility for their own actions. She also remarked that women who complained about harassment were 'sometimes accused of dividing the movement and losing their class perspective, by perceiving men — not the ruling class — as their main adversaries'. If the ruling class (and not men) are to blame, the corollary is that 'ruling class' women were more responsible than working class men for harassing railwaywomen, which clearly was not the case.

I contend that it was not social class but patriarchal attitudes — which were shared by managers and railwaymen alike — that caused the problems with men that were faced by women pioneers in traditionally male railway work. Boys were indoctrinated to believe that women were weak and would 'go to pieces' in emergencies and that women should not be out late at night and in all weathers, facing danger. Railway workers in many wages grades face terrible weather, work all hours day and night and face the many hazards of operating associated with speeding trains and, for many, electrified track. There is always the possibility of witnessing and having to cope with accidents and injuries, even

---

* In 1990 the author offered Ms Harrison space in this book to write her own piece. She declined, being 'too busy' at the time and has since made no contact.

† I disagree with Ms Harrison's claim that women were 'plonked into all-male workplaces', on two counts. Firstly, managers tried to divert women away from men's workplaces by offering them jobs as cleaners and clerks; secondly the women chose to work with men, but Ms Harrison makes them seem like helpless victims.

fatalities. Emergencies are certain to arise sooner or later in the career of everyone whose work takes him near the permanent way. In the years leading up to the recruitment of the first female train crew there were several highly publicised train crashes that resulted in multiple deaths, and thousands of incidents involving railway workers. (For example, 43 railway staff were killed on duty in 1979, while 6,122 suffered injuries.) Physical assaults on staff by passengers run at thousands per annum, in addition there are many more incidents in which staff are threatened and verbally abused. (In 2003 there were 3,581 reported attacks, nearly two-thirds of which were physical.)

Railwaymen knew they were expected to deal unflinchingly with whatever emergency arose, but they could not envisage women coping with the kinds of scenarios that could happen to anyone who works in the vicinity of the track, such as fires, obstructions, derailments and collisions. The lives and safety of many others depends on each employee keeping a clear head and carrying out the proper actions, even when in shock or injured. Many railwaymen did not feel comfortable that their own lives may one day have depended upon a female colleague's performing the correct safety procedures.*

There was also a feeling that, for their own welfare, it was not desirable for women — usually called 'ladies' in this context — to be in the firing line of abuse from passengers or placed in potentially dangerous situations. Men's reference point was their own families: they would not like their wives or daughters to face such hazards and they could not understand why any member of the 'fair sex' would choose such a harsh working environment, especially as she had softer options available in buffets and offices. To the argument that women could be trained to deal with emergencies, railwaymen's typical response was that it would be 'unladylike'.

Women were also perceived as damaging the machismo attached to male railway jobs. If women could do the work, it ceased to be men's work and, worse, it was no longer perceived as being difficult. Men feared that if women degraded railway operating to a job that 'even a woman could do' the value of the work might fall in the employer's estimation and that this would eventually lead to a reduction in wages.†

I believe that the pornography that was both sent to women and displayed on the walls, the lewd graffiti, the unwelcome fondling and the sexual assaults suffered by many female pioneers stemmed not from uncontrolled male libido but from an unconscious wish to remind both female staff and fellow railwaymen of women's 'proper' place in society: that of sex objects. The media's subversion of the 1960s sexual revolution served to encourage men to see women as little more than objects of male sexual desire. There was a huge increase in pornography and everywhere — even in national newspapers — there were images of topless, sexually provocative women. Even *Railnews* labelled female staff 'dolly-birds', habitually depicted them in mini-skirts and bikinis and set them to compete against each other in contests where physical appearance was the sole criterion. Is it any wonder that, having been indoctrinated by the media to see women in this way a number of railwaymen, when faced with a young woman entering their workplace, treated her accordingly? The 'dolly-bird' culture trivialised all women, and those who were trying to be taken seriously in the workplace found it difficult to counteract the view of women being constantly inculcated into men's minds.

It is hardly surprising therefore that male managers flinched at the thought of

---

* For example, if a train is derailed and obstructed an adjacent line, another train might collide with it if the crew failed to carry out the correct protection procedures.

† In fact, railway workers now enjoy the highest rates of pay they have ever received For example, train drivers currently (2005) earn over £36,000 per annum.

recruiting women to railway operating or that railwaymen on the 'shop floor' had so many adverse comments to make about their new female colleagues. It is unrealistic to expect anyone to disbelieve everything they have been taught, just because the law changes. It takes an exceptional person to rise above indoctrination and, by definition, the majority cannot be exceptional.

Railway managers, as well as being influenced by the media's trivialisation of women, found women in men's jobs to be a nuisance: they expected toilets to be provided; they complained of sexual harassment; they didn't like the feminine, fitted jackets or the ladylike berets designed for them and demanded masculine uniforms with capacious pockets, and caps with peaks to keep the rain and sun from their eyes. Some became pregnant, creating problems with uniforms and maternity leave. From the managers' point of view it would have been much simpler to get rid of the women rather than to tackle these seemingly never-ending problems. It was assumed that, in any case, they would all leave, probably sooner rather than later, to have children. It must have seemed an awful lot of trouble to build toilets, redesign uniforms and make special arrangements for maternity, let alone to educate over a hundred thousand railwaymen to take 'dolly-birds' seriously and to treat them as equals, all for a few temporary workers who, most men thought, shouldn't really be doing the job, in any case.

Exploitation, Betrayal and Triumph

Exploitation

There is no doubt that for the first century of their employment on railways women were exploited by the companies. This was, primarily, for their cheap labour, although the belief that they were more compliant and docile than men was a bonus. During the 19th century women were limited to low-skilled, low-paid jobs because their lack of education left them unfit for anything else: in all social classes, girls were denied the educational and training opportunities open to boys. Railway managers were simply doing their job by getting work carried out as cheaply as possible in order to maximise returns for the shareholders. They and every other industrial employer exploited the poor bargaining position that women held in the labour market, one that had evolved over centuries.

During both world wars women were engaged to take the place of men and, despite their successfully performing railway work for up to seven years, at the end of each war they were told in no uncertain terms that such work 'really' belonged to men and many were — ultimately — dismissed for nothing other than being the wrong sex. Their utilisation in war work was typical of how women were treated in other male-dominated workplaces.[6] Although in both wars women were used and discarded their exploitation pales into insignificance when compared with, for example, being sent off to die in the trenches as cannon fodder in a badly-managed war. Expert sources assert that many of the millions of troops who lost their lives during the First World War had no idea of what the war was about. At least war-working railwaywomen knew exactly why they were there, and 99% of them escaped not only with life and limb intact but with happy memories of their work.

Betrayal

Railwaywomen were betrayed mainly by men of their own class, in particular by their 'brothers' in the trade unions. For most of railway history, none of the industry's unions have consistently supported equality for women either in pay or in opportunity; on the contrary, before 1915 they were indifferent to the exploitation of women as cheap labour. Later, NUR officials betrayed female level crossing keepers by accepting their weekly subscriptions while agreeing to their being omitted from every improvement gained for their male counterparts; indeed, the union blatantly pursued improvements exclusively for male crossing keepers.

Only when companies wanted women to substitute for men during the First World War did the unions suddenly take an interest in their wages. Despite the fact that the (almost) equal pay gained for war workers was motivated by nothing other than concern for men (i.e. for male rates and male re-employment) both an officer and a historian of the NUR have since boasted to me that the union 'won equal pay for women' almost 60 years before it became a legal requirement, citing this as proof that the union has 'always' supported equal rights. The reality is that, over the years, NUR leaders have given consent to women being treated unequally in relation to pay, promotion, transfer, redundancy, uniform, pension schemes, sick pay and free travel. In some respects, ASLEF leaders acted more honestly. By refusing to recruit engine cleaners during both wars and making no promises to women they at least stuck to their principles. After each war, officers and members of the NUR and ASLEF made sure women were ejected from male grades and were content for them to revert to their former, inferior role, to be paid less than men in unisex grades and to be ghettoised in female grades.

The position of the RCA was different. Its officers wavered between supporting and opposing women's equality, but the cause was kept alive by the large number and vocal nature of its female members. They, however, often found themselves opposed by their union brothers, who moved anti-women resolutions, and by their general secretaries, one of whom openly announced his wish to block women from promotion to jobs he personally considered unsuitable for the female sex. If the union had not had so many female activists keeping women's cause alive, the situation might have been similar to that obtaining in the NUR.

All three railway unions when engaging administrative staff emulated other employers by advertising for male and female clerks separately and offering lower pay to the latter. Union leaders may have felt justified in not wasting their members' subscriptions by offering women higher pay than they would get elsewhere, but surely unions should have been setting the moral principle of equal pay, not colluding with the financial exploitation of women.

The RCA even dismissed one of its own employees in 1950 for getting married, at a time when the railways were abolishing the marriage bar.

Railwaywomen were among the millions of working women who, in the 50s and 60s, felt betrayed by the Labour party which, although its very existence was based upon improving the lot of the working classes, promised them equal pay when in opposition but found excuses not to deliver it when in power.

Railwaywomen were also betrayed by their employers. In 1955 the BRB told female salaried staff that they had won equal pay with men. However, when all the exceptions were excluded, only a quarter received it. The following year the BRB abolished women's grades, meaning that work could no longer be labelled as 'men's' or 'women's'. The BRB was able not only to grab the headlines at the time but would, in future press releases and promotional literature, be able to boast that they conceded 'equality' to women a full 20 years before British law required it. But, again, this turned out to be a hoax: women were still (unofficially) banned from promotion to positions that involved supervising or managing male staff, by 'gentleman's agreements' forged with the unions without consulting their female members.

Such gentleman's agreements were no secret; as has been seen in chapter 5, the NUR and TSSA leaders had publicly declared their opposition to women being promoted to positions in which they would be in charge of men, and this illustrates a further example of both unions' betrayal of women.

While it cannot be denied that the rank-and-file, the officers and the executive committees of the railway unions betrayed women and colluded with their exploitation, one needs to place their actions into historical, social and economic context. The unions were comprised of working class men, raised and educated to accept as true certain things about women that today's young, enlightened men (or older, 'reconstructed' men) do not believe. Trades unions are run by and for their members. Until 1915 the NUR's membership was entirely male, so it comes as no surprise that the priority of the union's officials was to protect their members from women's cheap labour, because it threatened to bring down men's rates and maybe even to displace men. One cannot blame them for wanting to ensure that their brothers in the forces had jobs to return to. To have acted any other way would have been a betrayal of their own members — a far worse offence than treating women in the same shoddy manner in which they were treated by comparable organisations.

Nowadays, political correctness dictates — in professional life, at least — that men may not openly treat women as inferiors, but this is a recent development that has filtered down from the professional classes to trade union officers, already under pressure from their growing female membership to distance themselves from traditional, working class, patriarchal attitudes. For most of the period covered by this book, however, the majority of the ordinary working men who joined railway unions and gained power and influence within them by becoming shop stewards, branch secretaries, conference delegates, regional officers and members of national executives took with them all the prejudices and beliefs about women that they had absorbed while being raised and educated in a patriarchal society. It seems unrealistic to expect them to hold views on women workers that were wildly different from those of their peers, their bosses and their counterparts in other industries and unions.

It is essential to look at the history of railwaywomen in the context of wider society, and to understand that factions fight their own corners, for their own ends. When one studies the motives and objectives of each party — employer, union, and worker — it becomes clear that each has its own agenda and the story of railwaywomen illustrates each sector behaving in ways that served itself.

No workplace exists in a vacuum; it is a reflection of the society in which it was created and in which it evolved; and there is nothing unique about the way women who worked for the railways have been treated; there is nothing unique about their employers, their unions or the way in which they eventually gained occupational equality with men.

TRIUMPH

Ultimately, railwaywomen have triumphed. They have equal pay and equal opportunities, from train maintenance depots to station platforms; from signalling technical departments to the boardrooms of the recently-privatised railway companies. There is probably no job on the railway that is not done by at least one woman somewhere in Britain.

In all grades, women have shown themselves little different from men as regards lateness, attendance, sick leave, coping with emergencies and other areas in which they had been predicted to be inferior, such as in the most traditionally-male area of train crew. Over the years thousands of trains have run with an all-female crew and, on 14th November 1995, Eurostar decided to celebrate its first anniversary by operating the 0813 from Paris to London with no men among its 18 crew members. Accompanying Driver Fiona Johns were Train Managers Emma Frank and Tracey Lynch, and 15 catering staff.[7] Women now clean, fire and drive steam locomotives, work that none was permitted to perform under BR.

In some cases women have proved to be better workers than men. Train Manager (i.e. Guard) Polly Robertson of Paddington beat the men to win several awards for customer service, including the Outstanding Personal Contribution category at the National Rail Awards 2003 and, less than four weeks later, was named Frontline Customer Service Professional of the year by the Institute of Customer Service, having already won a First Great Western Gold Award and other company commendations. Ms Robertson remarked, modestly: 'I am a little embarrassed by the awards ... It's a question of just doing my job.' In 2005 Rail Operator Doreen Sweeney was awarded an MBE for her 19 years' excellent service at Bexleyheath, London.[8]

It is perhaps ironic that the occupation most frequently singled out for remarks about women's superiority over men is that of train driver, the very job that has always had the most masculine image; the job that every schoolboy — and no schoolgirl — supposedly aspired to:

> London Underground recorded a record peak-time performance last month largely because of the impact of new women drivers. ... They have endured taunts from male colleagues and abuse from passengers, but the army of women drivers recruited by the London Underground have proved that they are better than men at making Tube trains run on time.
>
> The number of women driving Tube trains has almost doubled in the past year, and managers believe that their influence has helped to end a culture of absenteeism and militancy in the workforce. For the first time last month, London Underground recorded a week in which none of its 5,000 peak trains were cancelled because a driver had failed to turn up for work. ... The improved performance follows an 18-month recruitment drive that has concentrated on attracting female drivers with half-page advertisements in *Cosmopolitan*.
>
> An Underground spokeswoman said that much of the improvement could be attributed to the female recruits. ... 'There is evidence that suggests that women are very reliable employees and they do tend to have a very good work ethic', she said.[9]

Train Driver Carrie Simpson considered her female colleagues on LUL better workers than men: 'If you give a woman something to do they just get on with it. Women are less likely to call in sick and are more punctual'. She added that her male colleagues were much more likely than women to challenge the rules: 'I don't know whether it's the male ego or whether they feel they need to assert themselves'. [10]

Changes in its domestic and working environments have rendered the railway a more female-friendly workplace. Mess-rooms, traditionally gloomy and devoid of home comforts, are nowadays bright and clean; in place of dirty ovens and heavy iron kettles staff now enjoy instant water-heaters, cooled mineral water dispensers and microwave ovens. Staff accommodation now always includes toilets for both sexes and in some cases showers are provided. Warm, clean power-boxes with push-button controls have replaced the multitude of draughty old signalboxes with heavy levers. Dirty and smoky footplates have been replaced by well-upholstered, air-conditioned, double-glazed cabs. Dismal, grey-painted brakevans have disappeared, and guards (now called conductors or train managers) have bright, clean offices or sit with the passengers in carriages watched by CCTV cameras. The railways have become safer. Electric doors operated by crews reduce accidents to passengers. Cab-to-signalbox communications reduce the number of times drivers have to climb down onto the track. Staff now carry mobile phones, giving them more chance of summoning help quickly in emergencies. Changes in operational procedures mean that guards no longer have to walk about in marshalling yards. Automatic couplings make shunters' work less hazardous. Automated trains require much less effort to operate, as one LUL driver explained: 'There's nothing really heavy to lift, whereas the old Northern line trains had a big handbrake that you had to crank around.'[11] Uniforms have become less military; in some cases, unisex tee shirts and sweatshirts have replaced the traditional jacket, waistcoat, collar and tie. Although childcare continues to be a problem for shiftworkers, there are now crèches in some railway workplaces, mainly used by office staff.

These small changes when taken together have contributed towards the railways being transformed into a much more woman-friendly environment. Equally important is the reduction of astonished looks and comments from railwaymen and passengers that were at one time directed at women in traditionally male jobs. Being allowed simply to get on with one's duties and not having to endure the continual, tiresome remarks about one's gender has greatly improved the working environment and no longer is every woman in a formerly male job constantly reminded of her status as an oddity. Sarah Pinchen, who joined South West Trains in 2003 aged 18 and became a guard at Woking a year later, feels that she is treated the same as her male colleagues:

> I wouldn't say I'm ever treated unfairly because I'm a woman; I'm never advantaged or disadvantaged, never shown favour because of it. Same as a male guard, never treated differently. Most people are shocked when I tell them I have been assaulted (by a young lad) and say they thought that a woman wouldn't usually be a target for violence from passengers (not true!) If I did have to offer any advice to women thinking of joining the railway, I would say, make sure you have a sense of humour and are not easily offended![12]

In theory, since the early 1990s no woman need suffer any form of sexual harassment. Regulations and guidelines to that effect are now embedded in the rulebooks of the various private companies that run the railways. The policy has had a beneficial effect on the working environment, as South Eastern Trains Driver Jean Cochrane explained:

> When I first started in 1980 there wasn't a harassment policy, and women used to get harassed big time. Some railwaymen still have the same derogatory attitude towards women, but nowadays they can't actually say such things to you. Since the railway implemented the policy, men can get into a lot of trouble for saying those things, so they don't say them to us; they say them to each other behind our backs.[13]

Another woman, with two decades of railway service in various different jobs, looked back over her career:

> I found many difficulties along the way. I found the railway to be very male-dominated, and to succeed one had to adopt a 'mans way of thinking' or bow to male superiority, without compromise to one's female ways. Tact was the operative word, if one had to gain promotion; which was, mainly, having to prove oneself capable of the work allocated and, in some cases, allowing a male manager to believe it was his proposals that would succeed, and that it was through his guidance that you were able to carry out your duties. This, most of the time, was nonsense and could be quite frustrating. However, we are fortunate today as there are many employment laws which state that men must promote change within their way of working and thinking.
>
> I believe that the women before me were the forerunners for women's rights within the workplace. Gone are the days when those women at work on the railway must have suffered such jibes as 'you should be at home looking after the children' and 'you need chaining to the kitchen sink', not to forget the sexual innuendo that they must have endured, worse than in the last 20 years. It is to them that the accolades must go, for they are all heroines.[14]

The smart boardrooms and plush offices of senior railway management are a world away from the grime and danger of railway operating, and women staff meet with no more resistance and prejudice there than they do in any other business or industry. Alison Forster, Managing Director of First Great Western, feels her gender to be of so little significance that she declined to be interviewed for this book, for reasons explained by her Head of Corporate Communications:

> Alison feels that she has achieved her position within the industry through hard work, expertise and respect. She feels that the fact she is a woman in the rail industry is not an issue she wishes to be highlighted.[15]

In my opinion, women's greatest achievement in the history of railways was the appointment in April 2003 of Carolyn Griffiths (who in 1985 had been BR's first female engineering depot manager) to Chief Inspector of the Rail Accident Investigation Branch of the Department for Transport, just under a century since a woman crossing keeper was not even trusted to operate her gates when the Royal Train was due to pass through, and had to be replaced temporarily by a man.

Locomotive driver Margaret Radway. M. RADWAY

References

[1] See chapter 2.
[2] Holford, J. (1988) *Reshaping labour : organisation, work and politics - Edinburgh in the Great War and after*, (Croom Helm) p83.
[3] HMSO (1999) *Equality and Fairness in the Fire Service* (HMSO).
[4] *Morning Star* 12 April 1990.
[5] Ibid.
[6] See Braybon, G., and Summerfield, P. (1984) *Out of the Cage*, (Pandora).
[7] *Railnews* December 1995.
[8] *BBC news online* 10 June 2005
[9] *The Times* 6 June 2002
[10] *Metro*, 3 July 2001.
[11] LUL Driver Amanda Inwood, *BBC News Online*, 18 June 2002.
[12] Email to the author, 22 July 2005.
[13] Personal interview with the author, 2004.
[14] Email from Ms X, who wishes to remain anonymous, 28 July 2005.
[15] Elaine Wilde, Head of Corporate Communications, First Great Western, 8 June 2005.

POSTSCRIPT: RESEARCHING WOMEN'S HISTORY

> Women's past is at least as rich as men's; that we do not know about it, that we encounter only interruptions and silence when we seek it, is part of our oppression.
>
> DALE SPENDER

When I joined the railways in 1977, people told me that I and the few other women in uniformed grades were the first of our sex to work in the industry. A decade later I read several books about railway workers; women were barely mentioned in them. P.W. Kingsford's *Victorian Railwaymen*, for example, contains not a single word about railwaywomen.[1] One or two authors referred to war-workers in passing, and Dr Bagwell's 700-page history of the NUR included three short references to women. In one, he mentioned that over 100,000 replaced men during the Second World War. This statistic both startled and intrigued me: I wanted to know more, to establish whether they were the first women to work on Britain's railways and to discover what happened to them after the war. The meagre references in the written histories led me to believe that, if I was lucky, I might collect enough material for a short essay.

A male colleague informed me that if railwaywomen's story was 'worth' writing, it would already have been done, and a fellow railway researcher I chatted to in the café of the National Archives sniggered at my chosen topic and informed me that I was wasting my time. He asserted with confidence that, save for some temporary staff during the Second World War, women had not worked in the industry until recently. When I told him that I'd discovered over 13,000 before the *First* World War, he informed me that they 'didn't count' because they were probably 'only' carriage cleaners and office workers and not 'real' railway staff. Had I told him that, say, 250,000 men worked on the railways at that time, I doubt if he would have asked what proportion of them were cleaners and clerks and deducted them from the total, because they were not 'real' railwaymen.

As, clearly, he defined railway work as 'the manipulation of traffic',* I advised him that during the Second World War a large number of women worked in male uniformed grades, some holding the job for five or more years. He replied that they didn't count, either, because they were temporary. I reminded him that many thousands of men have also worked on the railways for just a few years; were they, also, not 'real' workers. 'Oh that's different, and you know it', he retorted as he left, clearly irritated that I could not comprehend something that, to him, was obvious: men (and not women) are real workers, and only his definition of 'real' was valid.

Shortly afterwards I was reading a book by Dale Spender when a shiver ran up my spine: it was as though she were analysing the conversation I'd had in the café. She

* A definition put forward by NUR leader Jimmy Thomas during the First World War.

contended that men's superior position in society enables them to make pronouncements on what makes sense, what is to be valued, and what is considered real, and what is not. My fellow researcher, it seems, was a 'text-book case'. Dr Spender also asserted that patriarchy depends on the experience and values of men being perceived as the only valid frame of reference and on preventing women from establishing their equally real and different frame of reference which is the outcome of different experience.[2]

In the course of their research, writers of previous railway histories must have discovered documents and photographs that proved women's participation in railway working since 1830, and decided to ignore (or should one say 'suppress'?) this information. Not only did they choose to omit women, they also failed to mention that they had excluded them or to reveal that there was another, completely different, story to tell. By concealing their omission of women, they led readers to believe that men's history is *the* definitive history of railway workers. My experience illustrates not only patriarchy in action, but how essential it is to look at primary sources (the original documents) because reliance upon secondary sources (books written after the event) allows others to filter information through their personal prejudices and bias, and suppress information that does not suit their ends.

Professor Deirdre Beddoe's comment that 'the history of men has been palmed off on us as universal history' has never been more true than when applied to railways. After all, what was expected to be a short essay has grown into this book and there is so much extra material that I am writing another: *Till The Boys Come Home: The Memoirs of Railwaywomen in Wartime.*

On 15th February 2005 I asked Murray Hughes, editor of *Railway Gazette International,* if he would participate in a promotion of this book by offering it for sale to his readers worldwide. He declined, claiming that 'our readers would not be interested in the subject.' What a sweeping judgment to make about thousands of people across the world, all of whom work in the industry or are interested in railways. As there are no previous books on railwaywomen that he might have promoted without success, one wonders on what he based his statement. Mr Hughes has thus contributed, in a very small way, to the invisibility of railwaywomen in history.

On 23rd June 2005 Keith Norman, acting General Secretary of ASLEF, remarked of this book: 'I doubt anyone will read it, anyway.'[3] Thank you for proving him wrong.

References

[1] Published by Frank Cass in 1970.

[2] Spender, D. (1990) *Women of Ideas.* (Pandora), p4

[3] Email to the author from Keith Norman at ASLEF HQ. The author has retained the email complete with full origination headers.

Sources and Bibliography

British Library; British Newspaper Library; Pre-grouping companies', Big Four, and British Railways' regional staff magazines; Gertrude Tuckwell Collection (TUC); Imperial War Museum; London's Transport Museum; National Archives; National Railway Museum; *Railnews*; Ashford Library; NUR archives, Unity House, Frant Place, Warwick University Modern Records Centre; Scottish Records Office, Edinburgh; The Women's Library;

Bell, R. (1946) *History of the British railways during the war.* Railway Gazette.
B. R. Press. *British Railways at War.* 1943-45.
Bagwell, P. S. (1988) *75 Years of Industrial Trade Unionism.*
Bagwell, P. S. (1963) *The Railwaymen* Vol.1 George Allen & Unwin.
Bagwell, P. S. (1982) *The Railwaymen* Vol. II George Allen & Unwin.
Bagwell, P.S. (1968) *The Railway Clearing House* George Allen & Unwin.
Blainey, J. (1924) *The Women Worker and Restrictive Legislation.* Arrowsmith.
Braybon, Gail. (1981) *Women Workers in the First World War* Croom Helm
Calder, A and Sheridan, D. (1984) *Speak For Yourself. A Mass-Observation Anthology*. Cape.
Carter E.F. (1964) *Railways in Wartime.* Frank Muller.
Clephane Irene. (1935) *Towards Sex Freedom.*
Clinker, C.R. (1977) *The Leicester & Swannington Railway.* Avon Anglia.
Cole, G.D.H. and Page Arnot, R. (1917) *Trade Unionism on the Railways: its history and problems.* FRD.
Coleman, T. (1965) *The Railway Navvies.* Hutchinson.
Darwin Bernard. (1946) *War on the Line.* SR.
Drake, Barbara. (1984) *Women in Trade Unions.* Virago.
Findley, George. (1899) *The Working & Management of an English Railway.*
Frater, A (1983) *Stopping Train Britain.* Hodder & Stoughton.
Gourvish, T.R. (2002) *British Rail 1974-97.* OUP.
Hamilton, J.A.B. (1967) *Britain's Railways in World War One*. George Allen & Unwin.
Hammertone, J.A. *A Popular History of the Great War.*
Hauf, Johann. (1980) *Women on the Railway* (in Germany). ITF.
Head F.B. (1849) *Stokers and Pokers.* Murray.
Hutchinson. S. (n.d) *Berney Arms Past & Present.*
Rolt, L.T.C. (1966) *Red For Danger* Pan.
Holtby, Winifred. (1934) *Women in a Changing Civilization.* Bodley Head.
Joby, R.S. (1984) *The Railwaymen.* David & Charles.
Kingsford, P.W. (1970) *Victorian Railwaymen.* Frank Cass.
Lewenhak, S. (1977) *Women and the Trade Unions.* Ernest Benn.
LTE. *Fifty Years of London Transport History.*
Manning, R. (1977) *The Book of Railways and Railwaymen*. Kestrel.
McKenna, Frank. (1980) *The Railway Workers.* Faber.
McKillop, Norman. (1950) *The Lighted Flame* Nelson.
Pendleton, J. (1894) *Our Railways.* Cassell.
Pratt, E. (1921) A *Britain's Railways and the Great War.* Selwyn & Blount.
Robbins, D. (1986) *Wanted: Railman.* HMSO.
Russell, J. (1983) *Great Western Railway Company Servants.* Wild Swan.
Sillars, S. (1987) *Women in World War One.* MacMillan.
Simmons, J. & Biddle, G. (1997) *The Oxford Companion to British Railway History* OUP.
Soldon, N. (1978) *Women in British Trade Unions.* Gill & MacMillan.
Strachey, R. (1928) *The Cause.* Bell & Sons.
Stretton, C. (1901) *The History of the Midland Railway.* Methuen.
Summerfield, P. (1984) *Women Workers In The Second World War.* Croom Helm.
Wallace, M. (1997) *Single Or Return? The Official History of the* TSSA.TSSA.
Whitbread, J. R. (1961) *The Railway Policeman.* Harrap & Co.
Williams, B. (1987) *The Railway Industry.* Batsford.
Westwood, J. (1980) *Railways at War.* Osprey.
Wojtczak, H. (2003) *Women of Victorian Sussex.* Hastings Press.

Index